CAMBRIDGE LIBRARY COLLECTION

Books of enduring scholarly value

Linguistics

From the earliest surviving glossaries and translations to nineteenth-century academic philology and the growth of linguistics during the twentieth century, language has been the subject both of scholarly investigation and of practical handbooks produced for the upwardly mobile, as well as for travellers, traders, soldiers, missionaries and explorers. This collection will reissue a wide range of texts pertaining to language, including the work of Latin grammarians, groundbreaking early publications in Indo-European studies, accounts of indigenous languages, many of them now extinct, and texts by pioneering figures such as Jacob Grimm, Wilhelm von Humboldt and Ferdinand de Saussure.

The Arawak Language of Guiana

This description of the Arawak language, once spoken widely across the Caribbean area but now restricted to some of the native peoples of Guyana, French Guiana and Suriname, was first published in 1928. C.H. de Goeje was a Dutch submariner whose work had taken him to the then Dutch colony of Suriname; on his resignation from the Dutch navy he continued to investigate its peoples and their languages, and was the recipient of a special Chair in languages and cultural anthropology at the University of Leiden. The book provides long vocabulary lists and a systematic exploration of grammar and phonetics; it also discusses the origin of the language and its differentiation from the other Carib languages of the region. An appendix gives anthropological data, including transcriptions and translations of Arawak myths.

Cambridge University Press has long been a pioneer in the reissuing of out-of-print titles from its own backlist, producing digital reprints of books that are still sought after by scholars and students but could not be reprinted economically using traditional technology. The Cambridge Library Collection extends this activity to a wider range of books which are still of importance to researchers and professionals, either for the source material they contain, or as landmarks in the history of their academic discipline.

Drawing from the world-renowned collections in the Cambridge University Library, and guided by the advice of experts in each subject area, Cambridge University Press is using state-of-the-art scanning machines in its own Printing House to capture the content of each book selected for inclusion. The files are processed to give a consistently clear, crisp image, and the books finished to the high quality standard for which the Press is recognised around the world. The latest print-on-demand technology ensures that the books will remain available indefinitely, and that orders for single or multiple copies can quickly be supplied.

The Cambridge Library Collection will bring back to life books of enduring scholarly value (including out-of-copyright works originally issued by other publishers) across a wide range of disciplines in the humanities and social sciences and in science and technology.

The Arawak Language of Guiana

C. H. DE GOEJE

CAMBRIDGE
UNIVERSITY PRESS

CAMBRIDGE UNIVERSITY PRESS

Cambridge, New York, Melbourne, Madrid, Cape Town, Singapore,
São Paolo, Delhi, Dubai, Tokyo

Published in the United States of America by Cambridge University Press, New York

www.cambridge.org
Information on this title: www.cambridge.org/9781108007689

This edition first published 1928
This digitally printed version 2009

ISBN 978-1-108-00768-9 Paperback

THE ARAWAK LANGUAGE OF GUIANA

BY

C. H. DE GOEJE

VERHANDELINGEN DER KONINKLIJKE AKADEMIE
VAN WETENSCHAPPEN TE AMSTERDAM
AFDEELING LETTERKUNDE
NIEUWE REEKS, DEEL XXVIII, N°. 2

UITGAVE VAN DE KONINKLIJKE AKADEMIE
VAN WETENSCHAPPEN TE AMSTERDAM 1928

PREFACE

The Arawak or Arowak [1]), whose language is dealt with in this work, inhabit the coastal districts of Surinam and British Guiana ; they formerly lived still further East, even as far as the mouth of the Orinoco and Trinidad.

Many vocabularies and a good deal of grammatical information have been published from Arawak, but very few sentences of the language usually spoken and no texts at all of myths etc. ; this paucity, however, is compensated for to a large extent by excellent translations from parts of the bible by the Moravian missionaries, and the English missionary Mr. Brett. The grammatical system, strictly adhered to in these bible-texts cannot possibly have been derived from the existing grammars (List of Litterature 5c, 18, 23b), and must therefore be attributed to the cooperation of an Arawak who assisted in the translation or in the correction of it. We may then consider them as being genuine Arawak (especially Brett's texts ; those of Schultz contain a freeer translation, which is not so easy to follow).

In this work Brett's texts (11. 5a, b) have been used in the first place, and an endeavour has been made, to discuss all the particularities of the language as found in those texts.

In the second place Schultz's texts have been examined, and all that deviates from Brett, or is not found in Brett, has been discussed here.

Of the remaining materials only such forms have been brought in, which appeared of sufficient interest.

Finally the Arawak language has been compared with the other languages of the Arawak-Maipure (A. M.) [2]) linguistic family.

The material is not sufficient for any deep investigation concerning pronunciation, pitch, stress and accompanying gesture ; the vocabularies are not complete ; it is not known whether the colloquial language and the

---

[1]) For the different ways of spelling, see List of Litterature 27 : the spelling "Arawak" is at present most in use, and is therefore adopted in this work.

These people call themselves *loko*, plur. *loko-no* (see § 164 a) [1])). The name "Arawak" is only used by other tribes (Kaliña: *Aruwăkŏ, Aɽowáka*, Warau: *Aɽuwʾkü*) and by the creole population of Guiana. If this word were originally Arawak, then it might be derived from *aroa*, jaguar, or *oroa*, to perform the functions of the medicine-man : the translation "flour-eaters" (v. Martius. ll. 15, I. 689 : *haru*, starch, *eke*, to eat) seems to be rather far-fetched.

[2]) "Maipure" (Lucien Adam), "Nu-Aruak" (von den Steinen), "Arawak" (Brinton, Rivet).

language of myths and magic formulas deviate from the language of the bible translations; etc., etc. Therefore this work cannot claim to be an exhaustive treatise on the language.

But Arawak is so singularly transparent, that notwithstanding this incompleteness, several phenomena may be traced back to their origin. This study may therefore perhaps be of some use to linguists in general, and to those who feel interested in the "pre-logical and mystic mentality" of primitive peoples (Lévy-Bruhl, ll. 67).

Those readers who have very little time at their disposal, might after reading Chapters I and II, at once proceed to Chapters XVIII—XX.

An Alphabetical Index has been added to facilitate the reading of the Arawak texts.

The English bible-texts have been taken from : The Holy Bible (British and Foreign Bible Society). Oxford, 1840. — Mr. J. Y. Steward of the Berlitz School, The Hague, assisted in the translation of the manuscript into English.

C. H. DE GOEJE.

The Hague. Oct. 1924—Sept. 1927

After the completion of this work, the author spent two weeks in Surinam, and was enabled to clear up several doubtful points. The results of these investigations are included in this volume ; a few myths in Arawak, and miscellaneous information, have been added to the Appendix.

I have to thank captain C. C. Käyser, in command of Hr. Ms. Hertog Hendrik (who is himself an explorer), for the opportunity of visiting this country, and the Roman Catholic mission in Surinam for its help in bringing me together with two Arawaks, and for its kind hospitality.

d. G.

CONTENTS

APPENDIX

Information collected in Surinam in 1907 and in 1928

LIST OF LITERATURE (ll.)

Am. C.   Proceedings of the International Congress of Americanists.
Ant.   Anthropos, Wien.
BLA   Bibliothèque Linguistique Américaine, Paris.
JGS   Journal of the Royal Geographical Society of London.
JSA   Journal de la Société des Américanistes de Paris, Paris.
P   De Periskoop, Paramaribo.
WIG   De West-Indische Gids, 's-Gravenhage.
ZfE   Zeitschrift für Ethnologie, Berlin.

Abbreviations used in this work: B., or nihil, Brett, 5; v. C., van Coll, 7; D, Dance, 8; G., de Goeje (collected in Surinam); Hi., Hilhouse, 12; Pen., Penard, 17. 69; Q., Quandt, 18; R., Roth, 19; S., Schultz, 22; Sc., Schomburgk, 21; Sm., Schumann, 23; I. Th., Im Thurn, 25.

Arawak

1. (Not consulted.) Lucien Adam, Grammaire de la langue arrouague. MS mentioned in K. W. Hiersemann's (Leipzig) catalogue 335; presumably unfinished. According to H. the sources for this work were the numbers 20, 23a, b, 22, 6, 5c, a, b, 4 of this ll.

2. (Not consulted.) C. H. Aveline, MSS, 1859, mentioned in N⁰. 27.

3. Adriaan van Berkel, Amerikaansche Voyagien. Amsterdam, 1695.

4. J. H. Bernau, Missionary Labours in British Guiana, London, 1847.

5. W. H. Brett,
a. Adaieli Wacinaci okonomuntu Ajiahu. London, 1856.
b. Questions on the Apostles' Creed, etc. London.
c. Arawak Grammar (dated 1849). The Guiana Diocesan Magazine, 1900—1902.
d. The Indian tribes of Guiana. London, 1868.
e. Legends and myths of the aboriginal Indians of British Guiana. London.

6. D. G. Brinton, The Arawak language of Guiana. Transactions of the American Philosophical Society. Philadelphia, 1871.

7. C. van Coll,
a. Primaria Fidei Catholicae Rudimenta, Arrowaccana lingua. Paramaribo, 1892.
b. A few Arawak words and expressions. MS.
c. Gegevens over land en volk van Suriname. Bijdragen tot de Taal-, Land- en Volkenkunde van Ned. Indië. 's-Gravenhage, 1903.
d. Matrimonia indigenarum Surinamensis. Ant. II, 1907.
e. Contes et légendes des Indiens de Surinam. Ant. II, 1907. III, 1908.

8. C. D. Dance, Chapters from a Guianese Log Book. Georgetown, 1881.

9. The voyage of Robert Dudley to the West-Indies 1594—1595. London. Hakluyt Society, 1899.

10. H. C. Focke. Iets over de Arrowakken en hunne taal. West-Indië. Haarlem, 1855.

11. C. H. de Goeje. In this volume.

12. W. Hilhouse, Notices of the Indians settled in the interior of British Guiana. JGS, 1832.

13. A. Kappler, Surinam. Stuttgart, 1887.

14. J. de Laet, America utriusque descriptio (Novus Orbis, etc.). Leiden, 1633.

15. C. F. von Martius, Beiträge zur Ethnographie und Sprachenkunde Amerika's. Leipzig, 1867.

16. Moravian missionaries: numbers 18, 22, 23. Moreover St. Luke XV, 11—32 in numbers 4 and 21a; 10 (taken from 18); 6 (taken from 22 and from a MS grammar written by Schultz); 15, I p. 686, II p. 307 (taken from 18 and from a MS). See number 27 concerning the works of the Moravians (not consulted), present at Herrnhut, Philadelphia, New York and London; here is to be noted, that in the Moravian archives at Paramaribo several Arawak MSS are to be found, which in substance agree with those that are in Herrnhut.

16 A. J. Mols (R.C. missionary in Surinam), Arawak words and expressions (collected by himself and by others). M.S.

17. Penard,
a. (F. P. & A. P.) De Menschetende Aanbidders der Zonneslang. Paramaribo, 1907, 1908.
b. (Th. E. & A. P.) Four Arawak Indian Songs. WIG VII, 1926.
c. (Th. E. & A. P.) European influence on the Arawak Language of Guiana. WIG VIII, 1926.
d. (Th. E.) Remarks on an old vocabulary from Trinidad. WIG IX, 1927.

18. C. Quandt, Nachricht von Suriname und seinen Einwohnern (dated 1807). Görlitz. (chapter: Nachricht von der Arawakischen Sprache, fac simile edition J. Platzmann, Leipzig, 1900).

19. W. F. Roth,
a. An enquiry into the animism and folk-lore of the Guiana Indians. 30th annual report of the bureau of American ethnology. Washington, 1915.
b. An introductory study of the arts, crafts and customs of the Guiana Indians. 38th do., 1924.

20. P. Sagot, Vocabulaire Français-Arrouague, BLA VIII, 1882.

21. Schomburgk,
a. (Richard) Reisen in Britisch Guyana. Leipzig, 1848.
b. (Robert H.) In N⁰. 15.

22. Th. Schultz, The Acts of the Apostles (written 1802). New York, 1850

23. Th. Schumann,
a. Arawakisch-Deutsches Wörterbuch (written about 1755). BLA VIII, 1882.
b. Grammatik der Arawakischen Sprache, do.

24. M. D. Teenstra, De Landbouw in de Kolonie Suriname. II. Groningen, 1835.

25. E. F. Im. Thurn,
a. Tables of Indian languages of British Guiana. Georgetown, 1878.
b. Among the Indians of Guiana. London, 1883.

26. Wyatt. In N⁰. 9.

27. J. Williams, The Arawak Indians and their language. Am. C. The Hague, 1924.

Other Arawak-Maipure languages

28. L. Adam,

a. (Not consulted.) Grammaire comparée des langues mojo et baure ; MS K. W. Hiersemann's (Leipzig) catalogue 335.

b. (& C. Leclerc), Arte de la lengua de los Indios Baures. BLA VII, 1880.

c. do. de los Indios Antis o Campas. BLA XIII, 1890.

29. J. C. Adelung—J. S. Vater, Mithridates oder allgemeine Sprachenkunde. Berlin, 1812.

30. M. M. Arvelo, Algo sobre etnografia del territorio Amazonas. Ciudad-Bolivar. 1908.

30 A. A. Balbi, Atlas ethnographique du globe. Paris, 1826.

31. R. Breton,

a. Grammaire Caraïbe. BLA III, 1878.

b. (J. Platzmann), Dictionnaire Français-Caraïbe, Dict. C.—F. Leipzig, 1892, 1900.

32. D. G. Brinton,

a. The American Race. New York, 1891.

b. Studies in South American native languages. Philadelphia, 1892.

32 A. D. J. Calcaño, Resumen de las actas de la Academia Venezolana. Caracas, 1886.

33. R. Celedon, E. Uricoecha, Gramatica, etc. de la lengua Goajira. BLA V, 1878.

34. J. Chaffanjon, L'Orénoque et le Caura. Paris, 1899.

35. A. T. Chamberlain, Nomenclature and distribution of the principal tribes and sub-tribes of the Arawakan linguistic stock of South America. JSA 1913.

35 A. W. Chandless, Notes on the River Purus. J. G. S., 1866.

36. H. Coudreau, La France équinoxiale. Paris ,1885.

37. G. de Créqui—Montfort, P. Rivet, La langue Saraveka, JSA, 1913.

38. J. Crevaux. BLA VIII, 1882.

39. P. Ehrenreich, Vokabulare von Purus-Stammen, 1897.

40. A. Ernst,

a. Die Guajiro-Indianer. ZfE 1870, 1887.

b. Ueber einige weniger bekannte Sprachen aus der Gegend des Meta und oberen Orinoco. ZfE, 1891.

c. Upper Orinoco vocabularies. American Anthropologist. New York, 1895.

41. W. C. Farabee, The central Arawaks. Philadelphia, 1918.

42. F. S. Gilij, Saggio di storia Americana. Roma, 1780—84.

43. R. de la Grasserie, Esquisse d'une grammaire et d'un vocabulaire Baniva. Am. C. Paris, 1890.

44. A. Jahn, Parauhanos und Guajiros, etc. ZfE, 1914.

45. Th. Koch—Grünberg,

a. Aruak-Sprachen Nordwestbrasiliens. Mitt. der Anthropologischen Ges. in Wien. 1911.

b. Ein Beitrag zur Sprache der Ipurina-Indianer. JSA, 1914.

c. Vom Roraima zum Orinoco. Berlin & Stuttgart. 1916—1928.

d. Indianermärchen aus Südamerika. Jena, 1920.

e. (& G. Hübner), Die Makuschi und Wapischana. ZfE, 1908.

46. P. Marban (J. Platzmann), Arte de la lengua Moxa. Leipzig, 1894.
— C. F. P. von Martius, see N⁰. 15.

47. F. Montolieu. BLA VIII, 1882, and N⁰. 40c.

48. Natterer, in N⁰. 15.

49. C. Nimuendaju, Die Palikur-Indianer, etc. Göteborg, 1926.

50. E. Nordenskiöld,
a. Indianerleben. Leipzig, 1912.
b. Deductions suggested by the geographical distribution of some post-Columbian words used by the Indians of South-America. Göteborg, 1922.

51. L. R. Oramas,
a. Contribucion al estudio de la lengua Guajira. Caracas, 1913 (with list of literature on Goajiro).
b. Estudios linguisticos. De Re Indica. Caracas, 1918.

52. J. E. R. Polak, A grammar and a vocabulary of the Ipurina language. London, 1894.

53. P. Rivet, P. Reinburg, Les Indiens Marawan. JSA, 1921.

54. P. Rivet, C. Tastevin, Les langues du Purus, etc. Ant. 1923—24 (with list of literature on the pre-andin group of A. M. languages).

55. C. de Rochefort, Histoire naturelle et morale des Iles Antilles. Rotterdam, 1658.

56. M. Schmidt,
a. Guana. ZfE, 1903.
b. Die Aruaken. Leipzig, 1917.

57. Schomburgk, see N⁰. 21.

58. Spix, in N⁰. 15.

59. K. von den Steinen, Unter den Naturvölkern Zentral-Brasiliens. Berlin, 1894.

60. B. Tavera—Acosta, En el Sur. Ciudad-Bolivar, 1907.

61. Wallace, in N⁰. 15.

Others works quoted

62. (F. de la Borde, in :) Recueil de divers voyages faits en Afrique et en l'Amérique. Paris, 1684.

63. P. Ehrenreich, Die Mythen und Legenden der Südamerikanischen Urvölker. Berlin, 1905.

64. J. van Ginneken, Principes de linguistique psychologique. Amsterdam, 1907.

65. O. Jespersen,
a. Language. London, 1922.
b. The Philosophy of Grammar. London, 1924.

66. J. P. B. de Josselin de Jong, De waardeeringsonderscheiding van „levend" en „levenloos" in het Indogermaansch vergeleken met hetzelfde verschijnsel in enkele Algonkin-talen. Leiden, 1913.

67. L. Lévy—Bruhl, Les fonctions mentales dans les sociétés inférieures. Paris, (Vme éd.) 1926.

68. P. Pelleprat, Relation des missions ...... dans les Isles, & dans la terre ferme de l'Amérique Meridionale. Paris, 1655.

69. A. P. Penard,

e. Wejumakon, P, 12 Sept. 1925, 14 April 1927.

f. Iets over onzen Caraibischen pujai. I—XXX. P, 1925—26.

70. P. Rivet, L'orfèvrerie Colombienne. Am. C. The Hague, 1924.

71. R. Steiner,

a. Sprachgestaltung und Dramatische Kunst. Dornach, 1926.

b. Eurythmie als sichtbarer Gesang. Dornach, 1927.

c. Eurythmie als sichtbare Sprache. Dornach, 1927.

72. A. Trombetti, Elementi di Glottologia. Bologna, 1923.

[1])

The writer feels indebted to several of the authors mentioned in this list, for the valuable suggestions contained in their works ; in this connection he wishes to mention also W. Ahlbrinck, H. Beckh, L. Bloomfield, R. Falb, F. N. Finck, W. von Humboldt, E. Sapir, C. C. Uhlenbeck and J. Vendryes

---

[1]) See also notes on pp. 240 and 241.

For the sake of completeness the following works are mentioned, which do not occur in the lists of literature in nos. 51 and 54 :

(Not consulted.) A. Jahn. Los aborigines del Occidente de Venezuela. Caracas, 1927.

(Not consulted.) J. P. Aza. Vocabulario Español-Machiguenga. Lima, 1923—24.

RULES FOR PRONUNCIATION AND ABBREVIATIONS

Brett : *a*, as in father, *e* as in prey, *i*, as in ravine, *o*, as in go, *u*, as oo in too, *ai*, as i in mile, *au*, as ow in how, *ci*, as che in cheer, *si*, as she.

S., Sm. and Q. very probably have used the German spelling ; *j* thus equals the sound of the *y* of B. Sm. gives in his grammar the meaning of the diacritical signs, but it is not certain whether S. has used them in the same way.

v. C. 7a, b, c and Pen. 17a have used the Dutch spelling; thus *j*∿ B. *y*, *oe* ∽ B, *u*, *u*∿ German ü, *ie* as ea in ear.

G. and Pen. 17b, c, d, 69 : ĭ, as in hill, *ü*, German ü, *u*, German u, å, as a in walk, о̊, between French eu and mute e, ŏ, French eu, *e*, French é, ĕ, as ea in heaven, ẹ, as e in written, χ, Dutch ch, Spanish j or x, ʕ, as ng in Dutch or German engel (angel) č, as ch in cheer, š, as sh in she, ž, as j in joy, ñ, Spanish ñ, λ, ρ, between l and r, ʲ, most closely resembling *l*, ρ most closely resembling *r*. ', accent, -, long, (, indistinctly articulated.

Sagot and v. C. 7e have used the French spelling; thus *ou*∿ B. *u*, *u*∿ German ü.

In this work the following abbreviations and signs are used:

Gen.	= Genesis	L.	= S. Luke
Mt.	= S. Matthew	J.	= S. John
Mk.	= S. Mark	Acts	= The Acts of the Apostles. ;

- separates the parts of compounds (only used for the purpose of elucidation) ; where B. uses this sign, it has been retained, for instance in *l'oforra-kita*, although elsewhere B. spells *loforrakitin*, *l'ofitikita* ;

( ) indicates : abusively not written in one word, for instance *abaptize da* (which ought to be *abaptizeda*) : *a-baptize()da* ;

| indicates : written in one word, although according to B.'s usual way of spelling, it ought not to be written in one word.

In the English text, a word or a sentence between ( ) means, that the English text does not contain this word or this sentence, but the Arawak text does contain it ; a word or a sentence between [ ] means that the English text contains this word or this sentence, but the Arawak text (or the part that is quoted) does not.

The ' 's used by B., especially with the pronominal prefixes, have been left out, because their application is not systematic (for instance *b'usweardoan*, thine oaths, *bu'sweardoa fa*, thou shalt swear), or even faulty (for instance *mibilokotu b'akada abu*, with thongs ; *mibilikotu* = narrow, *baka* = oxen. *(e)da* = hide, *abu* = with). See for the system of hyphens adopted in this work for separating a prefix, § 17.

* indicates a reconstructed word.

ALPHABETICAL INDEX

This index contains all words in Arawak, that are to be found in the texts of B. and S, even those which have not been specially discussed in this work; derived forms, such as the o-(n-wa) (§§ 4,5) and -kiti (§ 91) verbs and reduplications (§ 93) have generally not been mentioned.

The English words given after the Arawak words are the words of the English texts that have been translated by means of the Arawak word, and as a rule do not exactly express the inner meaning of the Arawak word.

The words have been arranged according to the first consonant; an *h* that shows an inclination to disappear, is in the index not reckoned as a consonant.

Sp. = of Spanish origin, cr. = of creole -Dutch (or negro-dialect) origin.

§		
2, 17, 185	*A*	the aspect of the world in its continual change
2	*a*	at some distance
28, 42	*a*	"Zeitwort", auxiliary verb
17	*a-*	prefix, announcing events
3.93	*a, aa, â*	end-vowel verbs: duration
82 *a*)	*-a*	possessive suffix
82 *A*	*-a*	resembling
5, 23, 132	*ia*	"let go": etherical
—	*oa, ua*	see *wa*
57, 184 *ff*	*B*	being at rest; the manner in which that which has been created manifests itself; the appearance
60	*ba,* S. *ba*	also, again
60 *d*)	*aba,* S. *abba*	some, other, another
60 c) 1)	*eba, iba*	the last, the end
60 *d*) 4)	*ababa, abbâba*	again
—	*aba warea-ci*	a stranger
64 *a*) 4) *IV*)	R. *o-bada,* Sm. *u-badda*	nail, claw
88 *k*)	*bajia,* S. *baddia, badja*	also
109	Sm. *baiwaru*	paiwarri, a beverage
180	*a-baptizedi-*	to baptize
179 *e*)	*baha*	perhaps
179 *e*)	Sm. *bahâ-sse, bahâ-ra*	perhaps, I think
(Sp.)	*baka,* S. *bàka*	cattle, ox
96 *b*)	S. *abbâ-ka-rén*	suddenly
161 *f*)	*bakilama,* S. *bakküllama*	(it is) evening
136 *d*)	*aba-koro,* S. *abba-kurru*	no; G. not a single one
135 *A*(Sp. ?)	S. *balla*	lead, ball
135 *A*	Sm. *ballalâ*	to be round
175 *d*)	*bali*	tree species (?)
(cr.)	*bali*	a vessel (for putting fish in)
60 *a*) 3)	Sm. *ballida*	a comb

60 a) 3)	Sm. a-ballidü-	to comb
116 b) 1)	balisi	ash
60 d) 7)	G. abaloko, abaroko	several
(Sp.)	bandola	a harp
60 e)	bania, banyia, S. bânja	lasting some time
64 a) 4)	o-banna	leaf ; liver
107 b) 6)	bara, S. bara	the sea
104 h)	ibara	to remain, to be left
107 b) 7)	o-barra, S. u-barra	hair, feathers
164 r)	G. barati	negro
152, 121 e) 4)	abar, aba(r)li (f. -ro, pl. -no), S. abba, abba-l-uwai (f. -r-uwai, pl. -nu)	a, one, the one, a certain, pl some
96 b)	abaren	straightway, forthwith, anon
182 (55)	Sm. baru	axe
152 c) 2)	abaro	to be one
60 d) 6)	G. abapoda	(roads) cross each other
160 c)	-ba-ro mairia	left side
145 a)	barri-ga, S. balli-ka	though
145 b)	bari-n, S. balli-n	certainly
164 d)	Sm. bassaban-ti (f. -tu)	boy (girl)
164 r)	G. basari	Kaliña
60 d) 5)	abati-	to alter
130 e)	bawhu, S. bahü	a house
130 e)	bawhu-yuho	a city
64 a) 4) I)	bawna- boho, R. to-banna-abu, Q. u-bannabuhü	tabernacle, banab, temporary shelter
116 a) 1)	bawhu-sibo, S. baha-ssubu-lle	door, gate
60 a) 5)	Sm. baijabu	centipede
60 a) 4)	Sm. baiara	saw-fish
184	R. baiyara-shiri	a certain fan-design
59	(i)be, S. (i)be	fullness, plentitude ; plurality
48 d) 2)	Sm. be	intensifying
59 a) 3)	ebe	to have done
164 n) 1)	Sm., Q., R. (e)bebe	honorific (vocative)
99 a), 186	bele, S. bele	to have the palsy, to be lame
99 a)	ebeli-	to lick
99 a)	R. bele-tto	anything soft or jelly-like
99 a)	Sm. ebelti-	to soften, to melt
99 a)	Sm. beltiri	beltiri, a beverage
38	bena, S. benna	when, after
59 c) 4)	abena	a portion
59 c) 2, 3)	ibena	to be a time ; a part
59 c) 2) II)	ibenata, S. ebentâ	to tarry
—	S. ebenda	to delay
164 n) 2)	S. eben-ti	a person of our (their, etc.) company, sect, nation
—	S. eberu-(nn-ua)	to deny, to betray
—	iberosoa	to groan
114 e)	besekin(i)	to be of little stature
125 c) 1 A)	ebeso-(n-wa), Sm. a-ebessu-(nn-ua)	to metamorphose oneself, to bloom
125 c) 1 A)	S., Sm. ebessu-(nn-ua)	to appear, to appear in a dream

164 n) 3)	S. *ebettira*	to be on friendly terms with, allied to
—	*beyukahu*	flute, pipe
58 a)	*(i)bi*, S. *(i)bi*	immediate past
58 c) 1)	*ibi*	to be ready, accomplished
58 c) 2), 91	*a-iibi-*, S. *a-übu-*	to leave
39	*bia*, S. *bia*	it will be, be it
39	S. *biaki*	kindness (?)
153	*biama*, S. *biama*	two
155	*bibici*, S. *bibiti*	four
58 d) 2)	*ibibidi-*, S. *ibébedü-*	to touch, to feel
58 d) 2)	Sm. *bibiri*	a dragon-fly
58 c) 2)	*iibidi-*	to prepare, to fulfill
153	*bihero*	to be adulterous
58 d) 2)	*ibihidi-*	to heal
58 d) 2)	*ibiki-*	to cut, to wound
125 c) 1)	Sm. *bikkibikki*	to grow up
58 f)	*ibi kibi*	almost, even
125 c) 1), 157 b)	*ibikido-(n-wa)*, S. *ibikidu-(nn-ua)*	to grow, to spring up (seeds)
98	*ibikidolia*, S. *ibikiddullia*	to be young
59 b) 2)	*ibikiti-*, S. *e-bekitti-*	to fill
69 a)	*ibi-li* (f. -*ro*)	small
58 d) 2)	*bilibiliro*	the lightning
103 i) 3)	*ibiloko*, S. *ibilugku*	breadth
103 i) 3)	*ibilokoto-*, *ibilogoto-*	to make broad, to spread, to strew
58 d) 2)	Sm. *bimiti*	humming-bird, colibri
58 b)	*ibi-n*	not long ago, already
58 d) 2)	Sm. *(i)bina*	remedy, charm
58 d) 2)	*ibini-*	to dance
58 d) 2)	*ibira*, S. *ibira*	to mock
125 c) 1)	Sm. *ibissi*	a slip (plant)
119 b) 6)	Sm. *bi-ssururu*	a remedy for curing small-pox
58 d) 1)	*ibici*, S. *ibiti*	for, to, unto, upon, after
58 c) 2)	*ibiti-*, S. *ibitu-*	to burn
153	Sm. *ibiju*	twins
62	*-bo*, S. *-bu*	remaining at rest for a time
7, 177	*bu*, S. *bū*	end-point pronoun II
7, 177	*b(u)-*, S. *b(u)-*	pronominal prefix II
65	*abu*, S. *abbu*	with, by, on, in
66	*iabo*	the outer (free) side
169 b)	*i(y)a-bo*	shadow
182 (125)	G. *buba*	paxiuba palm
67 c)	Sm. *buddahalalissi*	dead coal
67 c)	Sm. *buddali*	cassava-baking par
67 e)	Q. *u-buddalli-hü*	the knee, bone
67	*bodi*, *budi*	stiff; fish-hook
62 f) 4)	G. *bodya*, *budya*	a small remnant
62 f) 4)	G. *a-budia-či (-to)*	a corpse
7, 44 a)	*bui*, S. *bui*	emphasizing pronoun II
163 d)	*o-bugi-ci*	man's older brother
182 (79)	Sm. *buhiri*	a bat
44 h)	Sm. *bokkia*	pronoun II
120 g) 6) XII)	*aboku*	part, portion
120 g) 6) XII)	S. *abbukū-*	to receive

120 *d*) 4)	*aboa*, S. *aboa*	to be ill, foul, G. sickly, S. evil, sin, Sm. ill, bad
91	*aboadi-*	to destroy, to waste
91	*aboadikiti-*	to condemn
4	*aboado-(n-wa)*, S. *aboahüddu-(nn-ua)*	to perish
120 *d*) 5)	*aboaka*	perchance, haply
130 *a*)	*aboa-u-kili*	foul weather, winter
169 *c*)	*o-boea (boia-tu)*	odour, savour
65 *b*)	*abuie-* S. *abuja*	to feed
—	*abui-ua-hu*, S. *abuj-oa-hü*	[to find] pasture
65 *b*)	Sm. *abüja*	bush hog, Dicotyles labiatus
163 *g*) 7)	G. *boyan-to*	the first wife of a man
—	*C (a, o, u)*	see *k (a, o, u)*
90	*ci*	see *ti*
84, 184 *ff.*	*D*	to be firmly established, to stand, to be stiff, will-power manifesting itself by remaining motionless
7,177	*d(a)-*, S. *d(a)-*	pronominal prefix I
47 *A*	*da*	emphasis
89	*ada*, S. *adda*	tree, wood, staff
89	*eda*, S. *üdda*	skin, bark
89	*adafuji*	loin
109	*adagato-*, S. *a-hadakuttu-*	to require, to demand, to ask, to enquire for
182 (149 C)	G. *a-dahaka*	to urinate
45 *b*)	Sm. *daharu*	dorthin
7, 44 *a*)	*daii*, S. *dai*	emphasizing pronoun I
89	*adaia*	to have authority, to be a ruler
—	*adaia-hu* (pl. *adaiah-no*), S. *adaija-hü*	a deputy, a governor
89	*adaiana-sia*, S. *adaijana-ssia*	master, ruler
176 *a*) 4) II)	*adaie-l-ci*	a nobleman
—	*adaie-li*, S. *adaija-hü-li*	lord (vocative and nominative)
—	*adaie-li-wabu* (pl. *adaie-no-ci wabu*)	a king
—	*l-adaie-n*	his lord
—	*ororo adaie-n*	the deputy of the country
—	*adaierobi-ci*	a chief
—	*adaierobi-ci eragi-n*	a council
163 *g*) 2)	Sm. *adaün-ti*	mother's brother
126 *a*)	*adaili*, S. *haddali*	the sun
44 *a*)	S. *dailiwai*	I
175 *d*)	G. *dakamabali*	Andira inermis
44 *h*)	Sm. *dakia*	pronoun I
89	*idan*, S. *hiddan*	leg (under the knee)
89	*adanaina*	shoulder
180	*a-dankido-(n-wa)*	to thank
184	*adaridi-*, S. *a-dallidi-*	to run
118 *a*) 8)	*audasia*	to be with fever
121 *c*) 8)	Sm. *adawandu-(nn-ua)*	to be suspended in the air

B 2*

89	Sm. *idê*	gar sein
86 *b*)	*ajeago,* S. *adiáku*	upon
184	G. *dŏ(ĭdŏ(ĭ*	to be halting
117 *d*) 4), 184	*adedisaro*	an earthquake
184	*a-dehada,* S. *a-ddehiddi-*	to be leaping, to leap
173 *a*) 2)	*adeki-, adiki-,* S. *addiki-*	to see
89	Sm. *dele*	an anchor
89	S. *a-delledoa-hū*	a haven (anchorage)
89	*adenti-,* Sm. *adinti-*	gar machen
7,177	*di,* S. *de*	end-point pronoun I
85	*-di, -(i)ji,* S. *-di*	a fixed place or thing
86 *a*)	S. *adi*	upon
87	*aji,* S. *âdi*	more than
112 *e*)	*a-iidi-, a-iiji-*	to gird
88 *a*)	*jia,* S. *dia*	as
88 *l*)	*ajia,* S. *adia*	to speak, to say
140 *a*)	*jiali*	(who, what) like
88 *g*)	S. *dia-ma- ru*	as
88 *f*)	*jia-mu-ci (-mu-tu, -mo-tu-)*	such
132	*a-iadi-,* S. *a-ijahaddü-*	to move, to travel ; S. to walk, to go
131 *a*) 1)	*a-iaudi-...a,* S. *a-jaudi-...a*	to be beside oneself, to be mad
140 *b*)	*jiari*	(who, what) like
140 *c*)	*jiaro,* S. *diarru*	(who, what) like ; or
89	Sm. *idiballe*	smoke-dried meat
86 *f*) 1)	*adibeyo,* S. *addibeju*	belly, womb
86 *f*) 2)	*adiboloko*	a creek (?)
120 *d*) 1), 173 *a*) 1)	R. *adibua-hu*	omen, token, auguries
—	*adiga-ci*	a potter
86 *c*)	*adiki,* S. *a(d)dikki*	after
86 *e*)	*adiki*	the (lobe of the) ear
60 *a*)	S. *bahū addiki-balli*	the foundations of the house
---	*adikida-sia*	[a good measure,] pressed down
86 *c*) 2)	Sm. *adikki-hi*	footprints, track
86 *d*)	*adikiloko,* S. *adikkilukku*	instead of, in the room of
163 *g*) 1)	*adiki-ci*	younger brother
—	*a-dikiti-*	to wrap, to wind (in a cloth)
173 *b*)	*a-dimisi-*	to smell
88 *b*)	*jin,* S. *din*	as
86 *g*) 1)	*adina,* Sm. *adena*	arm, wing
86 *g*) 2)	*adinabo*	branch
—	*adina-hu*	a fathom
86 *g*) 4)	*ajinamu,* S. *adinamu*	to stand
86 *g*) 4)	*ajinama*	to stand, to rest (the ark upon the mountains of Ararat)
—	*l-ajinamada ia*	and to let him have liberty (Acts XXIV, 23)
86 *g*) 3)	*adinamun,* S. *adennamün*	near to, in the vicinity of
100	*a-dirika, a-diriko-(n-wa)*	to shave oneself
—.	Sm. *a-diriki-*	barbieren, abscheren
88 *c*), 118 *a*) 12)	S. *di-ssia*	to be a custom, a manner
84	*-do, -du*	something firmly established
109	Sm. *adu*	parasol
124 *b*)	*idju*	paps

122 e) 1)	a-odo-, S. a-hudu-	to die
184	Sm. dúbuli	sting-ray
122 e) 2)	Sm. hudu	krumm, gebückt sein
122 e) 2)	a-hododo-	to bow
179 f)	Sm. dukesi, dukara	freilich
163 g) 7)	G. dokara-to	the second wife of a man
89	Sm. u-dukku	der Schooss
163 e)	Sm. aduku-tti	grandfather
89	a-dokodo-	to loose, to forgive
89	a-dokoto-	to show
—	a-dokoto-(n-wa)	to appear
89	Sm., G. duli	root
40, 89	o-doma, S. u-dumma. u-dumã	because of
174 a)	adunku-, adunko-, S., Sm. adumki-, Sm. adunuki-	to sleep
89	adura, Sm. adüllebu	rib, side
89	Sm. addura	to plait
164 r)	G. dupi	negro
89	Sm. durrukoaru	yam
120 e) 10)	doada, S. doada	a pot
2,184 ff.	E.	sickly, delicate, tender, lingering, quality, heat
7,177	ie, S. je	end-point pronoun III pl.
83 a)	ie, S. je	tongue
69, 184 ff.	F, p, S. p	striving, aspiring, airily, lightly,
5	fa	future ; will
136 e) 2)	G.fa !	fy !
69 b)	Sm. ipa	duck
69 b)	a-fadakudi, S. a-paddukudu-, a-paddukuttu-,	to shake off
(cr.)	S. fadem	fathom
164 o)	G. papa	father
69 b)	Sm. papaia	papaya
69 b)	Sm. a-pappassü-	sich ausbreiten, gross werden
69 b)	Sm., R. appapu-rru	böses, wildes Wasser, R. bore, tidal wave
136 e) 2)	S. pahia	astonishing
—	S. a-pakütta	to pass
164 s) 1)	S. palle-ti	powerful, wise (?)
164 s)	Pen. faleto	a wise man, a stranger
69 b)	G. famodoa	to be floating
118 a) 6)	Sm. panasia	to be hungry, greedy
69 b)	Sm. parassa	a spear
164 s)	pareciyu, S. palettiju	barbarous people (Acts XXVIII, 1)
144	faroka, S. paruka	hypothetical
69 b), 159 f)	fata? S. patta(-hü) ?	how many ?
69 b)	a-fatadi-	to smite
197	pawmu	salt
(cr.)	penster, S. fenster	a window
(cr.)	S.offer ; offern	an offering ; offerings
(Sp.)	pero	a dog

(cr.)	*pesi*	pitch ; slime
69 *j*)	G. *fe, fĩ*	refuse, rubbish
69 *a*)	*ifi-li* (f. *-ro*), S. *ipi-lli* (f. *-rru*)	great
—	S. *ipilladü-*	to gush out
(cr.)	S. *Pinkstdaka*	the day of Pentecost
69 *a*)	*ifiro*, S. *ipiru*	the body ; a corpse
175 *f*)	*ifiro-koro*, S. *ipirru-kurru*	a feast
69 *a*)	*ifirota*	to enlarge
—	*ifiroto-(n-wa)* S. *ipirrutu-(nn-ua)*	to boast
(cr.)	S. *fiscal*	the townclerk
69 *a*)	*a-fitikidi-*, S. *a-puttikĩdi-*	to go forth, to go out
69 *a*)	*a-fitikiti-*, S. *a-puttikitti-*	to bring forth
—	Sm. *ipitti-*	fest machen ; anstecken
—	*ipitokoto-*	to seal
—	*c-ipito-koto-kwona-hu*	morter
(cr.)	*planka*, S. *planka*	a board
(cr.)	S. *plantasi*	possessions (a farm, plantations)
(Sp.)	*plata*, S. *platta*	silver, money
(Sp.)	Sm. *flauta*	European flute
180	*a-praisedi-*	to praise
(Sp.)	Sm. *práttana*	plantain
(cr.)	S. *prima-nnu*	fellows (Acts XVII, 5) (from cr. fri man, free man)
180	*a-prophesido-(n-wa)*	to prophesy
182 (78)	Sm. *puddi*, G. *fudi*	monkey
69 *d*), 186	*a-fudi-*, Sm. *a-ppüdü-*	to blow
69 *d*)	*afu-dyi* (f. *-du*)	ruler
69 *d*)	*afuji*	to surpass, to rule
69 *b*)	G. *fofaso-(n-wa)*	to soar
69 *f*)	*a-fogodo-, a-fokodo-*, S. *a-pukudu-*	to divide, to part, to separate
129 *c*) 3)	*pocoraro*, Sm. *pukuleru*	agouti
69 *d*)	*a-fullifullito-(n-wa)*	to be made smooth
69 *d*)	*a-folidi-*, S. *a-puldi-*	to loose
98	Sm. *pülli-lia*	shrubbery
136 *e*) 2)	Sm. *poi!*	astonishing !
69 *d*)	*a-fuili*	to loose, to unloose
69 *d*)	G. *funa*	greedy
69 *e*)	*a-forraa*	to strive
69 *e*)	*aforraa*	war
91	*a-forrakiti-*, S. *a-parrukitti-*	to put to death
—	*a-forri-ci*, S. *ka-pparka-tti*	a murderer
69 *e*)	*a-forri-*, S. *a-parru-*	to slay, to kill
69 *d*)	*a-furi*, Sm. *pulli*	to spring up (seed)
69 *d*)	*tu-furi*	the (its) blade
69 *d*)	*a-furiti-*	to bring forth (plants)
(Sp.)	*poroko*, Bernau *porku*	swine
(cr.)	*fort*, S. *fort*	castle
(Sp.)	Sm. *fortalissa*	eine von Leime geklebte Wand am Hause
—	S. *a-pussidü-*	to deliver, to loose (a prisoner)
69 *b*)	*fotobotori*, Sm. *púttuputtúli*	a nail
57	G. G. *g*, χ, *kh*, S. *gk*	see *k*

112 c) 2)	S. *ihime*	firewood
76 b) 2)	*himi*, Sm. *hime*	fish
54	S. *hinna, hiña*	events are proceeding
112 b)	Sm. *ihiri*	an eel
182 (94)	Sm. *hitti*	curassow bird
110 a)	*(hi)ti*, S. *hitti*	to desire, to will
112 c)	S. *hitti, ihittiattina* (?)	sepulchre
110 b)	S. *ahitti*	to be compliant, to believe
112 e)	Sm. *ihiti*	to ground fine
—	S. *ihittira*	to accuse
166 f)	v. C. *Hiwanama*, G. *Hiwanaka*	mythical man
24	*-hu, -ho, -ha, -he, -hi*	formative verbal nouns (abstracts, etc.)
7, 177	*hu*, S. *hü*	end-point pronoun II pl.
7, 177	*h(o)-, h(u)-*	pronominal prefix II pl.
151 a)	*uho*	quantity
7, 44 a)	*hui*, S. *hui*	emphasizing pronoun II pl.
112 e)	Sm. *a-hüidi-*	to press
44 h)	Sm. *hükia*	pronoun II pl.
122 d) 1) III)	G. *hulura*	swellings of a musquito-sting
184	G. *a-hüküdü-*	to clear one's throat
112 g)	Sm. *ue-hükkili, we-hikkili*	silkgrass
184	G. *hŏkŏkülisia*	to hiccup
76 d) 2)	S. *a-humadu-*	to rush (the wind)
164 k)	*o-ho-na-no-ci*	kindred, kin, cousins
(cr.)	S. *hondert*	a hundred
108A g)	*hori*, S. *wuri*	snake
109	Sm. *hüwa*	blow gun
2, 178, 184 ff.	*I*	1⁰. instantaneous, of very short duration, quick, free, no duration at all, principle, idea, intensively, accentuated, tiny ; 2⁰. masculine or human, rational, class
17	*i-*	prefix
3	*-i*	end-vowel verbs
41	*-i*	emphasizing suffix
7, 177	*i*, S. *i*	end-point pronoun III m.
91	*a-ii-, a-iiya*, S. *a-iji-, a-ija*	to weep
—	S. *J*	see *y*
84	B. *ji*	see *di, dyi*
57, 184 ff.	*K, g*	making its appearance in a positive manner, creation at work, the idea or the principle that becomes phenomenon
10	*k(a)-*	appearing, being present
5, 29	*ka, ga*	there is
125 a)	Sm *aka*, G. *ŏka*	to take a bath
136 e) 5)	Sm. *akka* !	ach !
55	*ika*, S. *i(k)ka*	a certain time ; there was once
163 b) 6)	*aiika*	to marry

133 b) 7)	aiika(h), S. haika, heika	death, to die
133 b) 3)	S. haika	peace
117 c)	S. aika-ru'mehli iwi	the wheat
134 d) 1)	kaba	to be saltish
183	R. kabadaro	jaguar
(Sp.)	kabaritu	goat
134 e)	(a)kabo, S. ü-kkabbu	hand (the forepart with the fingers)
(see abuie-)	k-abuea, k-abuia	field, country
176 a) 4) II)	k-abue-l-ci, S. k-abbujä-l-ti	house holder, citizen
154	kabuin, S. kabbuin	three
—	(a)kabokoto	hand (the full hand from the fingers unto the wrist)
105 a) 2)	Sm. a-kabburatikitti-	weit, geräumig machen
(cr.)	capitan, S. capitain	captain, centurion, magistrate
(Sp.)	Sm. kapussina	long beard ("Capucin")
(cr.)	S. kaputi, puti	garment, clothes
112 d)	ka-hili	quickly
133 e)	G. te-kaikai	whirlpool
170 b) 1)	G. kaki-ci	a human being
134 h), 166 g)	Sm. kaikuti	alligator; mythical man being; diminutive
34	ka-in(i), S. kan	
100 a)	kaiiri, S. kairi	island
134 cA)	G. kakali-ci	a man with curly hair
134 a) 4)	Sm. a-kkakardi-	to bite (a snake)
134 e) 2)	Sm. a-kakatta	to mix with hands
134 i)	G. kala	cicatrice
126 a)	Sm. kalekku, v. C. chale-kojeha	the white stones or pebbles of the medicine-man. v. C. the spirit of quartz
(Sp.)	S. kallena	chain
170 c)	R. kalli	cassava cake
126 a)	kalime, S. ü-kkalleme	light, glory, to be bright, to shine
134 f)	Sm. kamma	tapir
136 e) 3) II)	Sm. kamaije	vanilla
(Sp.)	S. kampanna	bell
134 f) 4)	Sm. kamudu	water-boa
(cr.)	kano	a vessel (for water)
104 c) 2)	Sm. karraba	Carapa guianensis
134 e) 3)	G. a-kapadi-	to stir up
134 c)	akarati-, akarate, akarata, S. akarratu-, akarta	to bury (a corpse)
130 e)	karau	grass, Sm. grass, savanah
134 a)	kari, S. karri	B. to suffer, to be vexed, S. to be ill
134 a) 2)	a-kariti-	to torment
134 a) 3)	karikona ... ajia-n	reproaching words
135 d) 1) VII)	Sm. karriman	black resin, pitch
135 d) 1) VII)	Sm. karraüru	Bignonia chica
126 b)	karime	to be black
(Sp.)	karina	a hen
(Sp.)	kaarta, S. karta	letter, book
108 A d)	karubo	a platter
108 A d)	Sm. karrupairu	snail-shell

120 *g*) 7)	*o-koborokwa (kwon),*	remembrance, consciousness
	S. *u-kkuburukkua*	
—	Sm. *a-kubudi-,* G. *a-kobodi-*	to miss (in shooting)
—.	S.*akodâ … o-kona*	to follow
129 *e*)	*kudi,* S. *kuddü*	to be heavy
129 *a*) 1)	*akudi-,* S. *akküddü-*	to drive out, to persecute
129 *a*) 2)	*kodibiyu*	bird
129 *e*)	*kudu*	a heavy thing
129 *aA*)	*(ikihi-) kudu*	fire-wood
129 *a*) 3)	R. *kudu-kudu-bari-lya*	a certain ant
128 *b*)	*akodo-, akoda,* S. *akkudu-*	to sew, to plaite, to weave
128 *c*)	*akodo-(n-wa),* S. *akudu-(nn-ua)*	to enter, to go (into)
128 *c*)	*akodoona-li*	a haven
169 *c*)	Sm. *kopaijoa*	copaiva
(cr.)	*koporo*	brass
(Sp.)	*kohoiyo, kohoiyu,* S. *kawaiju*	horse
125 *b*)	*o-koi*	spittle
128 *j*)	Sm. *kujama*	a fish trap
125 *b*)	*a-koidi-*	to spit
128 *i*)	*a-koio-(n-wa)*	to return (unto)
—	S. *akuju-, akuju-(n-wa)*	to depart, to return (unto)
—	*akoikiti-,* S. *akujukuttu-*	to cause to return
—	S. *akuikitta*	to repent (from)
—	*bibici t-akoina abu*	[a sheet let down] by four corners
172 *a*) 3)	Sm. *aku-ke*	eyelids
170 *a*)	*kokke,* S. *kakü*	life, to live
170 *a*) 2)	*(a-)kokketo-*	to quicken
128 *d*), 186	*k-okkituka-tu*	a thistle
170 *b*)	*kokota-n ono-roko*	foaming (an epileptic)
129 *d*) 1)	G. *kuλaboloko,* S. *tu-kulubulukku*	corner, angle
(cr.)	S. *gulden*	a piece of silver
99 *bA*)	Sm. *kule*	to be weak
129 *d*) 1)	Sm. *u-kkule*	little finger or toe
69 *bA*)	S. *a-kullebetü-*	to divide, to cleave
129 *d*) 1)	Sm. *ue-külle-kæbbu*	arm-pit
180	Sm. *kulekunnaru*	land-boa
129 *c*) 3)	G. *kuli(hi)*	rat
129 *c*) 2)	Sm. *hikkuli*	bush-tortoise
99 *bB*)	G. *kuliy̌*	muscular
166 *e*) 2)	Q. *Kulimina*	god or demi-god
—	G. *kulisa*	a pool of water
69 *bB*)	Sm. *u-kullissi*	a woman's knot of hair
99 *f*) 2)	Sm. *kuljara*	canoe
99 *b*)	*a-koldo-,* Sm. *æ-kul(lu)du-*	to dip a sop, to soak
99 *b*)	*kolo,* S. *kullu*	to be corrupt, to be soaked
103 *e*) 1)	*akoloko,* S. *akulukku, akulugku*	in
172 *a*) 2)	*ako-loko*	eyes
(Sp.)	Sm. *kulbara*	gunpowder
5	*koma,* S. *kuma*	there is (not quite certain)
—	*komaka*	silk-cotton tree
136 *e*) 3) II)	Sm. *kumaru*	Dipteryx odorata
(cr.)	G. *komiki*	a bowl
129 *f*)	*maba o-komodi*	an honeycomb
129 *f*)	*komogi*	to move, to be troubled

129 f)	Sm. *u-kumuju*	dust, dirt of a thing
129 f)	Sm. *u-kummu-luku-hu*	shine, lustre
129 f)	*a-komodwa(in)*, Sm. *a-kkummudü-*	to warm oneself (near the fire) Sm. to dry in the sun
129 f)	Sm. *a-kumurdu-(nn-ua)*	to fart
129 f)	Sm. *kumur-kû*	to fart
129 c)	Sm. *kummuttiri*	white ant-hill
37	*kona*	when
63 a)	*o-kona*, S. *u-kunna*	at, on, attached to, concerning
63 a) 2A)	*o-kona*	nearly
91	*akona*	to walk
91	S. *akunnu-, akunu-*	to depart, to go, to walk
172 b) 2)	*akonnabo-*, S. *akannabü-, akanabü*	to hear
164 s) 1) II)	G. *kunapalu*	a fish-poison
172 b) 1)	*akonnaki*, S. *akannakü, akanakü*	a loud sound
97 a) 3)	*o-konaria*	for the sake of
97 e)	*o-kona mairia*	over against
63 b)	*(o-)kon-di* (f. *-du*, pl. *o-no*), S. *kun-di (-du, -na-na)*	at, on in
128 b)	S. *a-kündü-*	to shine
128 b)	*ma-kon-do*	to be naked
(cr.)	S. *koning*	king
176 c)	S. *-kunnu*	forms substantives, pl.
127 e)	S. *kunuku*	forest
63 a) 4)	*o-konomun*, S. *u-kunnamün*	concerning
129 d) 2), 16 d)	S. *u-kurra*, Sm. *u-kkura*	S. bed, Sm. hammock
107 b) 5), 125 b)	*egura*	root
135 d) 1) VI)	Sm. *korabuli*	brown
108	*akurradi-, akurrada* S. *akarrida*	to break
108	*akorakali*	thunder
108	*a-korati-*, S. *a-kulattu-*	to knock, to buffet
135 d) 1)	*kore*, S. *kule*	to be red, ripe
99 f) 2)	Sm. *kurehara*	a certain tree
135 d) 1) III)	*koreli*, S. *kulleheli*	smoke
135 d) 1) V)	*kureme*	bête rouge
129 c) 1)	*ikori*, S. *hikkuli*	to be halt, maimed, lame
164 b)	*korilia-ci*	newly born child
125 b)	*(to-)korira*, G. *kulira*	the gall
142	*koro*, S. *kurru*	negation
175 f), 176 c)	*-koro*, S. *-kurru*	forms substantives
129 d) 1)	*o-koro*, S. *u-kurru, u-kkulu*	knee
142 b)	*a-korodi-*, Sm. *a-kül(li)dü-*	to break (a branch from a tree)
117 d) 2)	*a-korogasa ... o-kona, a-korogosa*, S. *a-kurrukussâ*	to tremble
—	S.*a-kurrukudu-(nn-ua)*	an uproar, a great dissension
135 d) 2) IV)	*korrokori*, S. *karrukulli üssa-be-ru*	gold
129 d) 1)	Sm. *u-kkuru lukku*	hollow of the knee
166 e) 2)	Sm. *Kurruruman*	god or demi-god
117 d) 3)	*a-kororoso-*, S. *a-kkurrurussu-*	to pull down, to fall down
—	*korotaga*	a locust
—	*a-kurowasito-(n-wa)*, S. *a-kullussibattoa*	to kneel
117 a)	*akosa*	on, at the side of

(Sp.)	akosa	a needle
61 d)	S. küssa	or
172 a) 1) I), 116 b)	akosi, S. akussi	eye
129 b) 2)	kuta	animal
129 b)	o-kuti, S. u-kutti	foot
170 d)	a-koto-, S. a-kuttu-	to eat
17 d)	Adaie-li o-koto-n	the Supper of the Lord
128 d)	Sm. akutta, aküttü	to prick
129 aA)	G. a-khoto-	to collect (firewood)
163 e)	Sm. aküttühü	grandmother
(cr.)	S. gouverneur	governor
143	kowa, Sm. kawa	to be absent
—	S. kawandu-(nn-ua)	[they were] brought to nought
167	koia	shy, wild (animals)
161 i)	Sm. katti u-kurrubu	full moon
167 a) 1) II)	Sm. kujara	deer
128 h)	Sm. u-kkuju	navel
167 a)	R. kuyuha, v. C. koeja	star or constellation of stars, spirit
128 g)	a-kuyuko, S. u-kkujukku	the ear (ear-hole or organ of hearing)
167 a) 2)	koiamoora, G. koyumoρo	manati
120 e) 4)	o-koa	a horn
120 a)	-kwa (-kwon), S. -koa (-koan)	yet
120 e) 6)	a-koado-(n-wa)	to be round
120 e) 7)	a-kwaiabo-, S. a-kujabu-	to beseech, to pray
120 e) 7)	a-kwaiabo-(n-wa), S. a-kujabu-(nn-ua)	to worship, to do a prayer
120 e) 5)	kwa(w)ma	a hat, a crown
97 g)	Sm. akkuaria	der Breite nach gegenüber
120 a) 2) II)	-kwon-ci (f. -tu, pl. -o-no-ci), S. -koan-ti (-tu, a-nu-tti)	a person which is continually doing the thing
120 a) 2) I)	-kwo(n)na-(hu), S. -koana	instrumentalis
120 a) 4)	-kwawa, S. -koawa	amongst each other, reciprocal
94, 178, 184 ff.	L, G. l, λ	1⁰. willing (and able) to move, loose ; 2⁰. masculine or human, rational class.
99 f) 1)	ala, Sm. hala	Indian seat, bench, footstool
69 b)	Sm. labba	paca
89	alaiti, S. aruleti	a candle, a light
122 c)	oolai, ooli	a hole
—	a-lakada	to pour out, to sow
99 f) 3)	G. halalu, R. hararo	spatula, stirrer, pot-spoon
161 e)	Sm.a-llammada	to joggle, to rock
(cr.)	lamp(u?) S. lampu	a light
—	S.allammulukkuda, alamulukkuda	to assault (a mob)
182 (121 A)	Sm. lana	black paint, Genipa americana
—	S. alantina	a seat (?)
82 b)	Sm. -le	possessive suffix
109	S. ma-halle	to be lacking
126 a)	Sm. auleara	chalk
184	Sm. a-leledü-	durch einander plaudern
(Sp. ?)	G. lemono	lime, Citrus medica lemon
180	S.a-lesedi-, a-lesidi-	to read

70, 184 ff.	M	hesitating, humble, mild
83 c)	S. m̃.	instead of mm
83 d)	-m	instead of -n
10, 28	m(a)-	negative or privative prefix
5, 138	ma	there is (not quite certain)
70 a)	ma-(n), S. u-mâ(n)	every, all, entirely
139 a)	ama, S. ha˜a	what
139 a) 1)	ama ibia, S. hamma-hü-bia	why
133 c)	aiima, S. a-ima	wrath
83 a)	Sm. ema, aema, uima	mouth of a river
71 a) 1)	o-ma, S. u-ma	with
182 (104)	Sm. uma	perai
134 d) 2), 186	maba	honey
69 j)	G. maba fe	bees wax
166 e)	Mabukulu, Mabekele	Orion
105 a) 2)	a-maboradi-	to throng
163 e)	o-maodogo-ci, Sm. u-madukur-ti	father in law
159 e)	S. mappa	not to be able
109	aimaha	to curse, to revile
104 b) 1) II)	ma-hara	quickly, with haste
180	G. mahŏleru	land-boa
166 j)	R. mahui	an evil spirit
133 b) 1)	maiika-ci (-tu)	deaf
35	ma-in	being (not quite certain) ; it hath been said
97	(a-)mairia, -mirea, S. -maria	side
74 d) 7)	a-mairikota, S. a-mallikutta	to teach
74 d) 7)	a-mairikoto-(n-wa)	to learn
71 c)	o-makana, S. u-mükanna	over against
166 e) 1)	Makanaura, Makanaholo	demi-god
48 e)	Sm. -make	intensifying
128 b)	makondo, S. makundu	to be naked
139 a) 2)	amakoro	nothing
120 a) 5)	-makwa, S. -maqua	alltogether, all, every
120 e) 8)	S. ma-kuahü	vain
120 e) 9)	Sm. makoali	a whip
—	S. a-makoalitedü-	to beat (to whip)
76 c)	Pen. o-mala	a stream
74 d) 8)	Pen. Mali	the mother of knowledge
74 d) 1)	mali	should, ought
74 d) 6)	S. malliku	to be able to
130 a)	malokon aukili, S. malukkunni-aukilli, mallugkunni-aukilli	the wilderness
103 i) 2)	a-malokododa	to be desolate
147	mamari, S. mammalli	to be impossible
74 e)	o-mana	edge (of a sword)
74 e) 2)	Sm. mannaka	manicole-palm
99 g)	Sm. mannako-la	manicole-palm-wood
74 e) 2)	Sm. mannali	sieve
88 d)	o-manjia, o-manjin	like
166 k)	R. mansinskiri	an evil spirit
148	manswa, S. manswa, mansua	to be exceedingly
74 e)	Sm. a-manti-	to sharpen
108	maraka	rattle

77. 184 *ff.*	*N*	firmness or substantiality of a neutral character
83 c)	S. *n*	instead of *nn*
83	*n*	alternating with ñ *y*, —
7, 177	*n*, S. *n*, G. *n*, *no*	end-point pronoun III f.
81 a), 26, 27	*-(i)n*	possessive suffix ; forms **verbal** nouns
81 *b)*	*-ie-n*, *-iâ-n*	possession
7, 177	*n(a)-*	pronominal prefix III pl.
79 a), 79 *b)* 1)	*-na*	continuation ; plurality
79 c)	*ina*, S. *u-ina*	end
79 a) 2)	*iana*	heel
131 *b)*	*iauna*, *iouna*, S. *üjauna*	value, price, reward
79 e) 1) II)	*oonaba*, S. *a-onnaba*	to answer
109	*aanabo*, *aanubo*, S. *ahannuba*	to be awake, to watch, to awake (intrans.)
79 c) 4)	*inabo*, S. *inabo*, *inabbu*	after
79 e) 1) I)	*onabo*, S. *wunabu*	low, the ground
184	G. *unabuse*	blindworm
79 e) 2)	S. *wunapu*	(to fall) to the ground
7, 44 *b)*	*naha*, S. *naha*	emphasizing pronoun III pl.
182 (53)	Sm. *nahallihu*	paddle
7, 44 a)	*naii*, S. *nai*	emphasizing pronoun III pl.
79 *d)*	*anaka*, S. *annakka*	the midst
—	*aunaka*	to hire
79 c) 3)	*inaka muniro*	backwards
79 e) 4)	*onnaka-ro*	burden
160 *b)*	*anaki*	South
79 e) 3)	*onnaki-*, S. *a-onnaki-*	to take
79 e) 3)	*aunaki-*, S. *anniki-*, *añiki-*	to receive
79 e) 3)	Sm. *anniki-*	to take, to carry
—	*aunaki ... o-ma*	to take with one
44 *h)*	Sm. *nakia*	pronoun III pl.
91	*onnakidi-*	to lift up
91	*onnakiti-*	to compel to bear
79 *d)*	*anaku*	the midst
79 e) 3)	Sm. *annaku-(nn-ua)*	to paddle
7, 44 c)	*naraha*, S. *narraha*	emphasizing pronoun III pl.
79 c) 2)	*iinata*	to begin
79 e) 5)	*onnawa*, S. *annuwâ*	to choose
80 a) 1)	*anda*	(two ways) meet
80 a) 2)	Sm. *andaka*	joint, articulation
80 a) 3)	*andakoto-*	to join, to cleave to
80 a) 4)	*andi-*	to come
80 a) 3)	*andi- ... abu*	to bring
(cr.)	*nete*	a net
25, 78 *d)*	*-ni*, S. *-ne*	something that really is or shall be
78 e) 1)	*ani*, S. *âni*	a thing
125 a)	*oni-abu*, *oini*, S. *wuni-abu*, *wuin(i)*	water
78 *f)*	*onnibit(i-?)*	to disperse
78 *f)*	S. *a-nebetu-(nn-ua) ... n-auri-koawa*	to be dispersed, scattered, divided
34	*onikain*	river
78 a)	*niikan*	a while

B 3●

78 c)	S. *nikebe*	to occur immediately, straightway, forthwith
78 a)	*niiman*	a while, a little
158 b)	-*ni-no*, S. -*nni-nu*	a group
78 b)	S. *ni rubu kurru*	a long time, no little, no small, not a few
(cr.)	S. *anker*	an anchor
79 b) 2)	-*no*, S. -*nu*, -*ñu*	plurality
176 b)	S. -*nu*	forms pl. substantives
7, 177	G. *no*	end-point pronoun III f.
79 a) 3)	*o-no*, S. *u-nnu*	neck
127 d)	*nokonne, nokonni*, S. *nukané*	sorrow, mercy
127 d)	*a-nokonnedi-*	to cause sorrow or sadness
127 b)	Sm. *hunnu-hunnu-li*	a certain fly
127 a)	*a-onnoda*, S. *a-huñahuñadü-*	to murmur
79 a) 3) II)	G. *honole*	tigerbird
79 a) 3) II)	G. *anula*	Ardea cocoi
158 a)	-*noma*	a group, a company
79 e) 1) III)	R. *n-onabo-kuanna*	a shield
80 a) 5)	Sm. *ansâ, ansî*	to grate
80 b)	*ansi*, S. *ansi*	soul, inner peace, love, to love
78 e) 1)	*anye, anyi*	a thing, a thing possessed
78 e) 1)	*onyi*	a thing, a thing possessed
78 e) 3)	*onyi*, S. *ani*	to do
78 e) 2)	*o(-)nyikau*, Sm. *anniku-hu*	goods
27, 120 g) 6) I)	-*n-wa*, S. -*nn-ua*	formative verbal nouns
166 g)	*Anuanai-tu*	mythical girl
166 g)	Q. *annoane*	vulture, carrion-crow
166 g)	*Anuanima*	mythical man
2, 184 *ff.*	O	see *U*
—	*oa*	see *wa*
—	*oe*	see *we*
130	*o*	alternating with *au*
69, 184 *ff.*	P	see *f*
—	Q	see *k*
94, 178, 184 *ff.*	R, G. *r*, *ρ*	1⁰. willing, but not able to move, motion being impeded: 2⁰. female or nature class
108 A	*r*	rotation
179	-*ra*	emphasizing particle, women
104, 107	*ra*	at a certain place or moment
104 b) 1)	*hara, ara*, S. *harra*	to be spent, ended, accomplished
107 b) 4), 125 b)	*ura*	juice
104 c) 1)	*(e)rabudiki*, S. *e-rabuddikki*	against, toward
104 c) 1)	*(e)rabodogo*	against, toward
104 b) 1) III)	*haradi-*	to spend
104 b) 1) IV)	*aradi-*, S. *arradü-*	to make fully, to complete
104 a)	*raia*, S. *raija*	appearance
108	*araga*	to cut off

108	*aragakoto-*	to separate, to divide
117 *d*) 2)	*aragasa*	to be shaken
117 *d*) 2)	*eragasi-*	to shake (transitive)
104 *b*) 2) IV)	*heraki, (h)eragi,* S. *hür(rü)kū*	to be together
104 *b*) 2) V)	*a-herakidi-, a-herakida,*	to come together, to
	S. *a-hürkida*	gather (together)
108	*(a)-iharakidi-*	to tear
108	*a-iherakido-(n-wa)*	to break (a net ; intrans.)
107 *a*)	*-(i)rako,* S. *irakku*	in
117 *d*) 2)	*arakosa,* S. *arrukussâ*	to be shaken
—	S. *Chios rallaboamün*	over against Chios
!04 *d*)	*arama,* Sm. *aruma*	the side
104 *b*) 2) IX)	S. *k-arrana*	to be mixed
161 *a*)	*aranaha-i,* S. *harrunaha*	the dayspring
(Sp.)	Sm. *aransu*	an orange
104 *b*) 2) IX)	*aranta*	to mix
184	G.*da-raraida*	I belch
108 *A f*)	*oraro,* S. *wuraru*	cloud
125 *b*)	G. *uraroni*	saliva
104 *b*) 2) II)	*a-herrati-*	to press
121 *c*) 7)	*arauadi-,* S. *araudü-*	to wipe
166 *d*)	*Arawanili, Arawidi*	sun-deity
104 *c*) 2)	R. *t-arbara-n*	(its) broadside
100	*ardi-*	to bite
108 *A b*) 2)	Sm. *aordü-*	to spin
96	*(i-)re,* S. *ré*	no motion
108 *A b*)	*(h)aure,* S. *haule*	perversed, maimed
164 *i*) 2)	*ire,* S. *irei*	to be married
96 *c*)	*ere-hi*	a snare
166 *b*) 1)	*ore-hi,* S. *wure-hū*	fornication
164 *i*) 3)	*ire-no*	little children
97	*-rea, -area, -aurea, -o-rea, warea*	from
104 *b*) 2) VIII)	S., Sm. *erekedi-*	to save, to keep
104 *b*) 2) VIII)	*eregi, erigi,* Sm. *erekê*	to gather up, to root up
104 *b*) 2) I)	*herre-n*	the press (of the multitude)
185 (59)	*rero,* G. λ*eru*	an organ, G. panpipe
184	G. *ĕerâdoa*	to yawn
184	*areroko. ireroko,* S. *ue-llerukku*	mouth
164 *i*) 2)	*ireyu*	the state of wife
175 *b*)	*-ri*	forms substantives
100	*-ri*	fixed
100	*airi*	tooth
100, 164 *i*) 1)	*iri,* S. *iri*	name
112 *b*)	Sm. *ue-iri*	backbone
100 *a*), 69 *j*)	*iribe,* S. *iribe*	uncleanness
100 *a*)	*a-ribeti-*	to pollute, to defile, to profane
163 *c*) 1)	Sm. *u-ribi-ti (u-ribia-tu)*	brother (sister) in law
108 *A c*)	*a-uribi*	to roll (transitive)
101 *a*)	*(e)ribo, (o-)rebo,* S. *ü-llebu*	waterside
101 *a*) 3)	*a-ribota,* S. *a-rubutti-*	to land
!80	*a-ridi-*	to read
(cr.)	S. *riem*	(rudder) bands
108 *A b*) 2)	*a-urid(i-?)*	to turn
!01 *b*)	*rifu*	waterside

163 c) 2)	Sm. *urihitti-ti*	a man's son-in-law
103 f)	*ariloko*, S. *arilukku*	in (between)
141	*arin(i)*, S. *âlin*	exercising a profession, a trade, a craft
125	*origahu*, S. *wullîkahu*	night
(from Sp. remo)	*a-rimodi-*	to row
126 a)	*arira*, Sm. *hallira*	to be white
166 f)	G. *Orliro*	mythical woman
126 b)	*oriroko-ho*, S. *wulliruku-hu*	darkness
126 b)	*a-orirokoto-*	to darken, to obscure
91	*iriti-*	to call one's name
166 d)	G. *Harliwanli*	sun-deity
166 b)	R. *oriyu*	goddess ; water spirit
102	*(i)ro*, S. *(i)ru*	stopped
175 c), 176 a, b)	*-ro*, S. *-ru*	forms substantives
108 A f)	Sm., R. *haru*	starch
164 h)	*aiero*, S. *a-haiaru*	to be in bondage, to be a slave
150	*robu*, S. *rubu*	only
150	*robuginai*	only (?)
—	*aroboti-*, S. *arubutti-*	to extract
122 d) 2)	S. *a-hurruda*	to come together
103 b)	*roko*, S. *rukku*	in
—	*a-rulaka*	to move
—	*a-rulako-(n-wa)*	to be moved
—	Sm. *ruli*	a stone axe
166 b) 2)	R. *oroli*	mythical big snake
—	*a-rulukokiti-*	to stir up
122 d) 1) III)	*to-horoman*	the hills
122 d) 1) IV)	*o-horomurrida-* ; *a-*	waves ; to be waves
122 d) 1) II)	*o-horora*, S. *u-hurrura*	land, farm, country
122 d) 1) I)	*ororo*, S. *hurruru*	earth, world
122 d) 1) V)	*ororoli*, Sm. *ruruli*	clay, mud
i22 d) 5)	*orosi*, S. *hurrussü*	to be filled with food
122 d) 5)	*a-orosidi-*	to fill, to suffice
117 d) 2 A)	G. *aroso*	washboard
117 d) 2 A)	Sm. *arrussuttu-*	to build up
122 d) 1) VI)	Sm. *hurrutu*	pumpkin
182 (64 A)	Pen. *iarowia*	Venus
120 b) 2)	*arua*, S. *aruwa*	jaguar
120 g) 1)	G. *oroa, owrowa*	to perform the functions of the medicine-man
166 f)	G. *Orlowama*	mythical man
120 e) 1)	*aroadi-*, S. *aroada*	to creep
139 c)	*arohai*, S. *haruwai*	here
113, 184 ff.	S	showing form, having a surface of its own, a scale or cuticle
114 b)	*a-sa*, S. *a-ssa*	to call (to give a name)
114 a), 164 c)	*(i)sa*, S. *ssa*	formed, sound, beautiful, good ; child, young animal, egg
114 a) 6) II)	*ka-sa*	to be with child, to conceive, to beget
104 c A) 2)	G. *sabadi-*	to trample flat

113	*isadi-*, S. *üüssadü-*	to heal, to save, to restore, to garnish
149	*sabu*, S. *sabu*	to be "very"
104 *c A*) 2)	*sapakana*	a long wooden sword
(Sp.)	*sapatu*, S. *ssappatu*	shoe
117 *e*)	*a-safodi-*	to trample, to tread
—	S. *üsseika-hü*	pleasure
29 *e*)	*isaigati-*	to please
176 *a*) 1)	*isaili !*	friend !
114 *c*)	*saka*	to wither, to be withered
(cr.)	*saka*	bag, scrip
117 *g*)	*a-sakada ... o-ma*, S. *a-ssakkadâ ... u-ma*	to meet
180	*a-sacrificedo-(n-wa)*	to do sacrifice
104 *c A*) 1)	G. *salabadi-*	to square wood
99 *i*)	G. *sale*	ancle (elbow, etc.)
119 *a*) 3)	G. *sale*	small lobster
160 *c*)	*iisa mairia*	right side
104 *c A*) 2)	G. *sapa-η*	smooth
—	S. *w-abunna-hü-ssia*	fruitful seasons (*) our-plantation)
	) assammukudoa	
116 *c*) 2)	Sm. *sammali*	a cassava grater
(Sp.)	Sm. *sambuleru*	hat
164 *c*)	*isan-ci* (pl. *isano-no-ci*, S. *issana-nu-tti)*	servant
114 *d*)	*a-saradi-*	to bruise, to grind
104 *c*) 4)	R. *sarapa*	three-pronged arrow, double bar-relled gun
119 *a*) 3)	G. *saρaρa*	small crab
100	*isa-ri b-a-li !*	farewell !
(cr.)	S. *Saterdaka*	Sabbath day
130 *a*)	*isa-u-ga, isa-u-kili*	fair weather, summer
130 *e)*	*isauka*	a kingdom
116 *d*) 10), 179	S., Sm. *-se*	emphasizing particle
182 (100)	Sm. *seberu*	a toad
115	S. *isehü*, Sm. *isehi*	a worm
75 *a*)	*seme*, S. *seme*	to be sweet, delicate
166 *h*) 1)	G. *seme(-he)*	good spirit
166 *h*) 2)	*semici-ci*, S. *semetti*	medicine-man, sorcerer
115	*esere, isere*	sores, leprosy
116 *d*) 9)	*serabokilio*, S. *seribokkilliu*	a tempest
(cr.)	*sesi*	a chariot
116 *b*)	*isi*, S. *issî*	seed ; top ; head
115	*isi*, Sm. *hissi, hüssi*	to stink
130 *b*) 1)	*a-usi-*	to go
130 *b*) 1)	S. *a-usu-*	to begin, to start, to depart
118 *a*)	*-sia*	indicates a trait of character, etc.
22	*-sia*	formative verbal nouns (result, etc.)
118 *a*) 10)	*a-sia*	to fish
118 *a*) 11)	*onnaki- ... (i)isia*	to comfort, to sigh
116 *a*) 3)	*siba*	stone, rock : also : prison
116 *a*) 1)	*isiba*	face
166 *f*)	G. *Sibarlojen*	mythical woman

93	S. *sibassibaru*	waves
116 a) 1)	*isibo*, S. *issỉbu*	in face of
120 d) 1A)	R. *shiboadda-hu*	child born with a caul
116 b) 3)	*(i)-sidi-tu*	roof
116 c) 3)	G. *siparali*	arrow with bamboo lanceolate head
116 c) 3)	I. Th. *siparara*, R. *shiparari*	do., iron
116 c) 3)	*siparari*, S. *siparalli*	iron
115	*sipe*	bitter
—	S. *sipeta-lli*	bitterness
116 a) 2)	*isifu*	in face of
116 a) 2) III)	*isifodo*	door, gate
116 a) 2) II)	*a-sifuda*, S. *a-ssipuddâ*	to turn away, against, about; to repent
116 a) 2) II)	*a-sifudo-(n-wa)*	to be interpreted, to be translated
117 f)	*wa-siga-te*, *wa-sika-te*	let us go
(cr.)	*sikapo*, S. *sikapu*	sheep
(Sp.)	Sm. *sikalu*	sugar
116 d) 1)	*a-siki-*, S. *a-ssiki-*	to put, to give
73 a)	S.*a-ssiki- ... ame*	to obey, to believe
136 e) 1)	*asikii*	interjection of disgust
91	*a-sikiti-*	to deliver
116 b) 4), 16 d)	*isikwa*, S. *ü-ssiqua*, *ü-ssikoa*	house, shelter
116 d) 5)	Sm. *sila*	to ache
99 e)	*a-silaki-*	to throw (dust into the air)
99 e)	Sm. *a-ssilikidü-*	to melt, to deliquesce
116 d) 2)	S. *a-ssimadü-*	to call
116 d) 2)	*a-simaka*, S. *a-ssimaka*	to cry
116 d) 2)	*a-simaki-*, S. *a-ssimaki-*	to call
116 d) 3), 184	Sm. *isimuddu*	electric eel
76 d), 116 c) 1)	*simara*	arrow
109	*simara-habo*	bow
116 d) 6)	S. *simika*, S. *simika*	to be jealous
116 d) 7)	Sm. *simittâ*	to laugh
115	S. *isin*	penis
116 b) 6)	*(i)siri*	nose; ruggedness
116 b) 6) III)	*isiribidi-*, G. *a-siribidi-*	to spin, to roll up
130 b) 2)	*ausiro*	idle
116 a) 4)	*isiroko*	flesh
175 d)	G. *ŝiruabali*	Nectandra
(cr.)	*slotro*	key
184	G. *ŝilotoρo wayurĭ*	padlock
135 f)	Sm. *subule*	to be green
119 b) 6)	Sm. *subuli*	a sore, ulcer
116 c) 4)	Sm. *sudi*	blow-gun arrow
119 a) 3)	S. *a-ssudu-*	to flay
119 b) 6)	Sm. *sukku*	Indian small-pox
119 a) 2)	*a-sogo-*, *a-soko-*, S. *a-ssuku-*	to hew down, to strike (with an axe or sword)
119 a) 1)	*isogo*, *isoko*, Sm. *aessuku*	small, little
119 b) 1)	*a-sogoso-*, S. *a-ssukussu-*	to wash
(Sp. or cr.)	*soldaro*, S. *soldaru*	soldier
(cr.)	S. *sûlu*	school
119 b) 3 A)	G. *a-solosolodo-*	to polish

116 *d*) 8)	*sumule*, S. *somole*	to be drunk
(cr.)	S. *Sondaka*	Sunday
119 *b*) 2)	S. *a-sonnuku-*	to pour out
119 *b*) 2)	*a-sonko-(n-wa)*	to be running out, to be poured out
(cr.)	S. *sura-bandi, sula-bandi*	an upper room
—	S. *a-ssurredü-*	to have diarrhoea
119 *a*) 3)	G. *isåρo*	small lobster
119 *b*) 4)	*a-sorobodi-*	to sweep (a house)
108 *A g*), 186	Sm. *a-ssürdü-,*	to spin
	a-ssürrissüridü-	
119 *b*) 6)	Sm. *surre*	diarrhoea
119 *b*) 5)	*a-sorokodo-*	to be shed, to well forth
119 *b*) 3)	Pen. *sorota-ro*	vampyr
119 *b*) 3),186	*a-soroto-,* S. *a-ssurtu-*	to kiss, to suck
(cr.)	S. *Statuta*	law
164 *l*) 3)	G. *šuwe*	friend, brother (vocative)
120 *f*) 2)	*a-soadi-*	to draw (a fluid)
180	*a-sweardoa*	to swear
120 *f*) 1)	*asoare*	withered
90, 178, 184 *ff.*	*T*	1⁰. motion directed towards an object, limited motion: 2⁰. female, or nature class
—	*ataba*, S. *a-tabâ*	to be scattered, dispersed
169 *a*) 4)	*tabisia*, S. *tabussia*	to slumber
(cr.)	*tapel*	table
45 *b*)	*taha*, S. *taha*	far off
121 *e*) 2)	*tahawai*	far off
104 *e*)	*t-itagara*	(its) wall
—.	S. *bahü ü-ttakarra*	the porch
—	*a-tagi-,* S. *a-ttakü-*	to cover, to close, to shut
99 *h*)	G. *tala*	lower jaw
73 *b*) 9)	*tamo-tu*	bowed
47	*tanahu*, S. *dannuhu, daⁿuhu*	now, to day, this day
(cr.)	*taraffa*, S. *treppa*	stairs
108	*atarata-hu airi-sibo,* S. *attarradu-n n-ari-ssibu*	gnashing of teeth
90 *a*)	*tata*, S. *(ü-)tatta*	hard
90 *b*)	*tata ... o-kona,* S. *(ü-)tatta ... u-kunna*	power, force, strength
90 *a*) 2)	*tatabudi*, S. *tattabuddi*	stiff
90 *a*) 3)	*itatadi-*	to harden
90 *b*) 2)	*a-tatadi- ... o-kona*	to strengthen
(cr.)	*tau*, S. *tau*	cord
90 *a*)	*ka-tau*	to be noble, wise (?)
166 *g*)	*Taukelŏlelio*	mythical woman
82 *b*)	Sm. *-te*	possessive suffix
82 *A*	*-te*	resembling
95	*-te*	limited motion
191	*ite*, S. *üttü*	blood
182 (23)	*itte.* S. *itte*	bowels
182 (123)	Sm. *itte*	ite (muriti) **palm**
175 *d*)	G. *itebali*	Vochysia tetraphylla

163 b)	Sm. *itte-boa-ti*	stepfather, father's brother
163 b), 120 d) 2)	R. *aiite-boa-chi*	stepson
—	*atedi-*, S. *attüddü-*	to flee, to go astray
184	Sm. *a-ttedi-*	to sneeze
110 b) 3)	G. *a-ttekedi-*	to advise
—	*itekia-hu*	a bloody flux
—	*a-tekida-*	to break, to put asunder
(Sp.)	Sm. *temona*	rudder
—	*atenaa*, S. *attenna*	to tread
191	*itena*, S. *ütenna*	blood (as a part of the body)
—	*atenabo-*	to borrow, to lend, to let out, to hire
—	*itendwa-ti-*, S. *attündu-*	to sink
(cr.)	*tenti*	a tent
159 a)	*atenwa*, S. *atennennua, atenénua*	the beginning
108	*aterakidi-*, S. *attürküdu-*	to rend
90 g), 125 c) 2)	*tere*, Sm. *ittere*	heat
164 o) 2), 16 d)	R. *tete*, Sm. *atette*	mother
90 d)	Sm. *tette*	to itch
184	G. *a-thethedi-*	to whisper
21	*-ci*	formative verbal nouns (agent nouns, etc.)
82 b)	*-ti*	possessive suffix
110 a)	*(hi)ti*, S. *hitti*	to desire, to will, etc.
91	*a-ti*	to drink
163 a), 16 d)	*ici*, S. *itti*	father
163 a)	Sm. *iti-ti*	a woman's son in law
163 a)	*itiu*, Sm. *itti-ju*	a woman's daughter in law
163 a)	*aii-ci*, S. *adi-tti*	son
91, 133 a)	*aici-*, S. *aditti-*	to know
—	*aici- ... o-konomun*	to understand
131 c)	*auti*	to suffer, to permit
—	S. *autu-(nn-ua)*	to get permission
—	*aciadi-*	to prick, to pierce
90 f) 3)	*itibi*, Sm. *ittebe*	a birth-mark, etc.
99 f) 5)	*tibo-kili*	a bush
99 f) 4)	*t-itiboko*	(bird's) nest
—	*itiga*, S. *attikaha*	to be drowned
—	*ittika*	excrements ; rust
11 d)	*a-cigi-*	to dig
11 d)	*a-ciga*	a ditch
91	*aiciki*	a token, a mark
131 d)	*aucigi-*, S. *a-uttiki-*	to find, to receive
118 a) 1)	*-cikibe*, S. *-ttikebbe*	theft
110 b) 3)	Sm. *a-ttikida*	to persuade
91	*a-tikidi-*, S. *a-ttikiddü-*	to fall, to cast, to pluck a leaf
110 b) 3)	G. *a-tikidikita*	to sing (a medicine-man)
163 c)	R. *ichiki-ci*	a woman's husband's sister's
91	*aicikiti-*	to warn, to betray
163 d) 2)	*a-ciligi-ci*	a woman's brother
90 f) 2)	Sm. *ittima(-hü)*	moustache, beard
—	*atima, atema*	to pass over
—	*atimi-*, S. *attimü-*	to swim
—	*itimi*	rope, bonds

17	o-	prefix announcing the not changing
7, 177	u, S. u	end-point pronoun I pl.
3	u, o	end-vowel verbs
17 d)	S., Sm., Q. Ü, ue	prefix
3	ü	end-vowel verbs
2, 185	W	vast, far away
136 e) 6)	Q. wa	affirmative word
4, 120, 188	-wa, -ua, -oa	stationary, in itself, independent
121	wa-	distant, exceeding, etc.
121 a)	Sm. oâ	to be long (time)
120 g) 3)	awa, S. awa	self
164 o), 16 d)	awa, S. awa	father
120 f) 5)	waa	to be dry
121 d) 1)	wabu, S. wabu	very, exceedingly, genuine ; honorific
121 a)	oaboddi-, S. a-wabaddu-	to abide, to wait, to tarry
121 a)	wabuji(-n), S. wâbudi	quickly with haste
121 a)	waboka	already, (just) now
121 b), 16 d)	waboroko, S. waburukku	a way, a road
121 c) 9)	G. u-wadawada	fins
121 c) 4)	auadi-, S. a-wadi-	to beckon
121 c) 1)	auadi-, S. a-wahüddu-	to go about, to seek
121 b)	wadi, waji, S. wadi	to be long
164 e)	wadili, S. wadili	a man (male)
121 c) 2)	S. t-awadu	wild (beasts)
121 b) 5)	auaduli, S. awadulli	wind
(cr.)	S. wagen	a chariot
(Sp.)	wela, S. wela	a sail
—	a-welado-(n-wa), S. a-weladu-(nn-ua)	to sail
121 a)	wahajia, S. wahaddia, wahadja	hereafter, by and by
121 a)	wahadu-tu	old (a thing)
121 f)	S. uahünnâ	a great quantity (?)
121 f)	S. uahüntu-(nn-ua)	to be added
121 e)	-wai	intensifying
2, 44 a)	wai, S. wai	emphasizing pronoun I pl.
120 g) 2)	-oaiya, -uaiya, S. -oaja, -waja	self
120 f) 5)	waiè, Sm. waija,	potters clay
120 f) 5)	Sm. waijeli	to fade
120 f) 5)	R. waiyari, Sm. waijali	knapsack
121 b)	waiikile	a far country
134 g)	wakaia	evil, to be evil
71 b) 2) VI)	wakaia ... omuni	woe unto
120 f) 6)	wakaukili	the dust (from the road)
44 h)	Sm. wakia	pronoun I pl.
121 a)	wakili, S. wakil(l)i	long ago, rather a long time ago
120 f) 4)	wakorra, Sm. wakarra	pining away, Sm. mager sein
121 a)	wakorrau, S. wakarruhu	now
120 c) 4)	oakudo-(n-wa), S. awakidu-(nn-ua)	to break (intransitive)
186	wakokwa	pigeon

121 *d*) 2)	S. *oâ-kurru seribokilliu*	a tempestuous wind
120 *c*)	*oa(l)la*	piece ; cheek
104 *c A*) 1)	G. *walaba*	Eperua falcata
—	S.*awallassa-ru meju*	broken pieces of the ship
120 *c*) 3)	*oalabaw*, S. *oallaboa*	the other side
100	*iwarikidikitti-*	to open the mouth (of a fish)
—	Sm. *a-warukudu-*	fortrücken, schieben, rutschen
—	Sm. *a-warukudukutt(u-?)*	to let down
121 *a*)	*wara-uara-tu eke-hu*	sackcloth
121 *c*)	*warea*, S. *waria*	from
121 *c*) 6)	*wariwari*	a fan
—	Sm. *wauriku*	speed
—	S. *wauriku-kû-n*	with all speed
120 *f*) 3)	Q. *oassini-hü*	the heart
125 *b*)	Sm. *oewedi-*	to spit
125 *b*)	Sm. *ueku*	resin
125 *c*) 2)	*iwerebe*	the heat
125 *c*) 2)	*eweribed(i-?)*	to be fervent
125 *c*) 1)	Sm. *iwera*	penis
125 *c*) 1)	*iwi*, S. *iwi*	fruit
—	Sm. *iwihi*	dead game
—	Sm. *iwihiti-*	to shoot
—	S. *n-iwihitta-hü-nni|je*	their stripes
(cr.)	S. *winu*	wine
125 *e*)	*wiru*	(turtle) dove
125 *c*)	Sm. *iwissi*	testicle
125 *d*)	*wiwa*, S. *wijua*	star
83 *a*)	Sm. *wijua*	Pleiades
175 *f*)	R. *wiwa-kihi-koro*	(Halley's) comet
184	G. *iwiwida*	to whistle
164 *l*)	*oe-n-ci (-tu)*, R. *wo-n-chi*	kinsman (woman), cousin
166 *f*)	Sc. *Wurekado*	mythical woman
118 *a*) 11)	S. *üwüssiati-*	to make lamentation
2, 45, 104 *g*), 123, 124, 185	Y-	"here"
169	*huia, ia*, Sm. *ueja*	principle of life, spirit
169 *b*)	*iya(bo)*, S. *ija*	shadow, image
125 *c*) 1)	*a-uiyi*, Sm. *a-oji*	to gather fruit
66	*iabo*	the outside, behind
169 *a*) 5)	*a-iaboda*	to broil
169 *a*) 4)	*a-iabos(i-?)*	to be drowsy
169 *b*)	*a-iaboti-*, S. *a-ijabutta*	to overshadow
184	Sm. *jadolle*, G. *yadoala*	a knife
45 *b*)	*yaha*, S. *jaha*	here
—	Sm. *jáhakanni-*	to be small
—	S. *jahakandu-ttu u-llua-hü abbu*	with humility
—	S., Sm. *a-(i) jakkad(d)a*	to lie in bed or hammock
97 *f*)	S. *jaha-maria*	here this side
102 *d*)	*yaha-mutero (-muntero, -muntiro)*, S.*jaha-mutero*	here
121 *c*) 10)	Sm. *jahu*	cotton
(cr.)	S. *jager-nu*	horsemen
45 *f*) 1)	*yakitaha*, S. *jakketa*	yonder

80 *b*) 6)	*a-iyurati-* ... *ansi,* S. *a-ijulattü-* ... *ansi*	to trouble, to be troubled, to be vexed, to care for
124 *b*)	*(o-?)iuri*	throat
124 *b*)	R. *yuro,* Sm. *juru*	cassava-squeezer
120 *e*) 3)	*yurua*	a thorn
124 *b*)	*yuyuokili*	a mist
124 *b*)	*a-iyuyuto-*	to water
123 *f*)	Sm. *aijoa*	late
96 *c*) 2)	*yu-warea,* S. *ju-waria*	from thence
123 *e*)	S. *a-ijuwedu-(nn-ua)* ... *u-mün*	to adhere to, to consort with

German words, in Schultz' texts

Apostel, apostle, *christianus,* a Christian, *engel,* angel, *evangelium,* gospel, *fest,* feast, *funfzig,* fifty, *gerber,* tanner, *gnaden,* grace, *Gutfurth,* The fair havens, *heidi-nu.* heathens, Gentiles, *judu,* Jew, *kaiser,* Cæsar, *kreuz,* cross, (*osser,* idol), *pingsten,* whitsuntide, *priester,* priest, *purpura,* purple, *stadt,* town, *stuhl,* seat, *stundu,* hour, *tausend,* thousand.

CHAPTER I

FINITE VERB

§ 1. Let us consider the following sentence:

H-adeka, d-imigoda hu sikapo wolf o-koboroko jin: ki-o-doma ka-
ye-see   I-send   you sheep   wolf among   as   this!-because affirmed-
koborokwa-li hu hori jin, ma-wakaia-li bajia hu wiru jin. To-moroa
wisdom-freely ye serpent as, withheld-evil-freely also ye dove as its-but
h-aitoa-li   loko-no o-mun. Behold, I send you forth as sheep in the
ye-beware-freely man-plural at
midst of wolves: be ye therefore wise as serpents, and harmless as doves.
But beware of men.

The action-words *h-adeka* and *d-imigoda* are composed of a pronominal
prefix *(h-, d-)*, a quality-word (quality, state or condition) or object-word
(ade, strong appearance, *imigo,* readiness, being ready), a consonant
which indicates in what way the preceding compound acts *(k* making its
appearance in a positive manner, *d* to be firmly established, to stand, to
be stiff) and a vowel indicating the general character of what is happening.

The words we here call action-words, are all composed in this way;
they all indicate an activity, and moreover a person can be indicated
who causes this activity or controls it, which person in the finite forms
is indicated by a pronominal prefix, or by an emphasizing pronoun or
object-word, which fulfills the same function and occupies the same place
as the pronominal prefix.

It is almost certain, that, for instance *lo-oda,* he died, and *h-adunka,* sleep
ye, also belong to this category; *a-odo,* S. *a-hudu-,* means: permanently firmly
established, or firmly established in space (which may refer to the body or to
the soul); *adunku-* may have a similar meaning, or it may mean "to snore".

Ka-koborokwa, ma-wakaia (see §§ 10, 18) we call quality-words, as
well as for instance *kokke,* to live; *kokke ka i,* he lives, probably denotes:
strength appears him.

§ 2. That the *a* is the real "Zeitwort", appears plainly from those
forms in which the *a* with the pronominal prefix is detached from the
remainder of the verb (see § 28); then the *a* acts as an auxiliary verb,
though not as a colourless copula, but with the meaning of "to happen".

The *a* occurs in numerous other forms, and in comparing them, we
find as a kind of greatest common divisor, that the Arawak language
uses the *a* to indicate: the aspect of the world in its continual change.
Not one single exception to this rule has been met with.

It has been found, that the *i* and the *u* or *o* are also used to express
definite principles. The Arawak uses the *i* to express: small dimensions
(in space and time) or high tension, the *u* or *o* to express: great dimensions
(in space and time) or low tension, whilst the *a* expresses that which stands
between the two principles, or partakes in the nature of both.

The Arawak makes no difference between time and space in the way we do ; the *a* may indicate both "happening", as well as a condition, or an object considered in its transitory character (Heraclitus *panta rei*). We shall use for this the abbreviation "time-bound reality" or "time-reality".

The *u* or *o* principle is independent of time ; it comprises as it were the whole time. We shall translate it, according to circumstances, by "great", "space", "the permanent", "motionless", "not changing", and the *w*, which is related to *u*, sometimes by "vast", "far away".

In the *i* principle, on the other hand, time is as it were, contracted into a single point, into the infinitesimally small. We shall translate it, according to circumstances, by "tiny", "quick", "instantaneous", "free", "principle", "idea", "intensively", "accentuated", and the *y*, which is related to *i*, sometimes by "here". *I*, "here", *a*, "at some distance", in the words *ikirikia*, our own nation, *akirikia*, a foreign nation, and perhaps in *ici*, father, *aiici*, son.

The *i*, and in contrast to it the *u*, *o*, are also used to mark the distinction between man (homo) and nature, or man (vir) and woman. This use of the *i* and the *u*, *o* and also that of the *l-* and *t-*, *r-* for the same purpose, we shall keep strictly apart from the remaining use of those sounds.

It seems that the *e* is used to indicate a principle, the nature of which may be illustrated by the following comparisons : *a* sound, healthy, somewhat relentless, hard — *e* sickly, delicate, tender ; *i* quick, idea, principle — *e* lingering, quality ; *i* light — *e* heat — *a* matter.

The deeper meaning of this use of the vowels in order to indicate definite principles, will be further discussed in §§ 185 ff.

The meaning of the *a* lies between the meaning of *i* and *o* or *u* ; the *e* lies between *i* and *a* ; it may be that Arawak also makes use of other intermediate sounds in order to express different shades of meaning. An indication of this may be seen in those words where *e* and *i* alternate, and in the metamorphosis of vowels before *-n*, *-in* (§ 81). Sm., S., Q. use besides the *u*, *o*, *a*, *e*, *i* also *ü* and *üü*, Sm. also *ue*, *uéü*, B. *ii* ; G. noted *ŏ*, *ŏ* (*ĭ*) or *ŏ* (*ü*) (a mixture of *ŏ*, *ü* and *ĭ*), *üĭ* or *ue*, *ĭ* and *ü*, and further in some words a distinct *o*, in others a distinct *u*.

Often, however, the immediate, and perhaps only cause of such variatons is the influence of the following vowels or consonants. It is especially plain to see, that the *i* has a trend to oust other vowels, and that it may exert a deteriorating influence upon *d* (§ 84), *t* (§ 90), *s* (§ 113), *n* (§ 83 [a])), perhaps also upon *b* (§ 125 [c] [1])).

§ 3. If the action-word denotes an action that passes quickly or does not end in a state of rest, then in some moods and tenses, the final *a* gives place to an *i* (table § 5, *i* group).

If the action-word denotes an action that passes slowly or ends in a state of rest, then in some moods and tenses, the final *a* gives place to an *o* (table, *o* group).

If the action-word denotes a prolonged action, then the final *a* is retained in all forms. In this case S. mostly writes *â* = long *a*, B. in the forms 6 and 9 sometimes *aa* ; therefore it is perhaps more correct to say that the final *a* gives place to long *a* (table, *a* group).

In reality, however, one cannot say of any action-word that it belongs to the *i, o* or *a* group, for in each case that presents itself, the vowel used is that which is suitable to that particular case. In this way the Arawak can express fine shades of meaning. Sometimes the difference of meaning also appears in the English verb, for instance *a-simaki-*, to call, *a-simaka*, to cry, *ikisidi-*, to judge, to measure, *ikisida*, to reckon.

In a few action-words an *u* is used instead of an *o*. The Moravians mostly use *u* when B. writes *o*, whilst the *i* group of B. is divided by them into an *i* group and an *ü* group ; no distinct difference of meaning between these *i* and *ü* groups has been discovered.

§ 4.   Compare the action-word *h-aiitoa*, beware (or : take heed) with *h-aita* [*omuni-ni n*], know [that it is near].

H-aiita is composed exactly in the same way as *h-adeka* and *d-imigoda* (*h-*, pronominal prefix ; *aii*, presumably "established security", § 133 ; *t*, motion towards an object ; *a*, time-reality).

H-aiit-a = *h-aiit* time-reality = (ye-) know.

H-ait-o-a = *h-aiit* stationary time-reality = (ye-) know, which remains in itself = (ye-) beware, (ye-) take heed.

Oa, ua or *wa* occurs in a great number of forms, see § 120 ; that one is justified in considering it as composed of *o*, stationary, and *a*, time-reality, appears from the forms 6—10 of the table in § 5, in which the *a* is lacking or is detached from the *o*.

These stationary forms (which we shall call *oa* forms) are applied :

a)   In action-words, if the nature of the action is "not moving from the place of origin", e.g. *l-idankidoa Wacinaci o-mun*, he thanked God, *ika ki t-akodwa, Adaie-li o-mun t-idankidwa*, and she coming in that instant gave thanks likewise unto the Lord, *bu-plate-n aboado fa bu-ma*, thy money perish with thee (comp. *Daii aboadi fa ie ororo abu*, I will destroy them with the earth) ;

b)   For the translation of reflexive forms ; the reflexive character is then expressed by *-oaiya*, self, e.g. *b-isadwa b-uaiya*, save thyself (comp. *b-isada-te di*, save me) ;

c)   Very frequently, by Brett, for the translation of English passive forms, e.g. *b-isadwa*, thou art made whole, *l-isado fa*, he shall be saved, *isado-ci m-aici-n goba i*, and he that was healed wist not who it was (comp. *lihi-ki isadi fa n*, the same shall save it, *isadi-ci ki di*, he that made me whole).

Now the *o* expresses the principle of low tension and the correlated principle of motionless, stationary, or in the soul : the principle of not active, expectant, passive (§§ 2, 190). In so far the *oa* forms really contain something of the passive. But they are not passive forms, neither are they intransitive forms (comp. example given under b)), and *bo-koborokwa di*, remember me). Their function is, to denote the principle of independency (§ 188).

§ 5.

Mood, tense etc. (approximate)	Action-words						Quality-words	
	i group	o group	a group	i group, oa	o group, oa	a group, oa	I[1]	II[2]
1. Imperative m.	-a	-a	-a	-oa	-oa	-oa	—	—
2. Indicative m., Perfect t.	-a goba	-a goba	-a goba	-oa goba	-oa goba	-oa goba	— goba	— goba
3. Abstract	-a-hu	-a-hu	-a-hu	-oa-hu ?	-oa-hu	-oa-hu	— hu	— hu
4. Indicative m., Present t.	-a	-a	-a-ga	-oa	-oa	-oa-ga	— ga	—
5. Potential m., Present t.	-a ma	-a ma	-a koma	-oa ma	-oa ma ?	-oa koma	— koma	— ma
6. Indicative m., Future t.	-i fa	-o fa	-a fa	-o fa	-oo fa	-oa fa	— fa	— fa
7. Present participle, Infinitive	-i-n	-o-n	-a-n	-o-n-wa	-o-n-wa	-oa-n	—(i) n	—(i) n
8. Agent-noun	-i-ci, f. -i-tu	-o-ci, f. -o-tu	-a-ci, f. -a-tu	-o-ci, f. o-tu	-oo-ci, f. oo-tu	-oa-ci, f. oa-tu	—-ci. f. -tu	—-ci. f. tu
9. Object-noun	-i-sia	-o-sia	-a-sia	-o-sia	-o-sia	-oa-sia	—-sia	—-sia
10. Hortative-Optative	-ia	?	-a-ia	-o-ia	-o-ia ?	-oa-ia ?	—-ia	—-ia
symbolic representations adopted in this work	adeki- (to see)	imigodo- (to send)	ikita (to serve)	adeko-(n-wa)	imigodo-(n-wa)	ikitoa	kokke (to be living)	isa (to be good)

1) The following have been met with : 1⁰. *Ialoko*, being a Spirit, etc. ; 2⁰. *d-ajcago*, being upon me, *ororo ajcago*, being in the world (upon earth), *isikwa o-loko*, being in the house, etc. ; 3⁰. *k-akosi*, having eyes. *m-akosi*, being blind, *ka-loko*, having contents, *ma-loko*, being empty, etc. (§ 10) ; 4⁰ *bari*, indeed, (Sm.) *aba*, to be different, *aboa*, ill. *ibi*, ready. *biama*, being two, *itili*, *itiro*, great, *(a-)furi*, springing up, *kari*, suffering, *kokke*, living, *kudi*, heavy, *kowa*, absent, *amaro*, afraid, *imeko*, ready, *misi*, right, *nokonne*, sorrowing, *orosi*, being filled with food, *-sabu*, very, *isi*, stinking, *isoyo*, small, *yuho*, being a quantity ; 5⁰. *alon*, *alomun*, where ?

2) The following have been met with : 1⁰. *ada*, being a tree, etc. : 2⁰. *lo-tokaini o-loko*, being in the (his) secret chambers ; 3⁰. *ma-yura*, having no root, *ka-koborokwa*, wise, *ma-koborokwa*, foolish, *ka-raia*, appearing ; 4⁰. *kalime*, being light, shining, *koro*, negation, *alikibe*, glad, *alikibi*, rejoicing, *alokosia*, thirsty, *amisia*, hungry, *murriya*, false, *isa*, good, *saka*, withered, *simika*, jealous, *taha*, fur, *yalu*, here, *wakaia*, evil ; 5⁰. *ama*, what ?

B4*

The final vowel that appears in the forms 6—10, appears also in the forms with -ni (verbal noun, § 25), -bi (Perfect tense, § 58 a)), -bona (Perfect tense, § 64 a) 2)), -ba ("also", § 60 b)), faroka ("if", § 144), sabu ("very", § 149), robu ("only", § 150), kwona-hu (instrument, § 120 a) 2) I)).

The a appears also in the forms with *(hit)ti* ("desiring", § 110).

Forms 4 : ga or ka, means "making its appearance in a positive manner — time-reality". This particle is used generally after a word that of itself is indefinite in regard to time (ikita, to serve, ikitoa, to be served, kokke, to live ; also after -n and -ni verbal nouns, §§ 28e), 29), in order to give it a definite sense. It is not used if the indefiniteness may remain (isa, to be good), or if definiteness is included in the construction and meaning of the word, so as with the i and o groups of the action-words.

Forms 5 : ma means "reluctant or hesitating — time-reality".

Forms 5 : koma is a combination of k(a) and ma ; presumably an o is used here, in order that a may only occur at the end ; analogous forms : goba, kona (§ 63), bona (§ 64), o-doma (§ 40), o-bora (§ 105).

Forms 2 : goba indicates a rather remote past ; g making its appearance in a positive manner, o not changing, ba, again (§ 60) ; see also § 128 k).

Forms 6 : fa means "striving (aspiring) time-reality".

Forms 10 : ia expresses : i, tension, (released into) a the calm flow of time (see § 132).

Forms 3, 7, 8, 9 : -hu, -n, -ci, -tu, -sia, see §§ 21—27.

Examples :

a) i, o, a groups.

lihi oonaba-ga (a, 4) kiana n, ajia-n (a, 7) na-mun, Daii bajia adagato fa (o, 6) hu abar amateli, h-oonaba-te (a, 1 ; te, § 95) kiana di, and he answered and said unto them, I will also ask you one thing ; and answer me : b-adeka (i, 1), d-imigoda (o, 4) d-imigodo-sia (o, 10) b-isibo o-bora, behold, I send my messenger before thy face, kena Wacinaci isadi-sia (i, 10) to-makwa isiroko-ho adeki fa (i, 6), and all flesh shall see the salvation of God, n-adagata goba (o, 2) i lo-dokoto-n (o, 7) bia na-mun a-dokota-hu (o, 3) aiomuni o-rea. L-oonaba goba (a, 2) n ajia-n (a, 7) na-mun, (they) desired him that he would shew them a sign from heaven. He answered and said·unto them, Wacinaci adeka goba (i, 2) kiana kalime-hi, and God saw the light, to-makwa yauhahu a-kwaiaba (o, 4) kiana i, Poroko o-lokomun b-imigoda (o, 1) u, and all the devils besought him, [saying], Send us into the swine, kena l-adeka (i, 4) ie tata kiben a-rimodi-n (i, 7), and he saw them toiling in rowing, tata-tu ajia-hu (a, 3) toho ; alika akonnaba ma (o, 5) n ? this is an hard saying ; who can hear it ? n-imisida ma (i, 5) koro kia ajia-hu (a, 3) n-ajia-sia (a, 9) da-konomun, neither can they prove the things whereof they now accuse me, alika-i koro ikita koma (a, 5) biama-no l-adaiana-sia : ... abar-li l-ikita fa (a, 6) ; l-ibiamti-ci l-imita fa (a, 6), jiaro. Mamari-ga (§ 147) h-ikita-n (a, 7) Wacinaci Mammon bajia biama-n, no man can serve two masters : ... or else he will hold to the one, and despise the other. Ye cannot serve God and mammon, *l-onnakia (i, 10) ifiro-tu b-eke bajia*, let him have thy cloke also, *a-ridi-ci (i, 8) aicia (i, 10) to-konomun*, let him that readeth understand (know it-concerning), *ho-dokoda (o, 1) i, l-ausia (i, 10)* loose him, and let him go, *bu-isauka andia-te (i, 10)* thy kingdom come, *Christ ... a-tokodia-te (o ? 10)*, let ... Christ descend, *naha yaha-ci kiana ajiaia (a, 10)*, let these same here say, *l-ahakaia (a, 10) na-mun to-konomun*, that he may testify unto them (L . XVI, 28) ;

     b) *i, o, a* groups : *oa*.

da-dankidoa (i?, oa, 4) bu-mun, I thank thee, *b-adeka, b-isadwa (i, oa, 4)*, behold, thou art made whole, *b-ikiduada Adaie-li Jesus Christ o-konomun, kena b-isado fa (i, oa, 6)*, believe on the Lord Jesus Christ, and thou shalt be saved, *kena hiaro isadwa goba (i, oa, 2) kia ikisi warea*, and the woman was made whole from that hour, *alika-i kiana isadwa ma (i, oa, 5)* ? who then can be saved ? *b-isadwa (i, oa, 1) b-uaiya* ! save thyself ! *aba-no l-isada barin, l-oaiya l-isadoia (i, oa, 10), kiana*, he saved others, let him save himself, *biama-ga c-isado-n-wa (i, oa, 7) kiana*, and both are preserved, *to-makwa bu-loa abu b-ikiduadi faroka, bu-baptize () doa ma (i, oa, 5)*, if thou believest with all thine heart, thou mayest (be baptized), *c-ibitoia (i, oa, 10) ibin ama d-ansi-ka kiana ?* what will I, if it be already kindled ? *toho origahu abu bu-ialoko adagatoo fa (o, oa, 6) b-aurea*, this night thy soul shall be required of thee, *naii k-ikisi-ka n-akonnabo-n-wa (o, oa, 7) bia yuho-ni n-ajia-n o-doma*, for they think that they shall be heard for their much speaking, *Rama mun ajia-hu akonnaboa goba (o, oa, 2)*, in Rama was there a voice heard, *penster aiomun-bonna-n-tu bajia a-torodwa (o, oa, 4)*, and the windows of heaven were opened, *ho-kwaiaboa (o, oa, 1), m-ausi-n h-a-n bia wakaia ikisida-hu o-lokomun*, pray that ye enter not into temptation, *to-moroa toho jiamutu koro a-fitikida ma, to-moroa a-kwaiaboa-hu (o, oa, 3) o-doma ma-koto-ni-hi abu to-fitikida ma*, howbeit this kind goeth not out but by prayer and fasting, *ama ibia ho-koborokwatoa ka (a, oa, 4) ho-loa o-lok-oa ?* why do thoughts arise in your hearts ? *loko o-loa a-koborokwatoa-n (a, oa, 7) wakaia-hu o-konomun l-iloni-ni warea o-doma*, for the imagination of man's heart is evil from his youth, *to-makwa lo-koborokwatoa-sia (a, oa, 9) ... lo-loa o-lok-oa*, every imagination of the thoughts of his heart, *d-adaiakitwa faroka* (same form as *a, oa, 6) da-uaiya, ausirobu-in d-adaiakitwa-ga (a, oa, 4)* : *Da-ci adaiakita di*, if I honour myself, my honour is nothing : it is my Father that honoureth me, *ma-sweardoa-n (a, oa, 7) h-a-li abaren : Aiomun koro abu bu-sweardoa fa (a, oa, 6)*, swear not at all ; [neither] by heaven (not shalt thou swear), *loko Aiici andi-n goba-te jin, l-ikitwa-n (a. oa. 7) bia koro, to-moroa l-ikita-n bia*, even as the Son of man came not to be ministered unto, but to minister, *a-sweardoa-hu (a, oa, 3) abu*, [he denied] with an oath, *a-nokondwa-hu (a, oa, 3)*, lamentation. *k-amunaiga goba kiana w-ajia-n ho-mun. kena hui koro a-nokonnedwa goba (a. oa. 2)*, we have mourned unto you, and ye have not lamented, *aiika-hu-sikwa sanoci a-nokonnidwa koma (a, oa, 5), ika tu ki aiika-ci na-ma-n ?* can the children of the bridechamber mourn, as long as the bridegroom is with them ? *h-aiitoa-li (i, oa, 1) kiana, h-ikitwa-hu (a, oa, 3) abu a-kwaiabo-n-wa (o, oa, 7),* take ye heed, watch and pray, *h-aiitoa, h-ikitoa (a, oa, 1) k-iitesia-sia o-rea,* take heed, and beware of covetousness ;

a-wa, in the following : *toho* ointment *a-iyugarawa ma yuho-ro bia barin,* for this ointment might have been sold for much, *biama ibiro kain kodibiyu a-iyugarawa koro,* are not two sparrows sold [for a farthing] ? *a-forrawa ti-n l-oaiya,* and would have killed himself ;

c) Quality-words, etc., *ga (ka), koma* class.

kokke ka (4) i ! he lives ! *kodibiyu-bi ... anda fa-te b-amun, b-ikita-n bia n kokki-n (7),* fowls ... shall come unto thee, to keep them alive, *tanahu isi-ga (4) i,* by this time he stinketh, *hui bajia nokonne-ga (4) tanahu,* and ye now therefore have sorrow, *nokonne-ga (4) yuho-li loko-no o-konomun di,* I have compassion on the multitude, *nokonne (1) wa-kona-n bu !* have mercy on us ! *kena hui nokonne fa (6), to-moroa ho-nokonne-hi (3) a-sifudo fa ahalikibi bia,* and ye shall be sorrowful, but your sorrow shall be turned into joy, *to-moroa ika tu yuho-li loko-no l-adeki-n nokonne goba (2) na-konomun i,* but when he saw the multitudes, he was moved with compassion on them ;

k-akosi ka (4) hu, mamari-ga h-adeki-n ? having eyes, see ye not ? *waii bajia m-akosi ka (4) ?* are we blind also ? *to-makwa sa-tu ada k-iwi-ka (4) sa-tu c-iwi ... sa-tu ada koro k-iwi koma (5) wakaia-tu c-iwi (§ 18),* every good tree bringeth forth good fruit ... a good tree cannot bring forth evil fruit, *k-iwi goba (2) kiana n,* and (it) brought forth, *mamari-ga t-adinabo t-oaiya k-iwi-n (7),* the branch cannot bear fruit of itself, *alika-i k-ire fa (6) kiana n,* whose wife shall she be ?

abar-timen siba oniabu eki a-sikoa goba yumun, Jew-no a-maribendo-n-wa o-loko-ji, abar ka-loko koma (5) biama firkin jiaro kabuin jiaro, and there were set there six water-pots of stone, after the manner of the purifying of the Jews, containing two or three firkins apiece, *abar-li yuho-ro k-amun-ci (8) akobain ka-loko goba (2) yuho-ro c-iwi.* the ground of a certain rich man brought forth plentifully, lit. one much possessing-person ground contained much its-fruit ;

to-moroa oniabu ki Daii a-siki-sia lo-mun. lo-loko fa (6) a-ciga (a-cigi, to dig) oniabu a-sorokodo-tu ma-iibo-n-wa-tu kokke-hu bia. but the water that I shall give him shall be in him a well of water springing up into everlasting life, *Da-ci sikwa o-loko (4) yuho-ro bawhu.* in my Father's house are many mansions, *lihi o-loko goba (2) kokke-hu.* in him was life, *ororo ajeago goba (2) i,* he was in the world :

Ialoko ka (4) Wacinaci, God is a Spirit, *kena abar-li hui o-rea-ci yauhahu ka (4),* and one of you is a devil, *l-augici iri goba (2) Jubal,* and his brother's name was Jubal, *Tubal-cain o-yuradatu goba (2) Naamah,* and the sister of Tubal-cain was Naamah. *ifili-ci fa (6) i,* he shall be great, *ki-o-doma naii ikisida-arin fa* (6) *ho-mun,* therefore they shall be your judges ;

d) Quality-words which do not take *ga (ka),* and take *ma* instead of *koma.*

isa (1), *W-adaiana-sia,* well, Master, *isa-li* (1) *kiana hu abaren,* be ye therefore perfect, *isa* (4) *b-ajia-n,* thou hast well said, *lo-boredwa-ga t-adinabo jin, kena saka* (4) *i,* he is cast forth as a branch, and is withered. *kena t-egura kowa-n tu-mun o-doma, saka goba* (2) *n,* and because it had no root, it withered away, *isa fa* (6) *hu,* ye shall do well, *isa-hi* (3) *jiaro. wakaia-hu* (3) *jiaro ? isada-hi kokke-hu jiaro, aboada-hu jiaro ?* to do good, or to do evil ? to save life, or to destroy it ? (L. VI, 9). *kenbena ama ibia koro sa-ma* (5) *n,* it is thenceforth good for nothing (Mt. V, 13). *waakoro fig ada saka-in* (7) ! how soon is the fig tree withered away ! *to-makwa kibi l-onyi-ka isa-n* (7), he hath done all things well ;

ifi-ro ka t-adinabo kiana, ki-o-doma kodibiyu-bi aiomun warea-tu ka-sikwa ma (5) *t-iya abomun,* and shooteth out great branches ; so that the fowls of the air may lodge under the shadow of it, *bara ma-iaukwa ma kiana,* and there was a great calm, *fox ka-sikwa* (4) *t-oolai o-loko,* foxes have holes (dwell its-hole in), *kena waii anda fa-te l-amun. ka-sikwa fa* (6) *lihi o-ma u,* and we will come unto him, and make our abode with him, *Cain ausa kiana Adaie-li isibo warea, Nod ororo mun ka-sikwa-n* (7), and Cain went out from the presence of the Lord, and dwelt in the land of Nod. *aiomun abomun-tu oniabu a-herakidaia aba-ro o-loko, ka-raia-ia* (10) *kiana waa-tu ororo,* let the waters under the heaven be gathered together unto one place, and let the dry land appear. *ma-gura* (4) *ie na-loa o-lok-oa, to-moroa m-ibena robu n-a oaboddi-n,* and (they) have no root in themselves (their heart), and so endure but for a time.

§ 6. The Arawak language does not distinguish between the active and the passive voice in the same manner as is done in English. The following means have been employed in translating :

a) The English active voice :

1) Ordinary action-word :

    I) No object : *l-adeka,* he looked up (Mk. VIII, 24), *d-ausa,* I go;

    II) Object fully affected : *d-imigoda hu,* I send you, *l-adeka ie,* he saw them ;

    III) Object affected in a particular manner ; it is indicated by one of the words denoting position, direction or time, enumerated in § 8, preceded by a particle or a word indicating the "person". e.g. with *ibici,* lightly touched : *h-imigoda d-ibici,* ye have sent for me, *l-adeka n-ibici,* he beheld them ;

    IV) (II) + III)) *d-imigodi fa-te i h-ibici.* I will send him unto you ;

2) *Oa* form :

    I) *t-eda botoli oakudwa,* the (leather) bottles break ;

    II) Does not exist :

III) *na-kwaiaboa da-mun*, they worship me ;

IV) — ;

V) Reflexive, see § 4 b) ;

3) Quality-word :

I) — ;

II) Subject (∼ the object fully affected in 1) II)) : *isa n*, it was good, *kokke ka i*, he lives ;

III) — ;

IV) Form II) + object affected in a particular manner : *nokonne goba na-konomun i*, he was moved with compassion on them, *wakaia ho-muni n*, woe unto you, lit. you-at it ;

b) The English passive voice :

1) The corresponding active voice has been translated, e.g. L. XXI, 16, ye shall be betrayed, *na-sikiti fa hu*, L. VIII, 5, it was trodden down, *n-atenaa goba t-ajeago* ;

2) An *oa* form is used, e.g. Mt. XV, 24, I am not sent, *d-imigodwa-te koro* ;

3) In order to emphasize the passive attitude, an *oa* form from a causative is used. Sm. gives this as the usual method, but in S. 's texts such forms are comparatively seldom met with. Examples : S. *na-maqua l-ansi-ssia-ñu ebekittoa üssa-tti üjahü abbu*, and they (his beloved ones) were all filled with the Holy Ghost (Acts II, 4), *ki-hia na-kujaba-ka Pilatus u-ria lu-parrükittu-nn-ua u-kunnamün*, yet desired they Pilate that he should be slain (Acts XIII, 28) ;

4) A durative form (a group) is used, e.g. L. I, 19, I am sent, *imigoda-ga te di*, L. XX, 18, he shall be broken, *lihi a-kurradaa fa* ;

5) S. makes use of a *-hu* verbal noun to do duty as a passive verbal root, after which the particles *ka, sia*, etc. are applied ; see § 24 ;

6) A *-sia* verbal noun is used, see § 22.

2) and 3) : If the English sentence gives the active subject, then it is translated by one of the words denoting position or direction *o-mun, abu* or *o-rea*, with a pronominal prefix or prefixed object-word ; examples, see §§ 71 b) 2) III), 65, 97 a).

CHAPTER II

CHARACTER OF THE ARAWAK WORDS

§ 7. The words *hu*, in the example of § 1, denoting persons, we shall call "end-point pronoun"; other similar words we shall call "emphasizing pronoun"; the particles *h-*, *d-* and *h-* we shall call "pronominal prefix".

	pronominal prefix	end-point pronoun	emphasizing pronoun
I	*d(a)-*	*di*	*daii*
II	*b(u)-*	*bu*	*bui*
III m.	*l(o)-*, *l(u)-*	*i*	*lihi, liraha*
III f.	*t(o)-*, *t(u)-*	*n* (G. also *no*)	*toho, toraha*
I pl.	*w(a)-*	*u*	*waii*
II pl.	*h(o)-*, *h(u)-*	*hu*	*hui*
III pl.	*n(a)-*	*ie*	*naii, naha, naraha*

The vowel between ( ) is used if it is not ousted by a stronger influence.

I   = the speaker,

II   = the listener,

III m. = one rational being or male person, other than the speaker or the listener,

III f. = one or more non-rational beings or things or one female person, other than the speaker or the listener,

 I pl. = two or more persons, the speaker included,

II pl. = two or more persons, one or more listeners included, the speaker excluded,

III pl. = two or more rational beings, the speaker and the listeners excluded.

Emphasizing pronouns and object-words may be used in the function of an end-point pronoun and in the function of a pronominal prefix, e.g. *wolf, loko-no.*

§ 8. Words denoting position, direction or time, such as *o-koboroko* and *o-mun,* fulfil the role of the prepositions and case-endings in European languages. Here follows a list of those words, with the English prepositions etc., for the translation of which they are used (most of them as given in Brett's grammar); for their real meaning, see the §§'s placed after them. After these words *ji* (§ 85) and *wa* (§ 120 g) 6)) may be added as suffixes.

bena, after, § 38

ibici, to, towards, § 58 d) 1)

ibiciro, to, towards, § 102 b)

abu, by, with, § 65

iabo, behind, beyond, § 66
aboloko, on the top of, § 103 c)
abomun, under, § 71 b) 7)
bonna, at the surface of, § 64 a) 1)
o-bora, at a certain future epoch, § 105 b)
o-boramun, at a certain future epoch or place, § 105 c)
aboroko, at the outside, § 103 d)
aji, more than, S. *adi*, upon, § 86 a)
ajeago, on, upon, § 86 b)
adiki, after, § 86 c)
adikiloko, instead of, in the room of, § 86 d)
adinamun, near to, in the vicinity of, § 86 g) 3)
o-doma, because of, § 40
ikira-ji, ikira-di, round about, § 106
S. *aku*, in (fire), § 103 e)
o-koboroko, among, § 103 h)
akoloko, in (fire, etc.), § 103 e)
o-kona, against, upon, § 63 a) 1)
o-konamun, at, upon, § 63 a) 3)
o-konomun, of, concerning, § 63 a) 4)
o-konaria, for the sake of, § 97 b) 3)
akosa, on, at the side, § 117 a)
o-loko, in, § 103 a)
i(y)aloko, against, § 103 g)
o-ma, with, § 71 a) 1)
mairia, etc., at the other side, § 97 d)
o-makana, over against, § 71 c)
mun, at, § 71 b)
amun, at, upon, over, § 71 b)
o-mun, to, for, by, § 71 b)
muniro, o-muniro, to, unto, § 102 b)
inabo, after, § 79 c) 4)
(e)rabudiki, (e)rabodogo, against, towards, § 104 c) 1)
(i)rako, in (a fluid), § 107 a)
irakomun, in (a fluid), § 107 a)
rea, ria, o-rea (aurea), area, warea, from, § 97
aramakona, at, § 104 d)
(e)ribo, rebo, at the waterside, § 101 a)
rifu, at the waterside, § 101 b)
ariloko, in (between), § 103 f)
roko, in, § 103 b)
isibo, in face of, § 116 a) 1)
isifu, in face of, § 116 a) 2)
o-tora, at the foot of, § 102 c)
o-toromun, at the foot of, § 102 e).

§ 9. In substance the pronouns are deictic expressions or demonstratives.

The pronominal prefixes and the end-point pronouns are short characteristic descriptions of the person ; from a comparison with other A. M. languages it appears probable that one kind of pronouns were formerly used for both functions. The emphasizing pronouns are compounds of a pronominal prefix with an emphasizing particle.

The pronominal prefixes are also used in a manner that reminds one of an article. The emphasizing pronouns are also used for the translation of English demonstratives.

That the pronouns denote place, appears also from the fact, that the emphasizing pronouns are composed in exactly the same manner as some words denoting locality, for instance *lihi*, he, this (m.), *naha* these. *yaha*, here (§§ 44, 45).

§ 10. The object-words and the proper names have the same character as the pronouns.

It may be, that in addition to the attributes connoted by an object-word. it is necessary to mention the person involved, as is the case with a thing possessed, a part of the body, a family relation. Then the person is indicated by a pronominal prefix, or by an emphasizing pronoun or an object-word. fulfilling the same function (*h-ada-n*, your staves. *d-akosi*, my eye. *lo-iyu*, his mother). Likewise the words denoting position, direction or time. enumerated in § 8 are always more particularly specified by a person (*wolf o-koboroko*, in the midst of wolves, *loko-no o-mun*. of men, *na-koboroko*, among them).

These words, without the prefixed particle or word. have no other value than to indicate a complex of qualities, and this explains how it is possible, that both object-words and the words denoting position. direction or time just mentioned, can be transformed into a word indicating a quality, state or condition, viz. with *k(a)-* (making its appearance in a positive manner) : the quality is appearing, is present ; with *m(a)-* (reluctant) : the quality is not appearing, is absent.

Examples : *(i)sa*, child, offspring, *ka-sa*, to be fruitful, being with child, *ma-sa*. to be barren ; *iwi*, fruit. *k-iwi*. to bring forth fruits, *m-iwi*, not to bring forth fruits ; *akosi*, eye, *k-akosi*, to have eyes. *m-akosi*, to be blind : *iri*, name, *ka-iri*, to be called by a name, *ma-iri*, not to be called by a name ; *o-banna*, leaf. *ka-banna*, to have leaves ; *o-koborokwa*, remembrance. consciousness, *ka-koborokwa*, to be remembering. to be wise, *ma-koborokwa*. to be foolish ; *o-loko*, in (or : inside. interior). *ka-loko*, to have contents. to be filled, *ma-loko*, to be empty.

§ 11. ᵃ) Emphasizing pronouns. object-words. proper names. words denoting position, direction or time. and quality-words can be used as a verb, denoting the state or condition to be, whatever the word expresses. The action-words with unalterable ending. namely the a group. and the verbal nouns. may be included in this category. Notionally they have in common : indefiniteness in regard to time ; in form : unalterable ending :

grammatically : that the different moods and tenses are formed in the same way (see §§ 5, 12, 21—27).

b) But the particles by which moods and tenses are formed, are even employed when the word is used in a function that may be fulfilled by a pronominal prefix or an end-point pronoun, e.g. *[David adaie-li-wabu ka-sa goba Solomon] Urias ire-tu goba o-mun*, [and David the king begat Solomon] of her that had been the wife of Urias ; see also the forms with (S.) *kuba, pa,* § 176 b) 2, 3), the forms with *ka,* § 29 a), with *bia,* § 39, and the *-hu* etc. forms, § 24.

c) Concerning the action-words with inflected endings, we have seen already, that the different end-vowels describe the different shades of reality. When we take this into consideration, we see that these words have nothing in their construction that distinguishes them from the other classes of words. Moreover the action-words are used in the sentence in quite the same way as the quality-words (see the examples in § 12), and furthermore certain quality-words may perform the function of action-words (§ 18).

d) In the following example we meet the Indicative mood, Present tense of an action-word doing duty as an object-word : *aiakatwa o-loko*, privily, in secret (parallel to *m-aiakato-n-wa o-loko*, public, openly), *ororo a-iiboa*, the end of the world (parallel to : *ororo a-iibo-n-wa o-bora-n*, unto the end of the world). Comp. also : *l-iciga goba*, he digged (*a-cigi-*, to dig), *aciga*, a ditch.

§ 12. Let us now turn our attention to the structure of sentences.

In Arawak the sentence consists of one or more words which indicate something that is new to the hearer (at any rate in this connexion, or under these circumstances), and often there is moreover indicated the thing that the hearer already knows, to which this new piece of information is added. That which is most intended to attract the attention of the hearer, is first said ; generally this is the most mobile or the most particular thing, or that which dominates the situation. The thing which is least mobile, which is already known, or which is in an expectant or passive attitude, is mentioned the last, unless it must be spoken first, in order to attract special attention. Word-order is determined by the emotional, in so far as reality, as the logical connexion between the things to be described, will permit.

a) 1) *lihi-ki Daii, [ajia-ci bu-mun]*, I [that speak unto thee] am he ;

2) *kenbena ada n*, and (it) becometh a tree, *Roman i*, [having understood that] he was a Roman, *Roman-o bari-ni waii*, being Romans (indeed we), *Peter bui*, thou art Peter, *Gabriel daii*, I am Gabriel, *Matthat aiici lihi*, which was the son of Matthat, *John l-iri*, his name is John ;

3) *yaha u*, we are present, *lo-tokaini o-loko i*, [they shall say : behold] he is in the (his) secret chambers, *lo-ma kiana u*, and (we) abode with him ;

4) *isa n* ! well done ! *wakaia i*, he is guilty, he is a debtor ;

5) *l-adeka ie*, he saw them, *d-imigoda hu*, I send you, *b-ikiduadi-n isada* (= *isa*, sound, *-d-a*) *bu*, thy faith hath made thee whole ;

b) 2) *lihi Jesus,* this is Jesus, *virgin iri Mary,* the virgin's name was Mary ;

4) *ororo wakaia,* it (the earth) was corrupt ;

5) *waii icinoci l-imigoda,* he sent out our fathers ;

c) *ho-bollita yaha,* sit ye here, *tanahu d-ajinama yaha,* now I stand (here), *yaha h-oabodda,* tarry ye here, *yaha a-kota-he h-amuni-ga ?* have ye here any meat ? *abar-timen kaci o-loko Wacinaci imigoda goba angel Gabriel abar bawhu-yuho mun i-ro Galilee mun-tu,* and in the sixth month the angel Gabriel was sent from God unto a city of Galilee, lit. sixth month in God sent angel G. a city unto Galilee-at-thing, *kia-n bena Jesus auciga temple o-loko i,* afterward Jesus findeth him in the temple, *n-auciga i temple o-loko,* they found him in the temple ;

d) Sentences consisting of a single word or compound :

Mary ! Mary ! *Cornelius* ! Cornelius ! *D-adaiana-sia* ! Master ! *Daii* ! it is I, *Bethlehem o-loko [Judea mun]* ! in Bethlehem [of Judæa], *h-adeka* ! behold ! *bu-prophesidoa-te* ! prophesy !

§ 13. If several action-words are to be placed in one sentence, then the Arawak expresses the most important action by a form with the ending -a (-a, -a goba, -i fa, -o fa, -a fa, etc.). Examples :

Acts XI, 25, 26, *Barnabas ausa kiana Tarsus mun i-ro, auadi-n Saul ibici.*
               B.   go   then   T.   unto   seeking S.   to
L-aucigi-n bena   i,   Antioch mun l-anda   l-abu. Kenbena abar wiwa
he-finding after   him   A.   at   he-come he-with and-after one year
na-herakida   church o-loko, a-mairikota-n yuho-li loko-no. Antioch mun
they-assemble church in   teaching   many men A.   at
atenwa a-mairikota-sia-no asoa   goba Christian-o, ma-in. Then departed
first   disciples   called   were Christians said, § 35.
Barnabas to Tarsus, for to seek Saul : And when he had found him, he brought him into Antioch. And it came to pass, that a whole year they assembled themselves with the church, and taught much people. And the disciples were called Christians first in Antioch, Acts XXV, 1, 2,
Festus andi-n bena l-ikita-sia bia   ororo mun, kabuin kasakabo adiki
F.   coming after his-ministry to-be earth at three day   after
Cesarea warea Jerusalem mun i-ro l-ausa goba. Priest-no afudyi
C.   from J.   unto   he-went   priests surpasser
Jew-no adaiana-sia-no mi-ci ahaka-ga kiana lo-mun Paul o-konomun,
Jews masters   with tell   then he-at P.   concerning
a-kwaiabo-n i. Now when Festus was come into the province, after three
beseeching him
days he ascended from Cæsarea to Jerusalem. Then the high priest and the chief of the Jews informed him against Paul, and besought him.

By this means the Arawak can single out one among several actions, as that which is to be represented as the most important or primary (see for further examples, § 27). And he even can focus the attention on the fact that an action occurs, by splitting up the action-word into a part containing the -a with the pronominal prefix, and a less vivid form, containing the description of the action (§§ 28, 42). See also §§ 55, 145, 147, 148, 151, 153.

§ 14. In the course of this work it will appear, that the great majority of Arawak words are built up from small particles, each of which represents a definite part of the total experience ; the same principles that rule the word-order in the sentence, determine the sequence of those particles.

Should one consider the Arawak word as a compound of the type -attribute[2]-attribute[1]-subject, -adverb-adjective-substantive, or (Jespersen, 65 b) -subjunct-adjunct-subject, -tertiary-secondary-primary, then it follows from this, that all Arawak words are object-expressions in which the ending represents the object. Now, however, that ending is always a vowel, or a vowel with a durative -n, and neither of these endings attains that degree of solid concreteness, which we connect with an "object".

The nature of the Arawak word is better described, when we say : the different peculiarities are mentioned one after another ; the sequence is, that the most striking, the most new (also : that which dominates the situation) goes first, and the least striking, the already known (also : that which is expectant or passive) follows.

When the speaker begins to speak a word, the plan of the whole word is already latent in his sub-consciousness, and it is already decided upon, what general or known idea will be expressed at the end of the form. Therefore the consideration which we had to reject just now, contains nevertheless a particle of truth.

Our first supposition would lead to the conclusion that Arawak has only prefixes ; our second supposition would lead us to the conclusion that Arawak has only suffixes. For the sake of convenience, however, we shall in this work make use of both terms.

§ 15. a) The following compounds of two object-words must be considered as junctions, because if a pronominal prefix is applied. it is put before the first word : *fig-ada*, fig-tree, *ada iwi*, the fruit of the tree. *fig-iwi*, fig (fruit) *c-iwi eda*, the husks (its fruit-skin), *t-eda botoli*, bottles (its hide-bottle), *m-ibiloko-tu baka-da*, thongs (un-broad-thing cow-hide). *hell ikihi*, hell fire, *ikihi-sikwa*, a furnace of fire, *ikihi-kudu*, sticks (fire-things). *yurua kwama*, a crown of thorns.

b) In the same way words denoting position. direction or time may be compounded. See the list in § 8 and : *bo-boreda bawhu-yura b-uaiya b-akosi o-loko area*, cast out the beam out of thine own eyes. *H-eta homakwa to-loko area*, [he took the cup ... saying] Drink ye all of it.

c) In the following examples a form combined with an end-point pronoun or with a word denoting position, direction or time, is used in a function which might also be fulfilled by a single pronoun or object-word : *kena adeki-ci, adeka imigodo-ci di*, and he that seeth me seeth him that sent me, *a-forri-ci i eke daii ikita goba bajia*, and (I) kept the raiment of them that slew him, *d-ausa imigodo-ci di ibici-ro*, I go my way to him that sent me, *oaboddi-ci da-kona*, he that abideth in me [bringeth forth fruit], *h-ansi-li k-aiima-ci-no ho-mun*, love your enemies, *ausi-ci lo-bora*, *ausi-ci bajia l-iinabo a-simaka goba, ajia-n*, Hosanna, and they that went before, and they that followed, cried, saying, Hosanna, *Roman i o-konomun d-akonnabo-n o-doma*, having understood that he was a Roman, lit. Roman he concerning my-hearing because, *l-adagata i alomun kondi-n i. L-aici-n bena Cilicia kondi-n i*, he asked of what province he was. And when he understood that he was of Cilicia, lit. he-ask him where of-a-place-being he. His-knowing after Cilicia of-a-place-being he, *kena, abaren kabuin-o wadili anda ibin yumun-tu di bawhu mun*, and, behold, immediately there were three men already come unto the house where I was.

d) Other examples of compound forms, used as a single word, are the following :

isa koro onnaka-he bia i, [Paul thought] not good to take him [with them], lit. good-not-taking to-be he, *tanahu warea k-iwi fa koro ada bu ma-iibo-n-wa-tu bia*, let no fruit grow on thee henceforward for ever, lit. now from with-fruit-future-not-tree thou not-ending-thing to-be.

§ 16. a) The pronominal prefix is attributive, and forms a compound with the word to which it is prefixed.

An emphasizing pronoun or an object-word can be used in the same function (and must then be put in the same place). Seeing that such a word attracts the attention much more than the pronominal prefix, the way in which it is felt perhaps more nearly approaches that of an English subject.

In the following examples the person indicated by the pronominal prefix, is (for our, European, analysis) in some cases subject, dominating, origin, in others object, subordinate, endpoint. But really the function of the pronominal prefix is always the same, viz. to indicate the person who is considered as being connected with the matter from its origin, the person who is in a strong position (in respect to a state of movement : active, in respect to a stationary condition : potential).

Examples :

l-imigoda ie, (he) sent them, *lo-baptize()da goba ie*, (they) were baptized of him, *da-dankidwa bu-mun*, I thank thee, *d-imigodwa-te*, I am sent (N.B. : these forms are not genuine passives, see § 6), *l-isi*, his head, *John Baptist isi*, John Baptist's head, *lo-bugici*, the (his) brother, *John o-bugici*, the brother of John, *da-sanci*, my servant, *d-Adaie-n*, my Lord, *ho-wakaia*, your sins, *loko o-wakaia*, the wickedness of man, *da-plate-n*, my money, *a-fogodo-ci-no plate-n*, the changers' money, *n-anda l-amun*, (they) come to him, *n-anda Jesus amun*, they come to Jesus, *Judea warea*, [he came] from Judæa, *Judea mun i-ro*, [he went] into Judæa, *Jerusalem mun*, [he was] in Jerusalem, *ǰauhahu bajia w-afuji-ga bu-iri o-doma*, even the devils are subject unto us through thy name, lit. devil also we-rule thy-name because, *w-afudyi-no*, the (our) rulers.

b) If a person who can be indicated by a pronominal prefix, is understood or must be understood to be there, the Arawak always mentions the person. Examples :

h-adeka, (ye) behold, *b-adeka,* (thou) behold (L. I, 31), *bui, da-sa,* thou, (my) child, *l-isanci ifili sabu-ka koro l-adaie-n aji,* the (his) servant is not greater than his lord, *l-oonaba goba n ajia-n na-mun, Abona-ci sa-tu t-isi, loko Aiici,* he answered (it) and said unto them, He that soweth the good (its) seed is the Son of man, *Adaie-li tanahu b-isiki fa Israel o-mun n-isauka ba ?* Lord, wilt thou at this time restore again the (their) kingdom to Israel ?

c) On the other hand the person is never indicated twice. One says *Jesus o-kuti,* the feet of Jesus, or *lo-kuti,* his feet, but never (as is customary in several languages, also in A. M. languages, see § 181) *Jesus lo-kuti.* A deviation is only made from this rule for the purpose of emphasis. Examples: *bu-iauda-a Paul,* Paul, thou art beside thyself, *ama w-onyi-ka waii ?* what do we ? (J. XI, 47), *b-ose bui,* go ! (L. X, 37), *to-moroa hui h-aiitoa,* but take ye heed (Mk. XIII, 23), *hui h-onnaka i,* take ye him (J. XIX, 6), S. *dai a-sseki-n|da|ppa bu-mün kiakéwai u-hurruru,* (I giving I-shall thee-to this country).

d) G. The words *bahü,* house, *hamaka,* hammock, *kabuya,* planted field, *waboroko,* path, *awa,* father, *tete,* mother, and perhaps others, do not take a pronominal prefix. If, however, a pronominal prefix must be applied, then the synonimes *sikwa, kura, akoban, abonaha, iči, yu* are used.

§ 17. In the composition of a prefix with a word, the vowel belonging to the prefix may be retained (*lo fa,* S. *lu-ppa,* he shall do).

If the word begins with a vowel which on account of the intrinsic meaning of the word cannot be left out, then this vowel supplants the vowel of the prefix (*l-a,* he did).

If the word contains many *i* sounds, then this sound often influences the vowel of the prefixes and suffixes (*isi,* seed, head, rounded surface, *m-isi,* to be straight, right, *h-imisi-hi,* your righteousness, *misi-ci-no,* the just, *m-imisi-ci-no,* the unjust ; *kidua,* to be true, *w-ikiduada,* we believe, *n-imikiduadi-n,* their unbelief).

Sometimes there is a sort of compromise between the vowel of the prefix and that of the word (*da-sikwa,* my house, *b-isikwa,* thy house, *ka-sikwa,* to dwell ; *sapatu,* a shoe, *l-isapatu-n,* his shoe ; *kaspara,* a sword, *bu-kaspare-n* thy sword, *l-ikaspare-n,* his sword ; Spanish *vela,* sail, *na-welan-wa,* (their) sail, *w-eweladoa,* we sailed, *ma-sogosoko-tu akabo abu,* with unwashen hands, *w-akabo,* our hands, *bu-kabo,* thy hand, *to-kabo,* her hand).

Sometimes both vowels are pronounced (*da-iiri,* my name, *bu-iri, l-iri, virgin iri*).

If there is no prefix, as with abstracts and agent-nouns or if instead of a pronominal prefix, an emphasizing pronoun or an object-word is used, then there are four possibilities :

a) The vowel is indispensable to the word, and is retained (*adeki-ci,* one who sees) ;

b) A vowel belonging to the word, is sometimes used and sometimes left out (*Peter isikwa*, Peter's house, *isikwa-hu*, villages, *Israel sikwa*, the house of Israel) ;

c) No vowel is applied (*atenwa-tu kaci*, the first month, *kena abar mihu o-lokomun l-iiga, Simon|i()mihu ia*, and he entered into one of the ships, which was Simon's) ;

d) An *a-* is prefixed to a word denoting an event, an *o-* to an object-word or a word denoting position, direction or time ; by this means as it were the general character of the word is announced (*lo-baptize()da goba ie*, (they) were baptized of him, *John a-baptizeda goba i*, (he) was baptized of John, *lo-bugici*, the (his) brother, *John o-bugici*, the brother of John, *a-burita-sia ... a-burito-n-wa Greek o-buri abu*, a superscription was written in letters of Greek, *wolf o-koboroko*, in the midst of wolves, *loko o-wakaia o-ma*, with man ('s evil), *camel o-barra*, camel's hair, *a-koto-*, to eat, *Adaie-li o-koto-n*, the Supper of the Lord).

The system of applying hyphens which has been adopted in this work will appear sufficiently from the examples given.

§ 18. The quality-words formed from object-words and words denoting position, direction or time, by prefixing *k(a)-*, to be with, or *m(a)-*, to be without (§ 10), may, if necessary, also perform the function of an action-word, see examples below. The English subject is then indicated by an emphasizing pronoun or an object-word that is placed before the word (a, b 1) II)). With the *k(a)-* forms a pronominal prefix can also be used : the prefix *k(a)-* is then left out, presumably because it then becomes superfluous (a, b) 2)). In case it is desired to use a pronominal prefix with the *m(a)-* form, the pronominal prefix is connected with the auxiliary verb *a* (b) 2)).

Ka-koborokwa, ma-koborokwa are indefinite in regard to time, and may remain so, at least in the examples met with : *k-ansi* and *m-ansi* are also indefinite in regard to time, but in the Indicative mood, the indefiniteness must be removed. For that purpose, with *k-ansi*, *ka* is added to form the Present tense (Potential mood *koma*), conformable to § 5 ; with *m-ansi*, *ma*, containing the element of uncertainty is added. Such forms are comparable to the action-words of the *a* group. In the same way *a-bolli*, to pass, and perhaps still more words.

a) *-Koborokwa*, remembrance, consciousness (§ 120 g) 7)) :

1) with the prefixes *k(a)-* and *m(a)-* :

I) as a verb denoting a state or condition :

ka-koborokwa-li hu, be ye wise, *abar-dakabo-no n-aurea ka-koborokwa goba abar-dakabo-no a-iiba ma-koborokwa goba*, five of them were wise, and five were (remained) foolish :

verbal nouns :

ka-koborokwa abu, in his right mind, *ka-koborokwa-hu*, wisdom, *ka-koborokwa-ci*, the wise, *ma-koborokwa-ci*, the foolish ;

II) as a verb denoting an action :

kena Peter ka-koborokwa goba Jesus ajia-n, and Peter remembered the word of Jesus ;

2) with a pronominal prefix :

as a verb denoting an action :

bo-koborokwa di, remember me, *loko-no a-ni robu-in bo-koborokwa,* thou savourest ... the things that be of men, *Lot ire-tu o-konomun ho-koborokwa-li,* remember Lot's wife, *kena ama ibia ho-koborokwa h-eke o-konomun ?* and why take ye thought for raiment ? *wa-koborokwa lihi a-murrida-ci ajia-n,* we remember that that deceiver said, *d-ajia-n da-koborokwa fa kiana,* and I will remember my covenant ;

verbal noun (*kwo-n,* see §§ 81 a), 120 a) 1)) :

to-makwa bo-koborokwon abu, [thou shalt love the Lord] with all thy mind ;

b) *Ansi,* inner peace, love, loving (§ 80 b)) :

1) II) *Da-ci k-ansi-ka di,* my Father love(s) me, *Daii k-ansi goba hu,* I loved you, *ki-o-doma ki ororo m-ansi ma hu,* therefore the world hateth you, *wakaia-be-ci k-ansi-ka k-ansi-ci ie,* for sinners also love those that love them, *m-ansi-ci di m-ansi ma Da-ci bajia,* he that hateth me hateth my Father also, *ororo warea-ci-n ka hu, ororo k-ansi koma t̗-amuni-sia-no,* if ye were of the world, the world would love his own ;

verbal nouns :

k-ansi-hi, love, *k-ansi-ci di,* he that loveth me, *m-ansi-ci di,* he that loveth me not, *abar-li lo-mairikoto-sia, lihi ki Jesus k-ansi-sia,* one of his disciples, whom Jesus loved ;

2) *h-ansi-li k-aiima-ci-no ho-mun,* love your enemies, *b-ansi ka di ?* lovest thou me ? *isa-tu-wabu a-bolliti-kwona-hu synagogue o-loko n-ansi-ka,* the chief seats in the synagogues (they love), *m-ansi n-a goba* (auxiliary verb a, § 28 a)) *di ausirobu-in,* they hated me without cause, *ororo koro m-ansi ma* (b) 1)) *hu : to-moroa Daii m-ansi t-a,* the world cannot hate you ; but me it hateth, *m-ansi d-a,* I will not (Mt. XXI, 29) ;

verbal nouns :

h-oabodda-li d-ansi-n o-loko, continue ye in my love, *d-aiici d-ansi-sia d-imigodi fa,* I will send my beloved son ;

c) *Ka-sa,* to be fruitful, to be with child, now changes its meaning into : to produce (a child), *k-iwi,* to bear fruits, becomes : to produce fruit. In the same way we might consider *ka-koborokwa* and *k-ansi,* when they fulfil the function of action-words, as : to produce remembrances, to produce inner peace ; and so with other words as well.

§ 19. The end-point pronoun is exclusively used :

1⁰. after a quality-word (word denoting a state or condition), and then it indicates the person who is in that state or condition ;

2⁰. after an action-word, and then it indicates the person who undergoes the action, or the object fully affected.

As the Arawak pronounces first the emotionally dominant, a sentence

of the type *kokke ka i !* he lives ! , has in reality the value : life (or vital
power) !!! appears !! (male third) person !

From this we may assume that some correlation exists between the place
behind the word of the end-point pronouns, their expectant, passive
function, and their short forms.

On account of this prescribed order of words, the combination of a word
with an end-point pronoun has something in common with a junction.

This appears still more strongly with the interrogative words m. *alika-i.*
f. *alika-n,* pl. *alika-ie* (§ 139 e)) in which the end-point pronoun remains,
even when the person indicated by it is already represented by an object-
word or an emphasizing pronoun.

S. always uses this construction :

lu-parra baddia kassiparra abbu i Jacobus Johannes u-hukiti, and he
killed James the brother of John with the sword, lit. he-kill also sword with
him Jacobus Johannes' brother, *lu-morrua Joseph u-ma kuba i Gott,* but
God was with him, lit. he-but Joseph with past-time he God, *na-ssimaki-n-
benna|je Apostel-nu n-ibiti ba,* and they called them, lit. their-calling-after
them Apostles them-to again, *bu-mallita-té wa-mallitta-koana-nu-tti bia|u,*
make us gods, lit. thou-make gods to-be-us, *n-assâ-ka kiahanna i Barnabas.
Jupiter, Paulus na-rita|i Mercurius,* and they called (him) Barnabas,
Jupiter ; and Paul (they named him), Mercurius.

Such pleonasms also occur in other A. M. languages. see § 181.

G. The end-point pronouns are generally pronounced as if they form
part of the preceding word.

§ 20. Before we plunge into the mass of forms, we shall make a few
supplementary remarks concerning the general character of the Arawak
word.

When, in § 1, we analyzed *d-imigoda,* I send, there remained a root
imigo, readiness, being ready. This root can again be split into *imi,* being
willing, and *g,* a force manifesting itself, *o,* permanently. And *imi* can be
split into *i,* quick, *m,* humble or new, *i,* quick.

In every analysis of a genuine Arawak word we experience the same.
It appears that the real psychological roots of Arawak, synchronistically
conceived, are : *a, e, i, (ü), o* or *u, y, w, h, (g), k, n, l, r, d, t, s, m, b,*
and *f* or *p,* each of which has a definite (and always the same) meaning, or
represents an elementary principle.

Such a word gives a short description of the thing. The description
begins with that which appears first in time or that which is considered
as the origin or the basis of the thing. The connexion appears from the
sequence, and in the sequence appear fluent transitions and contrasts. The
word may be compared to a sentence which has been contracted into a
single compound.

We may still mention the fact, that not one case has been met with, of a
sound having lost its original meaning when used in a compound (as, for
instance, hydrogen and oxygen in water have lost their gaseous quality).

With the exception of -n (perhaps also -r in abar, one), consonants are only used before a vowel; they model as it were the formless principle expressed by the vowel. For instance, the particles, *ba*, again, *bi*, just now, *bo* (to remain) at rest for a time, are composed of *a*, time-reality, *i* instantaneous, *o* permanent, with *b*, the way in which a surface, a shape, presents itself, or quiet, passionless appearance.

Two vowels express:

(1) *i—i*, quick, tiny, full of energy, (2) *a—a*, normal, (3) *u—u* or *o—o*, slow, great, little energy, (4) *i—a, i—u, a—u*, slowing down, widening out, relaxing of tension. (5) *a—i, u—i, u—a*, accelerating, narrowing, tightening.

Examples: (1) *hihi*, reed, *iri*, a name, *isi*, seed, *iwi*, fruit, *ibi*, ready, *ifi*, great (striving), (2) *ana*, the midst (in compounds), *ala*, Indian seat, *aba*, a, one, other, *ada*, a tree, *ama*, what, (3) *ororo*, earth, *a-odo-*, to die, (4) *ika*, "there was once", *ina*, a beginning, a continuation, *enu (A. M.), heaven, *eda*, bark, skin (loosely connected with the tree or the body), (5) *ani*, a thing, *airi*, a tooth, *adi*, something protruding (in compounds), *ona*, the ground (in compounds).

Now there is a habit of speech, which requires that, for instance in order to express "to send", one should always use the sound-sequence *imigod*, but it is quite probable that the Arawak feels this root more or less as *[(i-m-i)-g-o]d*.

When the European thinks, reasons and describes, then for him the most real, that to which everything else seems to be attached. is the "concrete object". Actions and qualities remain for him on another level of consciousness, in the sphere of feeling and will; and if he wishes to think about an action or a quality, he cannot do so without imagining an object which performs or undergoes the action, or possesses the quality. The use of abstract nouns is really an endeavour to transform an action or a quality into a mental image, namely to make an "object" of it. It remains, however, halting between the two opposites: imagination and thought (the motionless, the dead) and feeling and will (the living, the active).

The Arawak language expresses that which lies in the sphere of the feelings and the will.

The European of our time lives alternately in the sphere of imagination and thought and in the sphere of feeling and will; the Arawak probably lives chiefly in the sphere of feeling and will, and this explains how it comes that he expresses himself in elementary principles, which to us appear as abstractions. In § 184 we shall see that his feelings are transformed into a sort of gesture-language of the organs of speech, with the result that to each element of feeling, or elementary principle, corresponds a definite sound.

Considered from the outside, these elementary principles describe different shades of activity, and if we consider the ending of a word as its centre of gravity (§ 14), then we see that the words do the same. In accordance with this, endings which determine the character of an action-word (for instance *ki, di, ti* or *ci, li, -n*), may determine the character of an object-word as well, and we can now understand, how it comes that the European lines of demarcation between word-classes are non-existent in Arawak (§§ 9—11).

The following may be noted here, because it deviates from the accepted opinions as to the character of the languages of primitive peoples :

The Arawak can just as easily express what we call the abstract, as what we call the concrete.

He has special names for every sort of fish, every kind of tree, but he also has the words *himi* = fish, and *ada* = tree. These words describe "fish" and "tree" (see §§ 76 b), 89), and, so far as we can see, they are not the names for a special sort, which have later been applied to the whole group. Likewise the names for special sorts are in general not derived from *himi* and *ada*, although such forms occur (§ 199, names of tiger-cats and snakes).

In itself, the meaning of the Arawak word is as general as the value of its component parts permits. The habit of speech restricts that meaning, and also often requires the use of certain affixes, by which the meaning is further restricted. Ultimately the word is confined to a certain group of things, actions, etc., or even to one thing or one action, by the context and by the situation in general.

CHAPTER III

INFINITE VERB

§ 21. *-Ci (-tu)* can be suffixed to : [1] object-words and proper names, [2] words denoting position, direction or time, [3] quality-words, [4] action-words ; it adds to the meaning of these words the principle of "being active", "asserting oneself". Presumably the *t* (which with B. often turns into *c* before the *i*) has here again the meaning of motion towards an object (with a touch of will-power in it).

These forms (eventually with an end-point pronoun or a form fulfilling a similar function, behind them) are sometimes used as substantives, and often as adjectives. In the latter case they may be placed either before or after the word governed, and this forms a transition to such uses as remind one of participles and gerunds. They may moreover take the particles *fa*, *goba*, etc. as suffixes.

a) Examples.

[1] *ark isikwa-ci-n* (*-n*, possessive, § 81) *l-onnakida kiana Noah*, and Noah removed the covering of the ark, *Pharisee lihi, Gamaliel ci iri, a-mairikota-ci misi-tu-ahaka-hu*, a Pharisee (was he), named Gamaliel, a doctor of the law, *aba-ro hiaro, Martha tu iri*, a certain woman named Martha, *kia hiaro Greek goba, Syrophenicia tu akirikia*, the woman was a Greek, a Syrophenician by nation, *ikihi-tu kaspara*, a flaming sword, *siba-tu taraffa*, the (stone) stairs, *siparari-tu t-isifo-do*, the iron gate, *to-tokoro-tu kwawma*, garlands, *yurua-tu ada*, a bramble bush ;

[2] *abar-li l-Isa, Awa o-loa o-loko-ci*, the only begotten Son, which is in the bosom of the Father, *bo-loko-tu kalime*, the light which is in thee, *yaha-ci ikirikia bihero-ci wakaia-ci o-koboroko*, in this adulterous and sinful generation (Mk. VIII 38), *taha-tu ororo*, a far country ;

[3] *sa-ci lihi*, he is a good man, *Sa-ci Awa*. Holy Father, *sa-tu ajia-hu*, the gospel, *wakaia-ci*, the wicked one, *wakaia-tu c-iwi*, evil fruit, *kari-tu hori*, a viper, *aboa-ci*, sick people, *aboa-tu*, [a woman] being sick, *nokonne-ci aba-no o-konomun*, the merciful, *kokki-ci ialoko*, a living soul, *kokki-tu aiadi-tu*, the moving creature that has life. See also the names for family-relations, § 162 ff. ;

[4] See examples §§ 4 c), 15 c) ;

b) Different sequence.

[1] *imilia-tu a-odo-ci-sikwa*, a new tomb, *imilia-tu testament*, the new testament, *kokke-ci Wacinaci Aiici*, the Son of the living God, *imoro-tu*

abona-gira-hu, green herb, *alikibi bu, ibekito-tu isa-hi abu bui,* hail, thou that art highly favoured ;

2) *a-odo-ci-sikwa imilia-tu,* a new sepulchre, *Awa kokki-ci,* the living Father, *Awa misi-ci bui !* o righteous Father (thou) ! *to-makwa abona-gira-hu ka-si-tu to-makwa ororo ajeago-tu da-sika ho-mun, to-makwa ada bajia, k-iwi-tu ada ka-si-tu,* I have given you every herb bearing seed, which is upon the face of all the˙ earth, and every tree, in the which is the fruit of a tree yielding seed, *to-moroa na-loko wolf a-bokoti-tu naii,* but inwardly, they are ravening wolves, *Wacinaci, aici-ci wa-loa,* God, which knoweth the hearts, *Peter a-sifuda-ci adeka Jesus a-mairikoto-sia l-ansi-sia ausi-n l-iinabo,* then Peter, turning about, seeth the disciple whom Jesus loved following, *aba-no Greek-no goba andi-ci o-koboroko a-kwaiabo-n-wa bia ifirokoro ka o-loko,* and there were certain Greeks among them that came up to worship at the feast ;

3) The Arawak language has no adjectives. The forms with *-ci (-tu, -ci-no), -li (-ro, -no)* and *-sia* are used to translate English attributive adjectives etc. (*ikihi-tu kaspara,* a flaming sword, *biama-no k-augii-ci,* two brethren), but they are very loosely connected, as appears also from the fact that these attributive forms must give way to the pronominal prefix (*sa-ci d-adaiana-sia !* good (my) Master ! *sa-ci bu-sa Jesus,* thy holy child Jesus, *wakaia-ci oie-ci da-sanci bui,* thou wicked and slothful (my) servant, *to-makwa sa-tu ada k-iwi-ka sa-tu c-iwi,* every good tree bringeth forth good (its) fruit, *to-moroa na-uaiya m-arulaka ti n-a-n aba-ro na-kabo abu,* but they themselves will not move them with one of their fingers, *l-imigoda goba biama-no lo-mairikoto-sia-no,* he sent two of his disciples) ;

c) Plurality.

1) Persons : *-ci* :

adeki-ci n ahaka-ga kiana na-mun, and they that saw it told them, etc., *m-akosi-ci adeka, ikori-ci akona-ga,* the blind see, the lame walk ;

2) The same, but with a word that is already plural :

ka-sa-ci hiaro-no, them (women) that are with child, *Jew-no arulukokita a-kwaiaboa-ci hiaro-no adaie-ro-bi-ci bajia,* the Jews stirred up the devout and honourable women, *kena aba-no bajia, ikita-ci i n-amuni-sia abu,* and many others, which ministered unto him of their substance, *yuho-li botoba-ci hiaro-no goba,* many widows were, *kenbena Roman-o anda fa-te onnaki-ci wa-sikwa wa-kirikia bajia,* and the Romans shall come and take away both our place and nation, *na-makwa aboa-ci,* all that were diseased, *n-a( )alikibitoa k-amunaiga-ci ialoko,* blessed are the poor in spirit ;

3) Persons : *-ci-no* :

m-akosi-ci-no adeka, ikori-ci-no akona, the blind receive their sight, and the lame walk, *thousand-no k-ansi-ci-no di,* thousands of them that love me, *onnaki-ci-no, angel-no,* the reapers, are the angels, *mihu o-loko-ci-no,* they that were in the ship ;

4) Persons : *-no-ci, -na-ci* ; see § 79 b) ;

5) Mostly things : *-be-ci* ; also, though seldom : *-be-tu* : see § 59 a) ²) :

d) *-Tu* is only used to indicate one woman, or one or more non-rational beings or things.

aba-ro k-amunaiga-tu botoba-tu hiaro anda, and there came a certain poor widow, *wakaia-tu-wabu lihi ajia-ga*, he hath spoken blasphemy, *wakaia d-onyi goba, daii a-sikiti-ci ma-wakaia-tu ite*, I have sinned in that I have betrayed the innocent blood, *kia isadi-tu ajia-hu*, the word of this salvation ;

e) Different relations between a *-ci* form and the word connected with it :

1) *imigodo-ci di*, him that sent me, *onyi-ci kidua-hu*, he that doeth truth, *yuho-ro k-amun-ci*, a rich man ;

2) *k-aiima-ci bu-mun*, thine enemy, *andi-ci aiomuni o-rea*, he that cometh from above ;

3) *isogo-ci ikiduadi-n hui*, o ye of little faith, *l-imigoda-te di akurradaa-ci o-loa d-isadi-n bia*, he has sent me to heal the brokenhearted, *isa sabu koma bu-mun aba-ro-ci akosi bui akodo-n-wa kokke-hu o-lokomun, biama-ci k-akosi-n a-boredo-n-wa hell ikihi akoloko mun aji*, it is better for thee to enter into life with one eye, rather than having two eyes to be cast into hell, *tata-ci-o-kona*, a strong man.

§ 22. *-Sia* adds to the meaning of the word the principle of "the thing that has been realised", like *-ci (-tu)* adds the principle of "realising a thing". On account of this, such *-sia* forms are an easy means for the translation of English passive sentences (N.B. also other than *oa* forms are used for this purpose). *-Sia* probably means : *s*, form, *i*, free, *a*, time-reality (§ 132). Plural forms : *-sia-no* and *-sia-be* (§ 59 a) 1)).

Compare : *sa-ci*, f. *sa-tu*, plur. *sa-ci-no*, a good person or thing, with : *isa-sia ajia-n o-konomun*, [one] of good report, *isa-sia-no n-ajia-n o-konomun*, [men] of honest report. Also : *omuni-ga ie n-ausi-sia isikwa-hu mun i-ro o-rea, kena taha sabu ausi-ci bia jia l-a*, and they drew nigh unto the village, whither they went : and he made as though he would have gone further, lit. nigh-drew they their-go-*sia* village to from, and far more go-*ci* to-be as he-did.

Further examples :

a) *sa-tu onyi-sia t-onyi-ka da-mun barin*, she hath wrought a good work on me, *t-onyi-sia ma kiana t-onyi-ka*, she hath done what she could, *Jesus k-ansi-sia*, [the disciple] whom Jesus loved, *to-makwa d-amuni-sia bui k-amuni-ga*, and all that I have is thine ;

b) *i* group :

Wacinaci iibida goba l-imikeb-oa kia ki lo-murreti-sia, God ended his work, which he had made, *hui adeki-sia*, those things which ye see, *h-adeki-sia*, these things which ye behold, *da-ci-a-iibi-sia*, the inheritance, lit. his-father leave-*sia*, *h-auadi-sia ki ibici daii*, I am he whom ye seek, *Jesus daii, b-akudi-sia*, I am Jesus whom thou persecutest, *to-makwa Da-ci a-siki-sia da-mun*, all things are delivered unto me of my Father, *l-iaunti-sia l-isanonoci*, the (his) hired servants, *na-makwa l-aici-sia-no*, all his acquaintance, *l-isimakiti-sia-no*, them that were (by him) bidden, *da-simakiti-sia-no*, they which were (by me) bidden ;

c) o group :

lo-torodo-sia, the (his) bed *d-imigodo-sia*, my messenger, *a-sogoso-sia*, he that is washed ;

d) a group :

a-dokota-sia, a miracle, *ajia-sia goba*, it hath been said (Mk. V, 31). *b-ahaka-sia*, thy record, *w-ahaka-sia*, our report, *lihi koro Kalime ki goba. to-moroa imigoda-sia goba lihi, l-ahaka-n bia Kalime ki o-konomun*. he was not that Light, but was sent to bear witness of that Light, *to-makwa ada isa-be-tu adeka-sia bia*, every tree that is pleasant to the sight. *n-a( )alikibitoa akuda-sia-no misi-hi o-konaria*, blessed are they which are persecuted for righteousness' sake ; S. *ihittarra-sia*, he which is accused ;

e) e, in the following :

kia robu-in lo-mairikoto-sia-no a-iige-sia o-loko, [no boat] save that one whereinto his disciples were entered (*a-iige*, enter, *sia*. realised, *o-loko*. "in" place), *hui ikiside-sia jiaro ki abu, hui ikisido fa ba*, with what judgment ye judge, ye shall be judged, *auaduli aragase-sia hihi*, a reed shaken with the wind, *d-akoio fa da-sikwa o-lokomun i-ro da-fitikide-sia goba-te o-rea*, I will return into my house from whence I came out ;

f) oa principle, possessive pronominal prefix :

lo-mairikoto-sia, his disciple, *lo-mairikoto-sia⋅no*, his disciples, *waii a-kwaiabo-sia o-mun w-aiita*, we know what we worship, *lo-borago-sia*. his stripes ;

g) oa principle ; the person indicated by the pronominal prefix is the person who undergoes the action :

kia ki b-onnako-sia goba o-rea, for out of it wast thou taken, *alika-i koro a-siko-sia goba o-loko*, [a sepulchre] wherein never man before was laid. *na-makwa koro n-onnaka ma toho ajia-hu, to-moroa t-isiko-sia-no o-mun robu-in*, all men cannot receive this saying, save they to whom it is given (*t*, it, *isiko*, being given, *sia*, realised, *o-mun*, "at" place) ;

h) Miscellaneous examples :

l-Aiici onyi koma amakoro l-oaiya lo-doma wa, to-moroa l-adeki-sia Awa onyi-sia : lihi onyi-sia jiaro ki, l-Aiici onyi-ka ba. the Son can do nothing of himself, but what he seeth the Father do : for what things soever he doeth, these also doeth the Son likewise. *a-burita-sia ki iibidwa kiana, Ikisida-sia lihi wakaia onyi-ci-no o-ma*. and the scripture was ful-filled which saith, And he was numbered with the transgressors, *alaiti ibita-sia a-kalimeta-sia goba i*, he was a burning and a shining light. *k-amun-ci akuyuko l-akonnabo-sia bia abu, l-akonnabia-te*. he that hath ears to hear, let him hear, *alika-i koro a-timiti-sia ma*. no man could bind him, *Wacinaci k-amun-ci di, d-ikita-sia ; lihi angel ajinama da-mun kasakoda*. for there stood by me this night, the angel of God, whose I am. and whom I serve, *to-makwa lihi a-murreti-sia goba*. all things were made by him, *kena toho sa-tu ajia-hu isauka o-konomun-tu ajia-sia fa to-makwa*

ororo ajeago-ji ma-n, and this gospel of the kingdom shall be preached in
all the world, *ma-koborokwatoa-n h-a-li ho-kokke-wa o-konomun, ama
h-eki-sia bia, ama h-eti-sia bia, o-konomun ; h-ifiro-hu o-konomun bajia,
ama abu h-ekito-sia bia o-konomun,* take no thought for your life, what ye
shall eat, or what ye shall drink ; nor yet for your body, what ye shall put
on (for) ; Sm. *tú-maqua d-addiki-ssiä-bi,* das alles was ich heute gesehen
habe ; with *-buna, -kuba, -pa, -nu pa,* d.a.w.i. gestern g.h., d.a.w.i. vor-
längst g.h., d.a.w.i. sehen werde, alle die ich sehen werde.

Furthermore, both from the *-sia* and the *-sia-no* forms, an Infinitive can
be formed, by means of the suffix *-n.*

¹) Different sequence (parallel to § 21 ᵇ⁾).

¹) *abar-li n-aici-sia siba-loko-ci,* a notable prisoner, lit. one they-know-
sia stone-in-person, *aiita-sia-ma slotro-n h-onnaki-n n-aurea o-doma,* for
ye have taken away (from them) the key of knowledge, *n-isadi-sia boia-tu,*
the spices which they had prepared, *bu-imaha-sia fig-ada,* the fig tree which
thou cursedst, *bawhu a-murreta-ari-no a-borede-sia siba,* the stone which
the builders rejected, *l-akodo-sia bawhu,* the house where he entereth in ;

²) *Lihi d-Aiici d-ansi-sia,* This is my beloved Son, *hiaro b-isiki-sia
da-ma-tu bia,* the woman whom thou gavest to be with me, *bawhu na-
bolliti-sia o-loko,* the house where they were sitting, *kena kia l-adura,
Adaie-li Wacinaci onnaki-sia loko o-rea,* and the rib which the Lord God
had taken from man, *onabo l-onnako-sia o-rea,* the ground, from whence
he was taken.

See moreover for *-sia: a-sia,* § 30, *ma-mari-sia, bari-sia,* § 147, and
words denoting a human peculiarity, § 118 ᵃ⁾).

§ 23. *Hia,* also *ia,* S. *hüa,* adds to the meaning of the word the principle
of "existing condition" ; *h* means perhaps "gentle affirmation" (§ 109),
ia, free time-reality, etherical (§ 132).

Examples :

kena l-isimaka sa-be-ci botoba-ci bajia, a-siki-n kokke-hia na-muni n,
and when he had called the saints and widows, presented her alive (to
them), *ama ajia-hu toho h-ajia-ga ho-muni-kwawa, nokonne-hia h-akona-
ia ?* what manner of communications are these that ye have one to another,
as ye walk, and are sad ? *kenbena Jesus a-bolli-ci adeka goba loko m-akosi-
hia ka-raia-ci,* and as Jesus passed by, he saw a man which was blind from
his birth, *ika tu goba d-imigodo-ni hu m-amuni-hia plata-eke, saka bajia,
sapatu bajia ; amateli h-ansi goba ?* when I sent you without purse, and
scrip, and shoes, lacked ye any thing ? *daii ausa akero-hia ialoko abu,* I go
bound in the spirit, *ki-hia na-sikita goba di akero-ia,* yet was I delivered
(by them) prisoner, *l-iiba goba Paul a-timitwa-hia,* (he) left Paul bound,
adikito-ia lo-kabo lo-kuti l-akarato-sia kimisa abu, [he came forth], bound
hand and foot with graveclothes, *Herod ... eketoa-ia l-adaiakitwa-kwona-hu
eke abu,* Herod, arrayed in royal apparel, *ika ki aba-no Jew-no Asia warea-ci
auciga di maribe-ni-hia temple o-loko,* whereupon certain Jews from Asia
found me purified in the temple, *m-ikidoa-ni-hia,* I came without gainsaying,

ma-koto-ni-hia a-kwaiaboa n-a-n ka, and when they had fasted and prayed. *habe-ci ia di, d-ire-tu bajia habe ia*, for I am an old man, and my wife well stricken in years (L. I, 18), *toho hiaro kiana, Abraham o-tu ia. Satan akeri-sia*, this woman, being a daughter of Abraham, whom Satan hath bound, S. *l-irei-tu aditta-hüa lu-monnua*, his wife also being privy to it (knowing), *naha Prophete-nu üssanutti hüa hu*, ye are children of the prophets. *hama kurru l-amün-hitti-ka wa-uria-hüa*, as though he needed any thing. lit. thing not his-possession-wish-is us-from-*hüa*.

§ 24. *Hu* also adds to the meaning of the word the principle of "existing condition", but it lacks the free mobility which is expressed by *hia*; we feel the -*hu* forms as substantives. Compare:

ifili-ci capitan oonaba-ga n, Yuho-ro plata abu daii a-iaunta toho ma-iero-hu, main. To-moroa daii ka-raia goba ma-iero-hia, l-a Paul ajia-n lo-mun, and the chief captain answered, With a great sum obtained I this freedom. And Paul said, But I was free born;

Capitan ausa kiana a-bokota-ari-no o-ma aunaki-n ie m-aiima-hia, then went the captain with the officers, and brought them without violence. *m-aiima-hu abu b-osa*, go in peace (Mt. V, 34);

aucigi-ni|n a-oda-hia, found her dead, *alika-i jiali ikita faroka d-ajia-n, alika koro l-adeki fa a-oda-hu*, if a man keep my saying, he never shall see death;

a-sweardoa-hia l-ajia-sia waii icinaci Abraham o-mun ki. [to remember his holy covenant;] the oath which he sware to our father Abraham, *kenbena ki ba a-sweardoa-hu abu abakoro l-a goba ajia-n*, and again he denied with an oath;

Jesus adeka l-oonaba-n ka-koborokwa-hia, and when Jesus saw that he answered discreetly, *ibe-ci ka-koborokwa-hu abu*, filled with wisdom;

n-ateda, m-eke-hia, ibika-hia bajia, they fled. ... naked and wounded, *wadili da-forri-n o-doma ibika-hu abu di*, for I have slain a man to my wounding;

yuho-li murriga-hia ahaka goba lo-konomun barin, for many bare false witness against him (Mk. XIV, 56), *aba-no a-kenakwa kiana, ajia-n murriga-hu lo-konomun* (etc.), and there arose certain, and bare false witness against him, saying (etc., Mk. XIV, 57).

Hu, compared with -*sia*: *toho jia l-a goba ajia-n, a-dokoto-ci a-oda-hu lo-odo-sia bia abu*, this he said, signifying what death he should die, *da-konnaba ajia-hu ajia-sia da-mun*, I heard a voice speaking unto me (Acts XXVI, 14).

An object-word without -*hu* denotes a definite thing (or things); with -*hu* it denotes the thing in general or in a more solemn meaning.

Besides *isada-hu*, salvation, one also meets *isada-hi*; and with other words -*hi*, -*he* or -*ha* is invariably used. Probably this has something to do with the vowels of the word, but as every vowel of the word has a definite meaning, it may well be that -*hi*, etc. also express different shades of meaning from -*hu*.

Examples :

yumuni ki fa a-iiya-hu atarata-hu airisibo bajia, there shall be wailing and gnashing of teeth, *ikisida-hu,* judgment, *ikiduada-hu,* faith, *a-dokoda-hu,* remission (of sins), *a-dokota-hu,* a sign, a testimony, *a-mairikota-hu,* doctrine, *a-kenakwa-hu,* resurrection, *a-iyurati-ci loko-no ansi abu anda-hu jia h-a-te andi-n lihi abu da-mun,* ye have brought this man unto me, as one that perverteth the people, lit. stirrer people peace with come-*hu* as ye-do coming this with me-to, *kenbena adeka-hu abu l-anda goba,* and came seeing, lit. and sight with he-came, *Ajia-hu,* the Word, *Adaiakita-hu,* honour, *kidua-hu.* truth, *wakaia-tu o-loa-hu, a-forra-hu,* evil thoughts, murders (Mt. XV, 19), *kokke-hu,* the life [was the light of men], *kokke-hu ada,* the tree of life, *aboa-hu,* sickness, disease, *a-ciga-hu,* the tombs (Mt. XXIII, 29), *isikwa-hu,* a village (*isikwa,* house, shelter), *ifiro-hu,* body (also meat ; *ifiro,* great), *imikebo-hu,* work, *toho ki d-abona o-rea-tu abona-hu, da-siroko o-rea-tu isiroko-ho,* this is now bone of my bones, and flesh of my flesh (Gen. II, 23), S. *a-ssukussá-hü,* baptism (washing) :

a-kota-he, food, *akuda-he,* persecution, *a-iauda-he,* madness, *onnaka-he-bia-c-iwi,* [white already] to harvest ;

abona-ha, way (way of salvation, etc. ; a path through a wood etc. is called *waboroko*) ;

kalime-hi, light (Gen. I, 3), *misi-hi,* righteousness, *alikibe-hi,* joy, *Jerusalem warea ausa-hi bia to-kona,* beginning at Jerusalem, lit. J. from go-*hi* to-be it-against, *iri-hi,* name (Acts IV, 12), title (J. XIX, 19, 20), *ie-hi,* tongues (Acts II, 3, XIX, 6), *k-ansi-hi,* love, *nokonne-hi,* sorrow, *nokonne-hi na-konomun,* mercy (on them), *isa-n bajia akosi-hi o-mun,* and that it was pleasant to the eyes, *isa-hi,* good will, grace, holiness, *aici-n isa-hi wakaia-hu bajia,* knowing good and evil, *kari-hi,* disease, *tata-tu onyi-hi,* mighty work.

It is not quite clear, why in the following example *akosi* takes the suffix *-hi,* and *akuyuko* takes no suffix ; presumably this is to be attributed to the inner meaning of the words : *to-moroa t-a( )alikibitoa hui akosi-hi, t-adeki-n o-doma ; hui akuyuko bajia, t-akonnabo-n o-doma,* but blessed are your eyes, for they see : and your ears, for they hear.

S. and Q. use such *-hu* forms as passive verbs (Q. see § 91). Examples :

a) *Philippus a-uttika-hü|ka,* Philip was found, *l-ipiru akarta-hü|ka,* he (his body) is buried, *a-ijumünda-hü|ka|i.* he was taken up (Acts I, 9) ;

b) *a-ssika-hü|kubá,* [the stone] which was set :

c) *lü-ssiqua a-mallukududa-hü|pa* let his habitation be desolate :

d) *abba ikissida-hi-ttu kassakkabbu-hü.* a set day ;

e) *n-aditti-koana-wa ani-hü-ssia hidda Apostel-nu abbu.* and signs were done by the apostles, *kia ibenna-ria a-ssika-hü-ssia-kuba,* and distribution was made, *Joseph, Barsabas n-a-hü-ssia* (§ 30) *u-mün,* Joseph called Barsabas ;

f) *wa-méju a-bulleda-hü-n m-a-ni-ka* (§ 32), and when the (our) ship was caught, *a-pussida-hü-nni|bia|i lu-mün*, that he might loose him. lit. loosed to-be he him-by ;

g) *kiahaña adittikitta-hü-ka-hü*, be it known ;

h) *da-ijumujudá-ka-hüa-hü*, (I) publickly.

§ 25. -*Ni* adds to the meaning of the word the principle of "something that really is or shall be".

a) *to-moroa lo-mairikoto-sia-no m-aici-n goba Jesus ni*. but the disciples knew not that it was Jesus, *to-moroa n-aici-n kona Jew-ni*, but when they knew that he was a Jew.

S. uses *né* in the same manner : S. *Petrus Engel baha lihi né* ! it is his (Peter's) angel ! *ka-pparka-ti lihi né*, no doubt this man is a murderer. *iribé ti dia mutti lui né*, (he is unclean) !), *luilikewai né* ! (it is he !) ;

b) *ho-bokota-li i, isa-ni h-ausi-n l-abu*, take him, and led him away safely, lit. ye-take him, good-*ni* ye-going him-with, *akonnabo-ni abu h-akonnabo fa barin*, by hearing ye shall hear. *naii o-mun l-ajia-ga lo-mairikota-ni abu*, and he said unto them in his doctrine, *kena n-amunaigata-ni abu na-koiokota goba i*, and (they) sent him away shamefully handled. *toraha to-makwa d-ikita goba d-iloni-ni warea*, all these things have I kept from my youth up, *d-aimaha fa koro ororo loko o-konaria toho-ni warea ; loko o-loa a-koborokwatoa-n wakaia-hu o-konomun l-iloni-ni warea o-doma*. I will not again curse the ground any more for man's sake ; for the imagination of man's heart is evil from his youth ;

c) *Wacinaci lo-ma-ni o-doma*, for God was with him. *d-aiita ama d-onyi-ni wa* (§ 120 g) 6)), I am resolved what to do, *m-ansi w-a liraha w-adaie-ni wa*, we will not have this man to reign over us. *naii akonnabo-n kona kokke-ni o-konomun*, when they had heard that he was alive, *kena m-ikita-n-ci hu m-ikita-ni ma Daii bajia*. and he that despiseth you despiseth me ;

d) With an end-point pronoun :

b-ansi fa tu-muni bu ; b-adaiakiti fa n : isa fa b-ikita-ni n, wilt thou love her, comfort her, honour, and keep her. *m-aici-n w-a alo area-tu-ni n. n-a kiana oonaba-n*, and they answered, that they could not tell whence it was, lit. not-knowing we-do where-from-thing-*ni* it, they-did then answering, *b-ansi-ka w-ausi-n erigi-ni n* ? wilt thou then that we go and gather them up ? *kena h-akera ibiti-ni n*. and bind them [in bundles] to burn them. *na-makwa loko-no andi-ci adeki-ni n*, and all the people that came together to that sight ;

e) *tanahu maribe-ni hu*, now ye are clean, *m-amaro-ni bu*, be not afraid.

§ 26. -*In* adds to the meaning of the word the principle of "being continually present".

ika tu l-aradi-n ajia-n, loko-no akonnabo-in, now when he had ended all his sayings in the audience of the people. *liraha ki koro a-bolliti-ci goba a-kwaiabo-in* ? is not this he that sat and begged ? *t-aucigwa goba ka-sa-in Sa-tu Ialoko abu*, she was found with child of the Holy Ghost. *lihi ki k-iwi-ka yuho-in*, [he that abideth in me, and I in him,] the same bringeth forth much fruit, *ho-makwa h-afuji-ci isoko-in, lihi ifi-li fa*, for he that is least among you all, the same shall be great, *n-auciga l-isanci aboa-ci goba isa-in*, (they) found the servant whole that had been sick, *na-makwa n-aici-n Greek-in l-ici o-doma*, for they knew all that his father was a Greek (comp. *to-moroa l-ici Greek wadili goba*, but his father was a Greek (man)).

§ 27. *-N* adds to the meaning of the word the principle of "duration, vagueness in respect to time".

See examples in § 5, and the following :

l-idehada-ga kiana ajinamu-n, akona-n, temple o-lokomun a-kodo-n-wa na-ma ; akona-n, a-dehada-n, a-praisedi-n Wacinaci bajia, and he leaping up stood, and walked, and entered with them into the temple, walking, and leaping, and praising God ; *kena na-iinata goba a-kurradi-n marisi*, and (they) began to pluck the ears of corn, *kena t-akenakwa goba ikita-n ie*, and she arose, and ministered unto them.

In these sentences all the *-n* forms have no pronominal prefix ; the same may be the case with the *-ni* forms (§ 25 ᵈ). On the other hand a pronominal prefix is applied in : *d-ansi-ka b-isiki-n da-mun tanahu kibi John Baptist isi ifiro-tu karubo o-loko*, I will that thou give me by and by in a charger the head of John the Baptist, — because here the person connected with the secondary action-word is not the same as the person connected with the primary action-word.

In general a *-ni* form expresses the sharp, the pithy, an *-n* form more the indefinite, the vague. See also §§ 32, 33.

There is some relationship between the *-ci (-tu)*, the *-ni*, the *-n* and the *-in* forms ; if it is not absolutely indicated which of these forms has to be used, sometimes one and sometimes the other is met with, e.g. *Jesus aici-ci na-loa o-konomun ajia goba na-mun*, and Jesus knew their thoughts, and said unto them, *to-moroa ika tu Jesus aici-ni n, yu warea ki l-ausa goba*, but when Jesus knew it, he withdrew himself from thence, *ika tu Jesus aici-n l-oaiya lo-lok-oa lo-mairikoto-sia-no a-ononoda-n to-konomun*, when Jesus knew in himself that his disciples murmured at it, [he said] ; *yumuni ki l-auciga abar-li, Eneas ci iri, kabuin-timen wiwa-ci goba lo-torodo-kwona-hu ajeago, aboa-ci goba bele-n*, and there he found a certain man named Æneas, which had kept his bed (on) eight years, and was sick of the palsy, *biam-loko wiwa-n bena i*, and when he was full forty years old [it came in his heart to visit his brethren], *ika tu goba abar-mairia-kutihi wiwa-in Tiberius Cesar adaia-he-n*, now in the fifteenth year of the reign of Tiberius Cæsar, *Adaie-li isa-tu wiwa-in o-konomun d-ahaka-n bia*, [he has sent me] to preach the acceptable year of the Lord.

In the vowel preceding the *-n, the i, o* or *a* principle finds expression ; if that vowel is an *i*, then it is often uncertain, whether an *-in* or an *-n* form is meant. *Oa*, preceding *-n*, expresses a combination of the *oa* and the *a* principles. The *oa* principle alone, is expressed by substituting *o-n-wa* for *i-n* (*i* group) or for *o-n* (*o* group), e.g. *to-moroa kasakabo anda fa-te, ika tu fa aiika-ci onnako-n-wa n-aurea*, but the days will come, when the bridegroom shall be taken away from them, *biama goba kiana n-akosi a-torodo-n-wa*, and the eyes of them both were opened (comp. *Sabbath kasakabo barin ika ki Jesus a-murreta goba ororoli a-torodo-n l-akosi*, and it was the sabbath day when Jesus made the clay, and opened his eyes). These forms may be considered as *-n* forms : *a-torodo-n* and *onnako-n* (— the latter parallel to *onnaki-n*, and only used when *-wa* is suffixed —) with a suffix *-wa* having the meaning of "in itself", etc. (see § 120 ᵍ)).

The frequently used *-n-ci (-n-tu)* forms all indicate something including the principle of duration, vagueness in respect to time, together with the *-ci (-tu)* principle ; they are also used if there is an element of futurity in the action, the same as with the *ia* forms of § 5. Examples :

Adaie-li, d-ausia banyia to-bora, da-ci d-akarate-n-ci, Lord, suffer me first to go and bury my father (comp. *akarati-ci b-ire-ci*, them which have buried thy husband), *n-aiitᵤ barin ma-mairikoto-n-wa-ci naii m-aici-n-ci bajia*, (they) perceived that they were unlearned and ignorant men, *wakaia m-onyi-n-ci-n ka i*, if he were not a malefactor.

It is a matter of course that *-n-ci (-n-tu)* forms especially occur with such like negations.

Connected with these forms are the *-na-ci (-na-tu)* forms (§ 79 ᵇ) ; with both there is a disposition to substitute an *e* for the vowel *a* or *i* preceding the *-n*.

The *-ni, -ci, -tu, -sia, -hu* etc. forms can also take the suffix *-n*.

G. *wa-súko-sá-kona-či*, the priest (our baptizer, lit. we-wash-result-instrumental, § 120 ᵃ) ²) -agent).

CHAPTER IV

AUXILIARY VERB *a*

§ 28. *A* expresses : the aspect of the world in its continual change
(§ 2). It is the "Zeitwort" of the Arawak language, and is used with
pronominal prefixes as a verb "to do", "to be" (not as a copula "to be",
this does not exist in Arawak). In a separate word the doing or the being
may be paraphrased.

    a) Indicative mood, Present tense : *d-a, b-a, l-a, t-a, w-a, h-a, n-a ;*
       ,,   ,,   Past   ,,   the same, followed by *goba ;*
       ,,   ,,   Future   ,,   *da fa, bo fa, lo fa, tu fa, wa fa,*
                               ho fa, na fa ;
    Potential   ,,   Present   ,,   the same as Ind. m., Pr. t., followed
                                 by *ma.*

Examples :

bu-fitikida-te l-aurea, d-a bu-mun, I charge thee, come out of him, *isa
b-a te andi-n,* thou hast well done that thou art come, *toho jia l-a Adaie-li
da-mun,* thus hath the Lord dealt with me, *ki-jia n-a kiana,* which also they
did, *murriga-ci jia bo fa koro,* [when thou prayest] thou shalt not be as
the hypocrites are, *alika wa fa naraha ?* what shall we do to these men ?
alika lo fa-te naha kabuea-ari-no o-mun ? what will he do unto those
husbandmen ? *to-moroa tanahu akona kwa da fa,* nevertheless I must walk
to day, *kalime-hi fa !* let there be light ! *d-a ma koro, Adaie-li !* not so,
Lord ! (Acts X, 14, XI, 8), *alika l-a ma kiana Satan a-boredwa l-oaiya ?*
how can Satan cast out Satan ?

    b) This auxiliary verb *a* is often used, when, in describing an action,
it is meant to place in relief that an action is taking place, more than the
character of the action.

Examples : Usual form : Acts IX, 40, and she opened her eyes, *to-toroda
kiana t-akosi-wa,* lit. she-open *-a* then her-eyes-own. Form in which the
doing is placed in relief : J.. IX, 26, how opened he thine eyes ? *alika l-a
a-torodo-n b-akosi ?* lit. how he-*a* opening thine-eyes ? (comp. English
how did he open thine eyes ?).

    Further examples :

to-moroa d-ansi-sia-no d-a a-sa-ni hu. but I have called you friends,
kena toho jia bo fa a-murreti-ni n, and this is the fashion which thou shalt
make it of, *toho jia tu fa h-ikalime a-kalimeto-n-wa loko-no o-makana,
n-adeki-n bia sa-tu h-imikebo-sia,* let your light so shine before men, that
they may see your good works, *ki jia t-a aiomun iibido-n-wa, ororo bajia,*

thus the heavens and the earth were finished, *alika t-a b-akosi a-torodo-n-wa ?* how were thine eyes opened ? *ama-hu h-a k-ikisi-n Christ o-konomun ?* what think ye of Christ ? *kenbena manswa-ki n-a goba nokonni-n,* and they were exceeding sorrowful ;

c) The auxiliary verb *a* is also used in association with an Infinitive with the prefix *m(a)-,* e.g. Mt. XXIV, 2, *m-adeki-n h-a toraha to-makwa ?* see ye not all these things ? lit. *m-* (hesitating, reluctant, becomes in this place a negation) seeing ye-do this its-all.

Further examples :

wa-siki fa ? ma-siki-n wa fa botta ? shall we give, or shall we not give ? *m-onyi-n b-a ka-cikibe,* thou shalt not steal (commit theft), *bawhu-yuho muni-ro m-ausi-n b-a-li, bawhu-yuho kono-no o-mun, m-ahaka-n b-a-li,* neither go into the town, nor tell it to any in the town, *da-tu, m-amoto-n-wa b-a,* daughter, be of good comfort, *to-moroa yara anakabo-tu ada iwi o-konomun, M-iki-ni h-a-li kia, m-ibibidi-n h-a-li bajia kia, ma-odo-ni h-a-n bia, l-a Wacinaci ajia-n,* but of the fruit of the tree which is in the midst of the garden, God hath said, Ye shall not eat of it, neither shall ye touch it, lest ye die, *m-ibibidi-n b-a-te di,* touch me not, *b-ikisi-ka ma-kwaiabo-n-wa d-a ma Da-ci,* thinkest thou that I cannot now pray to my Father, *ma-bokoto-n h-a goba di,* and ye laid no hold on me.

d) If it is not intended to negative the single fact, but to negative privatively, then the prefix *m(a)-* is incorporated into the root of the word and prefixes may be applied in the usual way.

Examples :

a-maribendi-, to cleanse (from *iribe,* uncleanness), *a-maiero,* to be free, *a-maierodo-,* to make free (from *aiero,* to be in bondage, to be a slave), *imikiduadi-* to disbelieve (*ikiduadi-,* to believe), *n-imekida goba i,* they stripped him (*eki,* clothes), *a-masiidikiti-,* to (cause to) behead, (*isi,* head), Sm. *a-mabannadi-,* to strip off the leaves (*u-banna,* leaf), *a-maimadi-,* to propitiate (*aima,* wrath), G. *da-matéda-te hime,* I clean a fish (*-té,* intestines).

e) *A* with impersonal prefix *k-,* appearing in a positive manner.

1) See table, § 5, forms 4 : *a* group, *a* group with *oa,* quality-words I ;

2) *ama ibia waii* (emphasizing pronoun) *ma-koto-n ka yuho-ho-in, Pharisee-no bajia ; to-moroa bui a-mairikoto-sia-no ma-koto-n ka koro ?* why do we and the Pharisees fast oft, but thy disciples fast not ?

f) *A* with impersonal prefix *m-,* hesitancy.

1) See table, § 5, forms 5 ;

2) *m-ikita-n-ci hu m-ikita-ni ma Daii bajia,* he that despiseth you despiseth me (also), *ama-koro Wacinaci m-onyi-ni-ma ma,* for with God no thing shall be impossible, ... *ahaka-n na-mun, hui m-ajia-n ma-li abaren,* ... and commandeth them not to speak at all, *Adaie-li Ialoko onnaka goba Philip l-aurea,* eunuch *m-adeki-n ma goba kiana ba i,* the Spirit of the Lord caught away Philip, that the eunuch saw him no more :

(N.B. This would seem to be a double negative : in reality, however, it expresses a continual state of doubt; the same in §§ 18 b) 1) II), 29 b) 2), 30; comp. van Ginneken, 64, 199).

§ 29. a) Forms with ka as a definition of time :

ma-koto-ni abu Adaie-li n-ikita-n ka, Sa-tu Ialoko ajia-ga na-mun, as they ministered to the Lord, and fasted, the Holy Ghost said (to them), *kena ama a-dokota-hu fa-te kia andi-n ka ?* and what sign will there be when these things shall come to pass ? *h-onnaka ho-mun-wa isauka iibido-tu ho-bora mun ororo a-murreto-n-wa ka warea,* inherit the kingdom prepared for you from the foundation of the world, *passover ka,* at the passover, *a-kota-he ka,* at supper time, *kia-n bena Jew-no ifirokoro ka goba,* after this there was a feast of the Jews, *hui ausa-i-li toho ifirokoro ka ibici,* go ye up unto this feast, *kena amisia ka fa, aboa-hu ka fa, adedisaro fa alomun jiaro,* and there shall be famines, and pestilences, and earthquakes, in divers places, *tanahu abar-timen kaci ka-n, bari-ga ma-sa-tu n-a-ni goba a-sa-ni n,* and this is the sixth month with her, who was called barren.

b) Forms with *ka* as a condition (circumstance) followed by a form with *ma* or *koma,* indicating what will happen if that condition is fulfilled.

1) *d-ahaka-n ka ho-mun, h-ikiduada ma koro : Daii bajia adagato-n ka hu, h-oonaba koma koro di, h-ausikita ma koro bajia di,* if I tell you, ye will not believe : And if I also ask you, ye will not answer me, nor let me go, *h-aici-n ka toho, alikibi ma hu h-onyi faroka n,* if ye know these things, happy are ye if ye do them, *to-moroa t-ikaba kowa-ni-ka pawmu o-mun, ama abu t-ikabatoa ma ?* but if the salt have lost his savour, wherewith shall it be salted ? *to-moroa h-aici-n ka ma toho ki ajia-hu o-konomun ... ; m-aboadikiti-n h-a ma ma-wakaia-ci-no,* but if ye had known what this meaneth ... ye would not have condemned the guiltless, *na-sa-n ka goba k-abue-l-ci Beelzebub ma-in, aloman sabu kiana ki-jia na fa a-sa-n l-isikwa o-kono-no,* if they have called the master of the house Beelzebub, how much more shall they call them of his household ? *n-akudi-n ka goba ma di, n-akuda ma bajia hu ; n-ikita-n ka goba ma d-ajia-n, n-ikita koma bajia h-ajia-n,* if they have persecuted me, they will also persecute you ; if they have kept my saying, they will keep your's also ;

2) *isa goba ma lihi-ki loko o-mun, ma-raia-n ka goba ma i,* good were it for that man if he had never been born ;

c) *i-ka,* see § 55.

d) *isaigati-,* to please ; *isa,* good.

e) 1) *k-amunaiga-hu,* tribulation, *k-amunaiga-ni,* affliction, *k-amunaiga-ci-no,* the poor ; *amuna : m* humble ? comp. § 71 b) 5) (A.M. § 182, 134A) ;

2) *kena n-amunaigata-ni abu na-koiokota goba i,* and (they) sent him away shamefully, *l-amunaigatoa-n,* his humiliation, *h-amunaigato-n-wa bia,* to be (ye) afflicted ;

3) G. *minka-ko, minto-ko,* it is very (deep, difficult, etc.).

§ 30. A-sia.

l-isanci ki adaie-n anda fa-te kasakabo m-oaboddi-n l-a-sia o-loko o-bora, the lord of that servant will come in a day when he looketh not for him, lit. his-servant that lord come will day not-waiting he-*a-sia* in future moment, *abar virgin hiaro ibici, kia abar-li wadili ikisida-sia ma-ma-kwa|l-a-sia,* to a virgin espoused to a man, lit. which a man reckoned - thing not-with-yet he-*a-sia, tanahu robu-in w-adeka m-adeki-n|w-a-sia be !* we have seen strange things to day, lit. now only we-see not-seeing we-*a-sia* full, *to-moroa abar-li ajinama hui o-koboroko, lihi-ki m-aici-n h-a-sia,* but there standeth one among you, whom ye know not, *ma-koborokwatoa-n h-a-li alika h-a-sia bia oonaba-n, alika h-a-sia bia ajia-n o-konomun,* take ye no thought how or what thing ye shall answer, or what ye shall say, *ma-raia-tu a-odo-ci-sikwa jia h-a-ni o-doma, loko-no aiadi-ci t-ajeago-ji m-aici-n m-a-sia o-konomun,* for ye are as graves which appear not, and the men that walk over them are not aware of them, *lihi-ki waii icinoci m-akonnaba-ti-m-a-sia goba,* (he) to whom our fathers would not obey.

§ 31. *A-hu.*

alika-n ma-tata sabu ka ajia-hu, Bu-wakaia a-dokodwa b-aurea, m-a-hu jiaro ? B-akenakwa, kena b-akona, m-a-hu jiaro botta ? for whether is easier, to say, Thy sins be forgiven thee ; or to say, Arise, and walk ?

§ 32. *A-ni.*

a) *Wacinaci a-ni koro bo-koborokwon o-doma, to-moroa loko-no a-ni robu-in bo-koborokwa,* for thou savourest not the things that be of God, but the things that be of men, *bawhu sibo mun Solomon-a-ni n-a-sia a-sa-n,* in the porch that is called Solomon's, *kena da-korati fa koro to-makwa kokki-tu toho-ni warea, toho jia d-a-ni-n jin,* neither ... will I again smite any more every thing living, as I have done, *hiaro aiita m-aiakato-n-wa t-a-ni wa, to-korogoso-n abu t-anda kiana,* and when the woman saw that she was not hid, she came trembling ;

b) *Adaie-li, l-a-ni ka David a-sa-n i, alika l-a kiana l-aiici-n lihi-ki ?* if David then call him Lord, how is he his son ? *a-kwaiabo-n-wa, t-a-ni ka ma, c-ikisi ausi-n l-aurea,* and prayed that, if it were possible, the hour might pass from him, *kia abu na-murrida fa l-onnawa-sia-no, n-a-ni ka ma,* insomuch that, if it were possible, they shall deceive the very elect ;

c) *lihi Wacinaci o-rea m-a-ni-n ka, ama-koro l-onyi koma,* if this man were not of God, he could do nothing, *m-a-ni b-a, w-a lo-mun,* and we forbad him, lit. not-do-fact thou-do, we-did (said) him-to, *m-a-ni h-a-li ajia-n,* begin not to say, *Wacinaci a-maribendi-sia, ma-mariben-tu m-a-ni b-a-li a-sa-n,* what God hath cleansed, that call not thou common, *ika tu loko-no m-ansi m-a-ni hu ... ika tu n-imirita-ni hu,* when men shall hate you ... and shall reproach you.

§ 33. *A-n.*

ororo o-kona-tu o-konomun d-ahaka a-n-ka ho-mun. if I have told you earthly things, [and ye believe not, etc.], *ho-bollita yaha. ausa d-a-n ka yakitaha mun i-ro da-kwaiabo-n-wa bia,* sit ye here, while I go and pray yonder. *na-cikibe-sia goba i adunka w-a-n ka.* (they) stole him away while we slept. *a-kota n-a-n ka.* and as they did eat [he said]. *ajia kwa l-a-n ka. h-adeka ....,* and while he yet spake, lo ...., *m-andi-n d-a-n ka goba ma.*

m-ajia-n d-a-n ka goba na-mun, wakaia-hu kowa koma na-mun, if I had not come and spoken unto them, they had not had sin, *ika tu goba* ... *Pontius Pilate adaia-hu m-a-n Judea ororo ajeago,* now (it came to pass) ... Pontius Pilate being governor of Judæa, *kenbena, Apollos Corinth mun m-a-n ka,* and it came to pass, that, while Apollos was at Corinth, *kena n-anda goba a-baptize( )dikito-n-wa. John ma-siko-n-wa kwa m-a-n-ka siba o-loko o-doma,* and they came, and were baptized. For John was not yet cast into prison, *tora-jia ma-n t-a-n ka, d-ahaka goba ma ho-mun,* if it were not so, I would have told you.

§ 34. *Ka-in.*

saka goba n, ma-iyuyu-ka-in tu-muni o-doma, it withered away, because it lacked moisture, *a-boredi-n biama mite, kia abar farthing, isogo-tu ka-in plata,* and she threw in two mites, which make a farthing (*isogo-tu,* small, *plata,* money), *abar-dakabo ibi-ro ka-in kodibiyu a-iyugara-wa koro biama isogo-tu ka-in plata iauna ?* are not five sparrows sold for two farthings ? *biam-timen, yuho-ro koro himi ka-in bajia, n-a goba ajia-n,* and they said, Seven, and a few little fishes, *aba mihu ka-in bajia lo-ma goba,* and there were also with him other little ships.

Note the diminutive effect of *ka-in* in the last examples. Something of the same character might be seen in *oni-ka-in,* river (*oni, onyi,* water, § 125 a)), and in the following examples : *kenbena l-ausa goba taha sabu ka-in,* and he went a little farther, *m-ibena ka-ini ma-in t-adiki,* but not long after [a tempest arose], *lo-koto-n bena tata ka-ini ka lo-kona,* and when he had received meat, he was strengthened ; S. *elonti-kan,* a little child, *báhü-kan,* the tabernacle, shrine, *u-hurrura-kan,* a field.

§ 35. *M-a-in.*

a) *na-ma-ni ma-in aiika-ci, mamari koma ma-koto-n n-a-n,* as long as they have the bridegroom with them, they cannot fast, *na-herakida goba yuho-li loko-no l-amun, omuni ka-ini ma-in bara o-rea,* much people gathered unto him : and he was nigh unto the sea ;

b) After a quotation of something spoken long ago.

h-akonnaba goba n-ajia-n, B-ansi fa bu-ioci, m-ansi b-a-li k-aiima-ci bu-mun ; main, ye have heard that it hath been said, Thou shalt love thy neighbour, and hate thine enemy, *Adam main a-sa-n na-iri.* and called their name Adam, *a-herakida n-a-n ka, n-adagata kiana i. Adaie-li tanahu b-isiki fa Israel o-mun n-isauka ba ? main,* when they therefore were come together, they asked of him, saying, Lord, wilt thou at this time restore again the kingdom to Israel ?

§ 36. *Mo-tu,* after a quotation of something written long ago ; *o,* indicating space ?

kenbena na-sika goba l-isi amun ajia-hu lo-konomun-tu. LIHI JESUS JEW-NO ADAIE-N-WABU, mo-tu a-burita-sia. and (they) set up over his head his accusation written, This is Jesus the king of the Jews, *da-sikwa a-kwaiabo-hu isikwa, mo-tu a-burito-n-wa,* it is written, My house is the house of prayer (L. XIX, 46), *kena aba a-burita-sia, N-adeki fa na-ciadi-*

sia ibici ; mo-tu ajia-hu, and again another scripture saith, They shall look on him whom they pierced, *Jesus oonaba goba n|ajia-n, To-buritwa koro hui misi-tu ahaka-hu o-loko, Wacinaci jia mu-ci hui ; d-a goba ajia-n ; mo-tu koro ?* Jesus answered them, Is it not written in your law, I said, Ye are gods ?

§ 37. *-N kona,* when ; *ko,* the thing in question, *na,* continuation.

n-adeki-n kona, n-adeka siba auribisa-sia ibin, and when they looked, they saw that the stone was rolled away, *n-aucigi-n kona i, n-ajia-ga lo-mun,* and when they had found him, they said unto him, *naii akonnabo-n kona kokke-ni o-konomun, t-adeki-n bajia i o-konomun, m-ikiduadi-n n-a goba n,* and they, when they had heard that he was alive, and had been seen of her, believed not.

§ 38. *-N bena,* after ; *be,* full, fulfilled, *na* continuation.

n-adeki-n bena, n-aicikita ajia-hu l-ajia-sia na-mun korilia-ci ki o-konomun, and when they had seen it, they made known abroad the saying which was told them concerning the child, *n-akoio-n-wa bena,* and when they were departed [the angel appeareth], *to-moroa c-imeodo-n bena t-isa wa, ma-koborokwon t-a kari-hi,* but as soon as she is delivered of the child, she remembereth no more the anguish, *toho jia l-a-n bena ajia-n, lo-koida goba onabo ajeago,* when he had thus spoken, he spat on the ground, *biam-loko wiwa-n bena i,* and when he was full forty years old [it came upon his heart to visit his brethren], *toho-n bena da-sa fa koro hu da-sanonoci,* henceforth I call you not servants.

§ 39. *Bia* (after *ama : ibia,* § 139 a)) adds to the meaning of the preceding word (object-word, verbal noun) the principle of something that will be or will happen in the near future ; *b,* appearance, *i,* tension, (is relaxed into) *a,* time-reality.

aiomun kibilokoukili omuni fa kalime-be-tu, araga-koto-tu bia origa-hu o-rea kasakabo ; kia a-dokotoia, c-ikisi bia, kasakabo bia wiwa bia bajia, let there be lights in the firmament of the heaven to divide the day from the night ; and let them be for signs, and for seasons, and for days, and years, *c-ibikidwa kiana ifiro-tu ada bia,* and (it) waxed a great tree, *ibi-kibi b-isifuda()kota di Christian bia di,* almost thou persuadest me to be a Christian, *toho ki h-onyi-sia bia bari-n, to-bora-tu ma-iibi-n h-a-n bia bajia,* these ought ye to have done, and not to leave the other undone, *kena kia l-adura, Adaie-li Wacinaci onnaki-sia loko o-rea, hiaro bia lo-murreta n,* and the rib, which the Lord God had taken from man, made he a woman, *l-amuni-sia bia,* his inheritance, *kenbena na-murreta goba ajia-hu Jesus na-bokoto-n bia ka-ieniko-hu abu na-forri-n bia i,* and (they) consulted that they might take Jesus by subtilty, and kill him, *kenbena loko Aiici a-sikoa a-burrida-tu o-kona l-isiko-n-wa bia,* and the Son of man is betrayed to be crucified ;

S. *hama-hü h-ani-ssia-bia-pa,* [take heed] what ye intend to do. *abba Phoenicia muniru akunnu-ssia-bia-pa meju,* [finding] a ship sailing over unto Phenicia, *jumün-tu-pa ahaka-hü-n bu-mün b-ani-ssia-bia-pa u-kunnamün,* (that place-future) it shall be told thee what thou must do, *dai dá-waja a-dukuttu-n da|ppa-i hallika-kebé-ni-bia-pa* (§§ 139 e), 58 e)) *lu-julattü-n l-ansi-wa dai iri u-kunnaria,* for I will shew him how great things he must suffer for my name's sake.

Biaki, in the following sentences, = *bia,* let it be, *ki,* this ! (§ 48) (?)

S. *ni rubu kurru üsseika-kuba biaki-ka-n diarru|je jumün-kunna-na palettiju wa-mün,* and the barbarous people shewed us no little kindness, lit. a little only not kind-were *biaki-ka-n* such they that-place-persons barbarian, *Julius biaki-ka|kuba Paulus u-mün,* Julius courteously entreated Paul.

§ 40. *O-doma* adds to the meaning of the preceding clause, word or particle, the principle of reason or cause ; *do,* cause, origin, see § 40.

to-moroa t-a( )alikibitoa hui akosi-hi, t-adeki-n o-doma, but blessed are your eyes, for they see, *to-bolisi-n o-doma bu, to-bolisi kia ki b-akoio fa ba,* for dust thou art, and unto dust shalt thou return, *na-makwa kokki-ci o-iyunatu-n o-doma n,* because she was the mother of all living, *h-ausa yaha rea ; ma-odo-n t-a-n ilontu o-doma,* give place : for the maid is not dead, *alika-i koro aunaka-n o-doma u,* [we stand here] because no man hath hired us, *Noah akodwa kiana ... ark o-lokomun ; oniabu ifiroto-n-wa bia-n o-doma,* and Noah went in ... into the ark, because of the waters of the flood, *Lydda omuni-n Joppa o-rea o-doma,* and forasmuch as Lydda was nigh to Joppa, *lihi wadili isa-ni o-doma,* for he was a good man, *da-uaiya da-doma wa koro d-ajia-n o-doma,* for I have not spoken of myself, *ama-koro d-onyi koma da-uaiya da-doma wa,* I can of mine own self do nothing, *na-makwa n-ikiduadi-n bia lo-doma,* that all men through him might believe, *h-oaiya ho-doma wa koro h-ajia-ga,* for it is not ye that speak (Mt. X, 20), S. *ka-duma-ttu lui üüssadükittoa hidda-ba,* [examined] by what means he is made whole.

§ 41. In the following forms an *i* is added to *a,* presumably as an intensifying suffix. Sm. says of this : "Wenn es sich auf eine vorhergehende Rede bezieht, so ist in dieser Form gewöhnlich dass man es nicht durch *n* sondern *i* ausdrückt, z.B. *dapai* ich will, werde es thun oder sagen ; *bupai* du sollst es, etc. ; *lupai* er wird, oder soll es, etc."

da fa-i, maribe-n bu, I will : be thou clean, *da fa-i, l-a kiana,* and he promised, lit. I will, he did (said) then. *yaha kwa b-a-i wa-ma,* abide with us (L. XXIV, 29), *ki jiari ki* (§ 140) *l-a-i l-ibiamti-ci bajia.* likewise (did) the second also (Mt. XXII, 26), *ki jiari ki l-a goba-i ba,* and (he) did likewise (Mt. XX, 5), *bui imigodo-n goba ororo ajeago mun di jin, ki jiari ki d-a goba-i Daii imigodo-n ba ie ororo ajeago mun,* as thou hast sent me into the world, even so have I also sent them into the world. *ki jiari ki ho fa-i hui ba,* so likewise (do) ye (Mt. XXIV, 33), *ki jiari ki lo fa-i loko Aiici onnakido-n-wa ba,* even so must the Son of man be lifted up (J. III, 14), *h-ikiduadi-sia jiari ki tu fa-i ho-mun,* according to your faith be it unto you, *ki jiari ki l-a-i himi bajia aloman n-ansi-n,* and likewise (he distributed) of the fishes as much as they would, *ki jiari ki n-a ma-i priest-*

no afudyi, as also the high priest doth bear me witness, *Adaie-li, ha-jia|t-a-i toho wiwa*, Lord, let it alone this year also ; S. *ikka na-maqua — wa|ppa-i — mañ*, (then they all — we shall do — it was said), *ika k-abbukü-n hu|ppa-i üssa-tti üjahü ho-monn-ua-wa*, and ye shall receive the gift of the Holy Ghost.

§ 42. When in the narration a person is quoted as speaking, then the quotation is always followed by the verb *a*, to do, with a pronominal prefix indicating the person whose words are quoted, and often *ajia-n*, speaking, or such like. The same process is followed when two or more quotations are enclosed in each other.

Centurion oonaba goba n, ajia-n ... kena liraha o-mun B-osa, d-a ajia-n. l-ausa kiana ; aba-li o-mun ba, Ma-hara b-a-te, d-a, l-anda-te kiana ; da-sanci o-mun, Toho b-onyi, d-a ; l-onyi-ka kiana n ; l-a, the centurion answered and said ... and I say to this man, Go, and he goeth ; and to another', Come, and he cometh ; and to my servant, Do this, and he doeth it (Mt. VIII, 8, 9), *ika ki Adaie-li-wabu ajia fa l-iisa mairia-ci-no o-mun, Ma-hara h-a-te ... , lo fa*, then shall the King say unto them on his right hand, Come ... , *Peter bui, d-a ajia-n bu-mun bajia*, and I say also unto thee, That thou art Peter, *daii anda fa d-isadi-n bia i : l-a Jesus ajia-n lo-mun*, and Jesus saith unto him, I will come and heal him, *hiaro o-mun kiana hori ajia-ga, Ho-odo fa koro kidua-ni-n ; ... , t-a tu-mun*, and the serpent said unto the woman, Ye shall not surely die : ... , *alo mun Christ ka-raie-n bia ? l-a goba adagato-n ie*, he demanded of them where Christ should be born ;

S. Acts XVIII, 13, *n-a ihittara-n i*, they did accusing him, Acts VI, 14, *n-a mullika-hü abbu Stephanus amün*, they-did falsehood with Stephen concerning, Acts IV, 20, *n-a Petrus Johannes mu-tti na-mün*, they-did Peter John with-person them-to.

With the cautious *m-a* (comp. *ma-in*, § 35, perhaps also : S. *ka-maijana*, to be manifest, *a-maijanatâ, a-maijanattoa*, to preach, to teach, to tell, to make known) :

ki-o-doma Jesus a-mairikoto-sia l-ansi-sia, Adaie-li lihi, m-a ajia-n Peter o-mun, therefore that disciple whom Jesus loved saith unto Peter, It is the Lord, *yuho-li loko-no akonnabo-ci toraha ajia-hu, Kidua-n liraha Prophet ki ; m-a goba kiana ajia-n*, many of the people therefore, when they heard this saying, said, Of a truth this is the prophet ;

S. Acts III, 23, *l-a Moses — m-a Petrus*, Acts VIII, 33, *ma-ru Esaias*, Acts XIII, 47, *mo-rubu n-a Paulus Barabas mu-tti*, discreetly-only they-did P. B. with-person, Acts XV, 11, *mo-rubu l-a Petrus* (V, 9 *l-a Petrus*).

G. *moro, mora*, think, suppose, see §§ 215 (23, 35, 39). 219 (26). 221 (16).

Dialogue :

Adaia-hu oonaba goba n ajia-n na-mun, Alika-i h-ansi-ka da-dokodo-n bia ho-mun naha biama-no o-rea ? l-a. Barabbas, n-a goba ajia-n, the

governor answered and said unto them, Whether of the twain will ye that
I release unto you ? They said, Barabbas.

G. I ask A. : "did you go there this morning ?" he answers : "yes" ;
then I ask B. : "is it really so" ? B. answers : *l-á-ši* (§ 179 c)) or *l-á-diaru*,
surely, or *lú-mura-diaro* (§ 140 c)), perhaps (if A. were a woman : *tú-
mura-diaro* or *t-á-diaro-ka*, perhaps).

§ 43. Often English indirect speech is converted into Arawak direct
speech (especially in S.'s texts).

Mt. II, 7, Then Herod, when he had privily called the wise men, enquired
of them diligently what time the star appeared, *ika ki Herod a-simaka goba
ka-ieniko-be-ci aiakatwa o-loko, alika wiwa ka-raia goba ? l-a goba
adagato-n manswan ie*, lit. occurred ! Herod called wise-men hidden in,
"when star appeared?" he-did asking diligently them, Acts XXVII, 30,
under colour as though they would have cast anchors out of the foreship,
t-isiri warea wa-toboda-te anchor, n-a murriga-hu abu, lit. its-nose from
we-cast anchor, they-did lie with ;

S. Acts XXIV, 23, and he commanded a centurion to keep Paul, *ikka
l-issika Capitain, u-mün hi-ddia-mu-ttu adia-hü : b-ikittakutta-li-te|i Paulus*,
lit. occurred he-put captain, to thus word : thou-cause to keep -him Paul.

CHAPTER V

INTENSIVES, CONJUNCTIONS, ETC.

§ 44. The emphasizing pronouns consist of a pronominal prefix with an emphasizing particle.

a) *-i, -ii.*

I *da-ii,* II *bu-i,* III m., f. do not exist in this series ; in their stead the pronouns of series b) are used ; I pl. *wa-ii,* II pl. *hu-i,* III pl. *na-ii ;*

S. I *da-i,* II *bu-i,* III m. *lu-i,* III f. no examples have been met with ; I pl. *wa-i,* II pl. *hu-i,* III pl. *na-i ;*

b) *-h-* with vowel ; chiefly used as demonstratives.

III m. *l-i-hi,* III f. *t-o-ho,* III pl. *na-ha ;* S. III m. *l-i-hi,* III f. *t-u-hu,* III pl. *na-ha ;*

c) *-ra-ha,* demonstrative, at a definite place (*ra,* § 104) in space or time.

III m. *l-i-raha,* III f. *t-o-raha* (*t-o-ra,* § 104 f)), III pl. *na-raha ;* S. III m. *l-i-raha,* III f. *t-u-raha,* III pl. *na-rraha.*

G. *lihi, toho, naha,* indicate : near ;

liraha, toraha, naraha, indicate : somewhat further off ;

(*likitaha ?),* *tokotáha, nai,* indicate : still further off. not in the same space.

Examples a), b), c) :

m-aiima-hu da-iiba ho-mun, Daii m-aiima-hu da-sika ho-mun : ororo *a-siki-sia jia mo-tu koro Daii a-sika ho-mun,* peace I leave with you, my peace I give unto you : not as the world giveth, give I unto you ; *Lihi d-Aiici d-ansi-sia,* This is my beloved Son, *h-adeka lihi loko !* behold the man ! *lihi anda da-mun,* (he) came unto me (Acts XXII, 13), *lihi o-mun Paul ajia-ga kiana,* then said Paul unto him (Acts XXIII, 3), *liraha ajia goba,* this fellow said (Mt. XXVI, 61), *liraha,* this man (Mt. XIII, 54, 55, 56, J. VI, 52, VII, 15), *liraha wadili. liraha loko,* the man (Acts XXV, 17, 22), *Wacinaci liraha* (he is a god, Acts XXVIII, 6), *liraha b-aiici,* this thy son (L XV, 30), *toho,* this (Mt. XXIV, 48), *toho ointment,* this ointment, *toraha to-makwa,* all these things (Mt. XIII, 51, XIX. 20, XXIII, 36). *Ialoko toraha,* it is a spirit (Mt. XIV, 26), *kena Da-ci k-ansi fa i; kena waii anda fa-te l-amun, ka-sikwa' fa lihi o-ma u.* and my Father will love him. and we will come unto him, and make our abode with him. *naii b-amuni-sia-no goba ki,* thine they were. *Jerusalem mun ka-sikwa goba Jew-no a-kwaiaboa-ci wadili naii,* and there were dwelling at Jerusalem Jews. devout men (worshipping men they), *h-adeka, Galilee warea-ci koro na-makwa naha ?* behold, are not all these which speak Galiæans ? *naha biama-no o-rea b-onnawa-sia b-aicikita wa-mun.* shew whether of these two thou hast chosen, *naraha,* these men (Acts IV, 16, V, 38), *k-aiima-ci naraha da-mun,* those mine enemies (L. XIX, 27) ;

S. *lui* — *Moses akunnukutta Egypten u-lukku-waria je,* he (— Moses) brought them out (from Egypt), *lui Jesus, this Jesus, lu-morrua lihi baddia a-maraijattoa,* (but) he also perished, *n-addika baddia lihi üüssadükittu-lliä-ti,* and beholding (they behold also) the man which was healed :

d) S. *-wa-i ;* see § 121 e).

S. *dai\li-wai Adaija-hü !* I am here, Lord, *dai\li-wai,* I am he ;

e) S. one of the pronouns enumerated under a), b), or c), with *-ke, -kewai,* see § 48 b).

f) S. III m. *-ki-da,* f. *-ku-da ;* m. *-ki-da-ha,* f. *-ku-da-ha ; ki, ku* the person or thing in question, *da* firmly established. Probably the same construction in : B. *h-adeka, Christ yaha ; h-adeka li-kitaha,* lo, here is Christ ; or, lo, he is there. Also : B. *a-tukuda,* to command, to charge.

g) S. III m. *(lui)-li-kéwai.*

Examples f), g) :

S. Acts VII, 37, 38 *lihi-kewai Moses, adiâ-kuba-li Israeli-nu u-mün hiddin :,* this is that Moses, which said unto the children of Israel, *lui-li-kéwai\ba, naha mallukku-nni-aukilli-mün a-hurruda-kebé-mutti Israeli-nu ü-kkürküa annaka- ni-rukku-kubá-li, li-kidaha Jehovah u-ma-tti kuba i adia l-a-ni-ka Sina hurruru-müni,* this is he, that was in the church in the wilderness with the angel which spake to him in the mount Sina, lit. he-this also, those wilderness-in assembled Israelites nation in-the-midst-of-being, he Jehovah with-being he speak he-doing-when Sina mount-at, Acts III, 20, *Lui imékudu-n benna\i Jesus Christus, a-ijumuda-ssia hu-mün wakill lu-bura-mün, u-bura ba :* 21 *Lui-likéwai a-bukuttu-n lu\ppa kassakku lu-monn-ua,* 20 and he shall send Jesus Christ, which before was preached unto you, 21 whom the heaven must receive, Acts XI, 12 *likida Wadili üssiqua 'lukku,* into the man's house, *wahaddia tukuda addiki-ttu kassakkabbu-hü u-kunna ani-hü-nni-bia-pa\n,* and it shall come to pass in the last days, *tukkudaha Prophet David wakilli a-bulliti-ssia,* (this prophet David formerly written-thing), *tukkudaha ipirru-kurru ka-raija-ru-pa Adaija-hü ü-kkassakkabbu-n andi-n u-bura,* before that great and notable day of the Lord come ;

h) Sm. and Q. give the pronouns *da-kia, bo-kkia, li-kia,* (II f. is missing in this series), *wa-kia, hü-kia, na-kia.* These are probably antiquated forms; they are not met with in S., B. and G.

Examples : Van Berkel (in his description of the whip-ceremony) *bockja watilly !* lit. thou man ! *dackje wathia !* lit. I also (B. *bajia*). Translation of Genesis (Moravians, 16) : *dai ü-jaüale d-adinamukitta wuraru u-kuña, kia d-ebettira aditti-koana bia dakia wuñabu badia annaka-ni-ruku-di* (B. *da-simara-habo da-sika oraro o-kona, ajia-hu aiciki-n bia n Dai o-mun ororo o-mun bajia*), I do set my bow in the cloud, and it shall be for a token of a covenant between me and the earth. [*Likia* is also met with in Island-Karib].

§ 45. The emphasizing pronouns are composed in a similar way to the expressions indicating position, direction or time of the type *to-loko*, in it, "it-interior place", *na-mun*, to them, "they-humble place". Parallel to *na-mun*, Arawak has *yu-mun(i)*, a place ; here *y*, here, *u* space, takes the place of the pronominal prefix.

In a similar way, parallel to the pronouns treated of in § 44 :

b) 1) *yaha*, here, to be here (A. M. § 182, 132 C) ; examples, see § 12.

2) *taha*, far, to be afar off (A. M. § 182, 132 D) ; *taha-wai*, afar off, with the intensifying particle -*wai*, occurring under d). Presumably *taha* means not exactly "far", but rather another place than the place indicated by *yaha*, comp. S. *taha-maria* — *jaha-maria*, § 97 f). Sm. *táha-kûn*, there, *taha-mária*, on the other side ; *táha-ssábu-tu*, a little beyond the other side, *taha-wária*, from there, *dáha-ru*, thereto, *kü-ddaha-ru|ka|i*, he is there (comp. f)) ;

c) *yaraha*, the same as *yaha*, but somewhat further off (?)

yaraha abar-li ilon-ci, there is a lad here (J. VI. 9), *bui a-bollita yaraha ikisidi-n di*, [for] sittest thou (here) to judge me (Acts XXIII. 3), *yaraha kwa t-a ma*, it would have remained, lit. here yet it-is presumably ;

f) 1) *yakitaha*, S. *jakketa* in the following :

b-osa yaha rea yakitaha mun i-ro, remove hence to yonder place, S. *jakketa málukkuni-aukilli-mün*, (yonder) in the wilderness (Acts XIII. 18);

2) S. *hidda*, now, then ; Sm. it is also often used without especial meaning.

S. *ni-kebé-n t-a attikida Petrus u-kutti-mün, tu-húda hidda*, then fell she down straightway at his feet, and yielded up the ghost, lit. immediately she-did fall Petrus feet-at, she-die *hidda, bakküllama hidda-n u-duma*, for it was now eventide, *ikka hidda|ba*, (and also) [he has written], lit. occurred *hidda* again, *ikka l-adia-ka hidda|ba*, (and he said also).

§ 46. Parallel to the forms treated of in §§ 44, 45 b), *aha* with pronominal prefix ; we may also consider this as a durative (§ 3) of the auxiliary verb *a*. The only examples of these forms, that have been found in the texts are : *ibikido-lia b-aha-ni ka, bu-idwa b-uaiya*, when thou wast young, thou girdest thyself (comp. *yaha-ni ka bu*, if thou hadst been here, and § 32), *fig ada abomun b-aha-n ka, Daii adeka bu*, when thou wast under the fig tree, I saw thee, *bo-koborokwa, kokke kwa b-aha-n ka goba, isa-be-tu amateli b-auciga bu-mun wa*, remember that thou in thy lifetime receivedst thy good things.

§ 47. S. *dannuhu*, B. *tanahu*, now, to day, this day, *tanahu warea*, from henceforth. Presumably *da, ta* emphasizes, as in §§ 44. 45 ; *ana*, comp. *ana-ka (-ku)*, the midst, § 79 d).

§ 47 A. *Da*, emphasis ?

isa ma koro 'da di bu-sa-ni bia di b-aiici bia, (I) am no more worthy to be called thy son. *kia-n bena n-onyi koma koro 'da hu*, [them that] after that have no more that they can do, *kia abu da-koto fa koro 'da toho-ni bena*, I will not any more eat thereof, *l-oonaba-n o-doma na-bokwa ia, ma-*

iau-kwa n-a kiana 'da, and they marvelled at his answer, and held their peace.

§ 48. a) *Ki,* "the person or thing in question !"; *k,* appearing in a positive manner, *i,* principle.

hui ajia-ga, Daii ki, ye say that I am (L. XXII, 70), *lihi ki o-mun da-siki fa a-kolda-sia, da-koldo-n bena n,* he it is, to whom I shall give a sop, when I have dipped it, *toho ki abu Da-ci a-kalimetwa, yuho-n bia k-iwi-ni hu,* herein is my Father glorified, that ye bear much fruit, *Daii ki,* I am he [that ye seek], *bui ki d-Aiici d-ansi-sia, bui abu ki d-iisaigatwa,* thou art my beloved Son ; in thee I am well pleased, *naii-ki ajia-ga,* [two men stood by them] which also said, *toraha ki,* these things (J. XIV, 25, I, 28, XIX, 24), *Wacinaci ki a-murreti-ci ororo,* (that) God that made the world (Acts XVII, 24), *lihi o-doma ki kokke kwa w-a,* for in him we live (Acts XVII, 28), *kidua-n liraha Prophet ki,* of a truth this is the prophet, *liraha ki Christ,* this is the Christ, *b-isadi-n d-akosi adeki-n o-doma, b-iibidi-sia ki na-makwa loko-no isibo o-makana,* for mine eyes have seen thy salvation which thou hast prepared before the face of all people, *h-adeka Wacinaci Lamb, onnaki-ci ki ororo wakaia-hu,* behold the Lamb of God, which taketh away the sin of the world (comp. *kenbena Roma-no anda fa-te onnaki-ci wa-sikwa,* and the Romans shall come and take away our place), *ka-cikibe-ci-no bajia, a-burrida-tu o-kona-ci lo-ma, imirita ki goba i,* the thieves also, which were crucified with him, cast the same in his teeth ;

S. *ke,* the same as B. *ki : Matthias ké adittikitta-hü-ka,* the lot fell upon Matthias, *W-adaija-hü-n, bui kê Jehovah,* Lord, thou art God ;

b) S. *ke-wai, ke* with the intensifying particle *wa-i* (§ 121 e)).

S. *Jesus kéwai dai,* I am Jesus [whom thou persecutest], *kia kewai kassakkabu-hü,* the same day, *lui kewai,* him [hath God exalted], *lihi-kéwai,* the same [did God send], Bernau *tu-maqua dai ani|bui|ani kewai badja,* all that I have is thine ;

c) S. *-kei-se,* intensifying, see § 179 f).

d) 1) *-ke-n,* intensifying.

ababa, yauhahu onnaka i aiomun ke-n-tu ororo ajeago mun, again, the devil taketh him up into an exceeding high mountain, *kena to-makwa aiomun-be-ke-n-tu ororo aiomun abomun-tu ha t-itaga goba,* and all the high hills, that were under the whole heaven, were covered ;

2) Sm. *-kê-n, bê-n,* intensifying.

Sm. *ibi-n,* to be small, fine, *ibi-kê-n,* to be too small, too fine, *ipi-rru-n,* to be large, *ipi-rru-be-n,* to be somewhat larger ;

3) Sm. *-kê,* intensifying.

Sm. *m-oádi|ka|n,* it is too short, *m-oadi-kê|n,* it is very short, *karri-kê|n,* it aches very much, *k-aima-kê|n,* she, or it, is very bad ;

e) Sm. *-ma-ké* intensifying.

Sm. *üssa,* good, *üssa-maké|ma,* very good, *k-allikebbe-maké|d-a,* I am very glad ;

f) m. *l-iki-ni,* f. *c-iki-ni,* "the only one".

na-fitikita-bo-te abar-li a-odo-ci, likini-ka-ni lo-iyu aiici, there was a dead man carried out, the only son of his mother, *b-adeka-te d-aiici ibici, likini-ka-ini-n da-sa o-doma i,* look upon my son : for he is mine only child, *cikini ka-in lo-tu l-amuni-n o-doma,* for he had one only daughter ;

g) *c-iki-n,* at that same moment.

c-iki-n na-fitikidi-n, and as they came out (Mt. XXVII, 32), *c-iki-n n-andi-n t-eribo mun,* as soon then as they were come to land (J. XXI, 9), *c-iki-n Jesus a-simaka-n ki goba ba k-akonnaki-tu a-simaka-hu abu, l-isika goba l-iialoko wa,* Jesus, when he had cried again with a loud voice, yielded up the ghost ;

h) *oini ... (i)ki,* to rain ; *oini,* water, *(i)ki,* originating, condensing, comp. *-u-ki-li,* a natural phenomenon, § 130 a).

oini ki fa-te, h-a ajia-n, ye say, There cometh a shower, *kenbena oini iki-a* (§ 132) *goba,* and the rain descended, *ikihi brimstone o-ma-tu iki-a goba aiomun warea,* it rained fire and brimstone from heaven, *oini kiana aiomun warea-tu a-iibokotwa iki-n,* and the rain from heaven was restrained, *kena oini d-ikikiti* (§ 91) *fa,* and I will cause it to rain, *Adaie-li Wacinaci m-ikikiti-n kwa ma-n ka oini ororo ajeago mun,* for the Lord God had not caused it to rain upon the earth ;

i) *a-iigi ... mihu o-lokomun,* to go, to enter into a ship, *a-iigiti,* etc., to cause to go, etc. ; *mihu,* ship, *o-loko,* in, *mun,* place ;

j) *ikisi ; iki* with *si,* a point, or intensifying.

　　1) a certain moment.

　　　I) *daii ikisi m-andi-n kwa ma ibin o-doma,* for my time is not yet full come, *c-ikisi anda, loko Aiici a-kalimeto-n-wa bia,* the hour is come, that the Son of man should be glorified, *kia a-dokotoia, c-ikisi bia,* and let them be for signs, and for seasons, *toho ikisi,* this hour (J. XII, 27) ;

　　　II) Sm. *ikissi-hi,* knotted-string calendar (Kechua *kipu*) ;

　　2) *k-ikisi,* to think, to mean ;

　　3) *ikisidi-,* to judge, to mete, Sm., G. also : to taste ; *wakaia ikisidi-,* to tempt ;

　　4) *ikisida,* to number, to reckon ;

　　5) *ikisitoa ro* (§ 102) *l-a-n na-mun o-doma,* for he beckoned unto them, Sm. *ikissitú-(nn-ua),* belieben ;

k) 1) *ikita,* to keep, to have regard to, to serve ;

　　2) *imita,* to despise, to mock, to laugh ;

l) *kidua,* to be true (A. M. §§ 182, 149 B), *kidua-hu,* truth ; *ki,* this ! *d* standing, *ua* in itself (§ 120).

§ 49. a) *Kia,* "the person or thing in question", used as a relative pronoun ; *ki* with *a,* see § 132.

Esaias prophet ajia-n iibido-n-wa bia, kia l-ajia goba, that the saying of Esaias the prophet might be fulfilled, which he spake, *to-moroa Awa imigodo-ci di a-sika goba da-mun misi-tu ahaka-hu, kia d-ahaka-n bia, kia d-ajia-n bia,* but the Father which sent me, he gave me a commandment, what I should say, and what I should speak, *ika tu ki n-akonnabo-n kia o-konomun,* now when this was noised abroad, *hiaro b-isiki-sia da-ma-tu bia, kia a-sika ada iwi da-mun,* the woman whom thou gavest to be with me, she gave me of the tree, *kena hiaro isadwa goba kia ikisi warea,* and the woman was made whole from that hour, *kenbena, kia kasakabo o-loko, Cesar Augustus a-sika goba ajia-hu,* and it came to pass in those days, that there went out a decree from Cæsar Augustus ;

b) Sm. *ikiahâ,* to be avaricious ;

c) Sm. *ikiahaddi-* nöthigen zum da bleiben, von etwas zurückhalten, B. *ikiadi-* to forbid, to restrain from, to speak against, to keep from a purpose.

§ 50. Combinations of *ki* and *kia* with different particles.

Mary Magdalene o-mun l-iraiatwa goba atenwa wabu, kia ki biam-timen yauhahu lo-boredi-sia goba o-rea, he appeared first to Mary Magdalene, out of whom he had cast seven devils, *kia ki Mary a-luita goba Adaie-li ointment abu, kenbena t-arauada goba lo-kuti to-barra abu, kia ki aciligici Lazarus aboa goba,* it was that Mary which anointed the Lord with ointment, and wiped his feet with her hair, whose brother Lazarus was sick, *kia ki ikisi o-loko Jesus ajia goba yuho-li loko-no o-mun,* in that same hour said Jesus to the multitudes ;

to-moroa lo-dokoto-n-wa bia Israel o-mun, kia bia ki daii anda a-baptize()da ibici oniabu abu, but that he should be made manifest to Israel, therefore am I come baptizing with water, *d-ahaka fa aba bawhu-yuho mun Wacinaci isauka o-konomun, kia bia ki imigoda-sia-te Daii,* I must preach the kingdom of God to other cities also : for therefore I am sent ;

kia o-doma wadili a-iibo fa l-ici wa lo-iyu wa, therefore shall a man leave his father and mother (Gen. II, 24) ;

ki-o-doma ki bajia loko-no anda l-irabudiki, toraha a-dokota-hu l-onyi-sia o-konomun n-akonnabo-n o-doma. Ki-o-doma Pharisee-no ajia goba, For this cause the people also met him, for that they heard that he had done this miracle. The Pharisees therefore said (J. XII, 18, 19) ;

ki-hia na-sikita goba di akeroia Jerusalem warea Roma-no akabo roko mun, yet was I delivered prisoner from Jerusalem into the hands of the Romans (Acts XXVIII, 17), *ki-hia-ki onyikita-hu wakaia-hu anda fa-te,* for it must needs be that offences come (Mt. XVIII, 7) ;

kenbena ki ba a-sweardoa-hu abu abakoro l-à goba ajia-n. and again he denied with an oath (no he-did saying) :

Naii ki ka kabuini-no Noah sanoci, naii ki o-rea-ci onnibita goba to-makwa ororo ajeago-ji man, These are the three sons of Noah : and of them was the whole earth overspread ;

kenbena l-anda ki ka ba, l-auciga goba ie adunka n-a-n ka. and he came and found them asleep again, *l-ajia ki ka ba lo-mun biama-hi,* he saith to him again the second time ;

da-kalimeta goba n, da-kalimeti ki fa ba n, I have both glorified it, and will glorify it again ;

kenbena c-imeoda ki goba ba l-augici Abel, and she again bare his brother Abel ;

l-ausa ki kiana ba, a-kwaiabo-n-wa, ajia-n kia ki ajia-hu, and again he went away, and prayed and spake the same words :

l-akodwa ki koma ba biama-hi lo-iyu adibeyu o-lokomun, kena ka-raia ma i ? can he enter the second time into his mother's womb, and be born ?

n-aiita lihi-ki-n i a-bolliti-ci goba a-kwaiabo-n ie Isa-tu-wabu temple-isibo mun, and they knew that it was he which sat for alms at the Beautiful gate of the temple, *kenbena ika tu Jesus atima ki-n|ba mihu o-loko t-oalabaw mairia,* and when Jesus was passed over again by ship unto the other side. *kenbena Jerusalem mun d-anda ki-n bena ba,* and it came to pass, that, when I was come again to Jerusalem.

See also *ki jia, ki jin* etc., § 88 e).

§ 51.   a) *Kena,* and ; *ke* points to preceding events, *na* continuation :

b) *Kenbena,* and after that, thereupon ; *ke-n-bena* (§ 59 c)).

(In the narrative, beginning L. I, 5 :) *To-moroa angel ajia goba lo-mun, M-amaro-n bu, Zacharias, bu-kwaiabo-n-wa l-akonnabo-n o-doma, kena b-iretu Elisabeth ka-sa fa b-aiici wa, kenbena bu-iriti fa i John, ma-in.* But the angel said unto him, Fear not, Zacharias : for thy prayer is heard ; and thy wife Elisabeth shall bear thee a son, and thou shalt call his name John ;

c) *Kenbena ki.*

kenbena ki Jesus a-iinata goba ajia-n, H-isifuda, from that time Jesus began to preach, and to say, Repent (Mt. IV, 17).

§ 52.   a) *Kia-n bena.*

kia-n bena lo-fitikida, and after these things he went forth. *kia-n bena, Joseph Arimathea kon-di ... a-kwaiaba goba Pilate l-onnaki-n bia Jesus ifiro-hu,* and after this Joseph of Arimathæa ... besought Pilate that he might take away the body of Jesus ;

b) *Kia-ni warea* (§ 97 c)).

kia-ni warea ki Adaie-li ataba-kota goba ie, from thence did the Lord scatter them abroad, *kia-ni warea kwa l-a goba m-ajia-ni-n,* and (since he) remained speechless.

§ 53.   *Kiana,* "events are proceeding" ; *kia,* with *na.* continuation.

ika ki Pilate onnaka goba Jesus kiana ; lo-boraga goba i, then Pilate therefore took Jesus, and scourged him, *Jesus a-fitikida goba kiana, eketoia yurua kwawma abu, bonaro-tu waji-tu eke-hu abu. H-adeka lihi loko ! l-a kiana Pilate ajia-n na-mun,* then came Jesus forth, wearing the crown of thorns, and the purple robe. And Pilate saith unto them. Behold the man ! *m-aiima-hu ho-mun ; l-a ki kiana Jesus ajia-n na-mun ba,* then said Jesus to them again, Peace be unto you, *a-herakida n-a-n ka. n-adagata kiana i. Adaie-li,* when they therefore were come together, they asked of him. saying, Lord, etc., *na-bokwa kiana ia lo-mairikota-n o-bora.* and they were astonished at his doctrine ;

S. presumably uses *kiahanna,* corresponding to B. *kiana,* only in the signification given by Sm., viz. "darum, folglich".

Acts I, 21—22 *kiahanna ikissida-n wa|ppa-i,* wherefore (ordain we shall), V, 26 *kiahanna Capitain a-ussa hidda lü-ssananutti u-ma Apostel-nu ibiti,* then went the captain with the officers (to the Apostles), III, 19 *uüssadükittu-nn-ua rubu h-â-li kiahañ,* repent ye therefore, XVII, 19 *nabukutta kiahanna i,* and they took him, XVIII, 6 *maribe-ni-ka kiahanna de !* I am clean, XXVI, 3 *kiahanna da-kujaba bu-mün,* wherefore I beseech thee.

§ 54. *Hinna, hiña* is used by S. to indicate that events are proceeding ; *hi* gentle affirmation (§ 109), *nna* continuation.

Acts XIX, 25 *Wadili-nu, h-aditta hinna,* Sirs, ye know, etc., XIX, 34 *akannabü-n n-a-ni-ka Judu hinna i u-kunnamün,* but when they knew (heard) that he was a Jew, XXVII, 33 *bibitikuttihi-benna-li kassakkabbu-hü dannuhu hinna-n awâbaddü-n w-a-ni-ka m-äki-ni ma-hüa, ma-buju-nn-ua-kebé hinna u,* this day is the fourteenth day that ye have tarried and continued fasting, having taken nothing, II, 25 *David ahaka hiña kuba lu-buramün,* for David speaketh concerning him, V, 36 *lu-morrua heika hiña i,* who was slain.

§ 55. *Ika,* the time at which an event takes place ; comp. §§ 28 e), 29.

a) *abar-li Agabus ci iri, ajinama goba, Sa-tu Ialoko abu ahaka-n, to-makwa ororo ajeago-ji man ifiro-tu amisia-ika fa, ma-in : t-adiki amisia ika anda-te Claudius Cesar kasakabo o-loko,* and there stood up one of them named Agabus, and signified by the spirit that there should be great dearth throughout all the world : which came to pass in the days of Claudius Cæsar, *murriga-ci hui ! oraro o-konomun bajia h-aiita ia bari-n, alika h-a kiana m-aici-ni-n toho ika o-konomun ?* ye hypocrites, ye can discern the face of the sky and of the earth ; but how is it that ye do not discern this time ? *kena yuho-li loko-no a-kwaiaboa goba na-makwa t-isibomun, incense ika,* and the whole multitude of the people were praying without at the time of incense, *aloma t-a-n ororo yaraha-n t-iibo fa koro t-isi-ika, c-iwi-ika bajia,* while the earth remaineth, seed-time and harvest ... shall not cease, *a-kwaiaboa-hu ika,* at the hour of prayer ;

b) as an independent clause :

1) *ika wakaia-hu ikisida ie, na-tikida,* and in time of temptation fall away, lit. occurs evil tempts them, they-fall, *ika angel a-koiwa t-aurea,* and the angel departed from her (L. I, 38) ;

2) with *koro,* negation :

Adaie-li, yaha-ni ka bu : ika koro da-ciligici a-oda ma, Lord, if thou hadst been here, my brother had not died, *Wadili, Isa goba ma ho-mun h-akonnabo-n ka di, ma-dokodo-n-wa w-a-n-te Crete warea, ika koro h-auciga ma toho aboadwa-hu a-boredwa-hu bajia,* Sirs, ye should have hearkened unto me, and not have loosed from Crete, and to have gained this harm and loss ;

3) with *ki,* announcing a new part of the narration ;

4) with *tu* (comp. also *yumuni ki, yumun tu,* § 71 b) 4), *manswa ki, manswa tu,* § 148, *ama tu,* § 139 b) 1), *aloman tu,* § 139 b) 3) ; *tu =* its ?) and a secondary clause (action-word with the ending *-n* or *-ni*) :

ika ki lo-mairikoto-sia-no anda goba ajia-ibici lo-mun, then came his disciples, and said unto him, *kenbena ika tu lo-mairikoto-sia-no andi-n t-oalabaw mun, n-aiikasia goba meli n-onnaki-n bia,* and when his disciples were come to the other side, they had forgotten to take bread, *ika ki Herod tetrarch akonnaba goba ajia-hu Jesus o-konomun,* at that time Herod the tetrarch heard of the fame of Jesus, *kenbena ika tu Jesus akonnabo-ni n, yu warea ki l-ausa goba,* when Jesus heard of it, he departed thence, *ika tu Jesus a-fitikidi-n yuho-li loko-no l-adeka goba, nokonne goba na-konomun kiana i, kena l-isada goba aboa-ci-no na-mun,* and Jesus went forth, and saw a great multitude, and was moved with compassion toward them, and he healed their sick ;

c) *ika tu goba, ika tu fa, ika ki ba, ika tu ki :*

ika tu goba Pentecost kasakabo andi-n, abar o-loko goba ie na-makwa. and when the day of Pentecost was fully come, they were all with one accord in one place, *to-moroa ika tu fa n-akudi-ni hu toho bawhu-yuho o-loko, h-ateda-li aba bawhu-yuho o-lokomun i-ro,* but when they persecute you in this city, flee ye into another, *tanahu d-ahaka-ga ho-mun, t-andi-n o-bora, ki-o-doma ika tu fa-te t-andi-n, h-ikiduada ma lihi-ki Daii.* now I tell you before it come, that, when it is come to pass, ye may believe that I am he, *ika tu a-furi-ni n, k-iwi goba bajia n, ika ki ba ka-raia goba tare.* but when the blade was sprung up, and brought forth fruit, then appeared the tares also, *aiika-hu-sikwa sanoci ma-koto-koto-ni h-a ma kiana, ika tu ki aiika-ci na-ma-n ?* can ye make the children of the bridechamber fast. while the bridegroom is with them ? *b-adeka, ika tu ki b-ajia-n andi-n d-akuyuko o-lokomun, da-sa adehada-ga d-adibeyo o-loko alikibi o-doma !* for, lo, as soon as the voice of thy salutation sounded in mine ears, the babe leaped in my womb for joy, *toho ki ci-biamti-tu Jesus a-dokota-sia, ika tu ki l-andi-n Judea warea Galilee mun.* this is again the second miracle that Jesus did when he was come out of Judæa into Galilee.

§ 56. *-Moroa,* with a pronominal prefix, is used in order to express "but", "however", see § 120 b).

CHAPTER VI

K; B

§ 57. The *k* in Arawak implies activity; in contrast with this, the *b* is used to indicate "being at rest". The way in which *k* is used often reminds one of "creation at work", "the idea or the principle that becomes phenomenon", *b* of "the manner in which that which has been created manifests itself, the appearance".

G denotes the same as *k*, but is perhaps a degree milder (§ 5, forms 4; § 88 ʰ)).

It seems possible that the use of *χ*, *kh* (noted by G.), *gk* (used by some of the Moravians), *k* or *g*, is determined by the strength with which one wishes to express the *k*-principle. Moreover some influence probably comes from the other sounds of the word, and finally there may be personal differences in the speakers themselves and in those who wrote that down.

§ 58. *Bi ; b* appearance, *i* quick, light.

ᵃ) immediate past.

¹) *b-iki-bi kia ada iwi?* ... *ama toho b-onyi bi?* hast thou eaten of the (fruit of) the tree? ... what is this that thou hast done? (Gen. III, 11, 13), *ama l-onyi bi bu-mun?* ... *d-ahaka bi ho-mun ibi,* what did he to thee? ... I have told you already (J. IX, 26, 27);

²) *l-isiki bi ororoli d-akosi ajeago-ji, kena da-sogoso bi n, kena d-adika,* he put clay upon mine eyes, and I washed, and do see, *kidua-ni ka Adaie-li akenako-n-wa, Simon o-mun l-iraiato bi,* the Lord is risen indeed, and hath appeared to Simon, *da-burite-sia ki da- buriti bi,* what I have written, I have written, *Adaie-li, b-onnaki faroka bi yaha rea i,* Sir, if thou have borne him hence;

³) *ibi,* used in the same way as the auxiliary verb *a*.

m-adeki-n d-ibi yara o-loko lo-ma bu? did not I see thee in the garden with him? (J. XVIII, 26), *Daii ki, d-ibi ahaka-n ho-mun,* I have told you that I am he (J. XVIII, 8);

ᵇ) *ibi-n,* not long ago, already.

Annas imigoda goba ibin i akeraia Caiaphas priest-no afudyi o-mun, now Annas had sent him bound unto Caiaphas the high priest (J. XVIII. 24), *Pilate m-aiici-n ma alika l-a-n a-odo-n ibin,* and Pilate marvelled if he were already dead (Mk. XV, 44), *ikiduadi-ci i aboadikitoa koro : to-moroa m-ikiduadi-n-ci i aboadikitoa ibin,* he that believeth on him is not condemned : but he that believeth not is condemned already;

º) 1) *ibi,* to be ready, to be accomplished.

to-makwa ibi-ka, all things are ready, *ibi-ka, c-ikisi andi-n,* it is enough, the hour is come (Mk. XIV, 41), *to-moroa hui ikisi ibi-ka kasakabo man,* but your time is alway ready, *kena ibi-ci oaboddi-n* (to wait) *akodwa goba,* and they that were ready went in, *kabuin-timen kasakabo ibi-ka,* and when eight days were accomplished, *ma-hara h-a-te, to-makwa ibi-ni o-doma,* come ; for all things are now ready :

2) I) *a-iibi-,* to leave (A. M. § 182, 144), *a-iibo-(n-wa),* to end ;

II) *iibidi-,* to prepare, to fulfill, *iibido-(n-wa),* to be fulfilled, *iibidikiti-,* to cause to fulfill ;

III) *ibiti-,* to burn, *ibito-(n-wa),* to be burned, scorched :

d) 1) *ibi-ci.*

I) lightly touched (thing, place).

See examples in § 6, and : *ire-no andia-te d-ibici,* suffer the little children to come unto me, *fig-ada ibici h-adeka to-makwa ada ibici bajia.* behold the fig tree, and all the trees (L. XXI, 29), *Wacinaci adeka goba ororo ibici,* and God looked upon the earth, *h-adeka-li hui c-ibici.* see ye to it (Mt. XXVII, 24), *abaren d-imigoda b-ibici i,* I sent (him) straightway to thee, *d-ausa aiomun bonna-n, Da-ci ibici, hui Icinaci ki ibici,* I ascend unto my Father, and your Father, *loko-no o-rea da-borati fa bu, akirikia-no o-rea bajia, k-ibici-ci d-imigodo-ni bu tanahu,* delivering (lit. I will deliver) thee from people, and from the Gentiles, unto whom now I send thee :

II) done in a light manner (?).

kenbena lo-mairikoto-sia-no anda goba onnaka ibici l-ifiro-hu. n-akarata goba n, kenbena n-ausa goba ahaka-ibici Jesus o-mun, and his disciples came, and took up the body, and buried it, and went and told Jesus, *h-adeka, Adaie-li angel ka-raia Joseph o-mun, lo-tobonia, Egypt mun, Ajia- ibici, B-akenakwa,* behold, an angel of the Lord appeareth in a dream to Joseph in Egypt, Saying, Arise, *abar-li n-adaiana-sia anda goba a-kwaiaboa-ibici lo-mun,* there came a certain ruler, and worshipped him, (saying) ;

2) I) *ibibidi-,* to touch ; G. *ĕbébedi-,* to feel (transitive) ;

II) Sm.*bibiri,* dragon-fly ;

III) Sm. *bimiti,* humming-bird, colibri (A. M. § 182, 92) ;

IV) *bilibili-ro,* the lightning ;

V) *ibini-,* to dance ; (this might have a mystic meaning, comp. VI)) ;

VI) R. *bina,* Sm. *ibbihi, ibbina,* remedy, charm : B. *ibihidi-.* Sm. *ibbihiki-,* to heal (the medicine-man) (A. M. § 182, 137) ;

VII) *ibiki-,* to cut, to wound ;

VIII) *ibira,* to mock, Sm. spielen, scherzen, im Guten und Bösen ;

e) *ki-bi,* or *k-ibi,* very, exceedingly.

1) *kena isa kibi t-a,* and, behold, it was very good (Gen. I, 31). *ki-jia t-a aiomun iibido-n-wa, ororo bajia, to-makwa kibi to-loko-tu bajia.* thus the heavens and the earth were finished and all the host of them.

kenbena yuho-li kibi loko-no ausa goba l-iinabo, and there followed him great multitudes of people, *ama jia kibi l-a lihi ?* what manner of man is this ? (Mk. IV, 41), *ama kibi o-konomun-tu toho ?* what meaneth this ? (Acts II, 12), *isa-tu-kibi ajia-hu,* gracious words, *aloman kiana kari-kibi t-a da-mun c-iibido-n-wa o-bora !* and how am I straitened (*kari,* to suffer) till it be accomplished !

    ²) *kibe-n.*

oniabu a-murretia kokki-tu a-iadi-tu yuho kibe-n, let the waters bring forth abundantly the moving creature that has life, *abar hiaro k-amun-tu ka-iauna kibe-n-tu* ointment alabaster *kasa o-loko,* a woman having an alabaster box of very precious ointment, *t-aji-kibe-n-tu ajia-hu wakaia-hu o-rea-n o-doma,* for whatsoever is more than these (words) cometh of evil, *b-adeka alika kibe-n-tu siba yaha, alika kibe-n-tu ifiro-tu bawhu bajia,* see what manner of stones and what buildings are here, *aba-hi kibe-n.* in a moment of time (L. IV, 5) (comp. § 59 ᶜ) ²)).

    ᶠ) *ibi kibi, ibi kibi bo* (§ 62).

t-adiki-tu sabbath kasakabo o-loko ibikibi hara na-herakida-n bawhu yuho kono-no, akonnabo-n Wacinaci ajia-n, and the next sabbath day came almost the whole city together to hear the word of God, *da-tu ibi kibi bo a-odo-n,* my daughter is even now dead.

§ 59. *Be* is closely related to *bi,* and sometimes they are difficult to distinguish from each other. In so far as there is a difference in meaning, it seems that *be* implies more substantiality than *bi.*

    ᵃ) *be.*

      ¹) fulness, plentitude.

waii o-mun misi-ka n barin, w-onyi-sia-be iauna w-auciga waii; to-moroa amakoro wakaia-hu lihi onyi-be goba, and we indeed justly ; for we receive the due reward of our deeds ; but this man hath done nothing amiss ; *to-moroa toho, k-amunaiga-tu wabu barin a-boreda aradi-n to-makwa t-amuni-sia, c-ikitwa-sia be abu,* but she of her want did cast in all that she had, even all her living, *tanahu robu-in w-adeka m-adeki-n|w-a-sia be !* we have seen strange things to day. *yumun-tu be ꓭ-akwaiabo-n-wa,* where prayer was wont to be made, *l-aiici-n bia aloma-be-n-tu n-aucigi-n t-aji-sabu,* that he might know how much every man had gained [by trading] ;

    ²) plurality.

      ᴵ) *wakaia-be-ci, isa-be-ci bajia,* both bad and good (guests, Mt. XXII, 10), *isa-be-tu* pearls, goodly pearls, *imilia-be-tu wahadu-be-tu bajia,* things new and old, *kalime-be-tu bia kia,* let them be for lights, *ifiro-be-tu himi,* great whales, *to-makwa k-adina-be-tu kodibiyu,* every winged fowl, *to-makwa kokki-be-tu a-iadi-tu ororo ajeago-ji,* every living thing that moveth upon the earth, *ma-boredi-n h-a-li* pearl *h-amuni-be-tu poroko isibo-mun,* neither cast ye your pearls before swine, *na-iinata-ga kiana ajia-n aba-be-tu ajia-hu abu,* (they) began to speak with other tongues ;

II) *kudibiyu-bi*, the (i.e. a great many) birds, G. *hime-be*, fishes, *wiwa-be*, stars, *toho-be*, these (things, plural), *báka-be wabo* (§ 121 ¹) ¹)) *th-ábokoáwa*, a herd of cows, *kudibiyu-be wabo th-ábokoáwa*, a flight of birds ;

3) parallel to § 58 ª) ³), *ebe*.

kokke kwa d-ebe isa-hi abu Wacinaci isibo-mun tanahu kwon, I have lived in all good conscience before God until this day, *m-iitesia-n d-ebe alika-i jiali plate-n*, I have coveted no man's silver, *m-akonnabo-n w-ebe abaren ama Sa-tu Ialoko-hu-n*, we have not so much as heard whether there be any Holy Ghost, *m-aridi-n h-ebe*, have ye never read (Mt. XXI, 16) ;

b) *ibe*, to be full.

1) *to-moroa a-bota-sia abu ibe ho-lok-oa hu, wakaia-hu abu bajia*, but your inward part is full of ravening and wickedness, *Sa-tu Ialoko abu ibe fa i*, and he shall be filled with the Holy Ghost, *lihi ibe-sia o-rea*, of his fulness (J. I, 16), *Ajia-hu ... ibe-tu isa-hi abu kidua-hu abu*, the Word ...full of grace and truth, *nete l-aiyuraka goba ororo mun, ibe-tu ifiro-tu himi abu*, (he) drew the net to land full of great fishes :

2) *ibikiti-*, S. *e-bekitti-*, to fill ;

c) 1) *bena*, after, see § 38 ; *be*, full, *na*, continuation (§ 79 ª)) ;

²) I) *k-ibena*, to be a long time, *m-ibena*, to be a short time.

kena yumuni ki k-ibena goba i, and there he abode, *yumuni ki k-ibena goba na-ma i, lo-baptize()da goba*, and there he tarried with them, and baptized, *m-akosi fa kiana bu, k-ibena fa m-adeki-n b-a-n adaili ba*, and thou shalt be blind, not seeing the sun for a season, *k-ibena-n bena ma-koto-n n-a-n, but* after long (their) abstinence, *m-ibena di, kenbena m-adeki-n ho fa di ; aba m-ibena fa ba di, kenbena h-adeki fa di*, a little while, and ye shall not see me : and again, a little while, and ye shall see me, *m-onyi-ti l-a-n o-doma k-ibena goba i*, and he would not (do) for a time ;

II) *m-aici-n n-a ama ibenata-n i temple o-loko*, and marvelled that he tarried so long in the temple, lit. not-knowing they-did what to be a long time causing him temple in ;

3) *ibena*, a part.

ma-siki-n l-a goba ororo ibena lo-mun, and he gave him none inheritance in it, *vine-kabuea iwi ibena na-siki-n bia lo-mun*, that they should give him of the fruit of the vineyard, *isa-n bu-mun o-doma abar b-ibena aboado-n-wa bia*, for it is profitable for thee that one of thy members should perish :

4) *abena*, a portion (?) in :

h-isika wa-mun h-oili-a abena, give us of your oil, *na-makwa na-tata-o-kona m-aben-tu*, every man according to his ability.

§ 60. *Ba* ; *b* appearance, *a* time-reality.

ª) again, also.

1) *lo-sogoso-n bena na-kuti, l-onnaka goba l-eki wa lo-bollita goba*

ba, so after he had washed their feet, and had taken his garments, and was set down again, *to-moroa d-adeki fa ba hu*, but I will see you again, *c-iialoko anda kiana ba*, and her spirit came again, *aunaki-ci ki d-imigido-sia jiaro, aunaka Daii ba*, he that receiveth whomsoever I send receiveth me (also), *isa-hi h-onyi-li, a-tenabo-in, m-aucigi-n h-a-n bia amateli ba*, and do good, and lend, hoping for nothing again, *kena kaarta l-isiribida, l-isiki-n bia c-ikita-kwon-ci omuni ba n*, and he closed the book, and he gave it again to the minister, *kia-n bena aba jia l-a goba a-raiato-n-wa ba*, after that he appeared (again) in another form, *naii bajia ausa kiana ahaka-n aba-no o-mun, m-ikiduadi-n n-a bajia naii ba ie*, and they (also) went and told it unto the residue : neither believed they them, *m-ibena kiben t-adiki aba-li adeka ba i*, and after a little while another saw him (L. XXII, 58) ;

2) S., G. *a-balli*, B. *a-bolli*, to pass, to occur ;

3) Sm. *bállida*, a comb, *a-ballidü-*, to comb. S. *a-ballidâ-ni-bá-n*, speaking evil ("to comb out"?) ; (A. M. § 182, 58) ;

4) Sm. *báiara*, a saw-fish ;

5) Sm. *báijabu*, a centipede ; *iabo*, behind, § 66 ;

b) *b-anda-te, b-adeki ba- te*, come and see (thou), *h-anda-te, h-adeki ba-te*, come and see (ye), *b-osa, bu-simaki ba b-ireci wa, kenbena b-anda-te yaha ba*, go, call thy husband, and come hither, *w-asiga-te Bethlehem mun i-ro, w-adeki-ba-te toho*, let us now go even unto Bethlehem, and see this thing, *bui aunti ba w-ansi-sia ifirokoro ka o-bora*, buy those things that we have need of against the feast ;

c) 1) *iba, eba*, the last, the end (connected with § 58 c)).

yu warea mamari fa bu-fitikidi-n, plata iba-n isogo-tu ka-in b-aradi-n o-bora a-iaunti-n, thou shalt by no means come out thence, till thou hast paid the uttermost farthing, *kenbena ika tu fa-te t-eba-ni andi-n*, and then shall the end [of the world] come, *kasakabo iba-ni o-loko*, at the last day ;

2) *t-ebo-n-wa* in : *to-moroa oaboddi-ci t-ebo-n-wa o-bora, lihi-ki isado fa*, but he that shall endure unto the end, the same shall be saved (comp. also *a-iibo-(n-wa)*, § 58 c) 2) I), in : *kenbena ika tu Jesus a-iibo-n-wa ajia-n toraha*, and it came to pass, when Jesus had ended these sayings, *ma-iibo-n-wa-tu kokke-hu*, everlasting life) ;

d) *aba*, some, other, another.

1) *aba a-tikida goba waboroko-sa ... aba a-tikida goba yurua o-koboroko*, some (of the seed) fell by the way side ... and some fell among thorns, *ma-iaukwa l-a ki goba ba aba biam-timen kasakabo o-loko*, and he stayed yet other seven days, *ama ibia kiana w-ansi-ka aba ahaka-ci bia ba ?* what need we any further witnesses ? *Mary Magdalene aba Mary anda goba*, came Mary Magdalene and the other Mary, *na-iinata-ga kiana ajia-n aba-be-tu ajia-hu abu*, and (they) began to speak with other tongues, *akwaiaboa l-a-n ka aba mun*, as he was praying in a certain place, *bilibiliro a-kalimeti-tu aiomun abomun aba warea, aba mun i-ro aiomun*

abomun a-kalimeti-tu bajia, ki jiari ki lo ʄa-i loko Aiici lo-kasakabo o-loko,
for as the lightning, that lighteneth out of the one part under heaven,
shineth unto the other part under heaven ; so shall also the Son of man
be in his day ;

²) *aba, a,* one, *abar, abar-li, aba-ro, aba-no,* see § 152 ;

³) *aba-koro,* no, § 136 ᵈ) ;

⁴) *aba-ba,* again.

aba-ba, h-akonnaba goba wakili-ci-no ajia-n, again, ye have heard that
it hath been said by them of old time ;

⁵) *abati-,* to alter, *abato-(n-wa),* to be altered ;

⁶) G. *waboroko abáǫoda-(n),* two roads cross each other ;

⁷) G. *aba-loko, aba-roko,* several ;

ᵉ) *bania, banyia,* lasting some time ; *nia* continuing in a free manner.

ika tu yauhahu iibidi-n ikisidi-n wakaia abu i, t-iiba banyia i, and when
the devil had ended all the temptation, he departed from him for a season,
toraha l-ajia-n bena na-mun, Galilee mun kwa-re l-a bania, when he
had said these words unto them, he abode still in Galilee, *ire-no orosidoia
banyia,* let the children first be filled, *Adaie-li, b-oabodda da-bora banyia,*
Lord, have patience with me.

§ 61. *Ko* or *ku ; k* creative force, *o, u* remains at rest, or manifests
itself in space.

ᵃ) "faculty, power", for instance *ieni-ko,* cleverness, § 91, *ime-ko,*
readiness, § 73 ᵇ). S. *malli-ku,* able to, § 74 ᵈ) ; B. *ki l-eke o-mun t-akosa-ko
kowa* (§ 143) *goba,* now the coat was without seam (*akosa,* needle) ;

ᵇ) "place, position", for instance *o-loko, roko,* in, *ajeago,* upon ;

ᶜ) intensifying, in : Sm. *hallikebbe-kû,* or, *hallikebbe-maké,* to be very
glad (§ 48 ᵉ)), *hallikebbe,* to be glad ;

ᵈ) S. : also (and).

na( )ussa a-ijukarrâ-n na-ssiqua-i n-âni ku, and (they went) and sold
their possessions and goods, *Creta-kunna-na, Arabia-kunna-na ku,* Cretes
and Arabians, *hiaru-nu u-ma, Maria Jesus u-ju u-ma ku,* with the women,
and Mary the mother of Jesus.

In B.'s texts *ko* has been found only in the following sentences :
*aloman-ci da-ci a-iaunti-sia l-isanonoci wa k-amuni-ga yuhoro kibi meli
na-siki-sia ma ko, daii a-oda bo* (§ 62) *amisia abu,* how many hired
servants of my father's have bread enough and to spare, and I perish
with hunger, *priest-no afudyi-no, a-buriti-ci-no bajia lo-kona mun goba
habe-ci-no ko bajia,* the chief priests and the scribes came upon him with
the elders ;

ᵉ) S. *kü-ssa,* or ; *ssa* is probably an intensifying particle (§ 116 ᵈ) ¹⁰)).
comp. § 179 ᶠ).

lui l-oaja lu-kunnamonn-ua, aba u-kunnamün küssa baha ? [speaketh
he] of himself, or of some other man ? *a-hudu-tti mammalli-pa akünneku-
nn-ua ba, abbâ-kurru Engel. üjahü küssa jarraha badja,* [saying] there is

no resurrection, neither angel, nor spirit, *m-ansi-rubu|da|kubá|n platta,
karrukulli üssa-huabu küssa, äke-hu diarru hu-uria,* I have coveted no
man's silver, or gold, or apparel, *aboâ-ttu l-ani-ssia, ma-kuburukkua-hü
küssa,* [if it were] a matter of wrong or wicked lewdness.

§ 62. *Bo* adds to the meaning of a word the principle of "without
motion", "to remain at rest for a time".

a) *loko Aiici ausa-bo barin, ki-jia t-a a-burito-n-wa lo-konomun,* the
Son of man goeth as it is written of him, *h-ahaka-li Sion o-tu o-mun,
B-adeka, b-Adaie-n-wabu anda bo-te b-ibici,* tell ye the daughter of Sion,
Behold, thy King cometh unto thee, *wadili h-isiki-sia siba-o-loko ajinama
bo temple o-loko a-mairikota-n bo loko-no,* behold, the men whom ye put
in prison are standing in the temple, and teaching the people, *Jesus
Nazareth kon-di a-bolli-ga bo, n-a ahaka-n lo-mun,* and they told him, that
Jesus of Nazareth passeth by (L. XVIII, 37) ; G. *l-odó-ya-bo,* he is dying
(l-ōda, he has died) ;

b) *Jesus adeka bo ka l-ikira-ji wa,* and Jesus looked round about
(Mk. X, 23), *meli n-akurrada-bo goba bajia,* and (they) breaking bread
(*akurradi-,* to break), *akurrada-bo-ho meli abu,* [they continued] in
breaking of bread, *akurrada-bo-sia ibara-tu,* the fragments [of bread] that
remain ; G. *a-šifudá-bo-či,* one who hesitates ;

c) *kari-tu hori sanoci hui, alika aicikita ho-mun h-atedi-n bia-te
k-aiima-hu andi-tu bo-te o-bora-ji ?* o generation of vipers, who has
warned you to flee from the wrath to come ? *to-makwa abona-gira-hu
bo-in kia koro Da-ci aiomun kon-di abone-sia, erigo fa,* every plant, which
my heavenly Father hath not planted, shall be rooted up, *kena b-onnaki fa
bu-mun-wa to-makwa a-kota-he eke-sia-bu-in,* and take thou unto thee of
all food that is eaten ;

d) *Paul a-siki-n bo lo-kab-oa na-si ajeago, Sa-tu Ialoko bajia anda
n-ajeago mun,* and when Paul had laid his hands upon them, the Holy
Ghost came on them, *Galilee bara rifu-ji l-akona-n bo Simon l-adeka,* now
as he walked by the sea of Galilee, he saw Simon, *a-odo-ci sikwa mun
n-anda, adaili a-fitikidi-n bo,* they came unto the sepulchre at the rising
of the sun, *kidua-ni bo loko Aiici ausi-n barin, ki jiari ki t-a-n bia i,* and
truly the Son of man goeth, as it was determined, *na-forra-ti-n (ti, § 110)
bo i, aba-no ahaka-ga ifili-ci soldaro-no capitan o-mun,* and as they went
about to kill him, tidings came unto the chief captain of the band. *Paul
akodwa ti-n bo loko-no o-koboroko mun, lo-mairikoto-sia -no m-ausi( )kita
ti goba i,* and when Paul would have entered in unto the people, the
disciples suffered him not ;

e) *ika tu bo kasakabo hara-n,* and when the day began to wear away
(L. IX, 12), *ika tu bo l-itimati-n Achaia ororo mun i-ro,* and when he
was disposed to pass into Achaia (Acts XVIII. 27), *ika tu bo Peter
a-kodo-n-wa, Cornelius ausa l-irabudiki,* and as Peter was coming in,
Cornelius met him (Acts X, 25) :

ᵉA) G. *l-a-bo*, he was, did, said, §§ 214 (8), 215 (2, 18), S. *kiahanna d-a-bu-te hu-mün*, and now I say unto you ;

ᶠ) ¹) *a-bota*, to catch away, to spoil :

²) *a-bokoto-*, to lay hold on, to, hold ;

³) *a-bokodo-kwona-hu itimi*, the rudder bands, S. *abukudu-tti-kill*, the master (or mate) of the ship ;

⁴) G. *ka-budya*, little being left (for instance if· there is a lot of fruits of which many people have partaken, *bo-bódyatá-ya-da*. thou hast made it less, taken much) ; *a-búdia-či*, a corpse, *ho-bodya-to* (f.), your corpse, is said in a house where death has taken place, to avoid using the word *a-odo-či*; comp., however, *bodi*, stiff.

§ 63. ᵃ) ¹) *O-kona*, at, on, attached to, concerning ; *ko* with *na*, continuation.

Pareciyu adeki-n kona kari-tu a-iyuhodo-n-wa lo-kabo o-kona. and when the barbarians saw the venomous beast hang on his hand, *alika-i jiali a-siki-ci lo-kab-oa plough o-kona*, [no] man, having put his hand to the plough, *kena ama-koro to-bana robu-in l-auciga goba to-kona*, and (he) found nothing thereon, but leaves only, *a-burrida-tu o-kona l-isikoia*. let him be crucified, *kenbena na-kodo-sia yurua kwama na-sika goba l-isi o-kona*, and when they had platted a crown of thorns. they put it on his head,*ma-kona-ci eke-hu*, and (a man which) ware no clothes. *ororo o-kona-tu*, earthly things, *aiomun-tu o-kona-tu*. heavenly things. *nokonne wa-kona-n bu*, have mercy on us, *waii ka-kona-ia l-itena, wa-sanoci bajia ka-kona-ia n*, his blood be on us, and on our children, *to-moroa to-kono-n goba koro ie, n-ausa goba*, but they made light of it. and went their ways (Mt. XXII, 5) ;

²) *kona*, when, see § 37 ;

²A) *o-kona*, nearly.

G. *bikidólia-koná-yada|i*, he looks young, *hálira-kuna(η*, whitish, *hehe-khona(η*, yellowish, B. § 117 ᵈ) ²) *a-korogosa o-kona*, to tremble (= shake-like), § 90 ᵇ) *tata o-kona*, force, strength (= hard-like) ; § 134 ᵃ) ³) *kari-kona*, reproaching (= pain-like) ;

³) *o-kona mun*.

priest-no ... anda na-kona mun, the priests ... came upon them (Acts IV, 1) ;

⁴) *o-konomun*, concerning.

I) *m-aucigi-n wa kaarta bu-konomun-tu Judea warea, alika-i jiali koro w-augioci andi-ci a-dokota wakaia-tu ajia-hu bu-konomun*. we neither received letters out of Judæa concerning thee. neither any of the brethren that came shewed or spake any harm of thee. *isa goba kiana Adaie-li Abel o-konomun, l-isiki-sia o-konomun bajia. To-moroa Cain o-konomun goba koro i, l-isiki-sia koro bajia o-konomun*. and the Lord had respect unto Abel and to his offering : But unto Cain and to his offering he had not respect. *kabui-ni fa abakoro b-a-n ajia-n da-konomun*. thou shalt deny me thrice, lit. three future no thy-doing speaking me-concerning, *ho-makwa hui akatadi fa Daii o-konomun*, all ye shall be offended because of me, *baru bajia bore-kwa ma ibin ada egura o-konomun*, and now also the axe is laid unto the root of the trees ;

II) *Adaie-li, to-konomun ga koro bu ?* Lord, dost thou not care (L. X, 40), *to-moroa ama koro lo-konomun-ga a-forra-kiti-tu bia i akera-kiti-tu bia jiaro i*, but to have nothing laid to his charge worthy of death or of bonds ;

III) *ka-konaminda goba kiana na-bolliti-n*, and they sat down in ranks ;

b) 1) *o-kon-di*, pl. *o-kono-no ; di* firmly established, standing.

bui ma-luiti-n ka oili da-si o-kona, to-moroa toho hiaro a-luita ointment *da-kuti o-kon-di*, my head with oil thou didst not anoint : but this woman hath anointed my feet with ointment, *ointment tu-luita to-kon-di*, (she) anointed them (the feet) with the ointment, *kena na-koida goba lo-kondi*, and (they) did spit upon him, *abar-li wadili to-makwa lo-kon-di isere-ci*, a man full of leprosy, *Samaria o-kono-no bawhu-yuho-n o-lokomun ma-kodo-n-wa h-a-li*, into any city of the Samaritans enter ye not, *l-isikwa o-kono-no*, them of his household, *wadili-no Niniveh o-kono-no*, the men of Nineveh, *Nineve o-kono-no*, the Ninevites ;

2) m. *kon-di*, S. *kun-di*, f. *kon-du*, S. *kun-du*, pl. *kono-no*, S. *kunna-na*.

Wacinaci, aiomun kon-di bui, Our Father which art in heaven, *Egypt kon-di lo-korata kiana, a-forri-n i*, (he) smote the Egyptian, *yumun kon-di k-abue-l-ci ibici l-ausa kiana lo-ma-n bia i*, and he went and joined himself to a citizen of that country, *lihi-ki Samaria kon-di*, and he was a Samaritan, *alika ba bui Jew adagato-n bu-ta-ni-wa daii Samaria kon-du o-rea ?* how is it, that thou, being a Jew, askest drink of me, which am a woman of Samaria ? *Jew-no Samaria kono-no ma eraga-n ma-n na-muni- kwawa o-doma*, for the Jews have no dealings with the Samaritans, *Parthia kono-no, Media kono-no*, Parthians, and Medes, *yuho-li Israel kono-no*, many in Israel, *yuho-li aiomun kono-no*, a multitude of the heavenly host ;

3) *kon-tu* has been met with in : *Jordan eribo-kon-tu ororo ajeago-ji l-anda kiana*, and he came in all the country about Jordan ;

4) *kondi-tu* has been met with in : *wakaukili ho( )bawhu-yuho-n warea-tu wa-kondi-tu w-arauada wa-kona-rea w-a-n ho-konomun*, even the very dust of your city, which cleaveth on us, we do wipe off against you ;

S. *Pamphylia kundu-ttu Stadt*, a town in Pamphylia ;

5) in the following forms with *kondu, kondo*, the ending *u, o* perhaps does not point to the feminine gender, but to "space".

toho akabo-kon-du abu d-aiika-ga bu-ma, with this ring I thee wed, *kena akabo-kon-do-hu h-isika lo-kabo o-kona*, and (he) put a ring on his hand, *biama goba kiana ma-kon-do-n ie*, and they were both naked, *ma-kondo-ia di*, (I was) naked.

§ 64. a) 1) I) S. *u-banna*, surface, at the surface of.

S. *aijumün kassakku u-banna, wunabu u-bana baddia*, [wonders] in heaven above ... and in the earth beneath ;

II) *bonna*.

m-ibibidi-n b-a-te di ; m-ausi-n kwa d-a-n aiomun bonna-n Da-ci ibici o-doma, touch me not ; for I am not yet ascended to my Father, *totola a-sorokodo-kwona-hu kiana atagwa, aiomun bonna-n-tu bajia penster*, the fountains also of the deep and the windows of heaven were stopped, *ki-o-doma mihu o-loko l-iiga, a-bolliti-n bara bonna*, so that he entered into a ship, and sat in the sea, *kenbena ajia-hu lo-konomun ausa goba to-makwa toraha isikwa bonna-hi-ji*, and the fame of him went out into every place of the country round about ;

2) *bona*, S. *bunna*, past tense, less recent than *bi* (§ 58 a)), and not so long ago as *goba* (§ 5).

I) *ma-iakato-n-wa o-loko na-boragi bona u m-ikisidi-n n-a-ia u. Roma-no bari-ni waii*, they have beaten us openly uncondemned, being Romans (Acts XVI, 37) ;

II) *ama tata-o-kona abu, alika-i iri abu, b-onyi bona toho ?* by what power, or by what name, have ye done this ? (Acts IV, 7), *ama o-doma mamari bona waii a-boredi-ni n ?* why could not we cast him out ? (Mk. IX, 28), *aloman tu hour o-loko sa-sabu bona i ; l-a goba kiana adagato-n ie. Miaka, biam-timen hour o-loko audasia a-iibo bona i : n-a goba ajia-n lo-mun*, then enquired he of them the hour when he began to amend. And they said unto him, Yesterday at the seventh hour the fever left him ;

III) *h-auada d-ibici, a-dokota-hu h-adeki-n bona o-doma koro, to-moroa meli h-eke-n bona o-doma, orosi-n bona o-doma hu*, ye seek me, not because you saw the miracles, but because ye did eat of the loaves, and were filled, *m-amaro-ni hu : d-aiici-n h-auadi-n Jesus ibici o-doma, a-burrida-tu o-kona-ci ki bona*, fear not ye : for I know that ye seek Jesus, which was crucified ;

3) S. *u-bannamün, u-bannamân*.

S. *l-akannaba hidda|i lü-lesidi-n Esaia ü-kârta-n u-bannamün*, and (he) heard him read the prophet Esaias, *Judea u-bannamân*, [scattered throughout the regions] of Judæa ;

4) I) *o-banna*, leaf (A. M. § 182, 112) ; Q. *u-bannabu-hü*. R. *to-banna-abu*, banab, temporary shelter, B. *bawna-boho*, tabernacle ;

II) R. *o-banna(-hu)*, liver (A. M. § 182, 13) ;

III) *o-barra*, hair, Sm. *ú-bara*, hair, feathers (A. M. § 182. 115) :

IV) Sm. *ú-bbadda*, nail, R. *o-bada*, claw (A. M. § 182. 114) :

b) 1) S. *u-ban-di*.

S. *hurruru u-ban-di*, they that were [scattered] abroad (earth-surface). *n-amuda Sura-ban-di*, they went up in an upper room. *Samaria u-ban-di*.

[they passed] through Samaria, *kairi u-ban-di Paphos muniru,* [gone] through the isle unto Paphos ;

   ²) *bon-di.*

wa-malamalada goba Adria bon-di, as we were driven up and down in Adria, *n-ausa ki ka ba bara bon-di,* they committed themselves unto the sea ;

   ³) S. *u-banna-ttu.*

S. *w-anda Lycia u-banna-ttu Stadt — t-iri Myra — mün hidda,* we came tò Myra, a city of Lycia.

§ 65. *Abu ;* a time-reality, *bu* at rest, or *b* appearance, *u* in space.

ª) with, by, on, in.

bui ki d-Aiici d-ansi-sia, bui abu ki d-iisaigatwa, thou art my beloved Son, in whom I am well pleased, *wahajia h-adeki fa loko Aiici a-bolliti-n tata-o-kona iisa mairia, l-andi-n bo-te aiomun oraro abu,* hereafter shall ye see the Son of man sitting on the right hand of power, and coming in the clouds of heaven, *kena Beelzebub abu Daii a-boredi faroka yauhahu,* and if I by Beelzebub cast out devils, *siba abu l-ibikwa,* and (he) cutting himself with stones, *kena n-ekita goba i l-oaiya l-eke abu, kenbena n-ausa goba l-abu a-burrida-tu o-kona na-siki-n bia i,* and (they) put his own raiment on him, and led him away (lit. they went him-with) to crucify him, *h-erigi faroka tare, marisi bajia h-erigi fa t-abu,* lest while ye gather up¯the tares, ye root up also the wheat with them, *ho-bokota ho-kabo abu di,* handle me (L. XXIV, 39), *ama abu w-ekito fa ?* wherewithal shall we be clothed ? *misi-tu-ahaka-hu a-sikoa goba-te Moses abu barin,* the law was given by Moses, *hui a-baptizedo fa Sa-tu Ialoko abu,* ye shall be baptized with the Holy Ghost ;

   ᵇ) *abuia* or *abuie,* to feed (= calm appearance continuing for some time ?) ; Sm. *abüja,* bush hog (A. M. § 182, 90).

§ 66. *Iabo,* probably "the outer (free) side".

t-anda yuho-li o-koboroko l-iabo-mun, (she) came in the press behind (him), *b-osa da-iiabo mairia, Satan,* get thee behind me, Satan, *kena bu-pesidi fa n to-loko mairia t-iabo mairia bajia pesi abu,* and (thou) shalt pitch it within and without with pitch, *l-iiabo-area lo-kuti amun t-ajinama a-ii-n,* and stood at his feet behind him weeping, *adeki-ci l-iabo-muniro,* (a man) looking back.

§ 67. *Bodi,* stiff ; *bo,* at rest, *di,* to stand, to be stiff.

ª) *bo-bodi,* (thy fish-)hook, Sm. *tattá-ru búdde-hi,* iron (strong) fish-hook (A. M. § 182, 56) ;

   ᵇ) *tatta-budi-,* to be stiff (example § 79 ª) ³) I)) ;

   ᶜ) Sm. *búddali,* cassava-baking pan (A. M. § 182, 50A) ;

   ᵈ) Sm. *buddahalálissi,* dead coal (comp. *balisi,* ash, § 116 ᵇ) I)) ;

   ᵉ) Q. *u-buddalli-hü,* the knee, bone.

§ 68. *Botta,* or, rather ; *bo* quiet appearance, *tta* emphasizing ?

to-moroa h-ausa botta a-iyugara-ci-n ibici. but go ye rather to them that sell, *John baptism, aiomuni warea goba* ? *loko-no botta warea* ? the baptism of John, was it from heaven, or of men ? *misi-ka wa-mun wa-siki-n bia tribute plata Cesar o-mun, abakoro botta* ? is it lawful for us to give tribute unto Cæsar, or no ? *l-ajia fa koro botta lo-mun,* and will (he) not rather say unto him (L. XVII, 8), *to-moroa k-amunaiga-ci o-mun botta h-isika amateli h-amuni-sia ibena,* but rather give alms of such things as ye have, *ki-jia m-a-ni b-a-li botta,* but do not thou yield unto them (Acts XXIII, 21).

CHAPTER VII

F; P; B

§ 69. By means of the *f* or *p*, the Arawak expresses the principle of : to strive, to aspire, airily, lightly.

No difference in meaning has been ascertained between *f* and *p*. B. mostly writes *f*, Sm., S. and Q. mostly *p* ; G. has noted almost exclusively *f*, with the exception of foreign words ; in the writings of Pen. and Roth only *f* is to be found.

In order to show the character of the *f (p)*, different *f* forms are given below beside the corresponding *b* forms.

ᵃ) *ibi-li-no ifi-li-be-ci bajia*, from the least to the greatest (Acts VIII, 10), *ibi-ro*, something small, in : *lo-kab-oa ibi-ro*, his fingers, *biama ibi-ro ka-in kodibiyu*, two sparrows ;

m. *ifi-li*, f. *ifi-ro*, great ; *ifiro*, the human body ; *ifirota*, to enlarge ; Sm. *ipíru*, the body, *adda ippíru*, the stem of a tree ;

a-fitikidi-, to go forth, to go out, to come out, *a-fitikiti-*, to bring forth ;

ᵇ) *ba*, again, *aba*, some, another, *iba, eba*, being the last, the end, *ibara*, to remain, to be left ;

fa, future (§ 5), will (§§ 28, 41) ;

Sm. *a-pappassü-*, sich ausbreiten, gross werden ; G. *tó kudibiyu fófasoa a-morodo-n*, the bird is soaring ;

Sm., G. *papáia*, papaya (A. M. § 182, 124A) ;

Sm. *appapu-rru*, böses, wildes Wasser, heftige Brandung; R. *appapu-ru*, bore, tidal wave ;

Sm. *parássa*, a spear ;

a-fatadi-, to smite ;

a-fadakudi-, to shake (off — dust of your feet ; of his raiment) ;

G. *kuliala fámodoa-tu málada*, the boat is floating away upside down ;

G. *ifa*, Sm. *ipa*, duck (A. M. § 182, 95) ;

Sm. *labba*, water haas, paca (*lapa* or *lappe* in modern Trinidad creole) (A. M. § 182, 85) ;

A. M. (§ 182, 103) **kopa*, fish ;

foto-boto-ri, a nail ;

fata ? how many ? (§ 159 ᶠ)) ;

ᶜ) *bari-ga*, though ;

faroka, if ;

ᵈ) *bo, bu*, quiet, quiet in space :

a-burrida-tu, S. *ka-balladara-tu ada*, cross ;

S., Sm. *a-balti-, a-ballati-* B. *a-bolliti-*, to sit ;

bolla kwa (kwon), S. *ballâ-koa*, to be sitting ;

bore kwa (kwon), S. *pülla-koâ-n* (?) to be laying ;

Sm.*bórudi*, basket, trinket-box ;

a-boredi-, a-boridi-, to cast away, to lose ;

o-buri, letter, character, *a-buriti-*, S. *a-bulledu-*, to write ; G. *buüli*, to draw, to adorn, with colours or in black, *a-búleti-*, to have drawn, to write :

a-bolli, bolli, to pass ;

a-fudi-, to blow ;

Sm. *ehépudü-*, to sweep clean ;

afu-dyi, principal person, ruler, *afuji*, to surpass, to rule ;

a-furi, furi, Sm. *pulli*, to spring up (a seed) ; B. *atenwa tu-furi*, first the blade (Mk. IV, 28) ; *a-furiti-*, to bring forth (plants) ;

a-fulifulito fa, [rough ways] shall be made smooth ;

a-fuili, to loose, to unloose ; *lo-folida goba l-eki wa*, (he) laid aside his garment ;

G. *funá|i*, he is greedy, *fúna-či*, a glutton ;

e) *a-boragi-*, to scourge, to beat (A. M. § 182, 134B) ;

a-forri-, to slay, to kill (A. M. § 182, 134B) ; *a-forraa*. to strive, *aforraa*, war ;

f) *a-iibokota*, to rebuke, *a-iibokoto-(n-wa)*, to be restrained ;

a-fogodo-, a-fokodo-, to divide, to part ;

g) *sibo*, face, in face of, etc. (in rest) ;

sifu, do. (in motion) ;

h) *ribo*, water side (in rest) ;

rifu, do. (in motion) ;

i) S. *wunabu*, (at) the ground ;

S. *wunapu*, (to) the ground.

j) *iribe*, uncleanness ;

Sm. *úellipe*, refuse, G. *bahü-fǐ(h)*, a delapidated (straw) hut, *t-ǐfǐ(h*, a thing no longer fit for use, *mába fé*, bees wax.

CHAPTER VIII

M

§ 70. The *m* everywhere indicates something like "hesitating", "humble", "mild".

As a negative or privative prefix : *m(a)-*, §§ 10, 28 d).

As "uncertain" : *ma*, §§ 5, 28 f), 29 b), 32, 33, 138, *ma-in*, § 35, *mo-tu*, § 36.

Expressing surprise : § 136 e) 3), and perhaps also the following :

a) *ma(n)*, S. *u-mâ(n)*, every, all, entirely, the duration is indicated by the long *a*.

kasakabo ma n-a goba naii temple o-loko, and they, continuing daily with one accord in the temple, *kasakabo ma-n-tu bia n na-sa-sia-no o-mun*, for perpetual generations (Gen. IX, 12), *kenbena, h-adeka, kasakabo ma-n ho-ma di*, and, lo, I am with you alway, *l-ici lo-iyu mi-ci ausa goba Jerusalem mun i-ro wiwa ma-n, passover ifirokoro ka*, now his parents went to Jerusalem every year at the feast of the passover, *origa-hu ma-n kasakabo ma-n*, [with prayers] night and day ;

S. *lu-ma-ré lü-kkürküa u-mân*, and (with him) all his kindred, *manswa-ttu k-amonaika-hü ku a-ussa Egypten u-hurruru u-mân, Chanaan u-hurruru mâ baddia*, and great affliction (came over all the land of Egypt and Chanaan) ;

Sm. *dá-mân*, I quite *(bú-, lú-, tú-), wá-mân*, we quite, or each one of us *(hú-, ná-)* ;

b) *-ma-kwa*, all, see § 120 a) 5).

c) *-no-ma*, a group, see § 158 a).

§ 71. In the following forms *m* is used to indicate "to be (somewhere) in an unpretending manner" (with *a* time-reality, *o* or *u* space, *i* principle ; comp. also the interrogative words *ama*, § 139 a), *alo-man* and *alo-mun*, § 139 b)).

a) 1) *o-ma*, with (time-reality).

Pharisee-no anda goba Sadducee-no o-ma, the Pharisees also with the Sadducees came, *ama ibia b-ajia-ga to-ma*, why talkest thou with her ? *bui bajia Jesus Galilee kon-di o-ma-ci goba*, thou also wast with Jesus of Galilee, *hiaro b- isiki-sia da-ma-tu bia, kia a-sika ada iwi da-mun*, the woman whom thou gavest to be with me, she gave me of the tree (fruit) ;

2) m. (human) *mi-ci*, S. *mu-tti*, f. *mu-tu*, S. *mu-ttu*, combines two or more persons previously indicated, to one group.

Jesus ausa( )kita Peter, James, John mi-ci lo-ma wa, Jesus taketh with

him Peter, and James, and John, *kidua-ni ka Adaie-li a-kenako-n-wa,
Simon o-mun l-iraiato bi, mi-ci ajia-n*, saying, The Lord is risen indeed,
and hath appeared to Simon (L. XXIV, 34), *Lamech aija goba l-irenoci
o-mun, Adah Zillah mi-ci, h-akonnaba d-ajia-n*, and Lamech said unto
his wives, Adah and Zillah, Hear my voice, *l-ajia-sia Jesus o-konomun
o-doma Joseph lo-iyu mi-ci abokwa ia*, and Joseph and his mother
marvelled at those things which were spoken of him, *b-ici daii mi-ci a-uada
b-ibici*, thy father and I have sought thee, *n-aiakatwa kiana Adam l-iretu
mi-ci*, and Adam and his wife hid themselves, *auaduli oniabu mu-tu o-mun
l-ahaka-ga*, he commandeth even the winds and water, *b-auta w-ausi-n
t-abokwa-boa* (§ 120 g) 6) XII)) *mu-tu poroko o-lokomun*, suffer us to go
away into the herd of swine, *yuho-ro kibi b-amuni-ga maiaukwa-mu-tu*
(§ 131 a) 2)) *yuho-ro wiwa bia*, thou hast much goods laid up for
many years ;

3) perhaps connected with the afore-mentioned, S. *-mu-kille*
(§ 176 c)).

S. *gi-dia* (§ 88 h)) *lu-mükille adiâ-n l-akudoa*, and as he talked with
him, he went in (Acts X, 27), *gi-dia wa-mükille andi-n abba kairi — t-iri
Clauda — ü-jaboamün hidda*, and (we) running under a certain island
which is called Clauda (Acts XXVII, 16), *gi-dia na-mükille akannabü-n*,
when they heard these things (Acts VII, 54) ;

b) *mu-n*, with different prefixes is used in the following forms to
indicate "the place where a thing is or remains".

1) *mun(i)*.

*kia kasakabo o-loko prophet-no anda goba Antioch mun Jerusalem
warea*, and in these days came prophets from Jerusalem unto Antioch.
*akodo-tu loko o-noroko mun a-ribeta koro i ; to-moroa a-fitikidi-tu
lo-noroko o-rea, kia a-ribeta loko*, not that which goeth into the mouth
defileth a man ; but that which cometh out of the mouth. this defileth man,
abar-li Simon t-eda-isada-arin isikwa mun ka i, he is lodged in the house
of one Simon, a tanner, *tanahu b-isikwa muni-n fa di o-doma*, for to day
I must abide at thy house ;

2) *o-mun*.

I) *isa goba Julius Paulus o-mun*, and Julius courteously entreated
Paul, lit. good was J. P. *o-mun, kena ifiro-tu a-kota-he Levi a-murreta
l-oaiya l-isikwa o-loko lo-mun*, and Levi made him a great feast in his
own house, *kena na-kwaiaba tu-mun i*, and they besought him for her,
d-imisidi fa tu-muni n, I will avenge her ;

II) *a-kolda-sia l-isika goba Judas Iscariot Simon aiici o-mun*, he
gave it (the sop) to Judas Iscariot. the son of Simon, *l-a Jesus ajia-n
Simon o-mun*, Jesus said unto Simon. lit. he-did J. saying S. *o-mun, ho fa
ajia-n lo-mun*, shall ye say unto him, *Jesus oonaba-ga na-mun. ajia-n*, and
Jesus answering them said. *da-dankidwa bu-mun*, I thank thee ;

III) *daii a-baptize-dikitwa ti-ka bu-mun*, I have need to be baptized
of thee, *ma-baptize-dikito-n-wa-ci lo-mun o-doma ie*, [they rejected the

counsel of God], being not baptized of him, *h-adekito-n-wa bia na-mun,*
[do not your alm before men] to be seen of them ;

IV) *Wacinaci da-mun ama o-doma bu-iba di* ? my God, why hast
thou forsak(n me ? lit. God (our-father) me-*mun* what because thou-
leavest me, *Abraham o-mun Wacinaci,* the God of Abraham (L. XX, 37),
ororo o-mun kalime Daii, I am the light of the world, *bu-kalimeta
oriroko-ho wa-mun,* lighten our darkness ;

˙V) *omuni,* to be near, to draw near.

omuni-ga-te kia kasakabo barin, and the time draweth near (L. XXI, 8),
kasakoda anaka-in aba ororo o-rea omuni-ga u n-a matoroso-no, about
midnight the shipmen deemed that they drew near to some country, lit.
night midst-being one country from near is we they-said shipmen,
W-adaiana-sia ajia-ga, d-ikisi o-bora omuni-ga, the Master saith, My
time is at hand, *ika tu fa-te toraha to-makwa h-adeki-n, h-aiita omuni-ni
n,* when ye shall see all these things, know that it [the end] is near,
h-adeka a-sikiti-ci di omuni-n, behold, he is at hand that doth betray me ;

VI) *wakaia* (evil) ... *omuni n,* woe unto :

to-moroa wakaia lihi loko omuni n a-sikiti-ci loko Aiici, but woe to
that man by whom the Son of man is betrayed, *wakaia ho-muni n,
a-buriti-ci-no, Pharisee-no, murriga-ci hui !* woe unto you, scribes and
Pharisees, hypocrites !

³) *umuni* (u, space), has been met with in one example, viz.

*kena lo-bollita goba ikisida-hu a-bolliti-kwona-hu ajeago, umuni ki
a-soa-ga Imiselda-sia,* and (he) sat down in the judgment seat in a place
that is called the Pavement ;

⁴) *yumun(i)* (§ 123).

I) *k-ibena-n bena yumun i,* and after he had spent some time there;

II) (comp. *ki, tu,* § 55 b) ³, ⁴)).

yumun-tu jiaro a-odo-tu, yumuni ki eagle kodibiyu a-herakida fa, for
wheresoever the carcase is, there will the eagles be gathered together,
h-adeka yumuni ki goba loko asoare-ci kabo, behold, there was a man which
had his hand withered, *h-adeka-te yumun-tu Adaie-li a-torodo-n,* see the
place, where the Lord lay, *kenbena ika tu n-andi-n yumun-tu Golgotha,*
and when they were come unto a place called Golgotha ;

III) *yumuni,* to be in a place.

*kena b-ateda-li Egypt mun i-ro, kena yumuni fa bu d-ahaka-n bu-mun
o-bora,* and flee into Egypt, and be thou there until I bring thee word,
yumuni-n o-doma sa-tu h-amuni-sia, yumuni ki fa ho-loa ba, for where
your treasure is, there will your heart be also ;

⁵) *amun(i)* (a time-reality).

I) *ika tu l-andi-n t-amun,* and when he came to it (comp. *Jesus
oonaba-ga kiana ajia-n tu-mun,* and Jesus answered, and said to it, Mk. XI,
13 and 14), *a-siki-ni n apostle-no o-kuti amun,* and laid them down at the
apostles' feet, *ika ki Wacinaci ajia-n anda goba Zacharias aiici amun
malokon-aukili mun,* (then) the word of God came unto John the son of

Zacharias in the wilderness, *kenbena, ika tu loko-no a-herakida-n l-amun,*
and it came to pass, that, as the people pressed upon him, *l-anda goba*
l-amuni-sia amun, he came unto his own, *l-ajinama t-amun, a-iibokoto-n*
audasia l-ajia-n abu, and he stood over her, and rebuked the fever, *Sa-tu*
laloko a-tokoda goba-te l-isi amun, and the Holy Ghost descended ... upon
him (*l-isi,* his head), *kenbena na-sika goba l-isi amun ajia-hu lo-konomun-*
tu, and (they) set up over his head his accusation, *tanahu d-anda b-amun,*
and now I come to thee ;

II) *k-amuni,* to possess, *m-amuni,* to possess not.

to-makwa d-amuni-sia bui k-amuni-ga, all that I have is thine, *to-makwa*
Awa k-amuni-sia d-amuni-ga, all things that the Father hath are mine.
alika-i jiali k-amun-ci n, lihi-ki o-mun t-isiko sabu fa ba, kenbena yuho-ro
sabu l-amuni fa ; to-moroa alika-i jiali m-amun-ci n, lihi-ki o-rea l-amuni-sia
onnako fa, for whosoever hath, to him shall be given, and he shall have
more abundance ; but whosoever hath not, from him shall be taken away
even that he hath, *Cesar amun-tu,* [the image on the coin is] Cæsar's ;

III) *amunte, amute* (= *amun-ci ?*), to be wont.

kena l-ausa synagogue o-lokomun, l-amute-n be l-ausi-n jin, sabbath
kasakabo o-loko, and, as his custom was, he went into the synagogue on
the sabbath day, *lo-mairikota goba kiana ba ie l-amute-n.* and, as he was
wont, he taught them again, *kia ki ifirokoro ka ikisi o-loko adaia-hu*
l-amunte goba a-dokodo-n abar-li siba-loko-ci loko-no o-mun, n-ansi-sia
jiali ki, now at that feast the governor was wont to release unto the people
a prisoner, whom they would ;

6) *aiomun(i),* a high place ; *i,* free, *o,* space ? see, however, § 83 a).

I) *aiomun bawhu o-loko na-sika goba n,* they laid her in an upper
chamber, *kenbena l-anda n-abu aiomun-tu ororo ajeago mun,* and (he)
bringeth them up into an high mountain, *H-icinaci aiomun kon-di,* your
Father which is in heaven, *aiomun isauka,* the kingdom of heaven, *kenbena.*
h-adeka, ajia-hu aiomuni o-rea ajia goba, and lo a voice from heaven.
saying, *kena abar cubit o-loko b-iibidi fa aiomuni-ni n.* and in a cubit shalt
thou finish it [the ark] above ;

II) *aiomunti-,* to exalt ;

7) *abo-mun,* under ; *b* in rest, *o* space.

Wacinaci kiana a-murreta goba kibilokoukili, aragakoto-n kibilokoukili
abomun-tu oniabu, kibilokoukili amun-tu oniabu o-rea, and God made the
firmament, and divided the waters which were under the firmament from
the waters which were above the firmament. *da-sikwa-sidi-tu abomun,* [to
come] under my roof, *t-adina abomun,* [to gather] under her wings. *tapel*
abomun-ga pero, the dogs under the table, *n-abomun goba i.* (he) was
subject unto them, *ajia-hu abomun-ci loko daii barin. soldaro-no d-amuni-ga*
daii abomun, I also am a man set under authority, having under me soldiers:

c) *o-makana.* over against : comp. *o-ma.* with § 71 a) 1). *kona.*
against, § 63.

a-bolliti-n a-odo-ci-sikwa o-makana, sitting over against the sepulchre.

to-moroa abakoro l-a goba ajia-n na-makwa na-makanna, but he denied before them all, *b-iibidi-sia ki na-makwa loko-no isibo o-makana*, which thou hast prepared before the face of all people, *lo-makana-ci-no*, the (his) neighbours, *misi-n bia w-onyi-n b-akosi o-makana*, (we) to do always that is righteous in thy sight.

§ 72. *M* = holding in, holding back, hesitating, shrinking from.

a) 1) *amaro*, to be afraid, to fear ;

2) *amaronto-*, to threaten ;

b) *n-amoto fa d-aiici o-bora*, they will reverence my son, *m-amoto-(n-wa)*, to be of good cheer, to have courage, confidence ;

c) Sm. *u-mároa-n*, I. Th. *morowa*, arrow with blunt head for shooting birds (comp. *to-moroa*, but, § 120 b)) ;

d) *mimi*, to be cold, *mimi-li* the cold, winter, *imimidi-*, to cool, *imimido-(n-wa)*, to wax cool.

§ 73. *M* = submissive.

a) 1) S. *a-ssika ... äme*, to believe, to obey (*a-ssika*, durative to put, to give).

S. *abba-nu n-ebenna assika-ka hidda l-adia-ssia-bi-ru äme, kan abba-nu m-a-ni-rubu n-a*, and some believed the things which were spoken, and some believed not, *a-ssika-hü-ssia bia Wamallitakoanti, hui äme âdi-n*, we ought to obey God rather than men (you), *bu-morrua ma-ssika-n b-a-li n-äme*, but do not thou yield unto them ;

2) Pen. *b-ithe-fa-do d-ame-ni*, you will drink for me ;

b) 1) Sm. *imê-n*, willig, munter sein zu etwas, B. *hime-n*, oft (Mk. VII, 3), S. *Thessalonika-kunna-na âdi-kubá|je nai-kewai imé-n üssa-ttu ibiti*, (Acts XVII, 11 Thessalonicans more-than-were they they willing holy (word) touched) ;

2) *ime-wabu, imehi-wabu*, always ;

3) S. *iméniku-hu abbu*, gladly ;

4) Sm., S. *imenikuttu-*, to cause to be willing ;

5) *imeko ka di*, I am ready, S. *iméku-ka-hüa|de*, I am ready, *imeku-hu abbu*, diligently ;

6) *imigodo-*, S. *imekudu-*, to send ;

7) *k-imikebo*, to work, to toil, to till ;

8) Sm. *himekúne*, yam (napi), Dioscorea trifida ; (or : *hime-kune*, fish-like, § 63 a) 2A) ?)

9) *tamo-tu goba, mamari-tu imisido-n-wa*, (she) was bowed together, and could in no wise lift up herself (comp. *tata*, hard, and Island Karib *tamon*, prisoner, slave, *l-emon-hali*, he is bowed together, *tamonet*, crane (bird)).

§ 74. *M* = new, humble, discreet, cautious, fine.

a) —

b) *imeodo-*, to bring forth (children) ;

c) *imi-lia*, to be new ;

d) 1) *mali*, should, ought.

lihi wadili Jew-no a-bokoto-sia, na-forri-sia mali, this man was taken of the Jews, and should have been killed of them, *waii m-ikisi mali kiana Wacinaci korrokori jia-mu-tu bia,* we ought not to think that the Godhead is like unto gold ;

²) S. *ma-malli,* not to be able, not to be possible ;

³) *mari,* to be not certain (?, § 146) ;

⁴) *ma-mari,* to be not at all (§ 147) ;

⁵) S. *a-malliti-,* B. *a-murreti-,* G. *a-maliti-,* to bring forth, to create, to make (A. M. § 182, 144A) ;

⁶) S. *malliku,* to be able to ;

⁷) S. *a-mallikutta,* B. *a-mairikota,* to teach, B. *a-mairikoto-(n-wa),* to learn ;

⁸) Pen. (11. 17a III p. 105) *Mali,* the mother of knowledge :

e) ¹) *kaspara o-mana,* the edge of the sword, Sm. *ká-mana,* to be sharp, *má-mana,* to be blunt, *a-manti-,* to sharpen (A. M. § 182, 146) :

²) Sm. *mánna-li,* sieve, *mánna-ka,* manicole palm (A. M. § 182, 124) :

f) animals which cast their hide (? ; see § 168 ; A. M. § 182, 43) : *emena-hu,* worm, worms (probably "vermin", "insects"), *imina-ri,* scorpion, scorpions.

§ 75. *M* = tender.

a) *seme-tu amateli k-amun-ci,* (they which) live delicately, S. *seme-tu Evangelium,* the Gospel, Sm. *seme-n,* to be sweet ;

b) *miaumia-tu eke-hu,* soft clothing, *miaumia-ci ekc.* a man clothed in soft raiment, G. *toho múyamúya-ya,* this is soft.

§ 76. *M* = floating.

a) *amodi-,* to go up (into a mountain, out of the water) ;

b) ¹) *mihu,* a ship (A. M. § 182, 52) ;

²) *himi,* a fish (A. M. § 182, 102) ;

c) Sm. *málla-li,* current ; Sagot *malâ-li,* fall, Pen. *Koritini o-mala,* Corentyn stream ; B. *wa-malamalada goba Adria bon-di,* we were driven up and down in Adria, *na-tokodo( )kota kiana na-wela-n wa, a-mullidi robu t-a-n bia,* (they) strake sail, and so were driven ; S. *a-malladü-,* to float away ; B. *onikain mulla-n kia bawhu o-kona mun,* the stream beat upon that house ;

d) ¹) G. *simála,* Sm. *símara,* R. *shimara,* arrow (*si,* point, § 116 c) ; A. M. § 182, 54) ;

²) S. *a-huṁadu-* to rush (the wind) ;

e) *a-morodo-,* to fly (a bird) ;

f) *o-horomurrida,* waves, etc., see § 122 d) 1) IV) ;

g) ¹) *murriga,* to be false, to lie ;

²) *a-murrida,* to deceive, *a-murrida-koto-(n-wa),* to err ;

h) *camel ho-mokoda,* (you) swallow a camel.

CHAPTER IX

N

§ 77. The *n* is used in the Arawak language, in order to indicate "firmness or substantiality of a neutral character". The consonants give form, firmness, to the shapeless mass indicated by the vowels ; the *d, t, k, m* etc. do this, each in its own characteristic way ; the *n* does the same, but without any specific character.

§ 78. *Ni.*

ª) *nii-ka-n, nii-ma-n,* a while, a little.

niikan n-a k-ibena-n, and after they had tarried there a space [they were let go], *niiman t-adiki ajinama-ci-no yumun anda goba l-amun,* and after a while came unto him they that stood by, *h-ahakobu-in bia niiman,* [come] and rest (ye) a while, *kena lo-kwaiaba i l-icirikidi-n bia t-eribo-area niiman,* and (he) prayed him that he would thrust out a little from the land ;

ᵇ) S. *ni rubu kurru,* a long time, no little, no small, not a few ;

ᶜ) S. *ni-kebé,* to occur immediately, straightway, forthwith ;

ᵈ) *-ni,* something that really is, or shall be, see § 25 ;

ₑ) ¹) *ani, anye, anyi, onyi,* a thing, a thing possessed ; see examples in § 32, and :

alika-i koro ajia goba l-amuni-sia o-konomun, Daii a-ni toho, ma-in ; to-moroa na-makwa n-anye to-makwa, neither said any of them that ought of the things he possessed was his own ; but they had all things common, *b-onnaka b-anyi-re-n, kena b-osa,* take that thine is, and go thy way, *kenbena yumuni ki da-siki fa to-makwa d-anyi iwi, da-nyikau bajia,* and there will I bestow all my fruits and my goods, *wa-herakida w-onyi-wa,* we took up our carriages (Acts˙ XXI, 15), *k-onyi-li,* the owner (Acts XXVII, 11) ;

²) *onikau, o-nyikau,* Sm. *anniku-hu* goods, B. *sa-tu onyikau,* treasure ;

³) S., Sm., v. C. *ani,* B. *onyi,* to do (A. M. § 182. 139) ;

ᶠ) *onnibita* (or *onnibiti-*), to disperse, S. *a-nebetu-(nn-ua)* ... *n-auri-koawa,* to be dispersed, scattered, divided.

§ 79. *Na, no.*

ª) *-na,* continuation.

¹) *kena,* and (§ 51), *kenbena,* and thereupon (§ 51), *kiana,* events are proceeding (§ 53), S. *hinna,* do. (§ 54), B. *bena,* after, *ibena,* a time, a part (§ 59), *kona,* etc. (§ 37), *bona,* etc. (§ 64), *kwona,* instrumental (§ 120 ª) ²)) ;

²) *iana,* heel (§ 132), *adina,* arm (§ 86 ᵍ)), *itena,* blood (comp. § 187);

3) *o-no* means the neck (or the throat ?) (A. M. § 182, 20) :

I) *hui tatabudi-ci o-no-ro*, ye stiffnecked, *molo siba a-iiodokota-n ka lo-no-ro o-kona*, that a millstone were hanged about his neck, *onnaka-ro-hu h-isika ti-ka a-mairikota-sia-no o-no-ra-ji*, (ye wish) to put a yoke upon the neck of the disciples, *naha loko-no anda-te na-no-roko abu da-mun, n-areroko abu n-adaiakita di*, this people draweth nigh unto me with their mouth, and honoureth me with their lips ;

II) G. *honoli, anula*, herons (A. M. § 182, 21) ;

b) 1) *-na-*, plurality of a family-relation ; often the preceding vowel is metamorphosed, and also apocope of the *a* occurs :

ici, to be father to one person (indicated by the pronominal prefix).
ici-na-ci, to be father to more than one person, *wa-ci-na-ci*, our father ;

adaia, to have authority, *adaiana-sia*, master ;

isa, to be child, *l-isa-n-ci*, his servant ;

da-bogi-ci, Sm. *da-buki-ti*, my (man) older brother, *na-boge-n-ci*. Sm.
na-bukëi-n-ti, their older brother ;

2) *-no*, plurality (two or more) of rational beings (see also § 187) :

I) *wa-ci-no-ci*, Sm. *wa-tti-nu-ti*, our fathers ; *wa-boge-no-ci*, Sm.
wa-buke-nu-ti, our (man) older brothers; *-kwono-no-ci*, see § 120 a) 2) II);

II) *loko*, man, *loko-no* ; *hiaro*, woman, *hiaro-no* ; *akirikia*, nation,
akirikia-no ; *soldaro*, soldier, *soldaro-no* ; *publican, publica-no* ; *prophet,
prophet-no* ; *virgin, virgin-o* ; *Pharisee, Pharisee-no* ; *Jew, Jew-no* ;
Roman, Roman-o ; *Christian, Christian-o* ; *Christ, Christ-no* ; *angel,
angel-no* (all English words) ; etc.

In the same manner : *aba-no*, some, *biama-no*, two, *kabuin-o*, three, etc. ;
fata-no, how many — when used in relation to people ; *habe-ci-no*, the
elders, *a-buriti-ci-no*, the scribes, *lo-mairikoto-sia-no*, his disciples, etc.

Wadili, man, often takes no plural suffix :

Wadili, Sirs (Acts XXVII, 21), *biama-no wadili*, two men (L. XXIV,
4), *wadili Nineve o-kono-no*, the men of Nineveh (L. XI, 32), *wadili jiaro
hiaro-no jiaro*, whether they were men or women.

However : *wadili-no Niniveh o-kono-no*, the men of Nineveh (Mt. XII,
41), *wadili-no a-bollita goba kiana*, so the men sat down (J. VI, 10),
biama-no angel-no, two angels (J. XX, 12), *biama-no soldaro-no*, two
soldiers (Acts XII, 6).

S. gives, contrary to the principles of Arawak : *issehü-nnu* the worms.
Stadt-nu, cities, S. and Sm. *kuddibiju-nu*, fowls, birds, Sm. *üjehi-nu*, lice :

III) *noma*, indicating a group, see § 158 a) ;

c) 1) *ina*.

t-isiri kiana hatatwa ... to-moroa t-iina a-kororoswa, the [ship's]
forepart stuck fast ... but the hinder part was broken, *abar aiomun ina-rea
aba t-ina-rea ki ba*, from one end of heaven to the other, *a-sika-sia t-ina-
roko-tu bia*, which is become the head of the corner, *bawhu-yuho ina-roko
mun*, [standing] in the corners of the streets : S. *Gott aditti-ti wa-llua
u-ina-mün-tu*, God, which knoweth the hearts ;

2) *iinata*, to begin.

na-iinata-ga onyi-n toho, and this they begin to do, *a-iinata d-a-n ka ajia-n*, and as I began to speak ;

3) *inaka : n-akoikita goba na-iina-ka mun-i-ro*, they went backwards (J. XVIII, 6) ;

4) *inabo*, (following, etc.) after.

abaren na-iiba goba na-neti-n, ausi-n l-iinabo, and straightway they forsook their nets, and followed him, *ajia-hu n-imigoda l-iinabo kiana*, and (they) sent a message after him, *l-onnaki-n bia n Jesus inabo*, that he might bear it after Jesus, *kena l-isifuda-ga ajia-n l-iinabo-ci o-mun*, and (he) turned him about, and said unto the people that followed him ;

d) *anaka* (time-reality), *anaku* (space), the midst.

kasakoda anaka-in, about midnight, *kena t-isidi-tu anaka-roko-ji na-tokodo-kota i lo-torodo-kwona-hu ajeago anaka-bo Jesus isibo-mun*, and (they) let him down through the tiling with his couch into the midst before Jesus, *kena l-isika goba anaka-bo na-mun i*, and (he) set him in the midst of them, *Jesus anda goba anaka-bo l-ajinama goba*, came Jesus and stood in the midst, *yumuni ki anaka-bo ka Daii na-mun*, there am I in the midst of them, *kibilokoukili anaka-bo fa oniabu o-mun*, let there be a firmament in the midst of the waters, *anaka-bo-tu yara o-mun kokke-hu ada bajia*, the tree of life also in the midst of the garden, *a-iibi-n i anaku-ji a-oda-hu abu*, leaving him half dead, *kena anaku-ji abu l-anda*, and (he) brought a certain part, *anaku-ji-bo kiana lo-kurrada-ga*, he burst asunder in the midst, *kena aiakata-kwona-hu kimisa temple o-loko-tu a-terakidwa goba anaku-ji bo*, and the veil of the temple was rent in the midst ;

e) 1) I) *onabo*, low, the ground.

onabo o-bolisi, the dust of the ground, *a-buriti-n lo-kabo abu onabo ajeago*, and with his finger wrote on the ground, *onabo-ci*, them of low degree, *onabo-tu*, the low estate, *onabo-n-ci o-loa-n o-doma di*. for I am ... lowly in heart, *onabo-tu o-loa abu*, with all humility of mind ;

II) *oonaba*, to reply ; the object is always indicated, e.g. *centurion oonaba goba n, ajia-n, Adaie-li*, etc., the centurion answered and said, Lord, etc., *to-moroa ma-onaba-n l-a goba abar ajia-hu tu-mun*, but he answered her not a word, *ama koro b-oonaba-ga ?* answerest thou nothing ?

III) R. *n-onaba-kuanna*, a shield ;

2) S. *wunapu* in the following : *l-ittikida ... wunapu-ddi*, (he) fell down [from the third loft] ;

3) *onnaki-*, S. *a-onnaki-*, to take ; *a-odo-ci n-onnaki-kwona-hu*, the (their) bier ; *aunaki-*, S. *anniki-*, to receive ; Sm. *anniki-*, nehmen, tragen, Sm. *annakú-(nn-ua)*, to paddle ; see § 91 (A. M. § 182, 136) ;

4) *onnaka-ro*, burden ;

5) *onnawa*, to choose.

§ 80. *An, on*, having firmness, forms a part of :

a) 1) *waboroko anda-hi mun*, [they found the colt] in a place were two ways met, G. *waboroko andá-ka*, two ways meet ;

²) Sm. *andaka,* joint, articulation ;

³) *andakoto-,* to join, to cleave to ;

⁴) *andi-,* to come ; *andi- ... abu,* to bring, *ausi-ci Paul abu anda l-abu Athens mun,* and they that conducted Paul brought him unto Athens :

⁵) Sm. *ansâ, ansi,* to grate (cassava, etc.) ;

ᵇ) *ansi,* inner peace, G. (according to Baptist :) vitality ; Island Karib *ánichi,* heart, soul, life, *k-anichico,* wise ;

¹) love, to love, see § 18 ;

²) *na-tattada n-ansi-wa,* they comforted them, lit. they strengthened their-*ansi*-own, *bu-tattadoa-li b-ansi-wa,* be of good cheer :

³) *yura ... ansi ; yu,* §§ 123, 124, *ra,* §§ 104—108.

Jerusalem mun l-anda ti-n o-doma yura l-ansi Pentecost kasakabo o-bora. for he hasted, if it were possible for him, to be at Jerusalem the day of Pentecost, lit. J. place he-come wishing because *yura* his *ansi* P. day future point of time, S. *ni-kebé-ka jura-n w-ansi akunnu-n Macedonia-muniru.* immediately we endeavoured to go into Macedonia, Sm. *júra d-ansi.* I long for ;

⁴) S. *jura-kû d-ansi,* I must by all means ;

⁵) S. *jura-hü'lukku ansi,* he hastened, (he) was zealous ;

⁶) *a-iyurati- ... ansi,* Sm. *a-ijulattu- ... ansi.* to trouble, to be troubled, to be vexed, to care for ; also : *to-makwa ororo ajeago-ji lo-yurata Jew-no ansi,* a mover (lit. he moves) of sedition among all the Jews throughout the world.

§ 81. *-n, -in,* metamorphosed vowel + *n,* inserted vowel *-n ;* that which is indicated by the word, loses its mobility, its vividness, in the firmness of the *n ;* it becomes vague in regard to time.

ᵃ) behind object-words, when they indicate possession (alienable possession).

¹) *ada,* tree, stave, *h-ada-n,* (your) staves : *kaarta,* book, *l-ikaarta-n ; Galilee, akirikia-no Galilee-n,* Galilee of the Gentiles ; *sapatu,* shoe, *l-isapatu-n ; a-burrida-tu,* cross, *bu-burrida-tu-n ; temple, Diana temple-n,* the temple of Diana ; *sikapo,* sheep, *da-sikapo-n ; pound, bu-poundi-n ; priest, Jupiter priest-in,* the priest of Jupiter ; *lamp(u?),* lamp, *wa-lamp-en ; itena,* blood, *da-tene-n ; yara,* hedge, *l-iyara-in ; baka.* ox, cattle, *ho-baka-in ; plata,* silver, money, *bu-plate-n ; nete,* net, *na-neti-n ; kano,* vessel, *ti-kane-n ; tapel,* Sm. *tafel,* table, *da-tapelo-n,* Sm. *da-táfulu-n :*

²) *w-ikiduadi-n,* our faith, *n-imikiduadi-n,* their unbelief, *a-sogoso-n na-boragi-n,* and washed their stripes, *n-ajia-n.* their tongue, *bu-sweardoa-n.* thine oaths, *w-aboa-n,* our infirmities, *n-aboa-n,* their diseases, *b-aboa-n.* thy plague.

With some words, as for instance *kokke.* life, no *-n* is applied. Both forms, in the following examples : S. *a-huda-hü ü-karri-n.* the pains of death, *na-karri-n, na-karri,* their diseases, *lü-karri-n, lü-gkarri.* his disease :

ᵇ) *da-ie-n,* S. *da-ia-n,* mine, etc.

da-sa, b-osa, b-imikebo ba tanahu da-ie-n vine kabuea o-loko. son. go work to day in my vine-yard, *m-iitesia-n b-a bu-ioci iretu, l-ịkita-kwon-ci bajia, l-ikita-kwon-tu bajia, l-iie-n baka bajia,* thou shalt not covet thy neighbour's wife, nor his manservant, nor his maidservant, nor his ox, *n-ibilokota phylacterie na-iie-n,* they make broad their phylacteries, *kenbena aba-no ho-boragi fa h-iie-n synagogue o-loko,* and some of them shall ye scourge in your synagogues ;

c) in the particle *mun,* indicating place ;

d) 1) in order to take from the verb the definiteness in regard to time, see § 5, table, forms 7, and §§ 26, 27 ;

2) something similar in the forms *ji-n* (§ 88 b)) and *-kwo-n* (§ 120 a) 2). related to *-kwona*).

§ 82. a) With the following substantives, all ending in *i,* an *a* is added if they indicate possession :

korrokorri, gold, *lo-korrokorri-a ; logie,* garner, barn, *da-logi-a ; marisi,* wheat (maize), *lo-marisi-a ; meli,* bread, loaf, *wa-meli-a ; oili,* oil, *h-oili-a ; sesi,* chariot, *l-isesi-a ; warriwarri* (Roth), fan, *lo-wariwari-a ;* Sm. *borudi,* a basket, *da-borụdi-a ; hátti,* Cayenne pepper, *da-hatti-a ; horudi,* woman's basket, *da-horudi-a ; kekelli,* cassava-soup, *de-keh(?)lli-a ; kirahudúlli,* spindle, *ikiruhudúlli-a ; mánnali,* a sieve, *da-mánnali-a,* G. (creole *máti,* friend), *da-máti-a, kómiki,* a bowl, *da-kómiki-a.*

Beside *da-logi-a, da-logie-n* also occurs ; a difference in the meaning has, however, not been found. Sm. uses the *-n* with several words ending in *i,* for instance *dúbuli,* a ray, *dá-dubuli-n, hádduli,* a sort of rabbit, *b-áhadduli-n ; sikkisikki,* grass-hopper, *da-ssikkissikki-n ; siparálli,* iron, *dá-ssiparálli-n ; wáijoukássi,* small arrow, *d-oáijoakássi-n.*

b) *-Ti, -te, -le* (comp. *-ci,* § 21, *-li,* §§ 175, 176) have been met with in : *alaiti,* a candle, *ifiro-hu alaiti-ti,* the light of the body ; Sm. *ipa,* a duck, *d-ipa-te ; júli,* tobacco, *da-júli-te ; ikana,* bush rope, *d-ikána-te ; pimittika,* wax, *d-ipimitikka-le.*

§ 82 A. a) G. *fukuléǫuǫi-a,* snake *(uǫi)* resembling an aguti *(fukuleǫu);*

b) G. *warakaba aǫoa-te,* tigers *(aǫoa)* that look like or behave themselves like trumpet-birds *(warakaba).* Other examples, § 199.

Comp. also B. *ji-n, ji-a,* as, § 88. It may be that the Arawak considers an object in itself, the alienable possession, as a likeness, an image or a copy of the idea which it embodies, or as only the external form of its spirit.

§ 83. a) *-N-* (Arawak or A. M.) becomes *-ñ-, -y-,* — :

inabo (§ 79 c) 4)), *iabo* (§ 66), behind :

ani, anyi, onyi (§ 78 e)), *ie* (? § 81 b)), a thing, a thing possessed ;

S., Sm., v. C., G. *ani,* B. *onyi,* to do :

bania, banyia (§ 60 e)), lasting some time :

(**-augi-na-ci, *-augi-no-ci* ?), *-augi-o-ci,* Sm. *-huki-n-ti,* several brothers:

(**na, *ena* ?), *ie,* endpoint pronoun III pl. ;

A. M. § 182, 18 **enene, *ineñe,* Arawak *ie.* tongue ;

,,   ,,   17 **numa,* mouth, Arawak Sm. *ema. uima. aema-mün,* the   mouth of a river ;

A. M. § 182, 38 *eno, Arawak *iyu*, mother ;

,,   ,,   60 *eno, Arawak *a-io-mun*, heaven ;

,,   ,,   63 *iuina, Arawak Sm. *wiyua*. Pleiades ;

,,   ,,   32 *e(š)ina-ru, Arawak *hia-ro*, woman ;

,,   ,,   107 A, 107 B *haniu, Arawak *hayu*, wasp, gnat, ant ;

,,   ,,   120 *kaniri, Arawak Sm. *kalli*, cassava, *kanneki-ddi*, Cassabistöcke ;

b) -ng instead of -n :

G. *da-sikwa-ŋ*, my house, *ulalo tikidi-ŋ*, fog in the morning, R. *b-anshing-odóma|de*, if you like me, *hiaro-no-dulluhi-ng*, woman's pole (R. 19a. Sect. 155) ;

c) S. spells instead of -nn- also -ñ-, instead of -mm- also -m̃-: presumably we have to do here with a mark of abbreviation in the MS :

d) -m instead of -n :

S. *u-müm, amüm*, most often however *u-mün, amün ;* v. C. *isa-m bia* = B. *isa-n bia*, G. see § 193.

CHAPTER X

D

§ 84. The *d*, in the meaning of "to stand", "will-power manifesting itself by remaining motionless", we have already met with, when we considered the construction of the action-words (§ 1), and further in emphasizing particles (§§ 44—47A), as well as in the ending of object-words (*kon-di, kon-du, bon-di,* §§ 63 b), 64 b)). In the last-named function, also in :

afu-dyi, principal person, ruler, *afu-du-wabu*, queen, *ho-kuti-roko-do*, your sandals (*ho-kuti-roko-area*, (from) under your feet), *l-isi-bora-du*, a (his) pillow, *siba o-bora-do*, the foundations of the prison, *ma-bora-do ia*, (being) without a foundation, *isifo-do*, door.

Di sometimes alternates with *dyi* and *ji*, (phonetically *dzyi*) ; a corresponding phenomenon has been noted with the *t* and the *s* (§§ 90, 113).

§ 85. *-(I)ji, -di,* the preceding form is meant as a fixed place or thing.

to-makwa church-iji man na-sika habe-ci-no ikita-ci bia ie, and when they had ordained them elders in every church, *meli na-kurrada-bo goba bajia aba aba mun bawh-iji,* and (they) breaking bread from house to house, *n-ausa goba kiana na-uaiya na-sikwa-ji na-makwa,* and all went to be taxed, every one into his own city, *n-ausa kiana to-makwa bawhu-yuho-ji man ausi-n ajia-ci sa-tu ajia-hu, isadi-n to-makwa-ji,* and they departed, and went through the towns, preaching the gospel, and healing every where. *kena n-anda l-amun to-makwa-ji warea,* and they came to him from every quarter, *aba-ji-bo n-akoiwa goba na-uaiya na-horora mun i-ro kiana,* they departed into their own country another way, *aiomun-ji-tu kodibiyu,* [over] the fowl of the air [have dominion], *n-akonnaba Adaie-li Wacinaci ajia-n, akona l-a-n ka yara o-loko-ji mimi-aukili-di,* and they heard the voice of the Lord God walking in the garden in the cool of the day, *yuho-li akodwa to-loko-ji,* [broad is the way] and many there be which go in thereat, *Adaie-li kalime a-kalimetwa n-ikira-ji,* and the glory of the Lord shone around them, *ma-odo-ni bo fa Adaie-li Christ o-bora-ji b-adeki-n bia-te i,* that he should not see death, before he had seen the Lord's Christ, *l-adiki-ji,* the (his) younger son, the second (son), *taha-ji-be-tu ororo mun bajia,* and unto the uttermost part of the earth (Acts I, 8), *kena a-burrida-tu na-sika lo-nora-ji,* and on him they laid the cross, *alomun-ji jiaro fa ifiro-tu adedisaro,* and great earthquakes shall be in divers places, *yumun-ji ki lo-bolli-n fa-te o-doma,* for he was to pass that way, *kena Jesus akodwa goba a-bolli-n Jericho o-koboroko-ji,* and Jesus entered and passed through Jericho.

§ 86. *Adi, aji* (§ 20), protruding.

a) S. *adi*, upon (in an abstract sense).

S. *Gouverneur bia|i Egypten u-hurruru âdi, lü-ssiqua-mün-ti ádi ba,* governor (to be he) over Egypt and all his house, *hü-ttenna-wa andi-n-kebé ma-ppa h-issi âdi,* your blood be upon your own heads ;

b) S. *adiaku,* upon (in space), B. *ajcago,* upon ; *ku. go.* § 61.

S. *Paulus m-ani-beña a-ssiki-n lü-kkabbu na-ssibu adiaku, üssa-tti üjahü anda hidda n-âdi,* and when Paul had laid his hands upon them, the Holy Ghost came on them, *ahabula adiáku,* [to sit] on [his] throne ;

B. *aba a-tikida goba yumun-tu siba ajeago,* some fell upon stony places, *daii adeka goba Ialoko a-tokodo-n wiru jin aiomuni o-rea l-ajeago, oaboddi-n l-ajeago,* I saw the Spirit descending from heaven like a dove, and it abode upon him, *kia ki h-ajia-li bawhu ajeago-area,* that preach ye upon the house-tops, *Adaie-li Ialoko d-ajeago ka,* the Spirit of the Lord is upon me, *aloman ororo ajeago ka di,* as long as I am in the world (earth upon) ;

N.B. in other cases "upon" is rendered by *amun.* § 71 b) 5), or *o-kona.* § 63.

c) 1) *adiki,* after.

kena a-kota-he adiki, and supper being ended, *kenbena yuho-ro koro kasakabo adiki, l-adiki-ji l-aiici a-herakida to-makwa,* and not many days after the younger son gathered all together ;

S. *gi-dikki n-akujoa,* then returned they ;

2) Sm. *adikki-hi,* footprints, track ;

d) *adiki-loko,* instead of, in the room of ; after-in.

l-isiroko l-andakota kiana ba t-adikiloko, and (he) closed up the flesh instead thereof (Gen. II, 21), *l-ici Herod adikiloko,* [Archelaus did reign] in the room of his father Herod, *da-siki fa bu-muni n b-amuni-sia bia, bu-sanoci k-amuni-n bia b-adikiloko n,* he would (I will) give it to him (thee) for a possession, and to his (thy) seed after him (thee), *waii icinoci n-adikiloko-ci,* our fathers that came after (them) ;

e) *adiki,* the lobe of the ear ;

f) 1) *adibeyo,* belly, womb (§ 124) ;

2) *to-moroa t-adibo-loko n-adeka amudikile-hi jiamutu,* but they discovered a certain creek with a shore ;

g) 1) *adina,* arm, wing, Sm. *adena,* lower part of the arm, from the elbow unto the hand (A. M. § 182, 25) ;

2) *adinabo,* branch (A. M. § 182, 26) ;

3) *adina-mun,* near to, in the vicinity of.

t-adina-mun-ci, her neighbours (L. I, 58), *w-asiga-te t-adinamun-tu bawhu yuho mun, yumun d-ajia-n bia ba,* let us go into the next towns, that I may preach there also ;

4) *ajinamu-, ajinama,* to stand, to rest (the ark upon the mountain of Ararat).

§ 87. *Aji*, more than.

ᵃ) *b-a( )alikibitoa hiaro-no aji*, blessed art thou among women, *kia isogo-tu wabu barin to-makwa t-isi aji*, which indeed is the least of all seeds, *na-bolli goba kiana Mysia aji*, *Troas mun andi-n*, and they passing by Mysia came down to Troas ;

ᵇ) *kalime-hi sanoci aji-ka ka-ieniko-n toho ororo sanoci na-kirikia o-loko*, for the children of this world are in their generation wiser than the children of light, *a-kota-he aji-ka kokke-hu, koro ? eke-hu aji-ka ifirohu, koro ?* is not the life more than meat, and the body than raiment ? *t-aji-n bia hu*, and subdue it (Gen. I, 28), *kena l-aji goba n-ajia-n priest-no afudyi-no ajia-n bajia*, and the voices of them and of the chief priests prevailed, *n-aji-ti (ti*, § 110) *goba bajia na-muni kwawa*, and there was also a strife among them ; other examples, see § 149 ᵇ).

§ 88. ᵃ) *jia*, S. *dia*, doing as, becoming as.

toho jia l-a Adaie-li da-mun, thus hath the Lord dealt with me, *naii jia ho fa koro kiana*, be not ye therefore like unto them, *ajia-hu k-amun-ci jia l-a-n goba a-mairikota-n o-doma ie, a-buriti-ci-no jia l-a goba koro*, for he taught them as one having authority, and not as the scribes, *bilibiliro jia l-a goba ka-raie-n, kena snow jia t-a goba l-eke arira-n*, his countenance was like lightning, and his raiment white as snow (Note the word-order in the Arawak sentence, § 13), *ifili-ci-wabu hui o-koboroko, lihi isogo-ci-wabu jia ma fa*, he that is greatest among you, let him be as the younger ;

ᵇ) *jin*, S. *din*, being as (-*n*, form, comp. in the following example *atiki-di-n* and *bilibiliro ji-n*).

daii adeka goba Satan a-tikidi-n aiomuni warea bilibiliro jin, I beheld Satan as lightning fall from heaven. Other examples in § 1 ;

ᶜ) S. *di-ssia*, to be a custom, a manner ; G. *dai diša-ya ulisebe u-kili mautia anobo-(n*, I am accustomed to rise at daybreak, *l-idišadoa dá-ma*, this man has remained true to me ;

ᵈ) *o-ma-n-jia, o-ma-n-jin*, like.

loko wa-murreta-te wa-ma-n-jin, waii jia-mu-ci bia, let us make man in our image, after our likeness, *Wacinaci o-ma-n jia-mu-ci-n bia i lo-murreta goba i*, in the likeness of God made he him, *imilia-tu ibena to-ma-n-jia ma koro wahadu-tu o-kona bajia*, and the piece that was taken out of the new agreeth not with the old ;

ᵉ) Combinations of *ki jin* and *ki jia* with different particles (comp. § 50).

ki jin ki to-buritwa Adaie-li ajia-n o-loko, as it is written in the law of the Lord (L. II, 23), *b-ahaka-n o-loko-ji Jerusalem mun da-konomun, ki jin ki ba b-ahaka fa da-konomun Rome mun*, for as thou hast testified of me in Jerusalem, so must thou bear witness also at Rome, *ki-jin ki ba Abel anda atenwa-tu l-isikapo-n-isa abu*, and Abel, he also brought of the firstlings of his flock (Gen. IV, 4), *Adaie-li, tanahu b-ikita-kwon-ci b-akoiokota m-aiima-hu abu, b-ajia-n jin ki ba*, Lord, now lettest thou thy servant depart in peace, according to thy word, *ki jin ki goba h-icinoci, ki jin ki ba hui*, as your fathers did, so do ye, *Jesus n-a goba a-iriti-n i ; ki jia l-a-n goba angel a-sa-n o-doma i*, his name was called Jesus, which was so named of the angel, *ki jia l-a kiana a-kudi-n loko a-fitikiti-n*, so he drove out the man (Gen. III, 24), *kena ki-jia tu fa, na-makwa kokki-ci m-akonnaba-ti-ci lihi Prophet ajia-n aboado fa loko-no o-koboroko area*, and it shall come to pass, that every soul, which will not hear that prophet, shall be destroyed from among the people (Acts III, 23), *b-osa bui, ki-jia ba-n-ci onyi-n*, go, and do thou likewise ;

f) *jia-mu-ci*, f. *jia-mu-tu, jia-mo-tu*.

naraha jia-mu-ci omuni-n aiomun isauka o-doma, [suffer little children :] for of such is the kingdom of heaven, *ki-jia-mu-ci Awa k-ansi-n o-doma a-kwaiabo-ci bia lo-mun*, for the Father seeketh such to worship him, *ororo jia mo-tu koro Daii a-sika ho-mun*, not as the world giveth, give I unto you, *ki-o-doma tata-tu onyi-hi tora-jia-mu-tu l-onyi-ka lo-kabo abu ?* [what wisdom is this], that even such mighty works are wrought by his hands, *ki-jia-mu-tu ajia-hu*, a parable, *ki jia mo-tu koro h-icinoci eke goba manna*, not as your fathers did eat manna ;

g) S. *dia-ma-ru* (-ru, § 176).

S. *ipîrru-tu hallira-ru kimissa dia-ma-ru äke*, as it had been a great sheet, lit. great-thing white-thing cloth *diamaru* raiment, *Statuta dia-ma-ru adiâ-hu n-a-ni-benna a-lesedü-n*, and after the (their) reading of the law ;

h) S. *gi-dia* and *hi-ddia, gi-din* and *hi-ddin* = thus ; the *h* indicates "affirmation", but of a milder kind than is indicated by the *k* ; the *g* might possibly have an intermediate meaning (§ 57) :

i) *ha-jia*, thus.

da-sa, ama o-doma ha-jia b-a ? son, why hast thou thus dealt with us ? *ha-jia-t-a-i* (§ 41) *toraha*, suffer ye thus far (L. XXII, 51), *ma-iyurati-n h-a-li naraha ansi, ha-jia|naii*, refrain from these men, and let them alone, *ama o-doma ha-jia-mu-tu ajia-hu d-akonnaba bu-konomun ?* how is it that I hear this of thee ? (L. XVI, 2) ; G. *hadiá t-a séme-ŋ.* (the beverage) is too sweet ;

j) *ha-jia-ki*, gladly, willingly, with longing.

l-ajia-ga na-mun, Ha-jia-ki d-a k-ansi-n toho passover d-iki-n bia ho-ma kari-n o-bora di, and he said unto them, With desire I have desired to eat this passover with you before I suffer ;

k) *bajia*, co-ordinating word ; *ba*, again, *jia*, as.

atenwa-wabu Wacinaci a-murreta goba aiomun, ororo bajia, in the beginning God created the heaven and the earth, *naii ki o-koboroko goba Mary Magdalene, Mary James Joses bajia o-iyunatu, Zebedee sanoci o-iyunatu bajia*, among which was Mary Magdalene, and Mary the mother of James and Joses, and the mother of Zebedee's children. *biama goba kiana ma-kondo-n ie, wadili l-iretu bajia. ma-haburi goba bajia ie*, and they were both naked, the man and his wife, and were not ashamed. *kena na-synagogue o-loko l-ajia goba to-makwa Galilee ororo ajeago-ji man, yauhahu bajia lo-boreda goba.* and he preached in their synagogues throughout all Galilee, and cast out devils. (Note, how *bajia* is attached to *yauhahu*, and not to the verb) ;

¹) *ajia*, to speak.

§ 89. *ada* (§ 20), tree ; also staff, wood (A. M. § 182, 109) ; *ada-fu-ji*, loin ; *ada-na-ina*, shoulder ; *alaiti-adaia*, candlestick, torch (*alaiti*, candle, light, A. M. § 182, 132E) ; *adaia*, to have authority, to be a ruler ; *adaiakiti-*, to honour ; *adaiana-sia*, master, ruler ; *adaili*, sun ;

eda (§ 20, skin, bark (A. M. § 182, 7) ; *idan*, leg (below the knee), Sm. *idê*, gar sein, *adinti-*, gar machen, *idiballe*, smoke-dried meat, *dele*, an anchor, S. *üssa-kebé a-delledoa-hü*, The fair havens ;

o-doma, because, *a-dokoto-*, to show, *a-dokodo-*, to loose, to forgive ; Sm. *u-dúkku*, der Schooss ; Sm., G. *duli*, root (said from cassava and Ichnosyphon) (A. M. § 182, 110A), Sm. *dúrrukoáru*, yam, Dioscorea cayennensis, *kira-hudú-lli*, cotton spindle (*akkürrü-*, to bind), *addura*, to plait, B. *adura*, rib, *m-adure-ci*, the maimed, Sm. *addura-hü*, rib, *adüllebu*, the ribs, *m-adulle-ti*, a maimed person.

CHAPTER XI

T

§ 90. The *t*, in the meaning of "moving towards an object" (with a touch of will-power in it), we have already met with when we considered the construction of the action-words (§ 1). It occurs in a similar meaning in the particle *te* (§ 95), and in a great many words, for which we refer the reader to the Alphabetical Index, especially under *T*.

In some words and particles *ti* alternates with *ci* (phonetically *tsyi*). It is possible that *ti* is especially used if it is necessary to make the *t* principle appear plainly, or if the *t* principle is strongly felt, and *tsyi* etc. where that is not the case. Probably also euphony plays an important part in this phenomenon, e.g. *t-isi* (ph. *t-isyi*), its seed, *t-isa* (ph. *t-isa*), her child, *c-ikisi* (ph. *tsy-ikisyi*), (its) moment, *c-iwi* (ph. *tsy-iwi*), (its) fruit.

T in the meaning of "being active", "asserting oneself", in the verbal nouns ending in *-ci* (f. *-tu*).

T in the meaning of *d*, see §§ 44 f), 45 f), 47, 179 c), and with a similar meaning in the following :

a) 1) *tata-ni ho-loa o-doma*, for the hardness of your heart, *Daii tata-ci*, I was an austere man, *ma-tata-tu ialoko*, a spirit of infirmity, *tata kiana t-adeki-n l-ibici*, and (she) earnestly looked upon him, *to-moroa tata sabu goba l-ajia-n*, but he spake the more vehemently, *aba tata-tu-wabu auaduli*, a tempestuous wind, *tata-tu onyi-hi*, mighty works ;

2) *hui tatabudi-ci o-no-ro*, ye stiffnecked, Sm. *tatabuddi-*, stark sein, hart sein ;

3) *l-itatada goba na-loa*, (he) hardened their heart ;

b) *tata o-kona*, power, force, strength (*o-kona*, § 63 a) 2A) ; a similar construction in *a-iige-sia o-loko*, § 22 e), etc.).

1) *l-ajia-n o-kona tata-ni o-doma*, for his word was with power, *tata da-kona da-siki-n bia n*, I have power to lay it down, *tata ho-kona h-ete-n bia*, are ye able to drink [of the cup, etc.], *tata wa-kona*, we can, *koriliaci ibikidwa goba tata-ci bia o-kona ialoko abu*, and the child grew, and waxed strong in spirit ;

2) *a-tatadi-n na-makwa a-mairikoto-sia-no o-kona*, strengthening all the disciples, *bu-tatadi-n goba lo-kona jin*, as thou hast given him power :

c) *tau*, power (?) in : S. *ka-tau-ti Gouverneur*, most excellent Governor, *bui ka-tau-ti wabu Felix*, most noble Felix, G. *ka-tau-či*, a learned man, a saint ;

T in the meaning of "touched", in the following :

d) Sm. *tétte*, to itch ;

e) *ibici*, S. *ibiti*, lightly touched, § 58 d) 1) ;

f) 1) Sm. *ikitti(-hi)*, eyelash (eye-*iti*) (A. M. § 182, 11) ;

2) Sm. *ittima(-hü)*, moustache, beard (*iti*-mouth) (A. M. § 182, 12) ;

3) *t-itibi*, a tittle (L. XVI, 17), Sm. *ittebe*, a birth-mark, R. *tu-tebe*, "Mongolian spot" ;

4) *t-itibo-ko*, (bird's) nest (A. M. § 182, 111) ;

5) *tibo-kili*, a bush (A. M. § 182, 111).

g) *tere*, Sm. *ittere*, heat.

§ 90A. *Toko*, that which slowly falls or settles.

a) Sm. *tukkudun*, a mud bank in sea, B. *mo-togo*, sand (G. *mo-roli*, mud) ;

b) *a-tokodo-*, to come down, to descend, *a-togodo-tu*, the strangled (Acts XV, 29) ;

c) *o-toko-ro*, flower, G. *thokololo-n*, windfallen unripe fruit ;

d) *a-tok(o-?)*, to devour (fowls eating seed), Sm. *a-ttuku-*, essen mit saugen, z.B. Früchte, G. *a-toko-*, to bite (a snake).

Tik(i), that which quickly falls.

a) *itika*, excrements, rust (A. M. § 182, 13) ;

b) *a-tikidi-*, to fall, to cast, G. to pluck a leaf.

CHAPTER XII

FORMATION OF VERBS, ETC.

§ 91. We may now more closely examine the inner structure of the action-words, of which something has already been said in §§ 1 and 20.

Eke, to eat (§ 171 ᵃ⁾), is used wihout any inflexion, as a transitive verb : *d-eke kiana n*, and I did eat (it), *h-onnaka n*, *h-eke n*, take (it), eat (it) !. In other forms *eki* and *iki* prevail, and it is possible that the last *e* of *eke* is a slight indication that here an *a* ought to be used.

D-eke, I eat, belongs to the type : pronominal prefix — root. The type pronominal prefix — ending or particle (without root), is met with in : *l-a*, he did, *lo fa*, he shall do (§ 28), *d-ibi*, I did (a moment before) (§ 58 ᵃ⁾ ³⁾), *d-ebe*, I have accomplished doing (§ 59 ᵃ⁾ ³⁾).

In *a-ii-*, to weep (A. M. § 182, 150), the root consists only of a long *i* (felt as a sound-imitation ? see, however, A. M. § 182, 151, rain) : *Jesus a-iiya goba*, Jesus wept.

In *a-ti-*, to drink (A. M. § 182, 3), the root consists of a *t* with only traces of a preceding *e* ; *t(i)* indicates the motion of the fluid : *h-eta*, drink, *na-ta goba*, they drank, *da-ti fa*, I (will) drink, *da-tena a-ta-hi*, my blood is drink, *a-ta-kwona-hu*, a cup.

In *a-iibi-*, to leave (§ 58 ᶜ⁾ ²⁾), the root is *ib(i)*, quick, slight appearance (§ 58) : *na-iiba to-makwa*, they forsook all.

S. *akunnu-*, to depart, to go, to walk (Imperative *b-akun-te*, *h-akun-te*, *b-aku-te* ; *-ci* verbal noun *akun-ti*), B. *akona*, to walk, and Sm. *abbunü-*, B. *abone-*, to plant, to sow (A. M. § 182, 145), indicate something like "to be on the earth", the first in an active sense, and the second in a quiet or peaceable way ; comp. *kona* and *bonna*, §§ 63, 64.

The great majority of the verbs have *d, t* or *k* as endings, respectively indicating the principle of "standing", "movement towards an object" "appearing in an active, positive manner", with different vowels. Combinations also frequently occur.

Examples : *praise*, praise, *a-praisedi-*, to praise, *ikisi*, opinion, *ikisidi-*, to judge, *isa*, formed, good, sound, *isadi-*, to heal, *nokonne*, sorrow, *a-nokonnedi-*, to cause sorrow or sadness ;

eke, clothes, wrappage, *eketi-*, to clothe, *kari*, to suffer, *a-kariti-*, to torment, *iri*, name, *iriti-*, to call one's name, *kokke*, life, *a-kokketo-*, to quicken (J. V., 21) ;

a-ti-, to drink, *ma-teki-tu bajia iju*, and the paps which never gave suck ; *onna* (in compounds, § 79 ᵉ⁾), in a fixed place, *onnaki-*, to take (to appear in a fixed place), *onnakidi-*, to lift up, *onnakiti-*. to compel to bear, G. *lu-manikidoa*, he is proud, lit. he-not-lift up-self ;

ime, willingly. *imeko*, readiness, to be ready, *imigodo-*, S. *imekudu-*, to send ;

ie, presumably at one time *ieni*. § 83 a), tongue, *a-ientwa*, to sing, *ieniko*, cleverness, wisdom, *ka-ieniko*, to be clever, subtle, wise, G. to be an eloquent man, a crafty speaker, a poet (the Arawaks make poems), *ienikoto-*, to make wise (comp., however, § 80 b)), G. *ieni-hi*, song, *a-yentoa*, to sing ;

a-forra, to slay, *a-forrakiti-*, to put to death ;

akeri-, to bind, *akeraki*, bond, bands, *akerakiti-*. to cause binding ;

a-siki-. to put, to give, *a-sikiti-* to deliver ;

aici-, to know, *aiciki*, a token, a mark, *aicikiti-*, to warn, to betray ;

itimi, rope, bonds, *a-timiti-*, to bind, *abar-dakabo a-timitiki baka*, five yoke of oxen, Sm. *a-ttimetikitti-*. fest machen lassen ;

o-buri, letters, *a-buriti-*, to write, *a-buritikiti-*, to cause to write ;

aboa, to be ill, foul, *aboadi-*, to destroy, to waste, *aboada-be-tu wolf*, grievous wolves, *aboado-(n-wa)*, to be destroyed, *aboadikiti-*, to condemn, *aboadikito-(n-wa)*, to be condemned, *toho ki aboadikitoa-hu*, and this is the condemnation.

With regard to these forms, Sm. remarks : "Alle ihre Verba können in eine Form gegossen werden, die der Conjugation Hiphil ratione significatus correspondirt ; und davon wird das Passivum gemacht auf die Weise : *amalitin*, machen, *amalitikittin*, machen lassen, *amalitikittúnnua*, gemacht werden." It will be evident now (— see also §§ 4 c), 6 b) —), that this formula does not exactly get to the heart of the matter.

Q. states with more insight : "Activ. *a-ssukussu-(n)*, waschen, Passiv. simplex. *a-ssukussa-hü-(n)* (§ 24), Reciproc. *a-ssukussu-(nn-ua)*, sich selbst waschen, Activ *a-ssukussukuttu-(n)*, waschen machen, oder lassen, Pass. *a-ssukussukuttu-(nn-ua)*, machen, dass man gewaschen wird, wird aber auch oft als ein blosses Passivum gebraucht."

In each of the elements added, the vowel has a meaning of its own. All sorts of combinations occur, but it is a matter of course, that combinations of elements containing the same vowel-principle occur most frequently. Striking examples of this are : *a-tikidi-*, to fall, to cast. *t-itikidi-kiti-n i*, it hath cast him, *a-tokodo-*, to come down, to descend. *lo-dokodokoto-ni n*. and when he had opened it [the book].

It is possible that the wish to obtain harmony between the sounds is of some influence in those cases where the meaning would not thereby be placed in jeopardy.

In the application of the different forms, the Arawak is very precise. e.g. Mt. XXII, 4, Behold, I have prepared my dinner, has been translated by : *H-adeka, da-koto-n d-iibidi( )kita*, lit. Behold, my-dinner I -prepare-caused.

§ 92. Miscellaneous compound forms :

a) With an *-n*, indicating continuation or plurality (comp. the *-n-ci* forms, § 27) between the root and the *d* or *t* : *a-ma-ribe-n-di-*. to cleanse

(§§ 100, 28 d)), *amaro-n-to-*, to threaten (§ 72 a) ²⁾), *Damascus mun ka-sikwa-ci Jew-no lo-m-ajia-n-dikita goba*, (he) confounded the Jews which dwelt at Damascus (*ajia*, to speak) :

b) *to-moroa ika tu Pharisee-no akonnabo-n ma-iaukwa lo ma kiti-n Sadducee-no o-konomun*, but when the Pharisees had heard that he had put the Sadducees to silence, *ama jia wa ma koti fa Wacinaci isauka ? ama wa-siki fa kiana ki-jia t-a-n bia ?* whereunto shall we liken the kingdom of God ? or with what comparison shall we compare it ? *Daii ki-jia-ma koti fa i ka-koborokwa-ci*, I will liken him unto a wise man, *ki-o-doma aiomun isauka ki-jia-ma kotwa abar-li adaie-li-wabu jin*, therefore is the kingdom of heaven likened unto a certain king :

c) *ika tu yuho-li kibi loko-no eragi-n andi-n l-amun, to-makwa bawhu-yuho wa-rea-di-ci*, and when much people were gathered together, and were come to him out of every city (every city from-*di-ci*), *kia na-makwa Asia kono-no a-kwaiabo-sia o-mun tanahu barin, to-makwa ororo ajeago-di-ci bajia*, whom all Asia and the world worshippeth (all earth upon-*di-ci* also) :

d) *ama ibia koro isa u waii l-isanonoci*, we are unprofitable servants. *wakaia a-tekita-kwa-ma-ci na-sa wa omuni n.* woe unto them that give suck, lit. evil drink-cause-yet-with-person their-child own unto it :

S. *waikille*, far, *da-waikilledü-pa|hü*, I will carry you away ;

(B. *kidua*, true, *kidua-n*, verily, *kidua-in.* Amen), S. *kiduaheini-hü u-kunnamün*, [know] the certainty, *ikidduaheindi-.* to expound, to prove, *ikkiduaheinti-.* to give testimony.

§ 93. Reduplication is used in order to indicate "repeatedly" or "several".

to-moroa ika tu ho-kwaiabo-n-wa, m-ajia-n h-a-li kia ki kia ki ajia-hu ausirobu-in, akirikia-no ajia-n jin, but when ye pray, use not vain repititions, as the heathen do, *m-imite-n bia di t-andandadi-n o-doma*. lest by her continual coming she weary me. *akorakorada kwa l-a Peter*, but Peter continued knocking, *l-ahadadadi-kita yuho-ro ajia-hu abu i*. then he questioned with him in many words. *aiimahaimadi-n.* disputing. *onnakennakodwa-tu bara o-horomurrida-n abu.* [a ship] tossed with waves. *wa-malamalada goba Adria bara bo-n-di*. we were driven up and down in Adria. *ka-siri-siri a-u-kili waboroko a-fulifulito fa.* and the rough ways shall be made smooth. *aiomun-tu ororo abolokoloko ka-raia goba*, were the tops of the mountains seen. *m-ausi-n h-a-li aba aba mun bawhu mun i-ro.* go not from house to house. *ma-sogosoko-tu akabo*, unwashen hands (Mk. VII. 2). *k-augi-k-augi-mi-ci*, the brethren. *wariwari*, fan. *bilibili-ro*, the lightning. *tata*, hard. *ibi kibi.* even now. *ibibidi-.* to touch. *-kwawa.* reciprocal. *fotoboto-ri*, nails. *bibici*, four. S. *sibassiba-ru.* waves (*siba*, stone, rock) :

S. *na-ussa kiahañ adiadiadü-n Paulus ahaka-ssiä-bi-kurru ü-jalukku. imitamitadü-n badiä|n.* and (they) spake against those things which were spoken by Paul, contradicting and blaspheming. *ahakahakadü-.* to testify. to dispute (Sm. : viel reden machen). *a-ssimassimadü-.* to cry out (a multitude ; Sm. : to weep over the dead, without tears), *aimaimadu-*, to strive, to threaten repeatedly, *a-ijumujumuda*, to foretell, to prophesy (several prophets), *a-huñahuñadü-*, to murmur, *lu-ijulaijulattü-n-ti n-ansi*, (he) to vex (them), *anianidi-*, to do repeatedly, *a-ssikassikadü-*, to minister (daily, several persons), *akunnakunnadi-*, to travel, to pass through a country, *a-ijahaijahaddü-*, to pass through a country, *a-lammalaṁ adü-*, to be tossed (a ship by a tempest) ;

Bernau *jumün lui arrada tu-maqua l-amün-tu a-kuttakuttada-hü a-ttatada-hü mu-ttu*, and there he wasted his substance with riotous living (eat-eat drink-drink with) ;

G., see § 212 ff.

The long *a*, indicating duration (action-words *a* group, §§ 3, 5) may also be classed with the reduplications.

CHAPTER XIII

L; R

§ 94. *L* in Arawak generally indicates the principle of "loose", "willing (and able) to move", whilst *r* on the contrary indicates the principle of "fixed", "unable to move", "motion being impeded".

G. Arawak has an *l*, an *r*, and two intermediate consonants ; for the consonant most closely resembling *l*, the sign λ is used ; for the consonant most closely resembling *r*, the sign ǫ is used. It is possible that on further examination no real difference will be found between λ and ǫ.

L and *r* are used in places where the difference is of importance, for instance *-loko*, in (free), *-roko*, in (bound), *kalime*, shining, *karime*, black. It is, however, not clear, why they say *péro*, dog, and *kaǫina*, fowl, *báǫa*, sea.

In a few cases a word in a vocabulary contains an *l* where an *r* might be expected, and vice versa ; presumably these are simple mistakes resulting from indistinct pronunciation.

§ 95. *Te* added to a verbal form, denotes "limited motion" : *t* motion towards an object. *e* slowing down.

Li added to a verbal form, denotes "freely flowing forth" ; *l* loose, *i* principle or quick [1]).

Examples, with *ausa*, to go, or really "to form a void" (§ 130 b)).

a) *ma-heragi-n bena na-muni kwawa ie, n-ausa kiana*, and when they agreed not among themselves, they departed, *h-ausa ho-kona mairia-tu isikwa-hu mun i-ro*, go into the village over against you, *h-ausa, h-ahaka-li John o-mun ba h-akonnabo-sia o-konomun h-adeki-sia o-konomun*, go and shew John again those things which ye do hear and see :

b) *yu warea ki, w-augioci akonnabo-n bena wa-konomun, n-ausa-te asakada-n wa-ma Appii Forum mun*, and from thence, when the brethren heard of us, they came to meet us as far as Appii forum, *b-osa-te da-iinabo*. follow me (Mt. VIII, 22) ;

c) *h-adeka, w-ausa-i-li Jerusalem mun i-ro*, behold, we go up to Jerusalem (Mt. XX, 18), *h-ausa-i-li to-makwa ororo ajeago-ji man, ajia-n sa-tu ajia-hu na-makwa a-murreta-sia-no o-mun*. go ye into all the world, and preach the gospel to every creature (*-i-li* presumably is used, because

---

[1]) B. says in his grammar: "The termination *te* mostly denotes motion towards the speaker, the latter (*li*) from the speaker". Motion towards the speaker is of course a *te* motion; motion away from the speaker is very often a *li* motion, but it may be a *te* motion as well.

the preceding *a* has a durative meaning ; comp. *isa-i-li !* friend !, *ada-i-li,* sun).

An investigation has brought to light that the suffixes *te* and *li* are used absolutely independently of the grammatical gender of the persons concerned.

Other examples.

Adaie-li, b-isada-te u, Lord, save us (Mt. VIII, 25), *h-isada-li aboa-ci-no,* heal the sick (Mt. X, 8) ; *b-isika-te da-mun yaha John Baptist isi,* give me here John Baptist's head, *h-isika-te yaha da-muni-n,* bring them hither to me, *b-isika-li adagati-ci bu o-mun (bu-mun ?),* give to him that asketh thee, *ma-iauna h-aucigi-sia ma-iauna h-isika-li ba n,* freely ye have received, freely give ; *h-adagata-li, kena t-isiko fa ho-mun ; h-auada-li, kena h-aucigi fa : ho-korota-li, kena to-torodo fa ho-bora,* ask, and it shall be given you ; seek, and ye shall find ; knock, and it shall be opened unto you ; *ho-mairikota-li ie,* teaching (teach !) them (Mt. XXVIII, 20), *ho-mairikotwa-li kabuia o-loko-tu to-tokoro o-konomun,* consider the lilies of the field, *ore-hi o-rea h-ikitwa-li,* (abstain ye) from fornication, *bu-prophesidoa-te wa-mun, Christ bui, alika i a-fatada bu,* prophesy unto us, thou Christ, Who is he that smote thee ? ; *h-akonnaba-te, h-aiita-te to-konomun,* hear, and understand (Mt. XV, 10), *toho kiana h-aiita-li,* be it known therefore unto you (Acts XXVIII, 28), *m-iki-ni h-a-li,* ye shall not eat, *m-ahalikibi-li hu,* rejoice not.

In the nature of the case, *li* only occurs with the Imperative and in the Present Tense of the Indicative ; *te* on the other hand, occurs with all kinds of forms : *-ba-te* (§ 60 b)), *fa-te, faroka-te* (§ 144), *goba-te, ga-te, l-a-n ka-te, koma-te, ia-te, bena-te, bia-te, bo-te, -n-te* (this form occurs also in sentences with *o-doma*), *a-te, a-ia-te.* Further : *andi-ci ki te bui ?* art thou he that should come ? *d-Adaie-n o-iyu andi-tu-te d-amun ?* [and whence is this to me], that the mother of my Lord should come to me ? *d-ikiduada bui Christ, Wacinaci Aiici, andi-ci ki te ororo ajeago mun,* I believe that thou art the Christ, the Son of God, which should come into the world, *Lihi angel te jiaro, n-a kiana ajia-n,* Then said they, It is his angel (Acts XII, 15), *Cornelius imigodo-sia-no-te wadili adagata Simon isikwa ibici.* the men which were sent from Cornelius had made enquiry for Simon's house.

S. *-l-te, -li-te* :

b-addika-l-te b-a, receive thy sight. *b-ahaka-li-te|de.* or *b-ahaka-l-te|de,* tell me, *b-adepussudoa-li-té,* gird thyself. *hu-üboa-li-té.* refrain (leave). *b-ikittakutta-li-te|i Paulus,* keep thou Paul :

Sm. *bü-jahaddá-te,* or *bu-jahaddâ-l-te, hü-jahaddá-te* or *hü-jahaddâ-l-te,* walk ! *w-anssé-li-te wa-monne-koa-wa.* let us love each other.

§ 96. *Re, i-re,* denotes "no motion".

a) *isa-re b-a ikita-n i.* take care of him (L. X, 35 ; *isa.* good, sound),.. *isa-re l-a adeki-n,* he saw [in a vision] evidently, *isa-re t-a Sa-tu Ialoko ajia-n,* well spake the Holy Ghost, *w-auciga siba a-tago-n-wa isa-re-n,* the prison truly found we shut with all safety. *sa-re t-a Elisabeth o-mun ajia-n.* and (she) saluted Elisabeth, *toraha l-ajia-n bena na-mun. Galilee mun kwa-re l-a bania,* when he had said these words unto them. he abode still in Galilee, *to-moroa a-boredo re ki wa fa-i abar kaiiri o-kona,* howbeit we must be cast upon a certain island. *ajia-n, A-circumsise( )do re ki n-a fa ie.* saying, That it was needful to circumcise them, *ho-makwa hui m-ite-ci. kudi-ci k-onnaka-re-n bajia,* all ye that labour and are heavy laden. *ki-jia-mu-tu-re-n da-siki-n ho-mun o-doma,* for I have given you an example. *kidua-n i-re-n,* Yea (Acts III, 24; *kidua,* true), *kidua-h i-re-n,* yea (L. XIV. 26), *yuho-ro sabu Jesus onyi-sia goba, to-makwa to-konomun a-burito faroka, to-makwa i-re-n kaarta a-burita-sia bia ma-bora-n ma ororo ajeago. d-ikisi-ka. Kidua-in.,* And there are also many other things which Jesus did. the which, if they should be written every one. I suppose that even the world itself could not contain the books that should be written. Amen :

b) *aba-re-n,* straightway. forthwith, anon :

S. *abbâ-ka-ré-n,* suddenly ;

oma-re-n as soon as, immediately ;

c) *ere-hi,* a snare.

§ 97. *-Rea, -ria,* from ; *ea, ia,* § 132.

a) *o-rea, au-rea ;* with pronominal prefix *au-rea, au-ria.*

kena Wacinaci alomosa goba oriroko-ho o-rea kalime-hi. and God divided the light from the darkness. *Adaie-li Wacinaci kiana a-murreta goba loko onabo o-bolisi o-rea.* and the Lord God formed man of the dust of the ground, *kena n-akenakwa a-cirikida-n i bawhu-yuho o-rea.* and (they) rose up, and thrust him out of the city. *Wacinaci akenako-koto-sia a-odo-ci-no o-rea.* whom God hath raised from the dead. *alika naii biama-no au-rea-ci onyi goba l-ici k-ansi-sia ?* whether of them twain did the will of his father ? *to-dokodo fa l-aurea ... lihi koro o-rea to-dokodo fa.* it shall be forgiven him ... it shall not be forgiven him. *bu-wakaia a-dokodwa b-aurea,* thy sins be forgiven thee, *abaren l-esere ausa l-aurea.* and immediately the leprosy departed from him. *abar-dakabo-no n-aurea ka-koborokwa goba,* and five of them were wise, *ika angel akoiwa t-aurea.* and the angel departed from her, *alika-i koro anda ma da-mun. ma-siko-n-wa|tu faroka Da-ci o-rea,* no man can come unto me. except it were given unto him of my Father, *daii ajia-ga ororo o-mun d-akonnabo-sia l-auria.* I speak to the world those things I have heard of him :

b) *a-rea.*

1) *d-onnakia to-bolisi b-akosi o-loko area,* let me pull out the mote out of thine eye, *ho-fadakudi fa wakaukili ho-kuti-roko area.* shake off the dust under your feet, *kena wiru lo-fitikita ki goba ba ark o-loko area.* and again he sent forth the dove out of the ark. *tata-be-ci-o-kona lo-tokodo-kota na-bolliti-kwona-hu ajeago area. kena onabo-ci l-aiomunta.* he hath put down the mighty from their seats, and exalted them of low degree :

2) *yuho sabu-ci, w-asika yaha-rea. ma.* the more part advised to depart thence also. lit. much very-person, we-go here-from. said. *l-onnaki-n bia*

loko-no ajia-n kari-kona-tu da-kona rea, to take away my reproach among
men, *kena ajia-hu k-akonnaki goba-te aiomun bonna rea,* and a voice came
from heaven ;

   3) *o-kona-ria,* for the sake of.

   a-sorokodo-tu yuho-li o-kona-ria, [the blood] which is shed for many,
kia o-kona-ria, for which [hope's] sake [I am accused], *to-moroa alika-i
jiali a-boridi fa lo-kokke-wa Daii o-kona-ria,* but whosoever will lose his
life for my sake, *wakaia ororo o-muni n, onyikita-hu wakaia-hu o-kona-ria,*
woe unto the world because of offences ;

   c) *wa-rea, wa-ria ; wa,* distant, § 121.

   1) *Daii adeka goba Satan a-tikidi-n aiomuni warea,* I beheld Satan ...
fall from heaven (comp. *kenbena, h-adeka,ajia-hu aiomuni o-rea ajia goba,*
and lo a voice from heaven, saying), *isada-hu Jew-no warea-n o-doma,* for
salvation is of the Jews (J. IV, 22), *John baptism warea, l-onnako-n-wa
w-aurea o-bora,* beginning from the baptism of John, unto that same day
that he was taken up from us, *kia ikisi warea,* and from that hour (J. XIX,
27), *tanahu warea,* from henceforth, *abar-timen hour warea,* now from the
sixth hour [there was darkness]. *na-iakatwa kiana Adam l-iretu mi-ci
Adaie-li Wacinaci isibo warea,* and Adam and his wife hid themselves from
the presence of the Lord God, *aba-warea-ci goba di,* I was a stranger,
Thessalonica kon-di Macedonia warea-ci lihi, a Macedonian of Thessalonica
(he), *aba mihu Alexandria warea-tu,* a ship of Alexandria, *abar hiaro
Samaria waria-tu anda goba a-soadi-tu oniabu,* there cometh a woman of
Samaria to draw water, *lihi-ki atenwa waria d-ajia-sia ho-mun jin ki,* (he
is) even the same that I said unto you from the beginning, *ororo warea-ci-n
ka hu, ororo k-ansi koma t-amuni-sia-no ; to-moroa ororo waria-ci-n koro
o-doma hu ... ororo m-ansi ma hu,* if ye were of the world, the world would
love his own : but because ye are not of the world ... the world hateth you ;

   2) *yu warea w-ausi-n bena,* and when we had launched from thence
(§ 123) ;

   d) *ma-i-ria, a-ma-i-ria, m-i-rea : m-a* the inferior, *i-ria* from (?).

   Lybia ororo kono-no Cyrene mairia, and in the parts of Libya, about
Cyrene, *d-onnakiti fa kiana hu Babylon a-mairia sabu,* I will carry you
away beyond Babylon, *kena bu-pesidi fa n to-loko mairia t-iabo mairia bajia
pesi abu,* and (thou) shalt pitch it within and without with pitch, *abar-li
l-iisa mairia, abar-li lo-baro mairia,* [they crucify] the one on his right hand.
and the other on his left, *d-iisa mairia, da-baro mairia,* [to sit] on my right
hand, and on my left, *b-osa da-iiabo mirea, Satan,* get thee behind me, Satan;

   e) *o-kona mairia,* over against.

   h-ausa ho-kona mairia-tu isikwa-hu mun i-ro, go into the village over
against you, *Cilicia Pamphylia o-kona mairia-tu bara w-atima-n bena,* and
when we had sailed over the sea of Cilicia and Pamphylia, *omuni-ga
w-ausi-n Crete o-rea Salmone o-kona mairia,* we sailed under Crete, over
against Salmone ;

   f) S. *akudoa l-a-ni-ka taha-maria jaha-maria na-ssiqua u-llukkumün,* entering into every house, *lui kéwai a-ijahadda-kubá jaha-maria taha-maria*, who went about :

g) Sm. *akkuaria*, der Breite nach gegenüber.

§ 98. *Lia* denotes something newly arisen.

ibikido-(n-wa), to grow, *ibikido-lia b-aha-ni ka*, when thou wast young, *ibikido-lia-ci*, a young man, *ibikido-lia-be-ci*, young men, *ibikido-lia-tu*, maid, *burigo sa ibikido-lia-tu*, a colt, the foal of an ass ; *korilia-ci*, newly born, babe, infant ; *imi-lia*, new ;

Sm. *hemé-ru-llia-ttu*, a woman in childbed (*hemëu*, to bring forth a child) ; *pülli-lia*, shrubbery (*pülli*, to grow) ;

S. *ibikiddu-lliä-tti*, a young man, *abba-nu ibikiddu-llia-nnu*, the young men ; *üüssadükittu-liä-ti*, (the man which had been healed) ; *a-ssukussa-lia-ñu*, the persons that had newly been baptized (also : *a-ssukussu-tiä-li*): *andi-liä-tti-kubá-li Italia-waria*, lately come from Italy :

v. C. *bikidó-la-toe Maria*, the virgin Mary.

§ 99. *-L-*, to become soft or fluid ; easily removable.

a) *bele-ci aboa-ci*, a man sick of the palsy :

ebeli-, to lick, Sm. *ebelti-*, to soften, to melt, *ebêldi-*, to suck honey, *béltiri*, cassava-paste, a cassava-beverage, R. *beltiri*, do., *bele-tto*, anything soft or jelly-like ;

b) *kolo*, to be corrupt (decomposed, Acts XIII, 35-37), *a-koldo-*, to dip a sop (J. XIII, 26, 27), Sm. *kullu*, vom Wasser aufgeweicht sein : faul sein, verfaulen, *a-kulludu-*, *a-kuldu-*, durchweichen :

bA) Sm. *kule*, G. *khole*, to be weak. Sm. *a-kullebettü-*, to divide, to cleave ;

bB) G. *da-kuliyĭ*, my arm is muscular, *kuliŝi*, tangled or curled hair. Sm. *u-kúllissi*, a woman's knot of hair ;

c) *aluiti-*, to anoint ;

d) *t-isaradi fa i tule-n*, it will grind him to powder. Sm. *tüllüla*, fein sein. S. *(ü-)ka-ttulle-hü*, dust :

e) Sm. *a-ssíllikidü-*, to melt. B. *a-silaki-*, to throw (dust into the air) :

f) 1) *ala*, Sm. *hála*, footstool (Indian seat, bench) :

2) Sagot *kouli-ala*, I. Th. *coori-alla*. Sm. *kulj-ara*, canoe, corial : probably : *ala*, movable thing, with the character or likeness of a tortoise, Sm. *hikkuli*. Perhaps connected herewith : Sm. *kureháre*, a certain tree, very suitable for making canoes ;

3) G. *hála-lu*, R. *hará-ro*, spatula, stirrer, pot-spoon :

g) Sm. *mánnaka*, manicole-palm, Euterpe oleracea, *mannak-ola*, the wood when it has been split (for making hedges, walls, etc.) ; *oa-la*, a splinter :

h) G. *tala*, lower jaw ;

i) G. *da-sále*, ancle, Sm. *adenna-ssalle*, elbow, *ahara-ssale*, shoulder-blade.

§ 100. *Ri*, fixed.

isa-ri b-a-li ! farewell ! (also *isa-kibi h-a-li !* fare ye well !) ;

d-ahaki-n bia da-ri-wa ie. [let me go] bid them farewell. *w-ahaki-n bena wa-muni-kwawa wa-ri-wa,* and when we had taken our leave one of another, *l-ahaka-ga l-augioci l-iri-wa,* (he) took his leave of the brethren, *to-moroa l-ahaka l-iri-wa ie,* but (he) bade them farewell ;

iri, a name ; *imirita,* to reproach, to revile, to rail :

airi, tooth (A. M. § 182, 19) ; Sm. *ardi-,* to bite ;

kaiiri, island (A. M. § 182, 71) ;

iribe, uncleanness, *iribe-ci ialoko,* unclean spirits, *a-ribeti-,* to pollute, to defile, to profane, *a-maribendi-,* to cleanse ;

a-dirika, a-diriko-(n-wa), to shave oneself ; Dudley *a-rke-ano, a-rguecona,* scissors ;

a-iyeheriti- ... to-bara, to sheer (its-hair) (*iyehe,* A. M. § 182, 10) ;

ika tu bu-iwariki-dikiti-ni n, and when thou hast opened his mouth (a fish, Mt. XVII, 27).

§ 101. a) *Ribo, rebo, eribo, o-rebo,* waterside, without motion.

1) *lo-bollita goba bara rebo mun,* (he) sat by the sea side, *na-makwa loko-no ajinama goba t-eribo mun,* the whole multitude stood on the shore, *biama mihu l-adeka kiraha ribo mun,* and (he) saw two ships standing by the lake, *Jesus kiana m-ite-ci a-iadi-n jia ma goba a-bolliti-n a-ciga-oniabu o-rebo-tu ajeago,* Jesus therefore, being wearied with his journey, sat thus on the well ;

2) *kena l-iinata ki goba a-mairikota-n bara ribo kona,* and he began again to teach by the sea side, *Asia ororo eribo kona w-eweladoa ti-ka,* meaning (we wished) to sail by the coasts of Asia, *na-dokodwa kiana yu warea, a-welado-n-wa Crete eribo kona,* loosing thence, they sailed close by Crete ;

3) *a-ribota,* to land :

b) *rifu,* waterside, with motion (?) ; only found in the following example : *ika tu Jesus akona-n Galilee bara rifu-ji,* and Jesus, walking by the sea of Galilee.

§ 102. *Ro, i-ro,* stopped.

a) *h-adeka, imita-robu-mi-ci di hui, h-abokwa-li ia ; aboado-ro ho fa bajia,* behold, ye despisers and wonder, and perish :

b) *ama ibia ajinama kwa h-a adeki-n aiomun bonna-ro ?* why stand ye gazing up into heaven ? *bui bajia, Capernaum, onnakido-tu aiomun bonna-n i-ro, a-tokodo( )koto fa hell o-mun i-ro,* and thou, Capernaum, which art exalted unto heaven, shalt be brought down to hell, *Jacob ausa goba Egypt mun i-ro kiana,* so Jacob went down into Egypt (comp. *kena adaia-hu bia l-isika i Egypt ororo mun,* and he made him governor over Egypt). *kokke-hu o-muni-ro-tu waboroko,* the ways of life, *b-itikida-te b-uaiya yaraha-rea onabo-muni-ro,* cast thyself down from hence, *abar-timen hour warea oriroko-ho goba to-makwa ororo ajeago-ji. bibici-timen hour o-muni-ro,* now from the sixth hour there was darkness over all the land unto the ninth hour, *biama-no loko-no amoda goba temple o-lokomun i-ro na-kwaiabo-n-wa bia, aba-li Pharisee, aba-li publican,* two men went up into the temple to pray ; the one a Pharisee, and the other a publican. *kena na-makwa loko-no ausa l-ibici-ro*, and all the multitude resorted unto him :

ᶜ) (comp. *tu*, § 55 ᵇ⁾ ⁴⁾).

yumun i-ro tu Daii ausi-n, mamari-ga hui andi-n, whither I go, ye cannot come ;

ᵈ) (comp. *amunte*, § 71 ᵇ⁾ ⁵⁾ III⁾).

Galilee warea yaha mute-ro, beginning from Galilee to this place (L. XXIII, 5), *yaha-mute-ro h-adeka-te ! jiaro ; taha-ro h-adeka ! jiaro, na fa koro ajia-n*, neither shall they say, Lo here ! or, lo there ! (L. XVII, 21), *m-andi-n d-a-n bia-te yaha munti-ro a-soada ibici*, neither (that I) come hither to draw [water], *Rabbi, alika b-anda-te yaha munte-ro ?* Rabbi, when camest thou hither ?

S. *jaha-mute-ru*, hither [he that came], *kiani-benna na-llumussâ-pa ju-waria, jaha-mute-ru na-ssikâ-n-ti d-äme*, and after that shall they come forth, and serve me in this place ;

ᵉ) *toro ; to*, motion coming to rest, *ro*, stopped, in the following :

¹) *toro-tu ada*, a corrupt tree ;

²) ¹) *hajiatai toho wiwa, da-cigi-n bia c-ikira-ji, t-itika* (excrements) *bajia da-siki-n bia to-tora-ji*, let it alone this year also, till I shall dig about it, and dung it ;

II) *Jesus a-burrida-tu-n o-toro-mun lo-iyu ajinama*, now there stood by the cross of Jesus his mother, *a-mairikota-sia l-ansi-sia bajia ajinamu-n lo-toro-mun*, and the disciple standing by, whom he loved :

III) Sm. *ú-tturu*, the whole foot, handle :

³) *a-torodo-*, to lay down, to fall down (worshipping), *a-torodo-kwona-hu*, a bed.

§ 103. ᵃ) *O-loko*, in (not fixed) ; *l*. loose, *o* space, *ko* faculty, power, place.

Examples, see §§ 5 ᶜ⁾, 12, 10 :

ᵇ) *roko*, in (fixed) ; *r* not able to move, *o* space.

l-onnaka l-adina-rok-oa kiana ie, and he took them up in his arms, *lo-wariwari-a lo-kabo roko ka*, whose fan is in his hand, *aba-no a-fatada goba na-kabo roko abu i*, and others smote him with the palms of their hands, *ho-fadakudi fa wakaukili ho-kuti-roko area*, shake off the dust under your feet ;

ᶜ) ¹) *abo-loko*, on the top of ; *abo* appearance in space, *loko*, to be in a free manner at a place.

kena hihi aboloko l-isika goba n, and (he) put it on a reed, *t-aboloko warea onabo-mun-i-ro*, [the veil was rent] from the top to the bottom, *kenbena temple isi aboloko t-isika i*, and (he) setteth him on a pinnacle of the temple ;

²) the same principle appears in *aboloka-* (or *ga-*) :

l-itikida goba l-aboloka muni-ro, and (he) falling headlong, *n-ausa l-abu aiomun-tu ororo abologato-n-wa mun … na-boredi-n bia i l-aboloka muni-ro*, (they) led him unto the brow of the hill … that they might cast him down headlong, *abologato-n-wa bara rako-mun*, [the herd ran] down a steep place into the sea ;

d) *abo-roko*, at the outside.

a-ta-kwona-hu karubo bajia aboroko-ji ho-maribendi-n o-doma, to-moroa to-loko ibe kwa ma k-itesia-sia abu k-ikiha-sia abu, for ye make clean the outside of the cup and of the platter, but within they are full of extortion and excess, *atenwa a-ta-kwona-hu o-loko-ji karubo o-loko-ji bu-maribenda banyia, t-aboroko-ji maribe-ni-n bia bajia*, cleanse first that which is within the cup and platter, that the outside of them may be clean also ;

e) S. *aku* and *aku-lugku*, in (fire), B. *ako-loko*, in (*ikihi*, fire, *balisi*, ash, *ibiki*, wound, and perhaps other words). Presumably *ikihi* etc. indicate something tiny or slight, thin, or a principle (ending : *i*), and *ako* (see § 128), the principle of "entering into" has to be added before -*loko* can be applied.

kenbena ikihi akoloko mun to-boredwa, and (it, the tree, is) cast into the fire, *a-bolliti-n wara-uara-tu eke-hu abu balisi akoloko*, sitting in sackcloth and ashes (comp. *lihi a-baptize()da ſa hu Sa-tu Ialoko abu, ikihi abu*, he shall baptize you with the Holy Ghost, and with fire), *l-ausa kiana l-ibici, akera-n l-ibiki, a-sonko-n oili, wine bajia t-akoloko-ji*, and (he) went to him, and bound up his wounds, pouring in oil and wine ;

S. *Paulus a-hurrudukuttu-n benna ihime-wa, a-ssiki-n hikkihü aku badja|n, abba karri-tu wuri anda t-akulugku-waria Paulus ü-kkabbu u-kunna*, and when Paul had gathered a bundle of sticks, and laid them on the fire, there came a viper out of the heat, and fastened on his hand ;

f) *ari-loko*, in (between).

hihi bajia na-sika goba lo-kabo ariloko-ji, and (they put) a reed in his right hand ; Sm. *arilükku*, zwischen, *l-ábuna arilukku*, zwischen seinen Knochen ; S. *n-akunna abba waburukku üssiqua arilukku-tu u-llukku-di*, (they) passed on through one street, *Sondaka arilukku*, [that it might be preached] the next sabbath ;

g) *i(y)a-loko*, presumably means : *ia*, the free being, the essence (§ 132), *loko*, to be in a free manner at a place.

1) *a-dokota-sia bia lihi, ajia-sia iyaloko*, for a sign which shall be spoken against (no other example has been found with B.) ; S. *Gott ü-jalukku*, [to fight] against God, *Hebräer-nu ü-jalukku*, [a murmuring] against the Hebrews ;

2) *a-ialokoto-*, to change ;

3) *l-ialoko ialokodo bia*, [give] in exchange for his soul, S. *Judas ü-jalukkudu-wa*, (in the place of Judas), *lü-jalukkud-oa*, in his stead ;

4) S. *a-ijalukkududü-*, to build again (Acts XV, 16) ;

h) *o-kobo-roko*, among ; *ko*, the active, positive being (comp. *o-kona*, § 63), *bo*, without motion, in rest, (§ 62), *roko*, in (fixed) ; see also § 128 ^k).

kena ka-sikwa goba waii o-koboroko i, and (he) dwelt among us, *Peter bajia a-bollita na-koboroko*, Peter (also) sat among them : see also example, § 1 ;

i) derivations from *o-loko* :

1) *a-lokodo-*, to partake in, to part, *a-lokodo-tu iehi*, cloven tongues, *ka-lokodo-tu*, [a room] prepared, *ma-lokodo-tu*, desolate, *isauka* ... *ma-lokodo fa*, kingdom ... is brought to desolation, *l-iri a-lokodo-n-wa o-doma*, for his name was spread abroad ;

2) *l-isikwa a-malokododo-ia*, let his habitation be desolate, *a-malokododa-hu*, the desolation, *a-malokododa-tu o-bolli-tu*, the abomination of desolation passing ;

3) *c-ibiloko*, its breadth, *k-ibiloko-tu*, wide, broad, *m-ibiloko-tu*, strait, narrow (a way, a gate), *Wacinaci ajia-n k-ibiloko sabu ka kiana*, and the word of God increased, *k-ibiloko-u-kili*, the firmament, *ibilokoto-, ibilogoto-*, to make broad, to spread, to straw ;

4) Sm. *u-llukkude*, in the hand, *da-llukkude*, my staff.

§ 104. *Ra*, a definite place (in time-bound reality), generally at some distance from the speaker.

a) *ka-raia*, to appear, to be born ; *t-iraia*, the appearance (of things). *ka-raia-kona*, [he increased] in stature, *lo-maraiadwa*, he vanished. S. *ü-raija*, outward aspect ; also : a vision, a sight :

b) 1) I) *hara, ara*, to be spent, ended, accomplished :

II) *ma-hara*, quickly, with haste, *ma-hara kibi*, with all speed, immediately, *ma-hara b-a-te, ma-hara h-a-te*, go to (Gen. XI, 3, 4), *ma-hara h-a-te d-ibici, ho-makwa hui m-ite-ci*, come unto me, all ye that labour :

III) *haradi-*, to spend :

IV) *aradi-*, to make fully, to complete (a journey, a day, a repayment) ;

2) 1) *herre-n loko-no o-doma*, for the press [of the multitude] ;

II) *a-herrati-n bajia bu*, and [they] press thee :

III) *ka-heraka*, to keep company, to be friends with. G. *ka-kŏrkŏya to kúta*, animal species, *ka-körku-ada*, kind, *ka-kŏrŏkŏ-ya|da ye*, they are kind (*k* instead of *h*. comp. § 88ʰ)) ;

IV) *heragi, heraki, eragi*, to be together. G. *hüreka|de*, I am constipated ;

V) *a-herakidi-, a-herakida*. S. *a-hürkida*, to come together, to gather (together) ;

VI) *a-muirika*, Sm. *a-mühürka*, to be choked (under water) ;

VII) *akera, akere*, to bind, *akeri-*, to entangle ; (*k* instead of *h*. comp. § 88 ʰ)) ;

VIII) Sm. *erekê*, aufräumen, *erekedi-* bewahren, B. *eregi, erigi*, to root up, to gather up (the tares in the field) :

IX) *aranta*, to mix. S. *a-hürruküda-ti ü-ijuhu k-arrana-nɩ-bu Phariseer-nu, Sadduceer-nu u-mamünnikoawa*, the one part were Sadducees, and the other Pharisees :

c) *ra-bu, ra-bo, ra-ba*, in the following words, indicates the ͵(opposite)

side ; *ra*, yonder, *bu*, appearance ; comp. *re-bo*, *ri-bo*, waterside, § 101,
oalabaw, the other side, § 120 c) 3).

1) *(e, i)rabudiki*, *(i)rabodogo*, against, towards (on meeting).

na-makwa bawhu-yuho kono-no a-fitikida goba ausi-n Jesus erabudiki,
and, behold, the whole city came out to meet Jesus, *auaduli wa-rabuddiki-n
o-doma*, because the winds were (our) contrary, *abaren a-odo-ci-sikwa
o-loko area abar-li yauhahu k-amun-ci anda l-irabudiki*, immediately there
met him out of the tombs a man with an unclean spirit (Mk. V, 2), *lo-
tokodo-n bena t-eribo mun, abar-li l-irabodogo-ci bawhu-yuho warea
auciga i, wakili warea yauhahu k-amun-ci lihi*, and when he went forth to
land, there met him out of the city a certain man, which had devils long
time (L. VIII, 27), *ka-rabudika-tu bara n-aucigi-n bo*, and falling into a
place where two seas met, *ka-rabudika-ga n ajia-n. wakaia wabu-n*, con-
tradicting and blaspheming ;

2) *t-arbara-n*, (its, a paddle's) broadside ; Sm. *k-árraba*, Carapa
guianensis, the timber of which is very suitable for making the washboards
of canoes, etc. ;

3) R. *sarapa*, anything doubled ;   three-pronged arrow, double-
barreled gun ;

cA) 1) G. *salábadi-*, to square wood ;

G. *walába*, Eperua falcata, the wood of which is very cleavable and
is used in town for roof-shingles ;

G. *sálabalaba to-kónde*, a six-sided pencil ;

oalabaw, the other side, § 120 c) 3) ;

2) G. *sapa-ŋ*, smooth (a table) ;

G. *sábadi-, sábasabadi-*, to trample flat grass or shrubs, to wash by
beating with a piece of wood, *ada sábada da-kabo*, a piece of wood struck
my hand ;

sapakāna, a long wooden sword ;

d) *k-aiima-ci-no bu-mun a-cigi-n b-arama-kon-di akausakiti-n*, that thine
enemies shall cast a trench about thee, *a-odo-ci-sikwa arama-kona*, [Mary
stood] at the sepulchre, R. *t-arama-kon-di*, the lateral edges of a fan,
Sm. *n-akúnna húrruru áruma u-kun-di*, we (they?) sail along the coast.
kúljara áruma, the side of the canoe ;

e) *t-itagara*, (its) wall ; *a-tagi-*, to cover, to close, to shut ;

f) 1) *l-i-raha, t-o-raha, na-raha, y-a-raha* (§§ 44, 45) and *t-o-ra*.

kenbena ika tu tora-jia t-a-n ajia-n. and when she had thus said, *l-augici
fa i tora-jia-n-ci onyi-n*, (he) shall find (him) so doing, *tora-jin koro
publica-no onyi-ka* ? do not even the publicans the same ?

2) G. *toho yadowa dai-ni* (§ 78 e) 1)) *ra-da*, this knife belongs to me ;

g) (*y-*, see §§ 45, 123).

yara, a hedge ;

Sm. *jurada*, barbecue, rafter (A. M. § 182, 51) ;

bawhu-yura, a beam (house-tiebeam) ;

R. *to-yuranni*, wooden float ;

yura ... ansi, to hasten, *a-iyurati- ... ansi,* to trouble ; see § 80 b) ;

aiyurako-, aiyuraka, to draw, to hale, *oniabu kiana aiyura-kwa,* and the waters asswaged ;

Sm. *jura-hü,* the longing ;

h) *ibara,* to remain, to be left.

§ 105. *O-bora ; bo* in rest, *ra* a definite place.

a) room, place.

1) *b-isika lihi o-bora,* give this man place, *ho-korata-li, kena to-torodo fa ho-bora,* knock, and it shall be opened unto you, *kena a-korati-ci o-bora to-toroda fa,* and to him that knocketh it shall be opened, *ka-bora kwa t-a bajia,* yet there is room, *ki-o-doma ma-bora goba ie,* insomuch that there was no room to receive them ; S. *na-bulleda na-kkabbura u-ria baddia je,* and (they) expelled them out of their coasts ;

2) *a-maboradi-,* to throng ; Sm. *a-kabburratikitti-,* to make broad or wide ;

b) a certain point of time (indicated by the pronominal prefix or object-word) in the future.

kena tanahu d-ahaka-ga ho-mun t-andi-n o-bora, now I tell you before it come, *kena tanahu d-ahaka bi ho-mun to-bora,* and now I have told you before it come to pass, *ororo m-ansi faroka hu, h-aiita m-ansi t-a-n goba di, m-ansi t-a-n o-bora hu,* if the world hate you, ye know that it hated me before it hated you, *kenbena, h-adeka, kasakabo man ho-ma di, ororo a-iibo-n-wa o-bora-n,* and, lo, I am with you alway, even unto the end of the world, *andi-ci da-iinabo a-sikoa da-bora-ci bia ; da-bora-n goba o-doma i,* he that cometh after me is preferred before me : for he was before me, *to-moroa oaboddi-ci t-ebo-n-wa o-bora isado fa,* but he that endureth to the end shall be saved, *ika tu omuni-n c-iwi ikisi o-bora,* and when the time of the fruit drew near, *d-adaie-n k-ibena l-andi-n o-bora,* my lord delayeth his coming, *kabuea mun goba lo-bora-ji l-aiici,* now his elder son was in the field, *aba-li jiali koro da-simakiti-sia na-bora ikisidi fa da-koto-n,* none of those men which were bidden shall taste of my supper, *kena to-bora-tu a-fitikidi-n himi b-onnaka,* and take up the fish that first cometh up, *to-moroa ika tu na-bora-ci andi-n,* but when the first came (Mt. XX, 10), *to-moroa yuho-li na-bora-ci n-adiki-ci fa, kena n-adiki-ci na-bora-ci fa,* but many that are first shall be last ; and the last shall be first :

c) *o-bora-mun.*

na-bora mun n-anda kiana, and (they) outwent them, *lihi-ki iibidikiti fa b-abonaha bui o-boramun,* which shall prepare thy way before thee. *bawhu-sibo sikapo o-boramun Daii,* I am the door of the sheep. *k-ansi goba ie t-ebo-n-wa o-boramun,* he loved them unto the end.

§ 106. *Ikira-ji, ikira-di.* round about.

yara l-isika goba c-ikira-ji, and hedged it round about. *c-ikira-ji-tu ororo.* the country round about, *Galilee ikira-ji-tu ororo.* the region round about Galilee, *n-ikira-di-ci,* (they) that dwelt round about them. *a-bolliti-ci l-ıkira-di-ci,* them which sat about him, *l-adeka l-ikira-di-ci ibici kiana,* and he looked round about.

§ 107. *Ra* is also used in order to indicate, that something which has the nature of a liquid, is here considered as "a definite place".

a) *-rako, -irako,* in (a fluid).

kena abaren l-amodi-n oini-rako warea, and straightway (he) coming up out of the water, *a-tobadi-n nete bara rako-mun,* casting a net into the sea, *bara irako-tu himi,* the fish of the sea (comp. *b-osa bara mun,* go thou to the sea), *Jordan irako,* [to baptize] in Jordan, *aciga irako-mun,* [to fall] into the ditch ;

b) (comp. *oini ... iki,* to rain).

1) *oniabu ma-kira goba,* the waters were dried up, *ororo ma-kira,* the face of the ground was dry ;

2) *ikira,* tears ;

3) *kiraha,* a pool, a lake (A. M. § 182, 69) ;

4) *ura,* juice (A. M. § 182, 2), see also § 125 b) ;

5) *egura,* root (of a plant or tree) ; *abona-gira-hu,* a herb, see § 125 b) ;

6) *bara,* sea (A. M. § 182, 70) ;

7) *o-barra,* hair, see § 64 a) 4) ;

c) connected with the preceding :

S. *Jesus k-ansi-ssia-nnu akujabara- koaré n-a Gott u-mün lu-kunnamun akujaba-ra,* prayer was made without ceasing of the church unto God for him, *abba-nu ka-ijahadda-ra-ké rubu-mu-tti Judu-ñu,* certain of the vagabond Jews.

§ 108. *Ra* in the following words can be explained as indicating "a definite place", but it may also be sound-imitation.

araga, to cut off, *aragakoto-,* to separate, to divide ;

aterakidi-, to rend ;

a-iharakidi-, iharakidi-, to tear, *a-iherakido-(n-wa),* to break, intransitive (a net) ;

akurradi-, akurrada, to break ;

a-korati-, to knock, to buffet ;

akorakali, thunder ;

atarata-hu airi-sibo, gnashing of teeth ;

maraka, rattle (see also § 117 d) 2)).

§ 108A. By the combination of a free movement (*l* principle) and a restraining force (*d* principle), a couple of forces may arise which causes rotation. This accounts for the use of the *r* in words expressing a rotary movement.

a) see § 120 e) 1, 2) ;

b) 1) *aure-ci o-loa ikirikia,* perversed generation, *haure-ci-no,* those that were maimed ;

2) *l-a()aurida goba Galilee ororo mun i-ro,* he turned aside into the

parts of Galilee, Sm. *aordü-*, *aorda*, to spin, G. *to úri auǫoda*, the snake lies coiled up ; *yáho áurodo-(η*, to roll up a ball of string ;

c) *lo-uribisa*, he rolled, *a-uribi-sia*, rolled [the stone of the sepulchre]. G. *to úri ka-lebetoa*, the snake lies coiled up ;

d) *k-aru-bo*, a platter, Sm. *karrupairo*, snail-shell, G. *da-kérosa no*, I draw a çircle, *a-kerosó-to*, a circle, *karusa*, feather headdress :

e) G. *ka-ranalana-tu a-yáti-n*, to draw flourishes ;

f) *oraro*, S. *wuraru*, a cloud (comp. G. *úraroni*, saliva, Sm., R. *haru*. starch) ;

g) *hori*, S. *wuri*, snake (A. M. § 182, 41) ;

h) Sm. *a-ssürdü-*, to spin.

CHAPTER XIV

H

§ 109. The *h* is used in Arawak in order to indicate "gentle affirmation"; in some cases it means "to exhale"; in *ahe*, yes, both these meanings are included. In a few words the *h* has been found to alternate with *g* and *k* (§§ 88 h), 104 b) 2)).

ahe ! yea ! *ibi-ka bajia ie oaboddi-n ahe b-a-ni o-bora*, and now are they ready, looking for a promise, lit. ready-is also they waiting yes thine doing future-moment ;

S. *ehé*, yes, *t-aha-muté rubu t-adiâ-n*, but she constantly affirmed (her words) ; Sm. *ehé*, yes, *ehé-ka|d-a*, I say yes, G. *ehé* (nasalized), yes (A. M. § 182, 132A) ;

Sm. *hüwa*, blow-gun ;

ahaka, to tell, to command, to bring word, *ahaka ... bu-iri* (*l-iri*, etc.), to accuse thee (him, etc.), *misi-tu ahaka-hu*, the law (*iri*, name, *misi*, right) ;

ahaki- ... da-ri-wa (*l-iri-wa*, etc.), I (he, etc.) bid farewell ;

ahakobu-, ahakobo-, to breathe, to rest, *ahakoba-hu*, breath, rest, refreshing ;

l-ahako fa jiaro, when he should have swollen (or ... ; Acts XXVIII, 6), *abar-li ahako-ci*, a certain man, ... which had the dropsy ; S., Sm. *ahaku-(nn-ua)*, to swell ;

Sm. *hanna-hanna-(n)*, dick sein, *da-llerukku ahanna-hanna*, my lips, *d-adikka ahanna-hanna*, my ear-lap, *hán-iju*, gnat, mosquito (= swelling-producing) ;

Sm. *wuini burreha-ttu*, sour, strong paiwari, *báiwaru*, a fermented drink, prepared from cassava (creole *paiwari, tapana*) ; B. *a-boraada*, to leaven, *a-boraada-sia*, vinegar ; Sm. *búrreha*, to be sour, *a-búrahadü-*, to make sour ;

a-haburi, aburi, to be ashamed ;

(a)haduboci, perspiration, G. *hadufuci|ka|de*, I perspire ; Sm. *adu*, parasol ;

S. *ahannuba*, to be awake, to watch, B. *aanabo-, aanubo-*, to awake ;

Sm. *a-ehehebuda, a-eheherudunna*, to yawn ;

habe, S. *hebbe*, to be old (a person), *hebe c-iwi marisi*, the full corn in the ear, G. *hebé-ia č-iwi*, the fruit is ripe ;

ahalikibi, alikibi, joy, to rejoice, *alikibe*, to be glad, *ahalikibito-(n-wa)*, *a(\)alikibito-(n-wa),* to be blessed ; perhaps related to this : G. *tholebé ka i,* he is industrious, *tholebe-či-mekébo(η,* a pushing worker ;

S. *ma-hallê-ti,* (a person) that lacked, Sm. *ma-hallê,* not sufficient ;

S. *ahadakuttu-,* B. *adagato-,* to require, to demand, to ask, to enquire for ;

Sm. *ahabu,* backbone, Sm., S. *ahabula,* footstool, seat, B. *simara-habo.* bow (A. M. § 182, 54) (*simara,* arrow), *akera-n mihu t-ahabo* area. S. *tau abbu na-ttimetta meju ahabu u-kunna,* undergirding the ship ;

t-isiri kiana hatatwa, S. *t-issiri hatta kebé hiddan,* the [ship's] forepart stuck fast, S. *muttuku adiaku na-hattadoa-ma,* lest they should fall into the quicksands ;

aimaha, to curse, to revile (*aiima,* wrath).

§ 110. a) S. *hitti,* B. *ti, hiti,* to desire, to will, to hope, to seek, to be determined to.

S. *nai ké ikissida-hitti-ka|i Stephanus uiniku,* (they examine-wish him St. cleverness, Acts VI, 9), *bu-buruwattü-n-hitti-ssia k-amonaika-ti u-mün.* thine alms (thine help wish-sia poor-one unto, Acts X, 4) ;

B. 1) *liraha Jesus itena h-isika ti-ka wa-kona mun,* and (ye) intend to bring this man's (Jesus') blood upon us, *l-oaiya l-ikalimetwa ti-ka.* (he) seeketh his own glory, *lo-dokoda ti goba l-auroa kiana n aiakatwa o-loko.* (he) was minded to put her away privily, *alika-i jiali isada-ti faroka lo-kokke-wa, lo-boridi fa n,* for whosoever will save his life shall lose it. *h-atenabo faroka ie h-auciga ti-n n-aurea ba o-doma. ama kiana h-iauna wa ?* and if ye lend to them of whom ye hope to receive, what thank have ye ? *lo-iyu l-augioci ajinama goba maugili o-loko ajia-ti-n lo-mun,* his mother and his brethren stood without, desiring to speak with him :

kena alika-i jiali ifirotwa ti-ci lo-mun-wa, h-afudyi bia, lihi h-isanci fa. and whosoever will be chief among you, let him be your servant. lit. and who ever magnify-self wish-person him-at-self, your-chief to-be, he your-servant future. *kena m-anda-ti h-a Daii amun, kokke-hu h-amuni-n bia,* and ye will not come to me, that ye might have life, *ki-o-doma n-aboadwa ti goba,* and (they) were in jeopardy, *manswa ki l-a-ti goba aboko-n-wa ia.* and (he) began to be sore amazed ;

2) *a-mairikota-sia-no o-ma ti goba barin i,* he assayed to join himself to the disciples ;

3) *Satan k-amuni ti ga bu,* Satan hath desired to have you (thee) ;

4) *w-adagata ti sabu ka i, h-a-li lo-mun,* as though ye would enquire something more perfectly concerning him, lit. we-demand wish more is him. ye-do him-to, *ki-o-doma Jew-no a-forra ti sabu goba i,* therefore the Jews sought the more to kill him, *ki-o-doma na-bokota ti ki goba ba i.* therefore they sought again to take him ;

5) *kena tanahu warea n-onyi-hiti-sia koro ikiado fa n-aurea,* and (from) now nothing will be restrained from them which they have imagined to do, *m-onyi-hiti-ci l-ansi-sia.* [the which] neither did according to his will:

6) *ma-ti,* or *m-a-ti,* not willing, in :

to-moroa mati l-a goba Jesus, howbeit Jesus suffered him not, *da-sika ma koro n, mati l-a tu-mun,* he would not reject her (Mk. VI, 26), *to-moroa mati l-a,* he consented not ;

7) *iitesia,* covetousness (§ 118 a) 2)) ;

8) *(ka-)cikibe,* theft (§ 118 a) 1)) ;

b) 1) Sm. *ahitti,* to be compliant, *m-ihitê,* to be tired ;

S. *l-ahitti-ka Wamallittakoanti u-mün lu-llua u-llukk-ua,* (he) believed, lit. he-*ahitti*-was God at his-heart in own, *juhu-lli m-ahitti-ka Adaija-hü u-mün na-llua u-llukk-ua,* and many believed in the Lord, *lu-llua baddia ibé üssa-tti ü-jahü abbu, m-ahitti-kuma-hü abbu ba,* and (he was) full of the Holy Ghost and of faith. G. *mithé|de,* or *dai mithe,* I am tired, *mithé-ka̦di̯ hadī(η,* I am very tired ; B. *ho-makwa hui m-ite-ci,* [come unto me] all ye that labour, *imitedi-,* G. *imitedi-, imithendi-,* to be tedious to someone ;

2) S. *hitte : lu-morrua Saulus hitté l-a kubá a-tattadu-nn-ua lu-kuburukkua-monn-ua,* but Saul increased the more in strength, *d-a-n u-dumma hitte-kebe-pa adia-n d-awa m-ammarru-nni-hüa,* [therefore] I do the more cheerfully answer for myself, *Jesus k-ansi-ssia-nnu u-ijuhu hitté rubu m-a-ni-ka,* and in those days, when the number of the disciples was multiplied, *kiahanna d-akujaba bu-mün, mimi-hitté (mimi.* cold) *b-a-n-ti akannabü-n d-adiâ-n,* wherefore I beseech thee to hear me patiently ;

3) Sm. *a-ttikida,* to persuade, to speak kindly to someone, G. *a-ttekeda,* to advise, *da-tikidikita-ka,* I sing (a medicine-man ; see § 206).

§ 111. The *h* with *a* or *o* occurs further at the beginning of words if the *a* or *o* sound is specially important, e.g.

a) *ama, alika, alo,* interrogative words (§ 139), S., Sm. *hamma, hallika, hallu,* Sc. *hamma,* v. C. *ama, halika, halo,* Pen. *hama,* R. *hama, halleku,* G. *hama, halika, halo ;*

b) *adaili,* sun, Wyatt *hadaley,* Dudley *hadalle,* Laet *adaly,* S., Sm. *haddalli,* Hi. *hadalley,* Sc. *haddali,* I. Th. *adaili,* Sagot *hadali,* v. C. *adalie,* G. *hadali ;*

c) *ada,* tree, Wyatt, S., Sm., Sc., Sagot, R. *adda,* v. C., G. *ada,* Laet *hada ;*

d) Sm. *halpeléru,* a pin (Spanish *alfiler*) ;

e) 1) *ororo,* earth, Wyatt *arara,* S., Sm. *hurruru,* Bernau *harare,* Hi. *ororoo,* v. C. *hororo,* G. *hololo ;*

2) *o-horora,* land, farm, country, S. *u-hurrura ;*

f) *a-odo-,* to die, S., Sm. *a-hudu-,* v. C. *a-hoodo-, a-hoedoe-, oodo-.*
See further deictic or emphasizing *h* in §§ 44—47.

§ 112. a) *hihi,* reed (A. M. § 185, 127) :

b) Sm. *ihi,* tail (A. M. § 182, 29), *úe-iri.* backbone (G. : lower part of the back), *ihiri,* an eel ;

c) 1) *ikihi,* S. *hikkihü,* fire (A. M. § 182, 65) ;

2) S. *ihime,* firewood, v. C. *dai k-ime,* I have fire ; perhaps this word is the name for the apparatus for making fire, comp. § 73 b) ;

³) perhaps connected with the preceding (cremation ?) :

S. *l-üja majauqua|tu|ppa kurru l-ihittiattina u-llukku,* that his soul was not left in hell, *l-ihittiättina w-amunni-ka koa dannuhu baddia,* and his sepulchre is with us unto this day, *akkárrta-hü-ssia baddia kia hitti u-llukkumün,* and laid in the sepulchre [that Abraham, etc., Acts VII, 16] :

ᵈ) *ka-hile(n),* to be quickly, *kahili kibi t-a kiana ausi-n,* running (a ship, Acts XXVII, 16), *to-makwa t-abokwa-boa mu-tu poroko adarida goba kahili kibe-n,* the whole herd of swine ran violently ;

ᵉ) Sm. *ihiti-,* to ground fine, *a-hüidi-,* to press, to press out. B. *ifiro-tu kimisa a-huido-tu bibiten t-akoina mun,* a great sheet knit at the four corners, *a-iidi-, a-iji-,* to gird, *a-iido-(n-wa),* to gird oneself :

ᶠ) G. *a-hilesa,* to split cane ;

ᵍ) Sm. *ue-hükkilli, we-hikkili,* silkgrass, Dudley *huculle,* a bow string.

CHAPTER XV

S

§ 113. The *s* is used in Arawak in order to indicate "showing form", "having a surface of its own, a scale or cuticle".

Si (phonetic spelling) has an inclination to alternate with *syi* (ph. sp.).

§ 114. *Sa* (A. M. § 182, 148A).

ᵃ) 1) *m-isa kwa t-a-n ka* ororo *a-koado-n-wa*, the earth was without form, lit. not-*isa* yet it-being earth round-being ;

2) *isa*, sound, in Acts III, 7, 16 ;

3) *isa-ka-ni-ma-n* and [Moses] was exceeding fair, *kia ki Isa-tu-wabu n-a-sia asa-n*, [the temple] which is called Beautiful, *misi-ci a-odo-ci-sikwa sa-ke h-a-n ho-murreti-n o-doma*, because ye … garnish the sepulchres of the righteous ;

4) *isa*, good (the *i* is omitted in *sa-ci, sa-tu*) ; the word "holy" in the bible texts is also translated by *isa* ;

5) *isadi-*, to lay up (treasures), to save, to restore, to heal, to make whole, to garnish ;

6) I) *karina-sa*, an (hen's) egg, *karina a-herakidi-n t-isa-wa t-adina abomun jin*, as a hen doth gather her brood under her wings, *baka-sa*, a calf, *kabaritu-sa*, a kid ;

II) *isa*, child (offspring), *ka-sa*, to be with child, to conceive, to beget, *ma-sa*, to have no child, to be barren ;

ᵇ) *a-sa*, to call (to give a name) ;

ᶜ) *saka*, to wither, to be withered (a tree, a herb), lit. *ka*, making its appearance in a positive manner in time-reality, with the character of *sa*, showing form, scale or bark (in contrast with growing, living, soft things) ;

ᵈ) *a-saradi-*, to bruise, to grind ;

ᵉ) *bese-ki-n-ci-n o-doma i*, because he was of little stature. R. *base-ke-n-to hiaro*, short girl, Sm. *bêssekinni*, to be small, *bassa-ba-n-tu*, a little one (persons).

§ 115. *Se, si*, flesh (A. M. § 182, 4).

ese-re, ise-re, sores, leprosy ;

isi, Sm. *hissi, hüssi*, G. *hiši*, to stink, Sm. *ka-ssi*, to smell of fish ; *h* exhalation, *issi* flesh ? (A. M. § 182, 149A) ;

Q. *oassini-hü*, the physical heart ;

S. *issin*, penis ;

S. *isehü*, Sm. *issehi*, a worm ;

Perhaps also belonging to this category : *seme*, sweet, delicate, *sipe*, G. *šife*, bitter.

§ 116. *Si.*

a) surface.

1) *isibo*, in face of (without motion), *isiba*, a face.

l-isiba muni-ro lo-toroda goba lo-kuti isibo-mun, a-dankido-n-wa lo-mun, (he) fell down on his face at his feet, giving them thanks, *n-aiakatwa kiana Adam l-iretu mi-ci Adaie-li Wacinaci isibo warea,* and Adam and his wife hid themselves from the presence of the Lord God, *to-loa-sibo abu ka-koborokwa-ni n,* [Mary kept all these things, and] pondered them in her heart, *bawhu-sibo,* S. *baha-ssubu-lle,* door, gate, B. *l-adura-sibo,* his side (*adura,* rib), *airi-sibo,* (fore) teeth ;

2) *isifu*, in face of (with motion).

I) *oniabu isifu-ji Wacinaci Ialoko ausa goba,* and the Spirit of God moved upon the face of the waters, *t-ibibida goba l-eke isifu-ji,* and touched the hem of his garment ;

II) *a-sifuda,* to turn away, again, about, to repent ; *a-sifudo-(n-wa),* to be interpreted, translated ;

III) *isifo-do,* door, gate ;

3) *siba*, stone, rock (A. M. § 182, 75) ;

4) *isiroko*, flesh (A. M. § 182, 4) ;

b) 1) *isi*, seed (of a plant or a tree) (A. M. § 182, 119) ;

o-bolisi, dust (of the ground), chaff (*bolli,* to pass forth), *balisi,* ash (A. M. § 185, 66) ;

marisi, wheat (really : maize) (A. M. § 182, 122) ;

ako-si, eye, probably eye-ball (A. M. § 182, 15) ;

2) *isi*, head (A. M. § 182, 14) ;

3) *t-isidi-tu*, the (its) roof, *da-sikwa-sidi-tu,* my (house-) roof :

4) *isikwa*, a house, *ka-sikwa,* to dwell, to make one's abode, *ark isikwa-ci-n,* the covering of the ark, *b-elitada bu-kaspare-n t-isikwa o-lokomun,* put up again thy sword into his place. *Golgotha ... isii abona isikwa,* G. ... the place of a skull, *isikwa-hu.* village ;

5) *lo-kabo isi,* the tip of his finger, *temple isi,* a pinnacle of the temple, *a-modi-n sycamine ada-isi,* and climbed up into a sycomore tree, S. *hurruru issi,* mountain (top) ;

6) I) *isiri,* nose, also : the forepart of a ship (A. M. § 182, 16) ;

II) *ka-siri-siri a-u-kili waboroko,* the rough ways ;

III) *t-isiribida koro,* neither do they spin, *kaarta l-isiribida,* he closed the book ;

IV) *ka-siri-ma-n,* [a measure] running over :

7) I) *m-isi,* to be straight, right ; also : to be righteous, just, lawful, *misi-tu ahaka-hu,* the law, *misi-tu l-ahaka-n,* his commandment ;

II) *imisidi-,* to stretch forth (his hand), S. *imisidi-,* to expound, to declare, B. *imisido-(n-wa),* to be made straight, to be justified ; *imiseldá-sia,* the pavement (J. XIX. 13) (G. : masonry) ;

c) a point.

1) *simara,* arrow ;

2) Sm. *sámmali*, cassava grater (A. M. § 182, 50) ;

3) I) G. *siparali*, arrow with bamboo lanceolate head ; *para*, to kill ;

II) I. Th. *siparara*, R. *shiparari*, arrow with iron lanceolate head ;

III) *siparari*, iron [1]) ;

IV) Dudley *casparo*, S. *kassiparra*, B. *kaspara*, a sword [2]); *ka-sipara* or Spanish *espada* ?

V) Comp. Karib languages* *šipari*, sting-ray ;

4) Sm. *súdi*, blow-gun arrow ;

5) Q. *mussi*, R. *mossi*, a club ("and have sometimes on one side of the mussi a projection in the form of a little hatchet") ;

d) something sharp, sometimes unpleasant.

1) *a-siki-*, to put, to give ; G. *a-siki-*, to put before one (for instance food), and *a-kŏlŏk(ŏ?)-*, to reach (for instance an object), are used when we use "to give". According to A. P. Penard (verbal communication to the author), something similar occurs in Kaliña, and is rooted in the Indian belief that only what is required for one's personal necessities may be regarded as property. What his field, or the chase produces in excess of his needs, does not belong to him ; he is bound to give it away to those persons who are in need of it. He is also bound to lend a hand for any work, if necessary ;

2) I) *a-simaki-*, to call, *a-simaka*, to cry ;

II) S. *a-ssimadü-*, to call ;

3) Sm. *issimuddu*, electric eel ;

4) *yauhahu* (= bush-spirit, demon) *simaira*, a common expression denoting severe pain (B. 5e, 19) ;

5) Sm. *sila*, to ache ;

6) *simika*, to be filled or moved with envy, to be jealous ;

7) Sm. *simittâ*, to laugh, *amutta*, to disapprove of, to despise, B. *imita*, to despise, to mock, to laugh, *imitada*, to laugh ;

8) *su-mule*, to be drunk, *su-muli-kile*, drunkenness, *ma-muli-kille*, temperance ;

9) S. *oâ-kurru seribokkilliu*, a tempestuous wind ; *oâ-*, exceeding, *kurru*, think, *se*, sharp, *ribo*, waterside, *(o)kkilli*, natural phenomenon, § 130 a), *iu*, spirit ? ; B. *isogo-tu koro serabokilio*, no small tempest, *ifiro-tu goba serabokilio bara o-loko*, there arose a great tempest in the sea ;

10) Sm. *sè*, dictio enclitica, emphaseos causa adhibita, masc. gen. This

---

[1]) This explanation looks more plausible than the derivation from Wapisiana *tiipir*, a certain hard kind of wood, and *ari*, hard, rough, coarse (Nordenskiöld 50 b, 86). The Arawak nation has had much intercourse with the Spaniards, and the new metal might have been introduced to the other tribes of Guiana by the intermediary of the Arawaks. This would explain how it is, that the same word is in general use among the Indian tribes of Guiana.

[2]) Also this word is used by many tribes in Guiana : Island Karib *echoubara*, *coutelas*, has perhaps been brought over by way of Kaliña (Galibi) : *épée*, *cachipara*, *ousipara*, *soubara*.

sè is used very often, and attached to many words, so that hardly four to six words are pronounced, without this suffix *sè* being added in some way. for instance, *t-a dai-ssè*, I say, the matter is so, *kaka-ssè*, nothing at all. it is not there ; S. *wa-ppa kurru sé*, (we refuse, we shall do not *sé*), *Roma-kundi lirraha dai-se*, for this man is a Roman (I-*se*), *Judu kewai dai dai-se*, I am verily a man which am a Jew, *bele-ti-kuba-li lirraha sé* ¹ (it is the man that was lame !), *Judu-nnu kei-se*, (they were real Jews). *Judu kewai dai kei-se*, I am a man which am a Jew. See also § 179 ;

     ¹¹) *ikisi*, a moment, etc., § 48 ʲ).

§ 117. *S-*, perhaps with the meaning of "a definite place".

     ᵃ) *lo-bollita a-komodwa-in ikihi akosa* (comp. § 128 *ako*. entering into). he sat ... and warmed himself at the fire, *waboroko akosa-ci naii*, and these are they by the way side, *aba a-tikida goba waboroko-sa*, and some fell by the way side ;

     ᵇ) Sm. *a-ijakassa*, to kick with the feet, B. *iagasa*. to kick [against the pricks] ;

     ᶜ) *na-iikisa na-kabo rok-oa n*. (they) rubbing them [the ears of corn] in their hands ; comp. S. *a-ika-ru mehli iwi*, the wheat (Acts XXVII. 8 ; *mehli*, bread, *iwi*, fruit) ;

     ᵈ) ¹) Sm. *alomossa*, to move something from one place to another. S. *allumussa*, B. *alomosa* ; comp. *alomun*, § 139 ᵇ⁾ ²) ;

     ²) Sm. *all`küssi-*, schütteln, Sm. *a-rrakassü-*. B. *eragasi-*. to shake (trees, etc., transitive), Sm. *a-rrukussâ*, B. *arakosa, aragasa*, to be shaken. B. *a-korogasa o-kona*, to tremble. *lo-korogosa kiana o-kona*. and he trembling, G. *lo-korokosá-kona*, he trembles ;

     ²ᴬ) Sm. *arrussuttu-*, to build up. R. *arosutá-hu*. falca (canoe with washboards), G. *kuliála aróso*, or *thó-roso*, the washboards ;

     ³) *a-kororoso-*, to pull down, to fall down :

     ⁴) *ikihi-tu kaspara adidisi-n bajia a-sifudabo-tu to-makwa-ji*. and a flaming sword which turned every way ; *adedisa-ro*, an earthquake ;

     ᵉ) *a-safodi-*, to trample, to tread (under feet) :

     ᶠ) *wa-siga-te, wa-sika-te*, let us go ;

     ᵍ) *a-sakada ... o-ma*, to meet : *aba-ro ibikidolia-tu hiaro a-sakada-ga wa-ma*, a certain damsel ... met us.

§ 118. *Sia*.

     ᵃ) indicating a human peculiarity : a trait of character. or such like.

     ¹) *naha wadili abu yaha h-anda-te ma-cikibesia-n-ci temple o-rea amateli, ma-wakaia-ci ajia-n ifiro-tu ho-kwaiabo-sia o-mun o-konomun naha*, for ye have brought hither these men. which are neither robbers of churches, nor yet blasphemers of your goddess. *na-cikibesia goba i adunka w-a-n ka*, (they) stole him away while we slept (*-ciki*, comp. *a-cigi-*. to dig. *aucigi-*, to find, to receive : *be* plurality : *ka-cikibe. ka-cikibe-hi*. thefts. *m-onyi-n b-a ka-cikibe*, thou shalt not steal. *ka-cikibe-ci*, thieves) (A. M.. § 182, 149) ;

     ²) *m-iitesia-n b-a bu-ioci isikwa*. thou shalt not covet thy neighbour's

house, *k-iitesia-sia*, extortion, *Pharisee-no bajia*, *k-iitesia-ci*, and the Pharisees also, who were covetous (*hiti*, to desire, § 110) ;

3) *n-aiikasia goba meli n-onnaki-n bia*, they had forgotten to take bread, *m-aiikasia w-a-n bia*, lest we forget, *aba-ro jiaro koro k-aiikasia-sia Wacinaci isibomun*, and not one of them is forgotten before God (*aiika*, to disappear, etc., § 133) ;

4) *tabisia*, to be drowsy, etc. (§ 169 a) 4) II)) ;

5) *amisia*, to hunger, to be an hungred ;

6) Sm. *panassia(-en)*, to have hunger for something, especially for meat (§ 69 d)) ;

7) *alokosia*, to thirst, to be thirsty (perhaps connected herewith : *a-forra-tu|me-loko-ho na-ti faroka*, (G. *a-faro-to|ma-lokoho na-thüh faroka*), if they drink any deadly thing) ;

8) *audasia*, to be with fever ; G. *a-udasia|de* or *dai odasia*, I have fever — meaning : I am caught by death *(a-odo-)* ;

9) Sm. *jawahüssia(-en)*, to be beset with the *jawahü* (chimera, devil) ;

10) *a-sia-arin*, a fisher, *d-a-sia fa*, I go a fishing, *bo-tokodo kota buneti-n-wa bu-sia-n bia*, let down your nets for a draught ;

11) *n-onnaki-n c-isia o-doma*, and (they) comforted her, *n-onnaki-n n-isia o-doma na-ciligenci o-konomun*, to (they) comfort them concerning their brother, *onnaki-n l-iisia-wa*, he sighed (Mk. VII, 34), *manswa kiana l-onnaki-n l-iisia-wa l-ialoko abu*, and he sighed deeply in his spirit, S. *üwüssiati-*, to make lamentation ;

12) S. *dissia hinna kurru|je Roma-kunna-na*, it is not the manner of the Romans, *dissia-hü h-amün diarru u-kunnamün*, [if it be a question] of your law, *Herodes a-ssika üssa-ttu Koning dissia-ru äke lu-kunna*, Herod, arrayed in royal apparel, *heidi-nu dissia-ttu*, (the customs of the Gentiles), *ma-dissia-ttu*, special [miracles] ;

13) *synagogue o-loko-ci na-makwa adekisia-ga i*, and the eyes of all them that were in the synagogue were fastened on him ;

b) forming verbal nouns with the meaning of "the thing that has been realised", § 22.

§ 119. *So.*

a) *s* form, *o* in rest, not developed, (something that has) remained small ?

1) *isogo*, to be small, *isoko-ro*, a few [words], *abakoro iso kibi t-a jiaro ka wa-mun hui o-mun bajia*, lest there be not enough for us and you ;

2) *a-soko-*, *a-sogo-*, to hew down, to strike (with an ax or sword) ;

3) S. *a-ssudu-*, to flay, B. *yohau ho-sodo kota barin*, which (ye) strain at a gnat, Pen. *huli suduha-du*, the skin shed by a snake. G. *uri sódona-(n*, this skin is from a snake, *iså ̧o*, lobster, *sále*, small lobster, *sa ̧á ̧á*, small crab, Karib languages **išuru*, lobster, crab, Island Karib *achoularo*, shedding its hide (a serpent or a crab) ;

b) *s* form, *o* fluid, humid (§ 125) ?

1) *a-sogoso-*, to wash ;

2) S. *a-ssunnuku-*, to pour out, B. *a-sonko-(n-wa)*, to be running out, poured out ;

3) *a-soroto-*, to kiss, Sm. *a-ssûrtû-*, to suck, to kiss, Pen. *sorota-ro*, *a̅-sutaloko*, vampyr ;

3A) G. *a-sólosolodo-n*, polished (a new knife) ;

4) *a-sorobodi-*, to sweep (a house) ;

5) *a-sorokodo-*, to be shed (blood), *ifiro-tu totola a-sorokodo-kwona-hu*, the fountains of the great deep, *oniabu a-sorokodo-tu*, a well of water, G. *wuniábu sórokodo-n*, a fall or rapid ;

6) Sm. *surre*, diarrhoea, G. *da-súreda*, I have diarrhoea, Sm. *súbuli*, a sore, ulcer, *súkku*, Indian small-pox, *bi-ssurúru*, a certain wood, the shavings of which are laid upon the pocks.

CHAPTER XVI

VOWELS, DIPHTHONGS; COLOURS

§ 120. *Oa* or *wa*, stationary, separate among the events or things that partake in the passing of time ; *o, u* or *w*, motionless, *a*, time-reality.

a) not making headway, lasting.

¹) *kwa*, S. *koa* (parallel to *ka*), with auxiliary verb *a ; kwon*, S. *koan*, infinitive or present participle.

alomun kwa b-a ? where art thou ? (Gen. III, 9), *alon kwa|l-a ?* where is he ? (J. IX, 12), *b-isika bu-kab-oa t-ajeago, kena kokke kwa tu fa*, lay thy hand upon her, and she [being only dead in appearance] shall live (yet) (comp. *kokke ka i !* he is alive ! *alika-i jiali eke-ci toho meli kokke fa i ma-iibo-n-wa-tu bia*, if any man eat of this bread, he shall live for ever), *ama kwon kowa-ka d-amun ?* what lack I yet ? *aba-ro kwon kowa-ka b-amun*, yet lackest thou one thing, *abar-li abar-li kwon n-a goba a-fitikidi-n*, (they) went out one by one, *b-aiici kokke kwa|ma*, thy son liveth (J. IV, 51), *kokke kwon o-doma di, hui bajia kokke kwa|ma fa*, because I live, ye shall live also, *to-moroa Mary bolla kwa|ma goba bawhu o-loko,* [Martha went and met Jesus :] but Mary sat still in the house, *kena abar-li publican, Levi ci iri l-adeka bolla-kwon onnaki-ci bia custom plata*, and (he) saw a publican, named Levi, sitting at the receipt of custom, *Saul areroko o-rea a-fitikida kwa t-a amaronta-tu ajia-hu*, and Saul, yet breathing out threatenings, *Wacinaci a-borati-n o-doma di, tanahu ka-n kwa d-a*, having therefore obtained help of God, I continue unto this day, *l-akarato-sia o-loko yaha wa-ma tanahu kwon*, and his sepulchre is with us unto this day, *ika ki Sa-tu Ialoko ma-siko-n-wa kwa|ma : Jesus ma-kalimeto-n-wa kwa|ma-n o-doma*, for the Holy Ghost was not yet given ; because that Jesus was not yet glorified, *m-andi-n kwa t-a d-ikisi*, mine hour is not yet come, *m-andi-n kwon-ci Jesus bawhu-yuho o-lokomun. yumun-tu kwon ki Martha aucigi-n i*, now Jesus was not yet come into the town. but was in that place where Martha met him, *wakaia ka-sa-ci hiaro-no omuni n. wakaia a-tekita kwa-ma-ci na-sa wa omuni n, kia kasakabo o-loko*. and woe unto them that are with child, and to them that give suck in those days !

²) ¹) *-kwo(n)na, -kwona-hu*, S. *koana* (parallel to *-kona*).

ika tu tata-ci o-kona ka-forraa-kwona-ci ikita-n ifiro-tu l-isikwa. l-onyikau maiaukwa ma, when a strong man armed keepeth his palace. his goods are in peace, *l-onnaka to-makwa lo-forraa-kwonna m-amoto-n-wa l-a-sia abu l-aurea*, he taketh from him all his armour, *a-siki-n ie na-torodo-kwona-hu ajeago n-onnaki-kwona ie ajeago bajia*, and laid them on beds and couches, *yumuni ki ajia-sia ſa ba toho hiaro onyi-sia o-konomun. ka-koborokwa-koto-kwona-hu bia to-konomun*, there shall also this, that this woman hath done, be told for a memorial of her, *ikisidi-kwona-hu*, a bushel. *Daii onnaki kwona-hu*, my yoke, *aborage-kwona-hu*, a scourge ;

S. *Gott adaija-hü-koana*, the kingdom of God, *n-adaijana-ssia-koana*, the kingdom (Acts I, 6), *h-aditti-koana-wa*, by signs (Acts II, 22), *üüssada-koana 'lukku*, salvation (of man), *ahadakutta-koana bahü*, the council (questioning-house), *n-ebettira-koana-wa*, the covenant (their friend-*koana*-own) ;

II) m. *-kwon-ci*, S. *-koan-ti*, f. *-kwon-tu*, S. *-koan-tu*, plur. *-kwono-no-ci*, S. *-koana-nu-tti* (parallel to *-kon-, -kono-no-ci*).

ika ki lo-mairikoto-sia-no anda goba Jesus l-oaiya kwon-ci amun, ajia-ibici, then came the disciples to Jesus apart, and said, *to-loko amakoro b-imikebo ſa, bui, b-aiici, b-otu, b-ikita-kwon-ci, b-ikita-kwon-tu*, in it thou shalt not do any work, thou, nor thy son, nor thy daughter, thy manservant, nor thy maidservant, *naha loko-no aiomun-ci-wabu Wacinaci ikita-kwono-no-ci*, these men are the servants of the most high God ;

S. *kia ahaikada-koana-ttu kassakkabbu-hü*, (in that day of consolation), *ka-tattadü-koana-ttu bahü*, [they put them in] hold (fortified house) ;

3) Parallel to the forms of §§ 32, 33 :

ho-koborokwa l-ajia-n o-konomun ho-mun, Galilee mun kwa l-a-n ka, remember how he spake unto you when he was yet in Galilee, *adeka kwa n-a-n ka aiomun bonna-ro, ausa l-a-n ka, biama-no wadili arira-ci-eke ajinama na-mun*, and while they looked stedfastly toward heaven as he went up, behold, two men stood by them in white apparel, *toraha ki d-ajia goba ho-mun, ho-ma kwa d-a-n ka*, these things have I spoken unto you, being yet present with you, *toho ajia-hu d-ajia goba ho-mun, ho-ma kwa d-a-ni ka goba, to-makwa iibido-n-wa bia*, these are the words which I spake unto you, while I was yet with you, that all things must be fulfilled (etc., L. XXIV, 44), *ki-jia kwa l-a-n ka ajia-n*, while he thus spake ;

4) *kwawa*, S. *koawa*, reciprocal, among each other.

m-amaro-ni hu, hui iyuho-ci abo-kwawa, fear not, little flock, *Daii k-ansi-n goba hu jin, hui bajia k-ansi-n bia ho-muni-kwawa*, as I have loved you, that ye also love one another, *n-ajia goba na-muni-kwawa*, (they) spake among themselves, *n-ausia kiana ajia-n na-kona-muni kwawa*, let them implead one another, *lo-mairikoto-sia-no adeka goba n-ibici-kwawa*, the disciples looked one on another ;

S. *abbalüwai dia ré n-a kuba n-abbu-koawa*, they were all with one accord in one place, *n-adiâ-ka n-abbu-koawa*, they conferred among themselves, *na-maqua a-ssika-ti l-äme a-ñebettoa-kubá baddia n-aure-koawa*, and all, even as many as obeyed him, were dispersed :

5) *-makwa*, altogether, all, every.

bo-makwa bui ka-raia goba wakaia-hu o-loko, thou wast altogether born in sins, *lo-makwa ma-ribe-n ka i : hui bajia ma-ribe-n ka. to-moroa ho-makwa koro*, (he) is clean every whit : and ye are clean, but not all.

to-makwa yara o-loko-tu ada iwi b-iki ſa m-amoto-n-wa o-loko, of every tree of the garden thou mayest freely eat, *naii a-ſitikida kiana ajia-n to-makwa-ji,* and they went forth, and preached every where, *kia o-konomun ki waii wa-makwa ahaka-ga,* whereof we all are witnesses, *ki-o-doma na-makwa na-simaka ki goba ba,* then cried they all again, *na-makwa kidua-hu o-rea-ci akonnaba d-ajia-n,* every one that is of the truth heareth my voice, *na-makwa botobaci hiaro-no ajinama goba akausa-n i,* and all the widows stood by him ;

b) *to-moroa,* but, nevertheless ; *to-* its, *m* reluctant, *o* permanent, *r* motion being impeded, *oa* not making headway, or : in itself ; S. *-morrua* with different pronominal prefixes :

S. *da-morrua a-haiarudutti-pa|je b-adikkiti-ké u-mün, dai dá-waja a-ijaonti-n|da|ppa,* and the nation to whom they shall be in bondage will I judge, *bu-morrua ma-ssika-n b-a-li n-äme,* but do not thou yield unto them, *lu-morrua Petrus adiâ-ka lu-mün hiddia-mañ,* then Peter said (to him), *tu-morrua Prophet Joel wakilli adia-ssia-kubá-ru u-llukku-di rubu t-a tu-maqua-kebé, hi-ddia hé l-a kubá :* but this is that which was spoken by the prophet Joel, *wa-morrua wa-tulludu-n-benna|n, hallika-i kurru tu-llukkumünni-ka|n,* but when we had opened, we found no man within, *hu-morrua hu-mallikuttâ-n u-kunna|je abbu attabâ-ka Jerusalem u-mân,* and, behold, (but) ye have filled Jerusalem with your doctrine, *na-morrua m-ánniki-n rubu n-a na-monnua|n,* but they understood not ;

c) separate.

1) *t-oala,* the (its) crumbs, *mihu oalla,* broken pieces of the ship ;

2) *oala,* cheek ;

3) *oalabaw,* the other side.

to-moroa alika-i jiali a-ſatada ſaroka b-iisa mairia b-oala-kona, t-oalabaw abu b-isiſuda lo-mun, but whosoever shall smite thee on thy right cheek, turn to him the other also, *kenbena ika tu l-andi-n t-oalabaw mun, Gergese-no o-horora mun,* and when he was come to the other side into the country of the Gergesenes, *Jordan oalabaw warea,* [people followed] from beyond Jordan, *Jordan oalabaw mairia,* [the land] beyond Jordan :

4) *oakudwa* (Indicative m., Present t.) in : *t-eda botoli oakudwa,* the (leather) bottles break, *siba bajia oakudwa goba,* and the rocks rent ;

5) *na-tekida-bo-n bia Paul na-wa-ji-kwa-jia.* [fearing lest] Paul should have been pulled in pieces of them ;

d) *boa,* abnormal appearance.

1) R. *adi-bua-hu,* omen, token, auguries. G. *adiboá.* an omen (for instance in a dream, or when after hunting, a piece of game that was already dead and stiff, suddenly moves), *d-ádiba-ka,* I receive a sign (§ 173) ;

1A) R. *shi-boa-dda-hu,* child born with a caul (*isi,* head) ;

2) R. *d-aiite-boa-chi,* (my) stepson (*d-aii-ci,* my son), etc. ;

3) *maute-boa,* the day after to-morrow (*mauci,* morning) :

4) *aboa,* being ill, foul ; G. sickly (ill $=$ *kari*) ;

⁵) *aboa-ka*, perchance, haply, S. *aboâ-ka ; aboâ-kuma* (potential mood) ;

e) curved (see also § 108A).

¹) *to-makwa aroadi-be-tu ororo ajeago-ji*, every thing (animal) that creepeth upon the earth, *aroadi-tu amateli*, creeping things ;

²) *arua, harua*, jaguar (comp. also *airi*, tooth) ;

³) *yurua*, a thorn ;

⁴) *lo-koa*, a (his) horn ;

⁵) *kwama, kwawma*, hat, crown (A. M. § 182, 57) ;

⁶) *a-koado-n-wa*, being round (see ex. § 114 a) 1)), S. *abba akoada-ru wijua*, a whole year ;

⁷) *a-kwaiabo-*, to beseech, to pray, *a-kwaiabo-(n-wa)*, to worship, to do a prayer ;

⁸) S. *da-ija a-kkoahüddoa bu-kunnamün*, my tongue was glad (thee-concerning), *ma-kuahü-ttu aboâ-ttu*, vanities, *ma-kuahü-rubu-mu-ttu*, vain things ;

⁹) van Berkel *maquary*, whip used in the whip ceremony (also : torch), Sm. *makóali*, a whip, S. *a-makoalitedi-*, to whip (Karib languages : Cumanagota *macuare*, Kaliña *macoáli*) ;

¹⁰) *doada*, a pot ;

f) contracted, contracting, etc.

¹) *loko asoa-re-ci kabo*, a man which had his hand withered :

²) *a-soadi-*, to draw (water or wine from the pots) ;

³) Q. *oassini-hü*, the heart ;

⁴) *wakorra bajia i*, and (he) pineth away ;

⁵) *ororo waa goba*, was the earth dried, *waa-tu ororo*, the dry land, Sm. *wáija*, B. *waiè*, potters clay, Sm. *wajeli*, to fade. R. *waiyari*. Sm. *wáijali*, knapsack, plaited from palm leaves ;

⁶) *waka-u-kili*, the dust [from the road] (*u-kili*, § 130 a)) ;

g) in itself.

¹) I) *o-loa*, heart, mind, bossom. Q. *u-llua-hü*, Leben. Seele. Herz. G. *ka-loá-ma-ka-η uni-rako bu-dïdï-η* ? darest thou leap into the water ?

II) G. *oroa*, to study for, or to perform the functions of. a medicine-man (§ 205) ;

²) *-oaiya, -uaiya*.

kena n-ekita goba i l-oaiya l-eke abu, and (they) put his own (his) raiment on him, *w-akonnaba n-ajia-n w-oaiya w-ajia-n*, we do hear them speak in (our own) our tongues, *w-oaiya w-akonnabo-n o-doma i*, for we have heard him ourselves, *b-itikida-te b-uaiya onabo-muni-ro*. cast thyself down ;

b-isadwa b-uaiya, save thyself, *aba-no l-isada goba : l-oaiya mamari-ga l-isado-n-wa*, he saved others : himself he cannot save. *alika-i jiali ifiroto faroka l-oaiya lo-munwa, lihi isogoto fa*. and whosoever shall exalt himself shall be abased. *alika-i bia b-uaiya b-isikoa* ? whom makest thou thyself ?

isauka jiaro a-toroda-tu t-oaiya ma-lokodo|fa, every kingdom divided against itself is brought to desolation, *kenbena l-isika goba n l-oaiya l-a-n imilia-tu a-odo-ci-sikwa o-lokomun,* and (he) laid it in his own new tomb, *lo-mairikoto-sia-no anda goba l-amun na-uaiya robu-in,* the disciples came unto him privately, *kenbena l-anda n-abu aiomun-tu ororo ajeago mun n-oaiya kwa n-a-n bia,* and (he) bringeth them up into an high mountain apart, *kenbena h-iibo fa di da-uaiya robu-in ; to-moroa da-uaiya robu-in koro, Awa da-ma-ni o-doma,* and (ye) shall leave me alone : and yet I am not alone, because the Father is with me ;

3) *a-wa*

toho h-onnaka, ho-lokoda h-awa n, take this, and divide it among yourselves, *m-aiita-ni h-a-ia h-awa,* through (your) ignorance, *ika tu Peter aiita-ni l-awa, l-ajia-ga,* and when Peter was come to himself, he said, *n-onyikau n-amuni-sia na-iyugara goba, a-lokodo-n na-makwa n-awa n,* and (they) sold their possessions and goods and parted them to all men, *ika tu l-aiita-n l-awa,* and when he came to himself ;

4) *h-aiit-oa,* (ye) take heed, beware (§ 4 ; *h-aiit-a,* (ye) know), G. *d-aith-úa,* I am careful, *bahŏh ibit-oa,* a house is burning, *to 'niabu abuk-oa,* the water is boiling, (*d-aboka resi,* I boil rice) ;

5) *d-imigod-wa,* I am sent (§ 4 ; *d-imigoda,* I send) ;

6) I) *o-n-wa* infinitives or present participles (§ 27) ;

II) *b-ansi fa bu-ioci b-uaiya b-ansi-n-wa jin,* thou shalt love thy neighbour as thyself, *w-aherakida w-onyi-wa,* we took up our carriages (Acts XXI, 15) ;

III) *kia ho-muni fa h-iki-ni wa,* to you it shall be for meat (food) (comp. *Wacinaci aiita barin kasakabo ka-loko-tu h-iki-ni n, h-akosi a-torodo-n-wa fa,* for God doth know that in the day ye eat thereof, then your eyes shall be opened), *ki-o-doma da-kwaiaba hu amateli h-onnaki-n bia h-eki-ni wa,* wherefore I pray you to take some meat (comp. *kena lo-kurradabo-n bena n, l-iinata goba iki-ni n,* and when he had broken it, he began to eat, Acts XXVII, 34, 35) ;

IV) *kia o-doma wadili a-iibo fa l-ici wa, lo-iyu wa, kena l-andakoto fa l-ire-tu o-ma,* therefore shall a man leave his father and his mother, and shall cleave unto his wife (comp. *ika tu Jesus adeki-n lo-iyu kiana,* when Jesus therefore saw his mother, J. XIX, 26), *b-isimaka imikebo-ci-no, kena b-isika na-mun na-iauna-wa,* call the labourers, and give them their hire (comp. *kenbena misi-tu jiaro h-iauna h-aucigi fa,* and whatsoever is right, that shall ye receive), *b-akilaka ibiro-bu-kab-oa, kena b-adeka d-akabo ; b-akilaka bu-kab-oa,aciada-n d-adurasibo o-lokomun,* reach hither thy finger, and behold my hands ; and reach hither thy hand, and thrust it into my side, *h-onnakida 'h-akosi wa,* lift up your eyes (J. IV, 35) (comp. *n-akosi n-ataga bajia ; m-adeki-n n-a-n bia n-akosi abu,* and their eyes have they closed ; lest they should see with their eyes), *b-onnaka bu-kaarta-n wa,* take thy bill (L. XVI, 6) (comp. *ma-ridi-n h-a Moses kaarta-n o-loko,* have ye not read in the book of Moses) :

V) *-mun-wa, -mon-wa, -mon-owa.*

d-ikisi-ka da-mun-wa isa-ni bia daii bajia a-buriti-n bu-mun. it seemed good to me also ... to write unto thee, lit. my-opinion-is me-at-wa good to-be I also writing thee-to, *d-aunaki fa da-mun-wa hu,* I will ... receive you unto myself, *kena alika-i jiali isogoto faroka l-oaiya lo-mun-wa, lihi ifiroto fa,* and he that humbleth himself shall be exalted, *naii a-bokotwa goba to-monowa(-)tu aboa-hu abu,* that (pl.) were taken with divers diseases, *ororo a-fitikitia kokki-tu to-monwa-n,* let the earth bring forth the living creature after his kind, *to-moroa Paul na-sika lo-munwa-n bia ka-sikwa-n i,* but Paul was suffered to dwell by himself, *wakili na-makwa akirikia-no na-monwa goba akona-n, m-ikiadi-n l-a goba ie,* who in times past suffered all nations to walk in their own ways, lit. times-past they-all nations they-at-own past walking, not-preventing he-did them ;

VI) S. *u-ma-monnu-rua :*

na-onnaki-n-ti hebe-tti na-ttinutti Jacob lu-mamonnurua, and called his father Jacob to him, lit. they-taking old-one their-father J. him-to, *da-ija bo-onnaka-li-te bu-mamonnurua|n,* receive my spirit (thee-to it) ;

VII) *bui ahaka-ga b-uaiya bu-konomun wa,* thou bearest record of thyself, *t-isika kiana c-ireci omuni n to-ma wa,* and (she) gave also unto her husband with her, *l-aucigi-n bena n, l-adanaina ajeago wa l-isika n. alikibi abu,* and when he hath found it, he layeth it on his shoulders, rejoicing, ... *aunaka n-ibici wa,* [the Jews] took unto them [certain fellows], *l-aici fa a-mairikota-hu o-konomun. Wacinaci o-rea faroka jiaro n, da-uaiya da-doma wa d-ajia faroka jiaro n. Ajia-ci jiali l-oaiya lo-doma wa, l-oaiya l-ikalimetwa ti-ka,* he shall know of the doctrine, whether it be of God, or whether I speak of myself. He that speaketh of himself seeketh his own glory, *Awa bu-kalimeta-te di b-uaiya b-ab-ua,* Father, glorify thou me with thine own self, *toho ki ajia-hu h-isika ho-kuyuko o-lok-oa, loko-no akabo-roko mun l-isikito-n-wa fa loko Aiici o-doma,* let these sayings sink down into your ears ; for the Son of man shall be delivered into the hands of men, *l-ahaka fa lihi angel-no o-mun bu-konomun, kenbena na-kabo rok-oa n-onnaki fa bu,* he shall give his angels charge concerning thee : and in their hands they shall bear thee up (Mt. IV, 6), *yuho-li kibi loko-no l-ausa( )kita goba l-iinab-oa,* and (he) drew away much people after him (Acts V, 37), *l-onnaka l-adina o-kona wa i,* and when he had taken him in his arms, *a-bolliti-ci a-koto-n lo-ma ajia-ga na-koborokwa-ji-wa,* and they that sat at meat with him began to say within themselves ;

VIII) Instead of *au-rea, au-roa :*

kenbena b-akosi onyikiti faroka wakaia bu-mun. bo-ragasa n, bo-boreda b-auroa n, and if thine eye offend thee, pluck it out, and cast it from thee :

IX) Instead of *(o-)bora, (o-)boroa :*

ma-iikita-n b-a-li trumpet bu-boroa, do not sound a trumpet before thee :

X) Parallel to *-ro, roa :*

to-moroa ma-tata-roa na-kona, and they could not (L. IX. 40 : *tata o-kona,* § 90 b))), *amaro roa goba loko-no o-bora ie,* for they feared the people ;

XI) S. Twice *ua :*

h-akudukutta hu-kkujukku lukk-ua-monn-ua d-adia-ssia-pa, hearken to my words, lit. ye open your-ears in-*ua*-at-*ua* my-spoken-thing-future ;

XII) (*abu,* appearance, § 65 ; *aboku,* a part, a portion, *aboke,* to have part in, *k-aboki,* to receive inheritance, *abokwa-wa* § 120 a) 4)), S. *abbukü-,* to receive) ;

l-ahaka-ga na-mun kiana, Ho-bolliti( )kita ie n-abokwa-bi-ti-n imoro-tu karau ajeago, and he commanded them to make all sit down by companies upon the green grass ;

ikiduadi-ci kiana eragi goba n-abokwa-bo-n na-makwa, and all that believed were together, *yuho-ro poroko a-kota goba t-abokwa-bo-n,* there was ... a great herd of swine feeding ;

Judas aunaki-ci n-abokwa-boa-mu-ci loko-no, Judas then, having received a band of men, *t-ausa goba t-abokwa-boa mu-tu poroko o-lokomun,* they went into the herd of swine ;

S. *gi-dia l-a Wamallitakoanti k-anse-boa-kubá je heidi-nu ku,* then hath God also to the Gentiles granted [repentance unto life] ;

7) *o-koborokwa,* remembrance (or : consciousness, see Roth ll. 19 a Sect. 81) ; *kobo = goba,* past (*o* instead of *a,* see § 5, *koma*), *rok(o),* in (fixed), *wa,* self. Examples, see § 18 ; *-n* form : *o-koborokwon.* See also § 128 k).

§ 121. *Wa-,* distant, exceeding, etc. ; comp. §§ 120 c, d) separate, abnormal ; also : *w-,* vast, far away.

a) Sm. *oâ,* to be long (time) ;

wakili, long ago, rather a long time ago ;

wakorrau, now (from this moment on), only now, *wakorrau kibi,* of late, now (*koro,* negation, § 142) ;

oaboddi-, to abide, to wait, to tarry ;

waboka, already, now (just now) ;

wabujin, quickly, with haste, *ma-wabuji goba w-ausi-n,* when we had sailed (gone) slowly, *wabuji-ci-te andi-n,* and they came with haste ;

wahajia, hereafter, by and by (L. XVII, 7) ;

wahadu-tu eke-hu, an old garment, *wahadu-tu t-eda botoli,* old (leather) bottles, *wahadu-be-tu,* old things ;

wara-uara-tu eke-hu, sackcloth ;

b) *wa-rea,* from, § 97 c) ;

to-waji, its length, *kore-tu waji-tu eke-hu,* a scarlet robe, *waji-tu kasakabo b-amuni-n bia,* that thy days may be long, *kia kasakabo lo-mawajida,* he hath shortened the days (*a-mawajido fa,* shall be shortened), *l-iido-sia abu o-waji abu,* [the towel] wherewith he was girded;

kenbena waiikile l-ausa goba, and (he) went into a far country ;

waboroko, a way, a road ;

c) ¹) *auadi-*, S. *a-wahüddu-*, to go about ; *auadi-* ... *ibici*, to seek.
h-auada d-ibici, ye seek me ;

²) S. *t-awa-du [-mu-ttu]*, [and] wild beasts ;

³) R. *yawarri*, opossum ;

⁴) *auadi-*, S. *a-wadi-*, to beckon ;

⁵) *auadu-li*, wind (A. M. § 182, 67) ;

⁶) *wariwari*, fan ;

⁷) *arauadi-*, to wipe :

⁸) Sm. *adawandu-(nn-ua)*, to be suspended in the air (a falcon) ,

⁹) G. *hime u-wádawáda*, the fins of a fish ;

¹⁰) Sm. *jáhu*, cotton (A. M. § 182, 121) ;

d) ¹) *wabu*, very, exceedingly ; honorific.

aba tata-tu-wabu auaduli, a tempestuous wind, *isa-tu-wabu eke-hu*, the
best robe, *Aiomun-ci-wabu*, the Highest, *adaie-li-wabu*, a king, *adaie-n-wabu*, reigning (as a king), *ororo aji goba oniabu ifirotwa sabu wabu-n*,
and the waters prevailed exceedingly upon the earth, *kia kasakabo o-loko
ama-hu-wabu l-eke goba*, and in those days he did eat nothing, *isa-ci-wabu
adaia-hu Felix*, the most excellent governor Felix ;

S. *l-aditti-wâbu Jesus*, his Son Jesus, *kakü-tti-wâbu Wamallitakoanti*,
the living God, *Roma-kunna-na wâbu*, Romans (Acts XVI, 38), *lukku-hu
adia-n kurra turraha*, Gott *adiâ-n-wabu tuhu né*, it is the voice of a god, and
not of a man ;

G. *ikihi-khoda wabo*, genuine firewood, *loko-no wabo*, true Indians ;

²) S. *oâ-kurru seribokkilliu*, a tempestuous wind :

e) *wai*.

1) *isa-ni-wai*, well ! ; with the verb *a* : to be consenting ; S. *ussa-nü-wai*, it is good ; with the verb *a* : to praise :

2) *taha-wai*, afar off ;

3) *ke-wai*, emphasizing word, § 48 ᵇ) ;

4) S. m. *abba-l-uwai*, f. *abba-r-uwai*, with one accord ; one, a ;

5) S. *hara-wai hi-ddia-mu-ttu adia-hü lü-lesida-bu ikka-ké*, the place
of the scripture which he read was this, Sm. *hár-uai*, da ist es, da hasst du
es (*haru*, § 139 ᶜ)) ;

f) S. *hitté rubu t-a ka-uahünnâ-n*, and multiplied (Acts XII, 24),
ka- uaküña-n tu-maqua abba âdi-n ba, and prevailed (Acts XIX, 20), *ika
a-ssikâ-ti ujuhu hitté n-a a-uahüntu-nn-ua*, and believers were the more
added [to the Lord].

§ 122. *U*, the great, the vast, the motionless.

a) *u-ho*, to be a quantity, § 151 ᵃ⁾ ;

b) *-hu*, streaming, or breathing out into space : forms verbal nouns, § 24;

c) *hu-la*, etc. ; *l* loose, a time-reality, consequently : a deep hole.

1) Sm. *u-hulássi*, *tuhulai*, a hole, *bára u-ttula*, die Tiefe der See. B.
akosa oolai, the eye of a needle, *t-oolai*, a (its) hole, den, cave, gulf, *t-ooli*,
the rent, *tola-tu ororo*, depth of earth, *aciga-oniabu tola bajia*, and the well
is deep, *to-tola*, the deep, *tola-ci acigi-n*, and digged deep ;

2) a-holadi-, to break (a hole into the roof) ;

3) Sm. tuttulla, the lung ;

d) hu-ru, etc. ; r motion being impeded.

1) I) S. hurruru, B. ororo, earth, world ;

II) S. u-hurrura, B. o-horora, land, farm, country ;

III) Sm. húrruru, land, a mountain, B. to-horoman o-mun, and to the hills [they shall say ; L. XXIII, 30] ; G. hulurá, swellings of a musquito sting ;

IV) o-horomurrida-tu oniabu, the raging of the water, bara o-horomurrida-n, waves, bara manswa fa a-horomurrida-n k-akonnaki-n bajia, the sea and the waves roaring ;

V) ororo-li, Sm. rúru-li, clay, mud, G. roro, mud, or anything that is flowing sluggishly, róro-li, mó-ro-li, mud, ka-ró-tu tu-kúto-ŋ érẹ, a thick soup ;

VI) Sm. húrrutu, pumpkin, gourd ;

2) S. a-hurrudâ, to come together (comp. § 104 b) 2)) ;

3) I) S. hurussü, B. orosi, to be filled (with food) ;

II) a-orosidi-, to fill, to suffice ;

e) hu-du.

1) S. a-hudu-, B. a-odo-, to die (A. M. § 182, 138) :

2) Sm. hudù, to be bent, to be bowed, a-hudu-(nn-ua), to stoop, to bow down, B. a-hododo-, to bow (the head, the face), a-hododo-(n-wa), to bow, to stoop down, to be hanging.

§ 123. Yu, iu, a definite place ; y, i, here, u, space, motionless.

a) yumun, § 71 b) 4) ;

b) yu-warea, § 97 ;

c) 1) na-iuka (or na-iyuka) ... siba abu, they stoned, mihu a-iyuka onabo o-kona mun, (they) ran the ship aground ;

2) lihi-ki a-iyukontwa-ci lo-loa o-konomun, which also leaned on his breast ;

3) a-iyugari-, to sell (trans.), a-iyugara (intrans.) ;

d) yura, a-yurati-, § 104 g) ;

e) S. a-ijuwedu-(nn-ua) ... (u-mün), to adhere (to), to consort (with);

f) Sm. a-ijuehê, hújuehe, to be lazy, ma-júehê, not to be lazy, úejehi, a louse, aijoa w-andi-n, we come late, aijoa l-akunna. he has gone late, B. oie-ci, one who is slothful, G. hoyuwé, lazy, Sm. hau, a sloth.

§ 124. Yu, iu, a) united to its base by a thin link — the great, space, b) to enter into space (?).

a) 1) Sm. a-ijuhudu-, B. a-iiodo-. to hang (trans.): Sm. a-ijuhudukuttu-, B. a-iiodokoto-, id. causative, S. wuri juhu-a-koa|t-a-ni-ka lü-kkabbu u-kunna, the venomous beast (snake) hang(ing) on his hand ; G. yodoā-loko da-kuna-ka, I walk [over a beam and] balance myself [in going] ;

2) a big leaf (?): Sm. juli, tobacco, júlika, Montrichardia arborescens, ú-jule, cabbage (A. M. § 182, 129) ;

b) Sm. *hemëu*, B. *imeodo-*, to bring forth (children) ; *m*, see § 74 :
(A. M. § 182, 134C) ;

iyu, mother, *ire-yu*, the state of wife, § 164 i) ²) ;

adibeyo, belly, womb, § 86 f) ¹) ;

Sm. *hán-iyu*, gnat, mosquito, *ha-iju*, ant, = swelling-producing (A. M.
§ 182, 107A) ;

R. *yuro*, Sm. *júru*, cassava squeezer ;

a-iubosi-, to sieve ;

a-bokoto-n lo-iuri, and took him by the throat ; Pen. *ka-yor-ehe*.
consumption, Sm. *ittuli*, Pen. *ituri, itori, duli, dśuli*, howling monkey (=
strong throat ?) (A. M. § 182, 77) ;

S. *a-ijumudâ*, to prophesy ;

Sm. *idiju*, breast, *idiu-ssi*, paps, B. *idju*, paps, *a-te-ci-ju*, sucklings :

*to-moroa yuyu-o-kili a-fitikida ororo o-koboroko area a-iyuyuto-n
to-makwa ororo ajeago-ji*, but there went up a mist from the earth, and
watered the whole face of the ground.

§ 125. *Ui*, liquid, (to produce) fruit, (to produce) heat ; comp. also
§ 124 b) and § 153, *ibi*, small (produced by dividing).

a) S.*wuini, wuin*, water, B. *oini ... iki*, rain, *oni-ka-in*, river, *oini-rako*, in
the water, *oni-abu*, water as a substance, (A. M. § 182, 68) ;

Sm. *uima, aema, éma*, mouth of a river (A. M. § 182, 17) ;

G. *ŏka*, Sm. *aka*, to take a bath ;

b) Sm. *óewedi-, óëdi-*, to vomit ;

o-koi, spittle, G. *da-kúi*, (my) spittle, outside the mouth ;

Sm. *úeku*, resin ;

G. *dakχŏ*, (my) semen, *t-ŏkö*, pus ;

Sm. *limúne-éra*, limon juice, *idiúra*, milk, R. *nana ura*, pine-juice, *oludi-
ura*, cashew juice ; § 107 b) ⁴) (A. M. § 182, 2) ;

G. *úra-ro-ni*, saliva (inside the mouth) [or *uraro*, cloud, *oni*, water ?] ;

G. *kulira*, B. *to-korira*, bile (comp. also § 99 bB) ;

egura, root (A. M. § 182, 110 ?) ;

a-luiti-, to anoint ;

c) ¹) *iwi*, fruit of a plant or a tree (A. M. § 182, 118) :

a-uiyi, Sm. *a-oji-, a-uji*, to gather (fruit), B. *olive o-banna t-oi-sia*, an
olive branch plucked of, G. *d-oyu fä|n*, I shall pluck it (a fruit ; *da-tïkïdï fa
to-bána*, I shall pluck a leaf), Sm. *a-ohünti-*, to plant, Sm. *iwi-ssi*, testicle,
iwé-ra, penis, *k-iwéju-n*, R. *wayu-co*, woman's apron (a similar word is in
use with most Karib tribes in Guiana) ;

Sm. *bikki-bikki*, geschwind aufwachsen, stark werden (von Kindern).
B. *ibikido-(n-wa)*, to grow, (seeds) to spring up, *ibikidolia* to be young ;

    1A) Sm. *ibissi*, a slip (plant) ;

B., G. *ebeso-(n-wa)*, Sm. *a-ebessu-(nn-ua)*, to metamorphose oneself
(for instance a dog into a woman, § 224. D. a caterpillar into a butterfly,
Sm. an egg into a chicken, a flower into a fruit : Sm. to bloom ; S., Sm.
ebessu-(nn-ua), to appear, to appear in a dream ;

2) *Sa-tu Ialoko eweribeda goba i*, and being fervent in the spirit, *t-iwerebe*, the heat (of the fire ; Acts XXVIII, 3), Sm. *wérebê*, to be warm ; comp. B. *tere*, heat, *tere-tu*, the (day's) heat (e, § 2) ;

d) *wiwa*, star, also used for "year" (A. M. § 182, 63). This word may also mean : *w*, far away, *i*, tiny, *w*, far away, *a*, time-reality, or it may picture the sparkling of the stars ;

e) *wiru*, a turtledove (A. M. § 182, 93).

§ 126. a) *a-li, a-ri*, light (A. M. § 182, 132E), in the following.

ari-ra, Sm. *hálli-ra*, G. *halira*, white ;

Sm. *auléa-ra*, chalk ;

k-ali-me, light, glory, to be bright, to shine (§ 134 f)) ;

Sm. *k-alé-kku*, the white stones (or pebbles) of the medicine-man ; v. C. *ch-àle-kójehá* (§ 167), the spirit of white granite ;

Sm. *hikkihi e-hel-udu-n*, flame ; fire light-origin-possessive suffix ? ;

Comp. *a*, time-reality, *li*, freely flowing forth, *ahalikibi*, joy (*aha*, breathing out, *kibi*, very), *bili-bili-ro*, the lightning (*bi*, quick appearance), *adaili*, the sun (lordly light ?), G. *halitsi*, sweet potatoe (R. 19 a Sect. 108, "According to Carib tradition their Spirits of the Bush have a marked aversion to sweet potatoes") ;

b) *o-ri, u-li, ari*, dark (comp. *iri-be*, uncleanness, § 100), in the following.

ori-roko-ho, S. *wulli-ruku-hu*, darkness ;

ori-ga-hu, S. *wuli-ka-hu*, night ;

a-orirokoto-, to darken, to obscure ;

S. *wuli-ssebéju*, break of day, Sm. *wulissebë-u-killi*, evening or morning twilight ;

Sm. *wúlida*, to be dull, stupid ;

k-ari-me, G. *kh-are-me*, to be black (A. M. § 182, 133) ;

Comp. *o, u*, not moving, space, *ri*, fixed, and also §§ 122 d), 108A f).

§ 127. *Onno, hunnu, hunna*, murmuring, uneasy, unquiet, in the following.

a) *a-onnoda*, S. *a-huñahuñadü-*, Sm. *a-hunnuhunnuda*, to murmur ;

b) Sm. *húnnu-húnnu-li*, a big fly (G. : bumble-bee) ;

c) *m-onda-u*, a calm, *na-mundadwa kiana*, but they held their peace ;

d) *nokonne, nokonni*, sorrow, repenting, *a-nokon(ne)di-*, to cause sorrow, *la-nokonnedoa-n o-doma*, (he) being grieved, *a-nokonnedo-(n-wa)*, to lament, *nokonne goba kiana Jesus*, and Jesus, moved with compassion, *nokonne-ga kiana i*, and (he) had compassion, *nokonne-ga yuholi loko-no o-konomun di*, I have compassion on the multitude, *n-a()alikibitoa nokonne-ci aba-no o-konomun*, *nokonne-hi ſa ba na-konomun o-doma*, blessed are the merciful : for they shall obtain mercy, *nokonne da-kona-n bu*, have mercy on me (thou), *lo-koborokwon lo-nokonne-wa lo-konomun o-doma*, in remembrance of his mercy, G. *nŏkamó-ya|da|i*, he is in misery ;

e) Sm. *kúnnuku*, the forest (A. M. § 182, 76).

§ 128. *Ako, aku*, the principle of : entering into ; a time-reality, *k* making its appearance in an active manner (into) *u*, space.

a) S. *aku, aku-lugku*, in (fire), see § 103 e) ;

aA) Sm. *háku*, mortar (A. M. § 182, 50 B) ;

b) *akodo-*, to sew, to plaite, to weave ; *makondo*, to be naked (comp. S., Sm. *a-kündü-*, to shine, to radiate light) ;

c) *akodo-(n-wa)*, to enter, to go (into), *akodoona-li*, a haven (A. M. § 185, 72) ;

d) Sm. *akutta, aküttü*, to prick, to open the artery ; *aküttüka*, the long points of thorns, B. *k-okkituka-tu*, thistles, G. *tŏ-kŏtŏka*, a straight thorn. *ka-kŏtŏká-tu*, Melocactus ;

e) *akoba*, field, ground ;

f) Sm. *akkuba*, the core of a tree ;

g) *akuyu-ko, -kuyu-ko*, the ear (-hole) ;

h) Sm. *úkkuju*, navel (A. M. § 182, 22) ;

i) *akoio-n(n-wa)*, to return (into) ;

j) Sm. *kújama*, a fish trap ;

k) comp. *o-loko, roko*, in, *o-koboroko*, among, § 103 a, b, h).

§ 129. *Ku*, the principle of : power to move.

a) 1) *akudi-*, to drive out, to persecute ;

  2) *kodibiyu*, a bird (A. M. § 182, 91) ;

  3) R. *kudu-kudu-bari-lya*, a certain ant, used as a hunting-charm (ll. 19 a Sect. 236) ;

aA) G.*a-khoto-*, to collect (fire-wood), *o-kodoto-*, to keep up a fire, *ikihi o-kódo*, B. *ikihi-kudu*, fire-wood ;

b) 1) *o-kuti*, foot (A. M. § 182, 28) ;

  2) *kuta*, animal, game (A. M. § 182, 76 B ; comp. also *a-koto-*, to eat) ;

c) 1) *ikori-ci o-kuti jiaro bui, ikori-ci kabo jiaro bui*, halt (thou) or maimed (thou), *ikori-ci-no akona*, the lame walk, *ikori-hia*, (being) halt ; S. *hikkúli* (A. M. § 182, 140B) ;

  2) Sm. *hikkuli*, bush- tortoise (A. M. § 182, 96) ;

  3) G. *kuli(hi)*, rat, Sm. *pu-kulé-ru*, agouti (A. M. § 182, 83, 84) ;

d) 1) *o-koro*, Sm. *u-kkuru, u-kkulu*, knee ; Sm. *ue-kkülle-kabbu*, arm-pit. *ú-kkuru lúkku*, hollow of the knee, S. *lu-kullabu-lukku, tu-kullu-bu-lukku*, [a sheet knit at the four] corners, G. *tu-kuλabó-loko*, angle ;

  2) Sm. *ú-kkura*, G. *o-kūra*, hammock was explained as "a resting place" [but also : *da-kóra η* or *da-koró-ša*, it (hammock, clothes, food) belongs to me] ; comp. further *akera*, to bind, § 104 b) 2) VII) ;

e) *kudi*, to be heavy (A. M. § 182, 141) ; *kudu-sabu-tu amateli*, the weightier matters ;

f) *komogi*, to move, to be troubled (water, J. V, 3, 7) ; Sm. *kumúr-kû, a-kumurdu-(nn-ua)*, to fart, G. *kúmur-ka|de*. I am flatulent ;

Sm. *kummuttiri*, white ant-hill (emitting foam at certain seasons) (A. M. § 182, 108) ;

maba o-komodi, an honeycomb ;

Sm. *ú-kumuju*. dust, the dirt from something ;

Sm. *a-kkummudü-*, to dry in the sun, B. *a-komodwa*, to warm oneself (near the fire) ;

Sm. *u-kummu-lukku-hu*, the shine, the lustre, Pen. *komoloko*, light.

§ 130. *Au*, space with the character of time-reality (alternate use of *au* and *o* in : *au-rea*, *o-rea*, from, § 97 a), *wauaiya*, *woaiya*, ourselves, § 120 g) [2]), *h-ausa-ili*, go (ye), *b-osa-ili*, go (thee), perhaps also *aunaki-* to receive, *onnaki-* to take, to remove).

a) [1] *(a)-u-ka*, *(a)-u-ga*, to occur in space ; [2] *(a)-u-kili*, *(a)-o-kili* (§ 175 e)), occurrence in space ; [3] *-u*, occurrence in space.

[1] *isa-u-ga fa-te*, it will be fair weather, *monda-u ka kiana n*, and there was a calm ;

[2] *t-iibo fa koro t-isi-ika*, *c-iwi-ika bajia* ; *mimili, tere bajia* ; *isa-u-kili, aboa-u-kili bajia* ; *kasakabo, kasakoda bajia*, seedtime and harvest, and cold and heat, and summer and winter, and day and night shall not cease (*isa*, beautiful, good, *aboa*, foul), *tanahu aboa-u-kili fa*, it will be foul weather to day, *kena ifiro-tu monda-u-kili goba*, and there was a great calm (*m-onda*, § 127 c)), *ma-loko-n a-u-kili*, the wilderness (*ma-loko-n*, being empty), *ka-siri-siri a-u-kili waboroko*, the rough ways (*ka-siri-siri*, with rough points or pebbles), *n-akonnaba Adaie-li Wacinaci ajia-n*, *akona l-a-n ka yara o-loko-ji mimi-a-u-kili-di*, they heard the voice of the Lord God walking in the garden in the cool of the day (*mimi*, to be cold), *b-augioci ajinama ma-u-gili o-loko*, thy brethren stand without, *to-boredo-n-wa bia ma-u-gili o-lokomun*, to be cast out [and trodden under foot], Sm. *wulissebë-u-killi*, twilight, *ma-u-killi*, the sky, the starry sky ;

[3] *serabo-kili-o*, S. *se-ribo-kkilli-u*, a tempest (§ 116 d) 9)), S. *wuli-sse-bej-u*, break of day (§ 126 b)) ;

b) [1] S. *a-usu-*, to begin, to start, to depart, S. *ikka a-ussü-nn-üwa-i ba*, be it known therefore unto you (Acts XXVIII, 28), B. *ausi-*, to go ; presumably *u* space, *s* formed, consequently "to form a void" ;

[2] *ausiro*.

ausiro n-a ma ausi-n, they need not depart, *to-makwa ausiro-n-tu ajia-hu*, every idle word, *l-auciga goba aba-no ajinama-kwon-ci ausirobu-in*, and (he) found others standing idle, *m-onnaki-n b-a Adaie-li Wacinaci bu-mun iri ausirobu-in*, thou shalt not take the name of the Lord thy God in vain, *toro ausirobu-in-tu*, these vanities ;

c) *auti-*, to suffer, to permit, *m-auti-*, to forbid ;

d) *aucigi-*, to find, to receive ;

e) *m-au-ci*, early morning, see § 161 b) ;

onyikau, o-nyikau, goods, *sa-tu onyikau*, treasure ;

karau, grass, Sm. grass, savanah ;

kauri, a basket ;

akausa, to compass ;

isauka, a kingdom (comp. *isa-u-ga*, beautiful weather, § 130 a) 1)) ;

bawhu, house, *bawhu-yuho*, city (A. M. § 182, 116).

§ 131. *Iau ; i-a* let loose, *u* space.

a) 1) *a-iaudi-* ... *a* (§ 169 a) 2)), to be beside oneself, to be mad ; *bu-iauda-a*, thou art beside thyself, *manswa kibi d-a goba a-iaudi-ni-a na-kona mun*, and (I) being exceedingly mad against them, *lihi a-iaudi-ci-a*, he is beside himself, *a-maiaudo-(n-wa)*, to hold one's peace, to keep patience, *a-maiaudwa-hu*, [wars and] commotions ;

2) *ma-iau-kwa (-kwon)*, being in peace, quiet, silent ;

b) *iauna, iauna*, value, price, reward, *a-iaunti-*, to buy, to pay.

§ 132. *Ia* is used to express : *i* the preceding, appearing in a free manner (a principle or the momentary), *a* continues for some time.

-ia, Hortative-Optative, § 5, table, forms n⁰. 10 ;

-hia, -ia, existing condition, § 23 ;

word with the ending *i*, +*a*, separable possession, likeness, §§ 82, 82A :

bia, it will be, be it, § 39 ;

oini ... iki, rain, § 48 h), *mauci*, early morning, § 161 b) + *a*. Indicative mood, Present tense ;

-sia, the thing that has been realised, § 22 ;

-sia, a human quality or peculiarity, etc., § 118 a) ;

kia, relative pronoun, § 49 a) ;

lia, newly originated, § 98 ;

rea, ria, from, § 97 ;

nianna, season, § 161 j), *bania*, lasting some time, § 60 e), *o-tobonia*, dream, § 174 c) ;

h(ia), something airy or etherical, § 169 ;

boia, smell, savour, § 169 c), *raia*, appearance, § 104 a), *adaia*, to be a ruler, § 89, *abui(a or e)*, to feed, § 65, *a-kwaiabo-*, to beseech, to pray, § 120 e) 7), *a-iadi-*, to move, to travel, S. *a-ijahaddü-*, to walk, to go, *a-iako*, to pierce ;

comp. also *-i fa, -i ba* etc., § 5.

§ 133. *(H)ai, ai*, established security, peace (?).

a) *aici-*, to know, *d-aiita*, I know. S. *aditti-*, to know ;

b) 1) *m-aiika-ci-no*, the deaf, *m-ajia-n-tu, m-aiika-tu yauhahu bui*, thou dumb and deaf spirit ;

2) *aiikasia*, to have forgotten ;

3) S. *haika hidda na-kuburukku*, they held their peace ;

4) *ahaikata fa na-koboroko* (§§ 103 h), 120 g) 7)) *o-doma*, for they shall be comforted, *Ahaikata-ci ho-koboroko*, the (your) Comforter ;

5) *aiakati-*, to hide, *aiakato-(n-wa)*, to be hidden ;

6) *aiika*, to marry, *d-aiika-ga bu-ma*, I thee wed ;

7) *aiikah, aiika*, death, to die ;

c) *k-aiima-hu*, the wrath, *lihi koro k-aiima fa*, he shall not strive. *ama ibia akirikia-no k-aiima-ga*, why did the heathen rage ? *k-aiima sabu goba kiana ie,* and they were the more fierce, *k-aiima-ci-no wa-mun,* our enemies, *m-aiima-ci,* (a)meek(person), *m-aiima-hu ho-mun,* peace be unto you, *kena m-aiima-li ho-muni-kwawa hu,* and have peace one with another ;

aiimaha, tó curse ; *kena d-aiimatoo-koto fa ho-muni-kwawa bui hiaro o-ma, bu-sa t-isa aiimatoo fa na-muni-kwawa bajia,* and I will put enmity between thee and the woman, and between thy seed and her seed, *aiimawto-,* to offend, *aiimawto-(n-wa),* to be offended, to be wroth (*aiimaw = aiima-hu ?*), *aiimawto()koto,* to set at variance ;

d) *aiikita,* to pipe, to sound (a trumpet), to handle (harp and organ), comp. *ikita* to serve ;

e) G. *te̥-kaikai,* whirlpool.

§ 134. *Ka,* energetic action, sometimes relentless.

a) 1) *kari,* to suffer, to be vexed, *kari-hi,* disease, anguish, *kari-tu hori,* viper, *manswa-ci kari-bi-ci-n lihi a-kwaiaboa manswa sabu-in,* and being in an agony he prayed more earnestly (A. M. § 182, 132B) ;

2) *a-kariti-,* to torment, *na-loa a-karitwa,* they were cut to the heart ;

3) *karikona ... ajia-n* reproaching words, *karikona b-ajia-n,* thou reproachest ;

4) G. *háči karoa-ka,* the pepper is strong ;

5) Sm. *a-kkakardi-,* to bite (a snake) ;

b) *a-katadi,* to stumble, to dash (his feet against a stone), to be offended;

c) *akarati-, akarate, akarata,* to bury (a corpse) (A. M. § 182, 135) ;

cA) G. *kakali-či,* a man with curly hair ;

d) 1) *t-ikaba,* his saltness, *a-kabato-(n-wa),* to be salted (*pawmu,* salt, perhaps Karib, Sm. *ue-ssalá-ru,* salted meat or fish, Spanish or creole) ;

2) *maba,* honey (A. M. § 182, 105) ;

e) 1) *a-kabo,* hand (Sm. : especially the front part, the fingers) (A. M. § 182, 27) ;

2) Sm. *a-kakatta,* to mix with the hand ;

3) G. *a-káǫadi-,* to stir up ;

f) 1) *kaci,* A. M. § 182, 62 *kači, *kairi,* moon ; *ka* force, *či, iri,* fluid (tides, menstruation, etc.) (?) ;

2) *kalime,* light, glory, to be bright, to shine, § 126 a), A. M. § 182, 61 *kamu,* sun ; *ka,* force, *mu* origin of life, vegetative faculty ? (comp. § 135 d) 2)) ;

3) Sm. *kámma,* A. M. § 182, 88 *kama,* tapir ; (Pen. 17a, II, 57, III, 119, symbol of temptation, carnal lusts) ;

4) Sm. *kamúdu,* the big water-boa ;

g) *wakaia,* evil, to be evil ; § 188 ;

h) Sm. *káikuti,* alligator ; *ka* (biting) force, *ikuti,* halt, § 129 c) ? (A. M. § 182, 98).

§ 135. Colours.

[G. A paper with squares of different colours was placed before the

Arawaks. They (and also Waraus and a Kaliña), had great difficulty in giving the names of the colours, especially that for blue. "The rainbow has many different colours", they translated by *to yáwale abáloko diako ka-yá-n-da*, lit. this rainbow different upon with-image.]

a) *a-li*, light, white, see § 126 ;

b) *o-ri*, dark, *karime*, black, see § 126 ;

c) Sm. *úellihi*, to be black, G. *uülihi*, to be brown, Q. *illihiti*, R. *iri-to a-ta-hu*, a black beverage ;

d) 1) I) *kore*, to be red ;

II) *kore-tu marisi*, the harvest (*marisi*, maize, wheat), *to-kore-ka*, in the time of harvest ;

III) *oraro jiamutu kore-li*, vapour (cloud-like) of smoke, *flax a-koredo-tu*, smoking flax, S. *kulle-helli*, smoke ;

IV) B. uses *korrokori*, in translating "gold", but probably this word means a gold alloy, or the nose ornaments and pendants made of the same. G. *kálukuli*, brass, *kálukúli kulē-ro*, copper (*kule*, red), *puláta* (Spanish) or *góutu* (creole), gold, *puláta alidā-ru*, silver (*alida*, white), Sm. *kárrukulli*, brass, *karrukulli üssa-uábu*, S. *karrukulli üssa-be-ru*, gold (*üssa-uabu*, *üssa-be-ru*, precious). Comp. also : Cumanagoto *carcuriri*, oro baxo, *chuparari*, oro, *cappara*, hierro (§ 116 (·) 3)). Warau *corucuri*, brass, *borata šimu*, gold (*borata*, Spanish plata, *zimo*, red), *burata hoko*, silver (*hoko*, white).

The Island Karibs had nose ornaments and pendants made of a gold alloy, which they called *caracoli* or *calloucouli* : "c'est le butin le plus rare le plus prisé, qu'ils remportent de courses qu'ils font tous les ans, dans les terres des Arrouägues, leurs ennemis" (de Rochefort, 55, Livre II, Ch. 9).

See further for this gold alloy, Rivet, 70, and comp. Kechua *cori*, gold, Kampa (A. M. language) *quirei*, gold, silver.

V) Sm. *kureme*, bête rouge, Acarus Batatas ;

VI) Sm. *korabúli*, brown ;

VII) Sm. *kárraü-ru*, Bignonia chica, from which a red paint is prepared (A. M. § 182, 119A) ;

VIII) Sm. *kárriman*, black pitch prepared from the gum of Symphonia globulifera L. f.,Karib languages *paramani, mani ;*

2) I) *imoro-tu abona-gira-hu*, green herb, *imoro-tu karau*, the green grass, G. *imóro-to*, green ;

II) *ika ki t-adinabo moromorotwa*, when his (the fig tree's) branch is yet tender ; Sm. *múrmuru, murmuru-make, morumoru-make*, to be unripe, G. *imoro-koa|tha č-iwi*, the fruit is unripe ;

e) *bonaro-tu*, purple ; the origin of this word has not been ascertained :

f) Sm. *súbule*, to be green, see § 119 b) 7) :

g) Sm. *háehae, héhê*, to be pale, G. *hehé*, to be yellow (A. M. § 182, 134) ; Sm. *aehae, ehehi*, urine.

h) G. *ka-tuli*, to be gray (with-dust, § 99 d)).

§ 135A. G. *kabuin tu-kuλabóloko,* triangle (§ 129 d)), *bīši t.,* square, *badeχábu t.,* pentagon, *bátimaη t.,* hexagon ;

G. *abuλedá-tu,* cross (§ 69 d)) ;

G. *balalá,* ball, sphere, Sm. *bálla,* lead, shot, ball (Spanish ?), *bállalâ,* to be round, G. *bála,* lead, *tu-buelalădon-an,* circle ;

G. *a-kerosó-to,* circle (§ 108A d)) ;

G. *tu-kudibia-sadonan,* ellipse, lit. its-bird-egg-form ;

G. *tekáikaido-nan,* spiral (§ 133 e)).

CHAPTER XVII

CLASSES OF UTTERANCES; NUMERALS

§ 136. Command, prohibition, incitement, request, answer to a question, and exclamation, are composed in the same way as a statement. Probably there is some difference in intonation, and moreover, when one expresses a command, a prohibition or an incitement, use is frequently made of the particles -li and -te, which indicate the character of the movement, and at the same time show that the speaker means motion.

Every spoken utterance only completes what the hearer already knows, or what he can conclude by the gestures and actions of the speaker and others. Therefore we can easily comprehend that especially these sorts of utterances are often very short.

See examples in § 12, and also the following :

a) *b-adeka di, Adaie-li,* behold, I am here, Lord, lit. thou -see me, Lord, *h-onnaka n, h-eke n, toho d-ifiro-hu,* take, eat : this is my body, *b-osa !* go thy way ! *h-akenakwa-te, yaha-rea w-ausa-i-li,* arise, let us go hence, *da fa-i, ma-ribe-n bu,* I will ; be thou clean, *m-amaro-ni bu,* not afraid, *m-amaro-ni hu,* fear not ye, be not affrighted, *m-amaro-ni kiana hu na-bora,* fear them not therefore, *m-amaro-n bu, Paul,* fear not, Paul, *m-amaro-n bu, Sion o-tu,* fear not, daughter of Sion ;

b) *David Aiici,* The son of David (Mt. XXII, 42), *m-ansi d-a,* I will not, *d-ausa, Adaie-li,* I go, sir (Mt. XXI, 29, 30), *John Baptist isi,* the head of John the Baptist (Mk. VI, 24) ;

c) *Adaie-li, David Aiici bui,* O Lord, thou son of David ! *yauhahu bui !* thou unclean spirit ! *murriga-ci hui !* ye hypocrites ! *murriga-ci bui !* thou hypocrite ! *isa n, sa-ci, kidua-ci da-sanci bui,* well done, thou good and faithful servant, *Claudius Lysias, isa-ci-wabu adaia-hu Felix o-mun, imigoda toho ajia-hu ; Alikibi bu, ma-in,* Claudius Lysias unto the most excellent governor Felix sendeth greeting (sends this word ; Joy thee, *ma-in,* § 35), *alikibi bu !* hail ! (L. I, 28) ;

d) *ahe,* yes (§ 109) ; *aba-koro,* no (*aba,* one, a, *koro,* negation) ; *Ahe, Adaie-li, n-a goba ajia-n lo-mun,* they said unto him, Yea, Lord, *Abakoro : l-a oonaba-n,* and he answered, No, *to-moroa, Ahe, ahe ; Abakoro, abakoro ; h-a-li ajia-n,* but let your communication be, Yea, yea ; Nay, nay, *to-moroa abakoro l-a goba ajia-n na-makwa na-makanna,* but he denied before them all, *abakoro, l-a ki ka ba,* and he denied it again, G. *abákóro,* not a single one (*mani,* no ! § 32 c)) ;

e) 1) (from B. 's grammar :) "The interjections are chiefly uncouth sounds indicative of surprise, alarm, &c., many of which it would be difficult to express by letters. Some have a definite meaning, as *kimii* and *asikii*, the former expressing surprise with a degree of sorrow or alarm ; the latter denoting excessive disgust. But the majority are such as require the expression of the voice, and vary their meaning according to its intonation." (*kimii*, see under ³), *asikii*, G. *siki̯ !* comp. *isi*, to stink, § 115) ;

2) Sm. *poi !* word of astonishment, *poi ! d-a (b-a, l-a)*, I (thou, he) wonder, *poi ! d-ibi*, I have wondered to-day, *poi ! da-pa*, I will wonder, etc. ; S. *h-addika-te amuttâ-rubu-mu-tti|de, pahia* — *h-â-li*, behold, ye despisers, and wonder, *pahia !* — *ma na-kunnamüñ*, they marvelled (them-concerning ; Acts IV, 13), etc., G. *fá !* is said, when someone uses a bad word (see § 184) ;

3) I) Sm. *emè*, word of surprise, astonishingly ! S. *l-ani-ka baddia ipîrru-tu manswa-ttu* — *Eméme diamuttu* — *lukku-nnu u-mükaña, n-aditti-koana-wa*, (he) did great wonders and miracles among the people, lit. he-did-when also great thing very thing — *ememe* like — men before they-know-instrument-own (see § 184) ;

II) Sm. *aème*, the smell of a thing, *ká-maije*, vanilla, *k-úma-ru*, Dipteryx odorata, G. *th-éma*, it (a bush-hog) stinks, *n-éme*, they (a crowd) smell malodorously, *k-eméya-to dúϱi*, the negroes smell m. ;

4) *ah !*, ah (Mk. XV, 29) ;

5) Sm. *akka*, ach ! *akka|ka tuhu ! akka|ka-e !*, G. *akō*, word of surprise (A. M. § 182, 132B) ;

6) Q. : "In their meetings, their greetings and that which they have to say, is expressed in a singing tone, and is answered by the person to whom it is addressed, in the same singing, or rather plaintive tone, with a repetition of the last words with addition of *wa, ehekada* and *gideada*, as substantiation."

See moreover the words mentioned in § 179.

§ 137. Explanation :

Abona-ci sa-tu t-isi, loko Aiici ; Kabuea, ororo ; sa-tu t-isi, isauka sanoci ; to-moroa tare, wakaia-ci sanoci ; K-aiima-ci abona-ci n. yauhahu ; to-kore ka, ororo a-iiboa ; onnaki-ci-no, angel-no, He that soweth the good seed is the Son of man ; The field is the world : the good seed are the children of the kingdom ; but the tares are the children of the wicked one ; The enemy that sowed them is the devil ; the harvest is the end of the world ; and the reapers are the angels.

Other juxtaposition :

Daii, Da-ci, abar-li waii, I and my Father are one.

§ 138. Questions do not differ in the sequence of words from other sentences. Probably ambiguity is prevented by different intonation.

Daii ! it is I, *Daii ?* is it I ? *Christ bui.* thou art the Christ, *Christ bui ?* art thou the Christ ? *d-ikiduada bui Christ. Wacinaci Aiici*, I believe that thou art the Christ, the Son of God, *b-ikiduada Wacinaci Aiici ?* dost thou believe on the Son of God ? *m-aici-n d-a i,* I know him not, *bui a-mairikota-ci Israel, kena m-aici-n b-a toraha* ? art thou a master of Israel, and knowest not these things ?

With *ma,* expressing doubt (§ 5, forms 5) :

yauhahu a-toroda ma m-akosi-ci akosi-hi kiana ? can a devil open the eyes of the blind ?

With a negative form (perhaps in imitation of the English construction):

Joseph koro aiici lihi ? is not this Joseph's son ? *aba-ro t-aurea-tu atedi faroka, l-iiba koro bibici-loko bibici-timen kutibana t-ajeago ... ?* and (if) one of them be gone astray, doth he not leave the ninety and nine ... ? *ma-ridi-n h-a David onyi-sia o-konomun,* have ye not read, what David did ? (Mt. XII, 3), *m-adeki-n h-a toraha to-makwa* ? see ye not all these things ? (Mt. XXIV, 2), *Daii koro akabo a-murreti-sia goba toraha to-makwa* ? hath not my hand made all these things ?

§ 139. In the preceding sentences, the uncertainty is so well indicated, that the listener has only to answer "yes" or "no". When this is impossible or impractical, the uncertainty is indicated by a word denoting its class (interrogative word). The same words are used in non-interrogative sentences (in imitation of the English construction ?).

a) *Ama* denotes a person who "is", a thing that "is" ; *m* uncertain, unpretending, *a* time-reality.

1) I) *ama bu-iri* ? ... *Legion da-iiri,* what is thy name ? ... my name is Legion, *ama n-a loko-no a-sa-n di, Daii loko Aiici* ? ... John Baptist. *n-a aba-no a-sa-n bu ;* ... *To-moroa ama h-a hui a-sa-n di* ? whom do men say that I the Son of man am ? ... Some say that thou art John the Baptist ... But whom say ye that I am ? *ama toho l-ajia-ga* ? what is this that he saith ? *ama isa loko o-mun* ? for what is a man profited ? (Mt. XVI, 26), *ama ajia-hu abu b-onyi-ka toho* ? by what authority doest thou these things ? *ama w-onyi-ka waii* ? what do we ? (J. XI, 47), *ama jia kibi l-a lihi* ? what manner of man is this ? *ama ibia kiana, Elias andi-n bia-te to-bora,* why then say the scribes, that Elias must first come ? *ama o-doma* ? *ama wakaìa-hu l-onyi goba* ? why ? what evil hath he done ? (Mk. XV, 14), *ama tu* (§ 55 b) 4)) *kidua-hu* ? what is truth ? *ama-hu h-a k-ikisi-n* ? how think ye ? S. *hamma-hü-bia,* why ;

II) *ama l-a goba koro oonaba-ni-n,* [when he was accused] he answered nothing, *daii koro aiita ama b-a-n ajia-n,* I know not what thou sayest, *isiroko isa koro ama ibia,* the flesh profiteth nothing, *ama-hu l-a-n jiaro Adam a-sa-n to-makwa kokki-tu, kia ki t-iri,* and whatsoever Adam called every living creature, that was the name thereof :

2) *amisia-ci l-ibekita sa-be-tu ama-te-li abu ; kena yuho-ro k-amun-ci l-akoiokota ama-koro abu,* he hath filled the hungry with good things : and the rich he hath sent empty away ;

b) *alo* denotes circumstances ; *l,* loose, able to move, *o* space.

1) *alo-n,* where ?

I) *alon-ci bui* ? where dwellest thou ? *alon-ga|i ka-raia-ci Jew-no*

Adaie-n-wabu ? where is he that is born King of the Jews ? *alon-ga b-ici ?* where is thy Father ? *hiaro, alon-ga naii ahaka-ci bu-iri ?* woman, where are those thine accusers ? *alon kwa n-a bibici-time-no ?* but where are the nine ? (L. XVII, 17) ;

II) *auaduli a-fuda alon jiaro t-ansi-n, kena t-akonnakita-n b-akonnaba barin, to-moroa m-aici-n b-a alo area t-andi-n-te, alo mun i-ro t-ausi-n,* the wind bloweth where it listeth, and thou hearest the sound thereof, but canst not tell whence it cometh, and whither it goeth ;

2) *alo-mun,* where ?

I) *alo mun ka i ?* where is he ? (J. VII, 11), *alomun-ga bawhu adeki-ci bu o-bora-tu ?* where is the guestchamber ? *alomun ka h-ikiduadi-n ?* where is your faith ? *ama kiana bawhu ho-murreti fa da-mun ? l-a Adaie-li ajia-n, alomun-ga da-bora yumun-tu bia d-ahakobu-in ?* what house will ye build me ? saith the Lord : or what is the place of my rest ? *alomun kwa b-a ?* where art thou ? (Gen. III, 9), *alo mun Christ ka-raie-n bia ? l-a goba adagato-n ie,* he demanded of them where the Christ should be born, *Adaie-li, alo mun i-ro b-osa-bo ?* Lord, whither goest thou ?

II) *alomun jiaro ajia-sia fa sa-tu ajia-hu toho,* wheresoever this gospel shall be preached [this shall be told], *m-aici-n w-a alo mun i-ro b-osi-n,* we know not whither thou goest ;

3) *alo-man,* when ? how long ? how many ?

I) *aloman ho-ma fa di ? aloman d-onnaki fa hu ?* how long shall I be with you ? how long shall I suffer you ? *aloman tu hour o-loko sa-sabu bona i ?* (in which hour did he begin to amend ? (J. VI, 52 ; *tu,* see § 55 b) 4)), *aloman tu meli h-amuni-ga ?* how many loaves have ye ?

II) *aloman ororo ajeago ka di, ororo o-mun kalime Daii,* as long as I am in the world, I am the light of the world, *kena aloman tu kauri h-onnaki-n goba ?* [do ye not remember the seven loaves of the four thousand], and how many baskets ye took up ?

4) *alo-area,* whence ?

I) *alo area kiana tare t-amuni-ga ?* from whence then hath it tares ? *alo area liraha auciga ka-ieniko-hu toho ?* whence hath this man this wisdom ? *alo-area-tu kibi da-mun toho ?* and whence is this to me ? (L. I, 43) ;

II) *d-aici-n alo area d-andi-n goba-te o-doma, alo mun i-ro d-ausi-n fa ba,* for I know whence I came, and wither I go, *m-aiici-n l-a goba alo area-ni n,* and (he) knew not whence [the wine] was ;

c) *aro,* parallel to *alo* (*l,* loose, *r,* fixed), with emphasizing particle *hai, wai* (§ 121 ᶜ)).

II) *b-adeka, arohai bu-pound-in,* behold, here is thy pound, S. *haruwai Parthia-kunna-na, Medus-kunna-na,* etc., (there were) Parthians, and Medes, etc., *haruwai kirraha jaha-bu hidda,* see, here is water, G. *kharo(ho),* now ;

d) *halli-di,* in the following :

S. *lui kéwai a-ssiki-ssia na-mün ikissi-hü, patta-hü n-a kakü-n-ti, halli-di n-a ka-ssikoa-ni bia ba u-kunnamün,* (Acts XVII, 26, last part, lit. himself given-thing them-to time how-long they-do living-person, where they-do with-house-to-be also concerning), Sm. *halli-di wa-kúnnu-pa.* wie wollen wir gehen [*kuljara u-lluku hurrurá-di küssa.* im Corjar oder zu Land ?]

e) *alika,* denotes events; *li,* freely streaming forth, *ka,* if, when (§ 29 a)).

1) *alika, alika-a,* when ?

I) *alika tu bia toraha ?* when shall these things be ? (*tu,* see § 55 b) 4)), *alikaa l-anda fa-te ba ?* when shall he come back ? *alika w-adeka goba amisia-n bu ?* when saw we thee an hungred ?

2) with auxiliary verb *a,* how ?

I) *alika b-a ajia-n, Ho-maierodo fa ?* how sayest thou, Ye shall be made free ? *alika wa fa naraha ?* what shall we do to these men ? *alika h-a ma ikiduadi-n Daii ajia-n ?* how shall ye believe my words ? *alika t-a b-akosi a-torodo-n-wa ?* how were thine eyes opened ? *alika lo fa-te naha kabuea-ari-no o-mun ?* what will he do unto those husbandmen ?

II) *ho-mairikotwa-li kabuia o-loko-tu to-tokoro o-konomun ; alika t-a-n ibikido-n-wa,* consider the lilies of the field, how they grow, *alika koro t-adekoa goba torajiamutu Israel o-loko,* it was never so seen in Israel ;

3) with *mo-tu, mu-tu,* what manner of ? (comp. §§ 70 a) 2), 88 f)).

I) *alika mo-tu ajia-hu l-ajia-ga toho ?* what manner of saying is this that he said ;

II) *m-aici-n h-a alika mu-tu ialoko h-amuni-n,* ye know not what manner of spirit ye are of ;

4) with the end-point pronouns *-i, -n,* ie.

I) *alika-i bui ?* who art thou ? *alika-i loko hui o-rea-ci ?* or what man is there of you ? *alika i a-fatada bu ?* who is he that smote thee ? *alika-i abu h-isanoci a-boreda n ?* by whom do your children cast them (the devils) out ? *alika-n da-iiyu ? alika-ie d-augioci ?* who is my mother ? and who are my brethren ?

5) with *-i* and negation-word *koro,* indicating doubt.

I) *alika-i koro aboadikita bu ?* hath no man condemned thee ?

II) *alika-i koro anda ma da-mun,* no man can come to me.

§ 140. a) *Jiali,* (who, what) like, with motion ; *jia* (§ 88) with *li,* freely streaming forth.

ki-o-doma alika-i jiali akonnabo-ci toho d-ajia-sia, therefore whosoever heareth these sayings of mine, *m-amuni n-a goba alika-i jiali k-amunaiga-ci,* neither was there any among them that lacked, *kena m-ajia-n h-a-li aba-li jiali o-mun waboroko o-loko-ji,* and salute no man by the way. *kena a-siki-ci jiali,* and whosoever shall ye give ;

b) *jiari.* (who, what) like, without motion.

h-ikiduadi-sia jiari ki tu fa-i ho-mun. according to your faith be it unto you, *misi-tu-ahaka-hu o-loko-ji jiari ki n-a-n bia i,* [when the parents brought in the child Jesus]. to do for him after the custom of the law. *loko-no waii hui jiari-ki-n-ci waii ba,* we also are men of like passions with you. Other examples in § 41.

c) *jiaro,* (who, what) like, stopped.

1) I) *kabuin hour jiaro adiki l-iretu akodwa,* and it was about the space of three hours after, when his wife ... came in, *d-ausa fa bu- inabo alomun jiaro b-osi-n,* I will follow thee whithersoever thou goest, *alika jiaro k-aiima-ci ki ma-siki-n ma-n bia bu ikisida-arin o-mun,* lest at any time the adversary deliver thee to the judge, *alika-n jiaro bawhu-yuho o-lokomun h-akodo-n-wa,* and into whatsoever city ye enter, *alika-n jiaro aiita-sia ada c-iwi abu,* for every tree is known by his own fruit, *ki-o-doma amateli jiaro h-ansi-sia loko-no onyi-n bia ho-mun, tora-jin ki h-onyi fa na-mun,* therefore all things whatsoever ye would that men should do to you, do ye even so to them, *hui ikiside-sia jiaro ki abu, hui ikisido fa ba,* for with what judgment ye judge, ye shall be judged;

II) *aba-no wadili, bibici-hundred jiaro-no,* a number of men, about four hundred;

2) used for translating "or", after each of the coordinated terms.

kena alika-i jiali a-iibi-ci l-isikwa jiaro, l-augioci jiaro ... lo-horora jiaro, da-iiri o-konaria, and every one that hath forsaken houses, or brethren ... or lands, for my name's sake, *abar-li m-ansi lo fa, l-ibiamti-ci l-ansi fa, jiaro; abar-li l-ikita fa, l-ibiamti-ci l-imita fa, jiaro,* for either he will hate the one, and love the other; or else he will hold to the one, and despise the other.

§ 141. a) *Arin(i),* exercising a profession, a trade, a craft; *a* time-reality, *ri* fixed, *n* vagueness in regard to time.

ma-siki-n b-a oniabu da-kuti arini wa, thou gavest me no water for my feet, *kia ki arini o-doma i, na-ma goba kiana i, imikebo-n, tenti a-murreta-ari-no o-doma ie,* and because he was of the same craft, he abode with them, and wrought: for by their occupation they were tentmakers, *ada-arin,* carpenter, *plata-arin,* silversmith, *imikebo-arin,* workman, *t-eda-isada-arin,* tanner, *ikisida-arin,* judge, *sikapo ikita-arin,* shepherd, *bonaro-tu a-iyugara-arin,* seller of purple (woman), *kabuea-ari-no,* husbandmen, *asia-ari-no,* fishers, *a-bokota-ari-nno na-bokoto-n bia i,* officers to take him, *ajia-arin,* orator;

S. *purpura a-ijukarrâ-hü âlin-kurru,* a seller of purple, *lihi baddia kimissa akkudâ-hü âlini-n,* lit. he also canvas-sewing, *platta âlin.* silversmith, *ahaka-hü alini-nu,* the scribes, *Judu-nnu kerki ipilli-be-tti ikitta-hü âli-n.* the chief ruler of the synagogue, *na-ssika juhu-rru abujoa-hü w-adikk-oa wa-mün, wa-burugku alini-wa,* they laded us with such things as were necessary;

b) S., Q. *alin-ua,* superior (?) comp. *a(ha)li-kibi,* joy.

S. *ika ka-ijawa-ti-kill a-dallida n-ibiti, t-adaijahükitti-n-benna n-alinua,* and the man in whom the evil spirit was leaped on them, and overcame them, *meju u-lukkuaria t-alinua,* the tackling of the ship, Q. *hamma-kurru aboa-tu tatta-ni bia w-allin-ua,* let nothing evil overwhelm us (lead us not into temptation), *k-adanni-(n) alin-ua,* to overcome.

§ 142. *Koro,* negation ; *ko* affirms, knits up the event, the person or thing in question, *ro* stops.

M(a)- negatives a form which denotes a state or condition (§§ 10, 18, 28 ᵈ)) and may be compared to English "un-", or "without". *Koro* negatives a clause. The place of *koro* is chosen in accordance with the necessity of emphasizing the negation.

a) *Christ koro daii,* I am not the Christ (J. I, 20), *daii koro,* I am not (J. I, 21), *daii koro aiita lihi loko,* I know not the man, *ma-sweardoa-n h-a-li abaren : Aiomun koro abu bu-sweardoa fa,* etc., swear not at all ; neither by heaven, etc., *Sabbath a-murretwa goba loko o-mun, loko koro a-murretwa sabbath o-mun,* the sabbath was made for man, and not man for the sabbath, *h-adaiana-sia koro a-iaunta tribute plata ?* doth not your master pay tribute ? *Solomon, to-makwa l-ikalime-hi abu, ekitwa goba koro isa-n abar toraha jin,* even Solomon in all his glory was not arrayed like one of these, *c-imikebo ka koro, t-isiribida koro,* they toil not, neither do they spin, *ajia-hu k-amun-ci jia l-a-n goba a-mairikota-n o-doma ie, a-buriti-ci-no jia l-a goba koro,* for he taught them as one that had authority, and not as the scribes, *kidua-n, d-ajia-ga ho-mun, Torajiamutu ifiro-tu ikiduada-hi m-aucigi-n d-a goba ; abakoro, Israel akirikia o-loko koro d-auciga n,* verily I say unto you, I have not found so great faith, no, not in Israel, *to-moroa ma-dokodo-n ho faroka loko-no wakaia-hu. H-icinaci koro a-dokodo fa ho-wakaia h-aurea,* but if ye forgive not men their trespasses, neither will your Father forgive your trespasses ; see also § 138 :

b) *a-korodi-,* to break a branch from a tree.

§ 143. *Kowa,* S., G. *kawa,* to be absent : *k(a).* affirmed. *(o)wa.* distant, a void.

loko-no o-loa kowa fa, amaro-n o-doma ie, men's hearts failing them for fear (L. XXI, '26), *aba-ro kowa-ka bu-mun,* one thing thou lackest, *plata, korrokori mu-tu kowa-ka da-mun,* silver and gold have I none, *kena m-ansi t-a to-io-no ahikata-n to-koboroko, kowa-n o-doma ie,* and (she) would not be comforted, because they [the massacred infants] are not, *m-aiima-hu aiici yumuni faroka, hui m-aiima-hu yumuni fa ba ; to-moroa kowa faroka i, t-anda fa h-amun ba,* and if the son of peace be there, your peace shall rest upon it : if not, it shall turn to you again, *kena l-oabodda l-isikiti-n bia i na-mun, kowa n-a-n ka loko-no,* and (he) sought opportunity to betray him unto them in the absence of the multitude.

§ 144. *Faroka,* indicating the hypothetical, is used in the same way as *fa* (§ 5) ; *fa* points to the future, *ro* stops the flow of thought, *ka,* if, when (§ 29 ᵃ)).

Christ faroka i, [let him save himself], if he be Christ. *Adaie-li, bui faroka,* Lord, if it be thou. *b-ikiduada faroka, Wacinaci kalime-hi b-adeki fa ; d-a koro ajia-n bu-mun ?* said I not unto thee, that, if thou wouldest believe, thou shouldest see the glory of God ? *k-iwi faroka n, isa fa n ; m-a-ni tu faroka, t-adiki bu-sogo fa n,* and if it bear fruit, well : and if not, then after that thou shalt cut it down. *tata-o-kona koro b-amuni koma da-*

konomun, aiomuni o-rea ma-siko-n-wa tu faroka bu-mun, thou couldest have no power at all against me, except it were given thee from above, *abar-dakabo robu-in meli w-amuni-ga, biama himi bajia, m-ausi-n wa faroka a-iaunti-n a-kota-he naha na-makwa o-mun,* we have no more but five loaves and two fishes ; except we should go and buy meat for all this people, *kenbena alika-i jiali amateli ma faroka ho-mun,* and if any man say ought unto you, [ye shall say, etc.], *kena alika-i jiali Raca ma faroka ajia-n l-augici o-mun,* and whosoever shall say to his brother, Raca [shall be in danger], *alika-i jiali, Christ lihi, ma faroka,* if any man did confess that he was Christ, *Awa, tu faroka ma, toho a-ta-kwona-hu a-bollia d-aurea !* O my Father, if it be possible, let this cup pass from me.

§ 145. *Bari,* to be "really", indeed ; *ba* an existing state or thing, *ri* fixed.

a) *bari-ga wakaia-ni hu, h-aiita alika h-a-n bia a-siki-n sa-be-tu h-isanoci o-mun, aloman sabu kiana H-icinaci aiomun kon-di a-siki fa sa-be-tu amateli adagati-ci-no i o-mun ?* if ye then, being evil, know how to give good gifts unto your children, how much more shall your Father which is in heaven give good things to them that ask him ? *d-ajia-ga ho-mun, Bari-ga m-akenakwa-ti l-a-n a-siki-n lo-muni n lo-ioci-n o-doma i,* I say unto you, Though he will not rise and give him, because he is his friend (L. XI, 8), *bari-ga ama koro wakaia-hu d-onyi-n loko-no o-mun, bari-ga waii icinoci o-loko-ji d-ikita-n,* though I have committed nothing against the people, or customs of our fathers, *to-moroa bari goba lu-tukuda-n ie,* but the more he charged them, *bari fa na-makwa n-akatadi-n,* although all be offended, *bari koma da-odo-ni bu-ma, mamari fa abakoro d-a-n ajia-n bu-konomun,* if I should die with thee, I will not deny thee in any wise ;

b) *W-adaiana-sia, Adaie-li, h-a ia a-sa-n di ; isa h-ajia-n ; ki jia d-a-n bari-n o-doma,* ye call me Master and Lord : and ye say well ; for so I am, *yara o-loko-tu ada iwi w-eke ma bari-n,* we may eat of the fruit of the trees of the garden (Gen. III, 2), *na-makwa adagati-ci auciga bari-ni n,* for every one that asketh receiveth, *ahe bari-n,* yea rather (L. XI, 28), *b-aici-n ka goba ma, bui bari-n,* if thou hadst known, even thou ; *bari-sia,* see last example B. in § 147.

§ 146. *Mari-ga sa-n,* it is uncertain (?).

mari-ga sa-n na-munikwawa ie, (they) had disputation, *manswa kibi n-a-n bena ajia-n, mari-ga sa-n na-muni-kwawa ie,* and when there had been much disputing, *naha loko-no o-loa k-ikihi-n o-doma, mari-ga sa-n na-kuyuko akonnabo-n bajia,* for the heart of this people is waxed gross, and their ears are dull of hearing.

§ 147. *Mamari,* to be impossible ; see § 74 d).

mamari-ga m-ajia-n w-a-n w-adeki-sia w-akonnabo-sia mu-tu o-konomun, for we cannot but speak the things which we have seen and heard (non possumus), *mamari-ga h-ikita-n Wacinaci Mammon bajia biama-n,* ye cannot serve God and mammon, *tora-jin mamari-ga h-ikita-n da-ma abar hour robu-in ?* what, could ye not watch with me one hour ?

l-iimawto-n-wa o-doma, mamari-ga l-akodwa ti-n, and he was angry, and would not go in, *b-adeka, m-ajia-n-ci fa bu, mamari fa b-ajia-n, toho ibi-ni o-bora,* and, behold, thou shalt be dumb, and not able to speak, until the day that these things shall be performed, *mamari goba kabaritu-'sa jiaro b-isiki-n da-mun,* and yet thou never gavest me a kid, *lihi-ki Wacinaci akenako( )kota a-dokodo-n a-oda-hu kari-hi o-rea i. mamari-ni ma kia a-oda-hu a-bokota kwon o-doma i,* whom God hath raised up, having loosed the pains of death : because it was not possible that he should be holden of it, *kia imikebo-hu mamari-sia ma h-ikiduadi-n, bari-sia ma ahaka-hu o-konomun ho-mun,* a work which ye shall in no wise believe, though a man declare it unto you (comp. in this sentence *mamari-sia* and *bari-sia*) :

S. *ma-mmalli-nni-benna hürkü-nni|je n-abbukoawa tu-duma, aimahá-hitti|n-a-ni-ka ba,* and when there had been much disputing.

§ 148. *M-ans-wa,* to be exceedingly ; presumably *m,* without, *ans(i),* inner peace, *wa* in itself.

a) with *ki* and *tu* (§ 55 b)) :

kena manswa-ki n-a goba nokonni-n, and they were exceeding sorry, *manswa-ki t-a onnakennakidi-n u, kia maucia na-makudida kiana mihu,* and we being exceedingly tossed with a tempest, the next day they lightened the ship, *ika ki, Da-iialoko manswa-ki ma nokonni-n a-oda-hu bia. yaha h-oabodda, h-ikita da-ma, l-a ajia-n na-mun,* then saith he unto them. My soul is exceeding sorrowful, even unto death : tarry ye here, and watch with me, *ika ki manswa ki t-a-ni fa k-amunaiga-hu o-doma,* for then shall be great tribulation, *hiaro manswa tu b-ikiduadi-n,* o woman, great is thy faith ;

b) *manswa kibi* (§ 58 e)), *manswa sabu* (§ 149) :

mamari-ga isa-n l-akonnabo-ni n, manswa kibi t-a-n akonnakita-hu o-doma, and when he could not know the certainty for the tumult, *manswa sabu ki n-a a-simaka-n,* and they cried out the more exceedingly ;

c) *h-ausa-i-li, manswa h-a-li auadi-n koriliaci ibici,* go and search diligently for the young child ;

d) *ika tu wiwa n-adeki-n, manswa goba alikibi-n ie ifiro-tu alikibi abu,* when they saw the star, they rejoiced with exceeding great joy, *manswa gòba n-aiimawto-n-wa kiana,* they were sore displeased, *toho o-wakaia, yuho-ro bari-n, a-dokodwa t-aurea, manswa-n t-ansi-n o-doma di,* her sins, which are many, are forgiven ; for she loved much (me ?), *a-odo-ci-sikwa o-loko area a-fitikidi-ci manswa-ci k-aiima-n,* [two men] coming out of the tombs, exceeding fierce, *a-nokondwa-hu, a-iiya-hu, manswa-tu k-amunaiga-n ajia-hu,* lamentation, and weeping, and great mourning.

§ 149. *Sabu,* to be very ; *s* intensifying, *abu* appearance (?).

a) *l-ekiti sabu koma koro kiana hu ?* shall he not much more clothe you ? *to-moroa na-simaka sabu goba,* but they cried out the more. *alika-i k-ansi sabu fa i ? ... yuho-sabu-sia l-isiki-n o-mun, d-ikisi-ka,* which of them will love him most ? ... I suppose that he, to whom he forgave most, *to-moroa w-ikiada-li ajia-hu. m-ausa sabu-n t-a-n bia loko-no o-koboroko-*

ji, but (let us prevent the speaking) that it spread no further among the people, *lihi ajia-sabu-in o-doma*, because he was the chief speaker, *ki-o-doma m-amoto-n-wa d-a sabu ka a-onaba-n da-konomun wa b-isibomun*, (therefore) I do the more cheerfully answer for myself, *na-maiaudwa sabu ka kiana*, they kept the more silence, *t-ifirotwa sabu goba kiana oniabu*, and the waters increased, *alika-i jiali k-amun-ci n o-mun t-isikoa sabu fa*, for whosoever hath, to him shall be given, *a-iyuhotwa sabu-in kasakabo man*, and increased (increasing) in number daily, *Sa-tu Ialoko k-ansi-n o-loko-ji waii bajia k-ansi-ka, toho isa-tu aji* (§ 87) *sabu-tu onnaka-ro-hu ma-siki-n w-a-n bia ho-kona*, for it seemed good to the Holy Ghost, and to us, to lay upon you no greater burden than these necessary things, *biam-dakabo kasakabo aji sabu na-ma-n bena i*, and when he had tarried among them more than ten days, *toho ki k-amunaiga-tu botobatu a-boreda na-makwa n-aji sabu to-lokomun*, this poor widow hath cast in more than they all, *alika-n ma-tata sabu ka ajia-hu*, for whether is easier, to say, etc., *wahadu-tu isa-sabu ka*, the old [wine] is better, *aloman sabu kiana H-icinaci aiomun kon-di a-siki fa sa-be-tu amateli adagati-ci-no i o-mun?* how much more shall your Father which is in heaven give good things to them that ask him?

b) in contrapositions : the superior with *sabu*, the inferior with *aji* :

l-isanci ifi-li sabu ka koro l-adaie-n aji ; imigoda-sia ifi-li sabu ka imigodo-ci i aji, the servant is not greater than his lord ; neither he that is sent greater than he that sent him, *kena, h-adeka ifi-li-sabu-ci Jonas aji yaha-n*, and, behold, a greater than Jonas is here, *sa-sabu-ci koro hui kia aji?* are ye not much better than they? *kena toraha aji ifi-ro sabu-tu l-onyi fa*, and greater works than these shall he do, *loko aji sabu koma w-akonnabo-n Wacinaci*, we ought to obey God rather than men, *ororo aji goba oniabu ifirotwa sabu-in*, and the waters prevailed, and were increased greatly upon the earth, *ororo aji goba oniabu ifirotwa sabu wabu-n* (§ 121 d)), and the waters prevailed exceedingly upon the earth, *n-aunaka kiana na-ma wa i, a-mairikota-n i Wacinaci ajia-n o-loko-ji sa-sabu kibe-n*, they took him unto them, and expounded unto him the way of God more perfectly.

§ 150. *Robu* adds to a word the principle of "only" : *ro* stops, *bu* appearance.

a) *m-amaro-n bu, ikiduadi robu b-a*, be not afraid, only believe, *to-moroa t-egura kowa-ka lo-loa o-loko, m-ibena robu l-a oaboddi-n*, yet hath no root in himself, but dureth for a while, *H-ausa yaha rea : ma-odo-n t-a-n ilontu o-doma, to-moroa adunko robu t-a. l-a ajia-n na-mun*, he said unto them, Give place : for the maid is not dead, but sleepeth, *to-moroa a-bokoto robu n-a goba lo-kabo andi-n Damascus mun l-abu*, but they laid him by the hand, and brought him into Damascus, *a-baptizedo robu n-a goba Adaie-li Jesus iri abu*, only they were baptized in the name of the Lord Jesus, *lo-baptizedo-n-wa bena, Philip o-ma-robu l-a goba*, and when he was baptized, he continued with Philip, *a-odo-ci-no o-rea akenakwa-hu*

o-konomun n-akonnabo-n bena, imita robu n-a aba-no to-konomun, and
when they heard of the resurrection of the dead, some mocked, *aba aba
robu n-a goba a-simaka-n yuho-li o-koboroko,* and some cried one thing,
some another, among the multitude ;

b) *naha robu-in koro o-konomun da-kwaiaboa,* neither pray I for these
alone, *to-moroa lihi robu-in ki a-tokodo-ci aiomuni o-rea,* [no man hath
ascended] but he that came down from heaven, *kena l-ahaka-ga na-mun.
M-onnaki-n h-a-li amateli waboroko o-loko-ji bia, to-moroa aba-ro ada
robu-in,* and commanded them that they should take nothing for their
journey, save a staff only, *aba-no wadili bu-ibo fa na-makwa, lihi robu-ini
o-ma b-ikitwa fa,* (wilt thou) forsaking all other (man), keep thee only
unto him, *aba-no Jew-no a-iadi-robu-in-ci, semici-ci,* certain of the vagabond
Jews, exorcists ;

c) S. *m-aditti-nni rubu|n-a hallika-kebé t-a-ni-bia-pa,* they doubted of
them whereunto this would grow, lit. not-knowing *rubu* they-did, etc. *má-
ijaonti-n-rubu|b-á-li na-mün tuhu na-ma-ssika-ni-hü,* lay not this sin to
their charge, lit. not-rewarding-*rubu* thou-do them-to this their-not-obeying;

d) *robuginai* in the following examples ; perhaps *robu,* only, *gina,* there
is (comp. *kena,* § 51, *i,* end-point pronoun III m.).

alika-i koro sa-ci, to-moroa abar-li robuginai Wacinaci, there is none
good but one, that is, God, *abar-li robuginai Wacinaci ; kena aba-li
kowa-ka, to-moroa lihi robu-in,* for there is one God ; and there is none
other but he.

§ 151. a) *Uho,* to be a quantity (§ 122). Only example :
biam hundred penny plata meli uho ka koro na-mun, two hundred
pennyworth of bread is not sufficient for them ;

b) *yuho,* to be a quantity (§ 123).

1) *yuhoo-ka l-itikidi-n ikihi akoloko mun,* ofttimes he falleth into the
fire, *yuho goba d-aboadi-n ie,* and I punished them oft, *yuho goba
n-atimiti-n bari-n i,* [because that] he had been often bound, *ki-o-doma
yuho sabu goba l-isimaki-n i,* wherefore he sent for him the oftener, *yuho-
ho to-bokoto-n o-doma i,* for oftentimes it had caught him : S. *juhu-hu-
kû-n,* oft ;

2) *kore-tu marisi yuho ka bari-n, to-moroa ma-iyuho ka imikebo-ci-no,*
the harvest truly is plenteous, but the labourers are few, *Legion da-iiri :
yuho-ni waii o-doma,* my name is Legion : for we are many, *bari-ga yuho-
ni-n tora-jin,* for all there were so many, [yet was not the net broke]. *lihi-ki
k-iwi-ka yuho-in,* the same bringeth forth much fruit, *Adaie-li, ma-iyuho-ci
isadwa ?* Lord, are there few that be saved ? *lo-dokotwa kokke-hia naii-ki
o-mun lo-forrakito-n-wa bena ma-murrida-ni abu lo-dokotwa yuho-ho-n.*
to whom also he shewed himself alive after his passion by many infallible
proofs, *mamari-n n-andi-n omuni-n l-amun. yuho kibi n-a-n o-doma,* and
when they could not come nigh unto him for the press ;

3) S. *na-ijuhu,* the multitude, the more part (of men), *Jesus k-ansi-*

ssia-nu u-ijuhu, the number of the disciples, *naha Stadt-kunna-na u-ijuhu,* the multitude of the city ;

⁴) m. *yuho-li,* f. (non-human) *yuho-ro,* many.

yuho-li akodwa to-loko-ji, many there be which go in thereat (*ma-iyuho-ci auciga n,* few there be that find it, Mt. VII, 13, 14), *yuho-li loko-no,* the multitudes, *yuho-li Corinth kono-no,* many of the Corinthians, *yuho-li hiaro-no,* many women, *kena yuho-li sabu ikiduadi-ci anda goba Adaie-li amun, yuho-li kibi wadili hiaro-no bajia,* and believers were the more added to the Lord, multitudes both of men and women, *yuho-ro poroko,* (many) swine, *yuho-ro ajia-hu,* many words, *yuho-ro isogo-tu koro amateli,* many wonders (many small not thing), *yuho-ro wiwa adiki,* after many years, *kidua goba bu yuho-ro koro abu, da-siki fa bu b-ikita-n bia yuho-ro,* thou hast been faithful over a few things, I will make thee ruler over many things, *yuho-ro sabu Jesus onyi-sia goba,* and there are also many other things which Jesus did.

§ 152. *Aba-r, a,* one (§ 60 ᵈ)) (A. M. § 182, 131), m. *abar-li,* f. *aba-ro.*

ᵃ) ¹) *h-adeka, abar virgin ka-sa fa,* behold, a virgin shall be with child, *tanahu warea abar bawhu o-loko fa abar-dakabo-no ma-heragi-ci na-muni-kwawa,* for from henceforth there shall be five in one house divided, *ika tu !-ajia-n to-konomun imikebo-ci-no o-mun abar penny plata abar kasakabo iauna bia,* and when he had agreed with the labourers for a penny a day, *ika ki abar siba aba siba ajeago ibara fa koro,* there shall not be left one stone upon another ;

²) *to-moroa aba-re-n-ci isa-n l-adaiana-sia jia ma fa,* but every one that is perfect shall be as his master ;

ᵇ) ¹) *kenbena, h-adeka, abar-li anda goba,* and, behold, one came, *abar-li loko Wacinaci imigodo-sia goba,* there was a man sent from God, *abar-li priest goba,* there was ... a certain priest, *biama-no kabuea o-loko fa, abar-li onnako fa, abar-li ibara fa,* two men shall be in the field ; the one shall be taken, and the other left, *ajia-n lo-mun abar-li abar-li-n, Daii ?* and to say unto him one by one, Is it I ?

²) *aba-li anda kiana ba,* and another came (L. XIX, 20) ; see also example in § 102 ᵇ) ;

ᶜ) ¹) *biama-no a-saradi fa molo abu, aba-ro onnako fa, aba-ro ibara fa,* two women shall be grinding together ; the one shall be taken, and the other shall be left ; *aba-ro ibibida di,* somebody has touched me, *kena aba-ro Anna, prophet hiaro,* and there was one Anna, a prophetess, *aba-ro l-adura l-onnaka kiana,* and he took one of his ribs ;

²) *yuho-li loko-no ikiduadi-ci k-amun-ci abaro o-loa, abaro ialoko bajia,* and the multitude of them that believed were of one heart and of one soul, *naii abaro-n bia waii abaro-n jin,* that they may be one, even as we are one, *m-abaro-ka kiana l-isibo,* and his (Cain's) countenance fell, *ama o-doma bu-imawtoa ? a-mabarodo-n b-isib-oa ?* why art thou wroth ? and why is thy countenance fallen ?

ᵈ) *John Baptist, n-a aba-no a-sa-n bu ; Elias, n-a aba-no : Jeremias jiaro, abar-li prophet-no o-rea-ci jiaro, n-a aba-no,* some say that thou art John the Baptist : some, Elias ; and others, Jeremias, or one of the phophets.

§ 153. *Biama,* (followed by a word denoting a non-rational being or thing), two, *biama-no,* two rational beings (A. M. § 182. 132). Probably this word refers to the process of dividing something into two parts or portions ; *bi,* small, slight (i.e. small in comparison with the undivided thing), *ama,* something. Comp. *ibi-li,* a small person, *ibi-ro,* a small thing, *ibena,* piece, *ibiki-,* to cut, *bihero(-hu),* adultery, *beseki-n(i),* to be of little stature, Sm. *ibi-ju,* twins.

a) 1) *n-imigoda l-ibici biama-no wadili,* they sent unto him two men. *k-amun-ci biama eke-hu a-siki fa m-eke-ci o-mun aba-ro,* he that hath two coats, let him impart to him that hath none, *aba-li o-mun biama,* [he gave] to another two [talents] ;

2) G. *to hiāro biama-o̧ĭ ka-sá-ya,* or *to hiāro ĕméuda-ya biama-o̧ĭ-be,* this woman has given birth to twins ;

b) to be two :

biama-ga c-isado-n-wa kiana, and both are preserved. *biama goba kiana makondo-n ie,* and they were both naked, *n-anda na-mun. n-ebekita biama-n mihu,* and they came, and filled both the ships. *biama biama-in to-makwa isiroko-ho o-rea-tu,* two and two of all flesh [went into the ark]. *biama biama-h l-imigodo-n ie,* and (he) sent them two and two. *l-ajia ki ka ba lo-mun biama-hi,* he saith to him again the second time ;

c) the following forms might be considered as belonging to an action-word *biam(a)-t- :*

n-ibiamte-sia-no, their partners, *Simon ibiamte-sia-no.* partners with Simon, *l-ibiamti-ci,* the second [brother], *ci-biamti-tu.* the second [month, day], *ibiamtido-n-wa,* [the voice spake] again the second time.

§ 154. *Kabuin(i),* three (non-rational beings or things). *kabui-no,* three rational beings ; probably *kabu-in,* hand-being, i.e. a handful.

a) *kabuin bawnaboho,* three tabernacles. *biama-no jiaro kabui-no jiaro ahaka-ci areroko abu,* two or three witnesses ;

b) *l-ajia ki ka ba lo-mun kabuini,* he saith unto him the third time, *kabuini ka t-a-n da-mun,* and this [voice from heaven] was done three times (to me). *kabuini fa abakoro b-a-n ajia-n da-konomun,* thou shalt deny me thrice, *t-ekabuin-tu,* the third [day] ;

c) *na-kabuinti-ci,* a (their) third [servant], *t-ekabuinti-tu.* the third [day].

§ 155. *Bibici,* four (non-rational beings or things), *bibici-no.* four rational beings ; probably reduplication of *bi,* two (part). *ci* touched (§ 90) ?

bibici auaduli, the four winds. *bibici-no l-isanoci.* four (his) daughters. *da-sika lo-mun ba bibici-hi,* I restore him fourfold. *ci-bibici-tu,* the fourth [river, day] ;

bibite-n bia t-isiroko. [the river] became into four heads. *ahuido-tu bibite-n t-akoina mun,* knit at the four corners, *bibite-tu-o-kuti,* four-footed beasts.

§ 156. The numerals for 1, 2, 3 and 4 are not the names for special fingers or toes, though of course, in pronouncing those numerals, the Arawak may count on his fingers also. The higher numerals, however, bear witness of counting on fingers and toes :

5, *abar-dakabo,* one-my-hand ; 10, *biam-dakabo,* two-my-hand ; 6 *abar-timen,* 7 *biama-timen,* 8 *kabuin-timen,* 9 *bibici-timen* : *t-imen* = its-submissive or such-like, § 73, consequently 7 = one (at) the submissive (hand), one at the other hand (?) ;

11, *abar-kutibanna,* 12 *biam-kutibanna,* 14 *bibici-kutibanna ; o-kuti,* foot, *banna,* at the surface of ;

15, *abar-mairia-kuti-hi,* one-other side- foot-in general ;

20, *abar-loko,* one man, i.e. all the fingers and toes together ; 40, *biam-loko ;* 60, *kabuin-loko ;* 80, *bibici-loko ;*

100, *abar* hundred (English) ; 2000, *biam thousand ;* etc.

When rational beings are meant, *-no* (after an *n* : *-o*) is suffixed.

The plural suffix is omitted, perhaps because it is mentioned already in *wadili-no,* in : *naii a-koto-ci abardakabo thousand wadili-no jiaro goba, hiaro-no bajia, ire-no bajia,* and they that had eaten were about five thousand men, beside women and children.

The ordinal numbers from 5 onwards, are formed by substituting *dakabo-li* for *dakabo,* *time-li* for *timen* (*li,* § 175). Sometimes, however, the form which is used for the cardinal number, is also used for the ordinal, e.g. :

kenbena lo-fitikida goba kabuin hour jiaro, and he went out about the third hour, *abar-timen kaci o-loko Wacinaci imigoda goba angel Gabriel,* and in the sixth month the angel Gabriel was sent from God.

Numbers indicating more than 20, not being a full 20, 100 or 1000 :

Mahalaleel kokke kwa ma goba kabuin-loko wiwa (year) *ajeago* (upon) *abar-dakabo,* and Mahalaleel lived sixty and five years, *abar-hundred wiwa ajeago kabuin loko kia* (that) *ajeago* (upon) *biama,* 162 years. *kia mihu o-loko goba waii wa-makwa biam-hundred ajeago kabuin-loko kia ajeago abar-timen kutibana kokki-ci,* and we were all in the ship two hundred threescore and sixteen souls.

Sm. 11, *abba-kutti-hi-bénna, abba-kutti-hi-bénna-nu.* The complete form is : *biama-n-te-kábbe abba-kutti-hi-bénna tu-paküttâ-n* or *t-adi-wa-ku :* the fingers of both hands and one toe of the feet besides (which they all point out). Sm. *a-paküttü-,* to pass ; *t-adi-wa-ku :* its-more than-in itself-power.

S. *kabbuin lugku biama-dakkabbu tu-paküttâ-n* (B. *kabuin-loko-no ajeago biam-dakabo-no*), 70 ; S. *kabbuin lukku abba-maria-kutti-hi-benna-tti tu-paküttâ-n* (B. *kabuin-loko ajeago abar-mairia-kuti-hi*), 75 ;

v. C. *abba loekoe-noe-bena to-ppakita-n tó-joho,* 100, lit. one man-plural-after its-surpassing its-quantity.

§ 156A. G. *d-akósi-be* (§ 59 a) 2)), *biam-akáśi,* (my) two eyes (*d-akosi,* one eye) ; *aba karta oála* (§ 120 c) 1)), one sheet of paper, *aba karta ébena* (§ 59 c) 3)), half a sheet of paper ;

aba komiki wuniabu, one bowl of water (*komiki,* creole word), *anekidi-tu* (§ 79 d)) *uniábu komiki-lo ki,* a bowl half filled with water ;

biáma-thu kabuin-ki|da ba-dakábu ka, 2 + 3 = 5 ;

bián-ki kabuin|da ba-timaŋ-ka|de, 2 × 3 = 6 ;

tẹ-biči ibena (§ 59 c) 3)) *bian-ká|de,* ½ × 4 = 2 ;

tu-kabuin ebéna-ki|da aba-thó l-ab-oa|ká|de, ½ × 3 = 1½.

§ 157. a) Chronology, see § 27.

b) Age :

biam-kutibana wiwa l-ibikido-n-wa (his-growing) *bena,* and when he was twelve years old, *lihi Jesus abar-loko ajeago biam-dakabo wiwa jiaro ibikido-ci,* and Jesus himself began to be about thirty years of age, *biam-kutibana wiwa ibikido-tu-n o-doma n,* for she was of the age of twelve years ;

biama wiwa ka-raia-ci (being born-ci), *n-afuji-sabu-ci bajia,* [children] from two years old and under ;

Sm. *biama|kátti|ka|i lu-puttükidi-nni-bena* (his-going-forth-after), he is two months old, *danuhu biama wiju|ka|n tu-puttükidi-nni-benna,* she is now two years old ;

c) *o-bora,* being first, *adiki,* being last, see §§ 105 b), 86 c).

§ 158. a) *Noma* indicates a group, a company.

t-isifodo noma mun n-oabodda goba, and they watched the gates, *to-makwa ma-ribe-n-tu bibite-tu-o-kuti b-onnaki fa bu-mun wa biam-timen noma-in, wadili hiaro mu-tu,* of every clean beast thou shalt take to thee by sevens, the male and its female, *biama noma eke-hu m-onnaki-n h-a-li,* neither (ye) have two coats apiece, *ho-bollita( )kita ie biam-loko ajeago biam-dakabo noma-in n-abokwa-wa,* make them sit down by fifties in a company, *biam-timen kasakabo o-loko biama-hi noma da(-)ma-koto-ni-n, aba-ro noma da-sika biam-dakabo o-rea to-makwa d-amuni-sia o-rea,* I fast twice in the week, I give tithes of all that I possess ;

b) *nino* indicates a group, a company.

kena Herod ibira-ga lo-kona, lo-soldaro-nino bajia, imita-n i, and Herod with his men of war set him at nought, and mocked him (comp. *soldaro-no bajia imita goba i,* and the soldiers also mocked him). *biama-no o-mun k-aiima fa kabui-nino, kena kabui-nino o-mun k-aiima fa biama-no,* three against two (shall strive), and two against three (shall strive) : S. *nai biamattiba-nninu n-adinamukitta Apostel-nu issibumün,* whom (those seven) they set before the apostles. *na-parra baddia je a-ijumudaha-li-ninu.* and they have slain them which shewed (prophesied. Acts VII. 52) : Sm. *li-háiaeru-ninu,* his slaves ;

c) *ama-te-li,* something. *ama-koro,* nothing. see § 139 a) 2).

§ 159. a) *Ate-n-wa.* S. *atenennua-ttu,* the beginning : a. time-reality, *te,* limited motion, *n,* continuing, *wa* self (?).

to-moroa atenwa warea tora-jia t-a goba koro, but from the beginning it was not so, *atenwa-wabu Ajia-hu goba,* in the beginning was the Word ; *atenwa-ci, atenwa-tu,* the first ;

b) S. *m-attibia-ttu* or *m-attebia-ttu kassakkabbu-hü,* a few days, *m-attebia-tti wadili-nu kurru baddia,* and of men, not a few ;

c) *mata,* presumably = *ma,* entirely, § 70 a), *t-a,* it is.

biam-loko wiwa abar-timen t-ajeago ma-ta toho temple a-murreto-n-wa, forty and six years was this temple in building, *kasakabo ma t-a ma koro,* not always [shall my spirit strive with man] ;

d) *omata,* enough.

lo-mairikoto-sia omata bari-n l-adaiana-sia jia lo faroka, it is enough for the disciple that he be as his master, *kena bibici bia na-sika goba n, na-makwa soldaro-no omata-ni bia,* and (they) made four parts, to every soldier a part, *omata-i* (§ 41), *l-a kiana na-mun,* [behold, there are two swords]. And he said unto them, It is enough, *kasakabo omata t-oaiya to-wakaia,* sufficient unto the day is the evil thereof ;

e) S. *kañ mappa l-addiki-n,* he saw no man ; Sm. *mappa,* nicht können ;

f) *fata,* Sm. *patta,* how many ?

fata-no Wacinaci ? how many Gods are there ? Sm. *patta kuljara b-amünni-ka ?* how much coorials hast thou ? *pátta b-ánsi-ka ?* how much wouldst thou like to have ? *pátta-nu kalipi-na ?* how many Caribs ? *páttannu lukú-nnu ?* how many Arawaks ? *pátta-hü-kuba b-adunuki-n waburukku-lukku ?* how long, how many nights hast thou been on the way ?

§ 160. a) The three dimensions in :

kabuin hundred cubit ikisidi-kwona-hu fa to-waji (§ 121 b)) ; *biam-loko ajeago biam-dakabo cubit fa c-ibiloko* (§ 103 i) 3)) ; *abar-loko ajeago biam-dakabo cubit fa aiomuni-ni* (§ 71 b) 6)) *n,* the length [of the ark] shall be three hundred cubits, the breath of it fifty cubits, and the height of it thirty cubits ;

b) The four directions of the horizon :

n-anda fa-te adaili-a-fitikidi-n warea, adaili-a-kodo-n-wa warea. anaki warea, t-oalabaw o-kona-rea bajia, and they shall come from the east, and from the west, and from the north, and from the south.

East = sun coming out, west = sun entering, south = middle (§ 79 d)), north = the other side (the Arawak text mentions south before north, comp. *n-afudu-wabu anaki warea-tu,* the queen of the south, *ika tu auaduli a-fudi-n ma-tata-n anaki warea,* and when the south wind blew softly, *auaduli a-fuda anaki-warea,* the south wind blew).

South west and north west taken together in "west" :

kia akodoonali Crete mun, adaili akodo-n-wa o-kona mairia-tu, which is an haven of Crete, and lieth toward the south west and north west.

In another way :

S. *ju-waria eweledu-nn-ua w-a-ni-ka tü-llebu-maria. w-anda Rhegium mün hidda, abba kianibenna awadulli a(-)ussa wa-llebu-waria.* and from thence we fetched a compass, and came to Rhegium : and after one day the south wind blew, lit. thence-from sailing we-did-when its-waterside-inferior-from, we-come Rhegium at thus, other there-upon wind go our-waterside-from ;

Sm. *háddalli abumün*, the East, sunrise, *hadalli ab-uaria w-anda-te*, we come from the East, *hádalli u-tturu*, West (*hadalli*, sun, *abu*. appearance. *u-tturu*, foot.

c) Right : *iisa mairia*, good, beautiful side ; left : *-ba-ro mairia*, other side ; examples, § 97 d) ;

d) *aiomun-sabu-tu isikwa*, the highest room, lit high-very-thing shelter, *onabu-sabu-tu isikwa*, the lowest room.

§ 161. a) *aranaha-i*, the dayspring (L. I, 78), *ika tu goba-te aranaha-in*. as it began to dawn ; S. *harrunaha m-a-ni-ka*, or *harrunaha t-a-ni-ka*. and when it was day, *arrunnahadü-n|benna|i*, [awaking out of his sleep. Acts XVI, 27] ; Sm. *harúnnaha*, the light, the shine, *hádalli harúnnaha*. the sunlight, *harúnnaha-hü-ka bú-mün*, art thou in good spirits, merry ? Comp. *aro-ha(i)*, it is there, § 139 c), *na* plurality, continuity : also white, etc. (A. M. § 182, 132E) ;

b) *kena mauci-a* (§ 132), and the morning were (Gen. I, 8). *mauci abu n-a goba andi-n a-odo-ci sikwa mun*, very early in the morning they came unto the sepulchre, *lihi-ki a-fitikida goba mauci abu-in*, which went out early in the morning. *M(a)-*, without, *a-u* visible space, *-ci* asserting oneself ;

c) 1) *ka-saka-bo*, day ; *ka-*, with, *saka* to wither. *bo* quiet appearance :

2) *ka-sako-da*, night ; *sak-o*, withering stopped. *da* stands (?) :

ika tu ka-sako-n ie, and as soon as it was day (they : L. XXII. 66), *ka-sako-ni bena ie*, now as soon as it was day (they : Acts XII. 18), *mauci-abu-in, ka-sakoo o-bora l-akenakwa, a-fitikidi-n*. and in the morning, rising up a great while before day, he went out ;

3) *k-ibena goba l-ajia-n, a-kasakoto-n*, and talked a long while, even till break of day ;

d) *wa-mun adaili*. S. *haddali wa-mün*, at midday, noon ; *adaili*, sun, *wa-mun*. our-place ;

e) S. *haddalli a-llammada t-a-ni-ka*, three o'clock in the afternoon ; Sm. *a-llammada-n*, to sway. *háddalli a-llagmmada-ka*. they say of the sun from 12 to 3 o'clock in the afternoon ;

f) *kena bakilama, kena maucia*, and the evening and the morning were (Gen. I, 8), *ika ki bakilama*, so when even was come. *yaha kwa ba-i wa-ma, bakilama omuni-n o-doma, kasakabo bajia hara bo*, abide with us : for it is toward evening, and the day is far spent. Probably *bakilama* depicts the long shadows cast by the slanting rays of the sun. comp. *akilaka*. to reach. to stretch forth ;

g) *kasakoda anaka-in*, at midnight. § 79 d) :

h) *wa-mun- adaili a-kota-he jiaro. bakilama a-kota-he jiaro*. a dinner or a supper ;

i) 1) Sm. *kátti u-kúrrubu*, full moon ("round" ? § 108A d)) ;

2) Sm. *katti ú-bule*, new moon (comp. B. *a-bolli*, to pass) ;

j) Sm. *emessi-niánna*, the short rainy season (when *eméssi*, the big ants, fly) ;

Sm. *wijua-niánna*, the long rainy season (*wijua*, the Pleiades) ;

Sm. *joan-dâ-l-te*, the long dry season (*jóana*, iguana) ;

Sm. *mali-dá-l-te*, the beginning of the dry season (*mali*, a certain star or constellation).

CHAPTER XVIII

MAN

§ 162. Relationship is expressed in the following manner :

augi means "being a younger brother to a man", or "a younger sister to a woman" ; perhaps *au*, thing in space, *gi* active or emphasized. consequently *augi*, being in the same room, house or village with someone.

a) one man's brother, *-augi-ci* (Sm. *-huki-ti*) ; *l-augi-ci Abel*. his (Cain's) brother Abel ;

b) one woman's sister, *-augi-tu* (Sm. *-huki-ttu*) : *d-augi-tu*. my (Martha's) sister ;

c) several men's brother, *-augi-na-n-ci* (Sm. *-huki-n-ti*); *w-augi-na-n-ci*. (our) brother (Acts XXI, 20) ;

d) several women's sister, (Sm. *-huki-n-tu*) ;

e) one man's several brothers, *-augi-o-ci* ; *naraha d-augi-o-ci*. these my brethren ;

f) one woman's several sisters, (no example) ;

g) several men's several brothers *-augi-o-ci* (Sm. *-huki-n-ti*) ; *w-augi-o-ci*. our brethren ;

h) several women's several sisters, (Sm. *-huki-n-tti*) ;

i) to be brother, *k-augi* ; *ika tu Jesus akona-n Galilee bara rifu-ji, l-adeka goba biama-no k-augi-i-ci*, and Jesus. walking by the sea of Galilee saw two brethren, *k-augi-k-augi-mi-ci* (§ 71 a) 2)) *hui*. sirs. ye are brethren, *k-augi-k-augi-mi-ci o-koboroko*, among the brethren (J. XXI, 23).

Notes :

a) *-ci* is omitted with *ici*, father ;

b) *-tu* is omitted with *iyu*, mother, *o-tu*. daughter, *ireyu*, wife ;

c) regular ending *-na-ci* (§ 79 b) 1)) ; the *a* is often omitted, and the vowel preceding the *n* is often modified, in the same manner as in the *-n* forms of § 81 ;

d), e), f), g) regular ending *-no-ci* (§ 79 b) 2)).

§ 163. a) masculine *i*, feminine *u*.

ici, father. G. also : father's brother ;

iyu, mother. G. also : father's sister ;

aii-ci, S. *adi-tti*, son (§ 2) (A. M. § 182. 35). G. also : cousin :

o-tu (the root is *tu* or *to* : *da-tu*. *to-tu*. Aaron *o-to-no-ci*. the daughters of Aaron, *ho-to-no-ci*. your daughters). daughter (A. M. § 182. 36). G. also : cousin :

Sm. *iti-ti*, a woman's son in law. *itti-ju*. a woman's daughter-in-law. B. *t-itiu*, her d.-i.-l. ;

b) *-boa, -bua*, abnormal (§ 120 d)).

R. *da-te-bua-chi, da-iye-bua-to, d-aiite-boa-chi, da-tte-boá-to,* (man's or woman's) stepfather, stepmother or father's or mother's sister, stepson, stepdaughter, Sm. *itte-bóa-ti,* stepfather, father's brother, *ue-ja-bóa-tu,* stepmother, mother's sister, *uetta-bóa-tu,* stepdaughter, *ka-ttebóati-n,* to be the brother of someone's father, or the stepfather, G. *da-ya-boá-tu,* aunt (uncle's wife or mother's sister), *d-aiči-boa-či,* stepson ;

c) *-uri(bi),* turned (? § 108A c)).

1) Sm. *uribí-ti,* G. *da-uribí-či,* brother-in-law, Sm. *uribí-a-tu,* sister-in-law ;

2) Sm. *urihitti-ti,* G. *da-ueiti-či,* a man's son-in-law ;

d) 1) *-ki,* the person or thing in question (? § 48).

augi-ci, a man's younger brother, *augi-tu,* a woman's younger sister (§ 162) ;

o-bugi-ci, a man's older brother ; *bu,* appearance, *ki,* this ! consequently the big or strong one ? comp. Sm. *ú-bukü,* thigh, loin

2) *-liki ; li,* lively (?).

l-iliki-n, his cattle, Sm. *illiki-n,* living property ;

Sm. *wellikín-ti,* R. *da-lliken-chi,* grandson, Sm. *üllikín-tu,* R. *da-lliken-to,* granddaughter ; Sm. : the word is generally used to indicate a distant relative ;

aciligi-ci, a woman's brother ;

c) *-ku,* the same as *-ki,* but more distant, older, or venerated (?).

1) Sm. *aküttü-hü,* G. *da-kŏtŏ,* grandmother ;

Sm. *akkürrü-hu,* G. *da-ŏkürŏ,* B. *t-akiru,* a woman's mother-in-law (A. M. § 182, 38) ;

2) with *-du,* origin (?), authority (?).

Sm. *adukutti,* G. *da-dúkuči,* grandfather, *dukú-či, dokó-ko,* is also used when addressing an old man ;

3) with *m(a)-,* negation, i.e. "not my own", or *ma, mu,* with, i.e. "my companion's" ?

Sm. *u-mükuttü,* G. *da-makŏtŏ, da-muketé,* a man's mother-in-law ;

Sm. *úmadukúr-ti,* G. *da-madukure-tsi,* father-in-law, B. *Caiaphas o-maadogo-ci-n o-doma i,* for he was father-in-law to Caiaphas (A. M. § 182, 37) ;

f) *ra,* female (? comp. §§ 179, 163 c) 1)).

o-iyurada-tu, aiyurada-tu, a man's sister ;

da-tula-tu (t-itula-tu), a woman's older sister ;

g) Miscellaneous.

1) *l-adiki-ci,* his younger brother, R. *d-adiki-di,* a woman's younger brother, *d-adiki-do,* a man's younger sister ; *adiki,* after, § 86 c) ;

2) Sm. *adaün-ti,* G. *d-adaén-či,* mother's brother = lord, ruler, § 89 (see § 165, clan-system) ;

3) G. *wa-burá-na-no,* our ancestors, S. *wa-bura-tti,* our fathers ; *o-bora,* before, § 105 ;

⁴) S. *kubakadi*, the patriarchs ; *kuba*, past time ;

⁵) *wakili-ci-no*, G. *wakili-na-no, wakili-tsi, wakili-či-kuba* ; them of old time ; *wakili*, long ago ;

⁶) *botoba-tu hiaro, botoba-tu*, Sm. *buttuba-ttu*, G. *botoba-to*, a widow, *botoba-či hiaro*, widows, Sm. *butuba-tti*, G. *botobá-ci*, widower ; [G. In former times the widow was not allowed to marry any other person than a relative of her deceased husband. Should he have a brother, then the latter was obliged to marry the widow, eventually as his second wife.] Comp B. *a-bota*, to catch away, to spoil, and § 174 ᵇ˒ ᶜ), to fall in a trance, to dream ;

⁷) G. *tho-boyá-n-to*, first wife of a man ; *abuia*, to feed ?

G. *tho-dokára-to*, second wife of a man ; *tho-dokára-yó-tsi*, all the wives of a man, the first wife excepted ; *ka-dukará-či*, two men living with one woman [Baptist has once seen a case of this sort ; he disapproved of it] ; *dukara*, "rather", § 179 ᶠ) ?

§ 164. ᵃ) ¹) *loko*, individual of the Arawak nation, in the bible translations also used for "man" (human being) ; plur. *loko-no* ; *l*, loose, able to move, *o*, permanently, or : the same as the pronominal prefix III m. *l(o)-* ; *ko*, power, faculty ;

²) R. *lo-lo*, woman's younger brother, man's younger sister ;

³) R. lullaby song, sung by the mother : *b-adongka illor-lo papa o-bora*, sleep, child, father is coming ;

⁴) *d-iloni-ni warea*, from my youth, *l-iloni-ni warea*, from his youth, *iloni l-a-n ka*, of a child (Mk. IX, 21), *ilon-ci*, boy, *ilon-tu*, girl, *ilon-tu da-tu*, my little daughter ;

⁵) *o-loa*, heart, mind, bosom ;

ᵇ) *korilia-ci*, newly born (L. II, 12), *korilia-ci-no*, babes, infants, young children, (A. M. § 182, 34) ; *kore*, red, pointing to the red colour of the newly born, or *kori*, halt ? *lia*, newly arisen, § 98 ;

ᶜ) ¹) *(i)sa*, child, offspring ; the plural is frequently used for translating "sons" or "daughters" (§ 114 ᵃ⁾ ⁶⁾) ; G. in addressing a young man (woman), they often use the word *sá-či*, little brother (*sá-tu*, little sister) ;

²) *isa-n-ci*, servant, plur. *isa-no-no-ci* ; "child to several people" ; G. a headman (*wa-fúdyi*, our headman) calls his subjects *da-sa-na-nó-či* ;

ᵈ) Sm. *bassabá-n-ti*, a little one, or a boy of about 6—12 years, *bassaba-n-tu*, do. girl, *bassaba-nni-be-tti*, several boys (see § 114 ᵉ)) ;

ᵉ) *wadili*, a man (male person) (A. M. § 182, 30 ?) ; *wadi*, to be long, or : *wa*, exceeding, *di*, strong, firm ;

ᶠ) *hiaro*, a woman (A. M. § 182, 32) ; *hia*, soul, life, etherical ?

ᵍ) *ikita-kwon-ci*, manservant, *ikita-kwon-tu*, maidservant, *ikita-kwono-no-ci*, servants ; *ikita*, to serve, *kwon* § 120 ᵃ) ;

ʰ) *aiero-ci*, one who is in bondage. *L-aiici kiana a-maierodo faroka hu, kidua-n a-maiero fa hu*, if the Son therefore shall make you free, ye shall be free indeed. Sm. *háiaeru*, a slave, G. *haiéro*, a slave, a convict (A. M. § 182, 39) ; *ai*, established, *ro*, stopped ?

i) 1) *iri*, name ; *r*, fixed, *i* principle ;

2) *ire*, the state of husband or wife, *ireyu*, the state of wife ; *ire-ci*, husband, *ire-tu*, wife, G. *m-ére-tsi-tå*, widow, *m-éreyu-či*, widower ;

3) *ire-no*, little children ;

j) 1) *kirikia*, kind, *ikirikia*, sort, tribe, people, own nation, *akirikia*, a (foreign) nation (§ 2), *akirikia-no*, kindreds, nations, the heathen, Sm. *ükkürrküa-hü*, nation ; § 104 b) 2) III) ;

2) Sm. *kirtia-ti*, ein Blanker (~ Christian ?), plur. *kirtia-na*, G. *kirtiádo-nå*, white people ;

k) Presumably connected with *iyu*, mother (see § 165, family-system) :

1) *o-io-ci*, friend, neighbours, kindred, people, plur. *o-io-no* ; S. *lu-ijuhu-nnu*, his friends ;

2) *o-ho-na-no-ci*, kindred, kin, kinsfolk, cousins ;

3) G. *thúyu-či*, a grown-up man, *thoyó-ya-korro kayará-n-da*, he looks like a grown-up man, S. *tuju-kû-ti*, elders ;

l) 1) *oe-n-ci*, kinsman, *b-oe-n-tu Elisabeth*, thy (Mary's) cousin Elisabeth, R. *da-wo-n-chi*, (man's or woman's) brother's or sister's son, *da-wo-n-tu*, do. daughter ;

2) Pen., G. *da-yéna*, my sister (rather archaic word), plur. *da-yéna-no;*

3) G. *šuwe* is used as a vocative in addressing a person of one's own age, or a brother ;

m) B. *habe*, being old, other authors generally *hebe*, is often used with the suffixes *-ci*, *-tu*, *-li*, *-ru*, to denote an old man or woman, a grandfather, a grandmother ; also : *habe-ci l-imigoda l-ibici*, he sendeth an ambassage ;

n) 1) Sm., Q., R., G. *ebebe*, *bébe*, honorific (Vocative), especially used by young people in addressing older people (see § 184) ;

2) S. (*w-*, *n-*, etc.) *ebe-n-ti* or *ibe-n-ti*, a person of (our, their, etc.) company, sect, nation ;

3) S. *ebettira*, to be on friendly terms with, in peace with, allied to, G. *d-ebetére-či*, my friend (comp. *ra* in G. *na-bukutára*, their slaves or prisoners ; *a-bokoto-*, to lay hold on, etc.) ;

o) 1) *awa*, father, especially Vocative ; G. *awa* is the archaic word, the modern word is *pápa ;*

2) R. *tete*, Sm. *attétte*, mother, Vocative, term of endearment ; G. *téte* is also used when addressing an old woman ;

p) Sm. *aha-ti*, comrade, *l-ahá-ti*, his countryman, *aha-nu* comrades, playmates ;

q) Q. When children or close relatives speak of their elders, then they use the plural, for instance they are not there, they have gone hunting, etc., instead of : he, or she is not there, etc.

r) G. *dūǫi*, a negro (hinting at the woolly hair, § 89 ?) ;

G. *baráti*, a negro ; *bara*, sea ?

G. *basári*, plur. *bassári-no*, Kaliña ; origin not ascertained ;

G. *wărau*, Warau ;

G. *k-arána-to*, a half-caste, lit. mixed ;

s) *fale*, powerful (magic power ?), wise, in the following expressions :

1) I) S. *h-akussi-wa abbu h-addiki-pa balli-n, tu-murrua palle ti dia tu-ppa hu-münni-n, m-aditti-pa|n*, and seeing ye shall see, and not perceive: presumably : your-eyes-own with ye-see-shall verily, but power quality it-shall you-to not-know-shall it ;

II) G. *faru-thu-má-lokó-ho*, a poison or charm for working evil on someone ; *kuna-palu*, fish-poison, Euphorbia cotinoides ;

²) Sm. *pále-tti*, masc., *pále-ttu*, fem., *pále-tti-ju*, plur., is the collective name for those Indian tribes¹) which are ever on a war-footing with the Kalepi-na or Kalevi-te-nu ; *kalipi-na má-pale*, the Caribs are not pálettiju : G. *fáleto*, any stranger (white man, negro, Kaliña), plur. *falétyu(h-nå* or *falétu-be*, Pen. *faretho*, a wise man or a stranger ;

³) Pen. *faretho, fareto, faleto* is used in combinations with other words to designate certain mythical Indian tribes as *Itori-faretho* (Howling Monkey Indians), *Papaya-faretho* (Papaw Indians), and many others : B. has used *Pareciyu*, S. *Palettiju*, for translating "the barbarous people" (Acts XXVIII, 2).

§ 165. Formerly the Arawak nation was subdivided in families or clans. At present this seems to be falling into disuse. [G. In Surinam it is still in operation. A child is considered to belong to its mother's clan. and a man who marries becomes subject to his father-in-law ; comp. § 164 k) kindred. *o-io* ~ mother, § 163 g) ²) mother's brother, *adaen-či* ~ lord, ruler, and also that curious custom, by which an Arawak man is not allowed to look at his mother-in-law or to speak to her, and vice versa : *wadīli lu-mukŏtŏ u-ma koro lü-dia-kuma, l-ikisidá-ya-fa to lú-mukŏtŏ-uwa-da*, a man may not speak to his mother-in-law. he must be respectful to her (see also § 216 and a similar statement by Q. 18, 251 and v. C. 7 ᶜ).

The *káluafú-na* clan (plur. ; a man is called *káluafú-di*, a woman *káluafú-du*) belongs to a group of eight. It is forbidden to marry any person of the same group. if dwelling in the same country, and any one of the same clan, no matter where he or she lives. It is also prohibited to marry a child of the full brother of one's father. Thy clan = *bu-kurukuya, bu-kürkiya* (§ 164 ʲ)), or *b-ibithadu* (comp. § 164 ⁿ)). In order that marriages may be possible. families belonging to different clans are living in the same village.]

A similar clan-system has been reported also from the Palikur. Goajiro and Achagua ; presumably it was already in existence among the old Arawak-Maipure. It is possible. however, that the names of the different clans are not so old as the system is.

The following types of Arawak clan-names occur :

---

1) The *Máhanau* (Manao). *Úttumaku* (Otomake). *Akuliju* (Trio). *Assawánu* (?). *Saliwánu* (Saliva), *Addaráia* (Atorai). *Sáimakúttu* (Chayna), *Kumáiya* (?). *Nipuju* (Nepoio), *Waijána* (Guayana).

a) name of a place + yo (family, mother, § 164 k)) : *Maratakayo*
(Marataka, a river in Surinam), etc. ;

b) name of a plant + fo (ruler, or offshoot, § 69 d)) : *Haiawafo*
(*hayawa*, incense tree), etc. ;

c) name of a plant or of an animal + ka (when, § 29, or little, § 34 ??) :
Mibika (*mibi*, vine-rope), *Barakataka* (*barakata*, small armadillo), etc. ;

d) miscellaneous : *Ebesowa, Koroboha, Demare*, see §§ 224, 167 b).

For lists of the Arawak clan-names, see Hi., I. Th., v. C., R., and § 196.

§ 165A. Proper names, see § 176 a) ²).

§ 166. a) It seems that the old Arawaks acknowledged a First Cause ;
however, (B. 5e, 6) they never called upon this deity : "to Him for succour
none can fly. He is so high above". The titles for this Supreme Being :
Aiomun Kon-di, Dweller in the Height, *Ifili-ci Wa-ci-na-ci*, Great Our
Father, *Wa-murreti-kwon-ci*, Our Maker, may perhaps be due to the
influence of Christian missionaries ;

b) ¹) *Orehu*, Pen. *huliu*, R. *oriyu*, G. *oriyu, uriyu*, probably indicates the
cosmical mother-principle. "Bright Orehu ... her beauty rare", the unborn
virgin (having no navel), ever renewing herself, like a serpent which casts
its skin, appears to the medicine-man in his greatest illumination ; see
B. 5e, 18, Pen. 17a, III, 102, 162, and especially 69g VII, VIII.

The same word is generally used to indicate spirits of a less exalted
state, water-spirits, described to the author as "a dragon, a huge serpent
with feet and wings".

The Kaliña term *Okoyumu* is probably composed of *okoyo*, serpent,
yumu, spirit, and so we may translate *Oriyu* by *ori*, serpent, *yu*, mother
(-spirit) ; but *ori* may also hint at "darkness" (§ 126 b)) or "rotation"
(§ 108A), she being the "mother of time".

Speaking of the common water-spirits, R. (19a, Sect. 186) says : "Like
the Spirits of the Forest, the Oriyus have strong sensual predilections.
Every night, in their anthropomorphic form, both males and females may
come after Indians of the opposite sex". This perhaps accounts for the
fact that the biblical term "fornication", has been rendered by *orehi*, S.
wurehu (comp., however, also German Hure, English whore) ;

²) R. *oroli*, G. *horoli*, is the name of a big snake which endowed man
with the hunting-charms *(bina)* ; it is the same as the *halamali* of the
Kaliña, a drawing of which is given by Roth, 19a Sect. 235. Comp. A. M.
§ 182, 42 ;

c) It may be that the heavens are considered to be the abode of the
cosmical mother-principle. Indians told v. C. that in the height the wisdom
of the vulture (§ 166 g)) is found. The Maipure consider heaven as being
of divine nature. Comp. also Arawak *iyu*, mother, *a-io-mun*, heaven
(§ 71 b) 6)), A. M. *eno, *ina*, mother, *eno*, heaven. The Arawaks trace
descent through the mother ; evidently this is expressed in the word *o-io*,
kindred, people ; it might also be expressed in A. M. *eina-ri*, man (homo
or vir), *ino, *ina-ru*, woman or wife (§ 182, 33, 60, 30, 32) ;

^d) G. *Harliwanli*, v. C. *Haliwálika, Halwanli*, R. *Hariwalli*, B. *Arawânili.*
Arawidi, probably all indicate the powerful deity to whom inanimate things
and irrational beings are subject (v. C.), who metes out justice (§ 212),
and became afterwards the sun (*adaili*, which expresses lord or lordly
light). The name reminds one of *hali*, light, *wa*, own, *li*, free or male ;

^e) By an action of the sun(-deity), a woman became pregnant with twins
(§ 213) ; from one of them, the human race, or the Arawak nation is
descended.

The adventures of the demi-god, or of him and his brother, or of two
animals, form the subject of a great many legends of the Arawaks and
other tribes (see Ehrenreich 63, Koch-Grünberg 45d, Roth 19a). In Arawak
tales we find the following names :

¹) D. *Maconaura*, v. C. *Macanaholo, Macanaura*. Probably the same
is meant by G. *makuranale*, "the proper name of the big otter in the fable",
and the word might also be contained in G. *waǫu-maká(nre*, big species of
bat, and *wáliti-maká(ŋro*, small ant-eater. It bears moreover a strong
resemblance to the Makusi (Karib) name for the same hero, *Makuna-ima*.
The origin of the word has not been ascertained ;

²) Sm. *Kurrúruman*, der hiesige Indianer Grosvater ; Q. *Kururuman*,
the creator of men, *Kulimina*, the creator of women. Hi. *Aluberi* (comp.
this §, ^d)) is the supreme being, and *Kururumanny* the god or patron of the
Arawaak nation. See A. M. § 182, 40. The Maipure name *Purrùnaminàri*
might mean great lord or great soul ;

³) *Mabukulu* (without thigh), after he has lost one leg and has
become Orion ;

⁴) The man who roasted his wife (§ 214) is probably the same hero;
but a name has not been given ;

^f) Hi., Sc. *Kururumanny* had two wives, called *Wurekado* and
Emisiwaddo (night-female and morning-female ?). v. C. A girl asked the
sun in marriage ; the girl was impatient and opened the sun's box ;
instantly the light of the first day appeared.

Harliwanli had two wives who committed sin with his two brothers. One
wife, G. *Sibarloyen*, v. C. *Sibourouyan* (rock-soul ?) could not stand the
heat of the fire, and was changed into a porpoise, *kasekoyah*, § 167 a) ²),
the animal which is alternately below the water, and rises to the surface
(comp. the remarks about repeated incarnations in § 168, and the legend
told by v. C., 7c, 519, of the men who, by way of punishment, were changed
into fishes in such a manner that at times their human nature appeared
above water). — The other wife, G. *Orliro*, v. C. *Ouriro* (fornication-
female ? or darkness-female, water-spirit) could not remain in earnest, and
was changed into a caracara-falcon, *beletata* (probably a sound-imitation
and also *bele*, lame, *tata*, strength). — One brother, *Orowama*, G.
Orlowama, v. C. *Ourwanama* (fornication-lord ? or darkness-lord ; comp.
Akawai *Oroan*, Taulipang *Olozan*, the demon of darkness who causes

eclipses, B. 5e, 189, Koch-Grünberg 45d II, 55, III, 171, IV, 34) was banished to a desolate part of the world of spirits. — The other brother, v. C. *Hiwanama*, G. *Hiwanaka* (from *hiwa*, bamboo ??) was banished to a place where spirits lived who extracted his bones; ultimately he was delivered by *Harliwanli*;

R. 19a, Sect. 183. Two sisters had a tapir for a sweetheart (— according to Pen. this animal is the symbol for carnal lusts). Their brother killed the tapir, and when the women discovered what had happened, they threw themselves into the water; one sister turned into a manati, and the other into a porpoise;

g) The demi-god married a girl, got into trouble with her clan, and finally escaped with the loss of one leg, and became Orion. The girl is *Anuanaitu* (vulture-daughter), her mother *Anuanåyo* or *Anånoyo* (vulture-mother-spirit) or *Taukelŏlelio* (condor-mother-spirit), her father *Anuanima* (vulture-lord ?) or *Kaikoutji* (caiman; however, in a Karib version he is the tiger, Karib *kaikuši). [The name of the vulture or carrion-crow, Q. *annoane* probably means: heaven-being];

h) 1) G. *seme, sémehe*, the good spirits which inspire the medicineman. A similar word with a similar meaning is found in Island Karib, and Pelleprat has mentioned it in his Kaliña vocabulary; it has also been reported from the Great Antilles. The word might be the same as *seme*, sweet;

2) G. *sémi-či*, Sm. *seme-tti*, medicine-man or doctor-priest. In the bible translations: B. *semici-ci*, S. *seme-tti, seme-tti-kill*, a sorcerer, B. *semeci-hi*, witchcraft;

3) Twice the greater part of living men has been destroyed, because of their sins; the first time by fire, the second time by water (B. 5e, 10, v. C. 7c, 515). *Mārerewāna* survived the big flood. This name reminds us of the A. M. name for medicine-man *mariri (§ 182, 49), which probably means "wise man" or "teacher";

i) 1) R. *yawahu*, G. *yáwahŏ*, the Arawak generic term for forest spirits or bush spirits, Sm. *jáwahü*, "the Indian's nightmare of something which does them harm, that makes them ill, etc.; we call it the devil", S. *jawahü*, B. *yauhahu*, (biblical) devil, unclean spirit (Acts V. 16); *y. i.* freely, *auha, awa*, roaming through space, *hu* forms verbal nouns, § 24, comp. *auaduli*, wind, *a-iaudi- ... a*, to be beside oneself, to be mad, § 131;

2) *yaware*, a rainbow (A. M. § 182, 48); nature-spirit — no motion;

3) Sm. *da-hudu|paruka jawale bia da-ebessu|pa baba*, when I die I shall perhaps resurrect as an opossum (said a heathen Arawak), lit. I-die if roaming spirit (the same word is used also for opossum and for rainbow) to-be I-transform future again;

j) R. *mahui*, an evil spirit, the *kanaima* of the Macusi, etc. (A. M. § 182, 46);

ᵏ) R. *mansinskiri*, a particular nature-spirit ; *m-*, without. *ansi*, soul, inner peace, love, *kiri*, active being (§ 175 ꞏ)) ?

ˡ) R. *ekkekuli*, a certain kind of nature-spirits, Pen. *ekekoli*. the man-eaters ; *eke*, to eat ?

§ 167. ᵃ) Certain groups of stars are called by the Arawaks (R.) *tu-kuyuha*. Each of these has its particular name, consisting of R. *-kuyuha*. G., Pen., v. C. *-kuya*, *-koya*, preceded by the name of an animal or plant. The life and activity of that animal or plant species comes from its eponymous *-kuyuha*. G. The *-kuya* is a sign, not a spirit ; when, for instance, the *hitsi-kuya*, the Southern Cross, appears, the curassow-birds *(hitsi)* begin to pair.

We surmise that the old Arawaks regarded each constellation as the visible sign of the spiritual connexion between the heaven-world and the animal or plant and called it : *tu-*, its, *kuyu*, navel, *u(h)a*. own. "Navel" as a symbol for a spiritual contact is also used by the Kaliña (Pen. 17A III, 137).

The same word is used to indicate :

1) I) the shyness or wildness of an animal or bird, or as a verb *ka-koia*, Sm. *ka-kuja*, G. *ka-kuyá*, to be shy or wild, Sm. *a-makujadi-*, to tame;

II) Sm. *kujára*, deer ;

2) aquatic mammals, often mythical : Sm. *bara akkujaha*, a huge sea-beast, *aruwa-kujaha*, a sea-beast shaped like a tiger. *peru-kujuha*, seal (Seehund), *t-akujaha*, whale, R. *kassi-kuyuha*, a white or black variety of porpoise, embodying a good or an evil water-spirit ; Sm. *kassi-kuyuha*, porpoise, G. *káse-kuya*, dolphin. *koyumóꝓo*, manati ;

3) R. *konoko-kuyuha*, bush-spirit, *adda-kuyuha*, tree-spirit ; these spirits generally have a bad name :

4) G. the following mighty spirits :

I) *yóli-kuyáha*, the spirit of tobacco *(yúli)* ; "true Indians treat tobacco with awe and smoke but little ; lack of awe may cause illness" ;

II) *hiáλi-kuya*, the spirit of the takini-tree *(hiali)* ; "a true Indian will not touch this tree, out of awe" ;

III) *khaléko-kuyá*, the spirit of the white pebbles in the medicine-man's rattle (which mostly come from the uplands) ; "*hamaru-ka|ie khaléku bura*", they (i.e. persons which still believe in these things) are afraid of those pebbles.

IV) v. C. *hóroro-kojáha*, the spirit of the earth ;

V) v. C. *kiringhá-kojá-no*, the spirit which opposes those spirits which bereave a man of his strength (comp. § 166 ᶠ): muscular. § 99 ᵇᶦᶦ)) ;

ᵇ) Several myths of the Arawaks and neighbouring tribes speak of a time when animals were men. and I. Th., when discussing the clan-system. tells us that "most Arawaks ... assert that each family is descended — their fathers knew how, but they themselves have forgotten — from its eponymous animal. bird or plant".

Whereas animals are supposed to be still connected with the heavenly

world, the connexion of man with this world has been severed, as is told in
the following legends (B. 5e, 178) :

¹) The *Koroboha-na*-clan "originally came from above the clouds. The
weight of a heavy woman broke the rope by which they were descending ;
(comp. the navel-string symbol, § 167 ^a)) ; and communication was thus
cut off between those who had reached the ground and those remaining
above. The Great Spirit, pitying the latter, supplied them with wings and
plumage ; and they came down, to colonise the trees above the heads of
their brethren — still privileged to live near, and to converse with them,
though changed into *koriouka*-parrots" ;

²) A *Korobohá(na)* man married a *Demare-du,* an elphin-maiden, a
daughter of the earth, and from this union the *Demaré*-clan has sprung.

Koroboha might indicate the firmament (§ 108A ^d)) ; in *demare* the *d*
may indicate "heavy" or "compressed".

Comp. also D. 8, 102 : In the Arawak country there lived two sisters.
One day they saw a creature whom they had seen before only in their
dreams and worshipped and loved as a god. He was the first man they
had ever seen in bodily form. He told them that his country was above the
clouds ; that while hunting he came to a cave, descending which led him
to them. This first man taught them to cultivate the cassava, etc. (all trades
and implements). From these three persons sprung the Arawaks, [and ever
since bigamy has been a custom, or almost a law of the Arawaks] ;

^c) In the heaven-world, or some intermediate world, the *yu,* the mother-
spirits of the several animal- and plant-species reside. v. C. (7c, 517) the
galej-ojo, cassava-goddesses formerly served man. G. After death, before
the human soul goes to the world of God, it meets those spirits. If a man
in his life has been kind to a dog, then, when he comes to *péro-o-yu šikwa
bana,* dog-mother-spirit house surface, this dog (even if it died long ago)
meets him, wagging its tail *(pero čwa halikibetoá-ŋ),* and gives him many
things, and *kaširi* to drink. But if the man has badly treated a dog, then the
dog tells the dog-mother-spirit, and she judges him, and he gets nothing ;

^d) There is a tradition that animals are men, who on account of their
wickedness have been changed into animals. In the legends birds often
play the role of heavenly messengers ; in Sm.'s vocabulary *kuddibiu.* bird.
is the only name for an animal which takes the plural suffix -*nu* of the
rational beings, and the word itself might mean : *kudi.* driving. racing. *bi,*
tiny, quick, *yu,* spirit. We suspect that the same ending *yu,* meaning a
spirit, occurs in the word *serabokilio,* a tempest, § 116 ^d) ⁹).

§ 168. All Indians believe that after death the soul continues to live
(Sc., 21a, II, 319). The following facts might be remnants of an ancient
belief in repeated incarnations :

^a) v. C., 7c, 512 : The first men ... were happy ; there was no sin, and
neither were sickness and death. Every day God descended among them.
If someone entered heaven, then he was obliged to die first, because the

human eye is not fit to contemplate God. To those Arawaks who had entered heaven and had to return, God gave a new life :

b) G. Formerly, when an Arawak child died, and a new child was born, the parents sometimes said *to šuku-to a-kóyua kikatéba*, the little one returns again ;

c) De la Borde, 62, 15 : The Island Karibs believed that one of their several souls after death went to heaven and took a new young body :

d) Pelleprat, 68, 77 : Among the Kaliña there was a belief that when they died, their soul entered into the body of a child which entered this world ;

e) The Arawaks, and also the Tamanacos (Q., 18, 257, Gillij, 42, III, 5) had a tradition, that man on account of his wickedness has been deprived of everlasting life, which was given to the animals which change their skin (snakes, cockroaches). A Carib legend, told by Brett (5e, 107) tells that before the great flood came : "if age brings evil on you ... Youth renewing, bright and fair : As the serpent glideth clear From the slough he scorns to wear". Pen. 69f, V : The soul of the Kaliña changes its body, like a snake changes its skin ;

f) G. The suffix *-mi* (= new, § 74 ?) after the name of a person or animal, indicates that that person or animal is no longer in the land of the living, for instance *da-yó-mi*, my late mother, *da-boketsi-mi*, my late brother, *d-epéro-mi*, my dead dog. The Maipure equivalent, *-mine*, is almost the same as *meni, mene*, field, plantation, and *umeni*, a snake (A. M. § 182, 49A, 43).

§ 169. G. *ü-ya*, 1⁰. that by which plants, animals and men differ from dead matter, 2⁰. something etherical (shadow, image, aroma, etc.) : possibly *ü-ya* expresses something intermediate between *u-yu*, mother-spirit, and *a*, time-reality.

a) 1) *kia n-onyi faroka huia-tu ada o-mun, ama-hu saka-tu omuni fa ?* for if they do these things in a green tree, what shall be done in the dry ? Sm. *uéja*, to be living, fresh, *üja-tu hime*, fresh fish, *ka-hüa*, bread being well-seasoned, not sour, I. Th. *eeya-to*, raw, fresh, G. *uüya-to hime*, fresh fish, *uüya-to kúta-ha*, fresh meat, *uüja-to khalli*, newly dug-out cassava-root (but : *na-korolia-sa*, §§ 164 b), 22, *khalli*, fresh cassava-bread) :

2) Sm. *abuku-nn-ua üja-hü*, to be uneasy (*abuku-nn-ua*, to be boiling), *kia abuká-ka da-iya*, that has caused me anxiety, *d-abuku-nn-ua üja*, I am anxious ;

B. I) *h-abokwa-li ia !* wonder (ye) ! *n-abokwa ia na-makwa*, and they were all amazed, *l-aboko-n-wa ia o-doma*, for he was astonished, *m-aboko-n-wa b-a ia*, marvel not ;

II) *ama o-doma abokwa-ga hu-ia toho o-konomun ?* why marvel ye at this ?

III) *kia adaiahu adeki-n bena, l-ikiduada kiana: Adaie-li o-konomun-tu ajia-hu abokoto-n l-iia o-doma*, then the deputy, when he saw what was done, believed, being astonished at the doctrine of the Lord :

IV) *ma-kariti-n ia i*, [the devil came out] and hurt him not ;

V) *a-iaudi-* ... *a*, to be beside oneself, to be mad (§ 131) ;

VI) S. *pahia*, word of astonishment ; *pa* blowing away (?) ;

3) *ma-ia-kwa*, being easy, in peace ;

4) I) Sm. *a-ijabussü-*, to be drowsy ; B. *Wacinaci a-iabosa kia wakaia-hu o-konomun*, God winked at (that evil) ;

II) Sm. *t-abussia-hü*, the sleep, the sleepiness, B. *t-abisia goba na-makwa, kena n-adunka goba*, they all slumbered and slept ;

III) *Peter, lo-ma-ci bajia t-abo-kibi ma goba adunku-in*, Peter and they that were with him were heavy with sleep, *t-abo-kibe-n-ci adunku-in*, being fallen into a deep sleep ;

IV) *l-itabotwabo ka adunku-in*, he sunk down with sleep ;

5) Sm. *a-ijabudü-*, braten, B. *a-iaboda-sia himi ibena*, a piece of broiled fish ;

6) Sm., *üeja, úeja-hü*, S. *üja*, G. *üyá-hü*, spirit, S. *üssa-tti üja-hü*, the Holy Ghost, *da-ija-wa*, my (own) Spirit (Acts II, 17) ;

7) R. *(h)iyaloko*, a dead person's spirit, G. *na-ialoko*, the spirits of the dead, B. *ialoko*, spirit ; the word may be the same as *ialoko*, instead of (§ 103 g)), or it may express *ü-ya*, spirit, *loko*, man.

Examples : *Sa-tu Ialoko*, the Holy Ghost, *Ialoko ka Wacinaci ; a-kwaiabo-ci-no a-kwaiabo fa lo-mun ialoko abu kidua-hu abu*, God is a Spirit : and they that worship him must worship him in spirit and in truth, *ama isa loko o-mun, to-makwa ororo l-auciga faroka, kena lo-boreda l-oaiya l-ialoko-wa ?* for what is a man profited if he shall gain the whole world, and lose his own soul ? *Ialoko* in an unfavourable sense, has only been met with in : *ika tu iribe-tu ialoko a-fitikidi-n loko o-rea*, when the unclean spirit is gone out of a man (Mt. XII, 43). On the other hand Mk. V, 2 *abar-li yauhahu k-amun-ci*, a man with an unclean spirit ;

b) Sm. *üeja, úeja-hü*, shadow, image *(da-ija, bu-ja*, etc., plur. *üjahú-nnu)*, *da-bulliti-pa béju üja*, I will paint a deer. G. *thü-ya*, picture, image in a mirror, shadow, *d-adekáh da-yá-wa*, I see my image in the mirror, *kakü-či üya*, photograph of a man, *üya-hü*, the shadow of a man, *da-khábo-roko th-üyada-η*, the lines in the palm of my hand, *a-yati-*, to picture, B. *a-iata-hu*, image, idol, R. *(h)iyá*, a person's shadow, B. *t-iya abomun*, [the fowls lodge] under the shadow of it, *a-bolliti-ci a-oda-hu iyabo mun o-mun*, to them that sit in the shadow of death, *Peter a-bolli-n bo l-iya a-iabota ma aba-no jiaro*, that at least the shadow of Peter passing by might overshadow some of them ;

c) 1) I) *ointment o-boea*, the odour of the ointment, *boia-tu*, a sweet savour, Sm. *bùhujae*, to emit a balmy smell ;

II) Sm. *kopáijoa*, a tree which emits a delicious smell (copaiva) ;

2) G. *hiaǫi*, the takini-tree (see § 205) ;

3) Sm. *háiali*, fish poison ;

4) Sm. *háiawa*, incense tree, Protium heptaphyllum.

§ 170. a) *kokke*, Sm. *kaku, kakü*, G. *kakü*, life, to live, is used when speaking of human beings or animals ; however, G. *kakü kan,* may be said when a newly planted tree is alive ; *ka, ko,* to appear in a positive manner, force, *ke, kü,* emphasis ?

b) 1) G. *kaki-či,* a human being in general (see also §§ 219, 9 : 222, 3, 7), v. C. *kakhi-tsji bia l-ebéésowa koeba,* pro nobis factus est homo. G. *üe-kákü-hü,* human (perhaps also animal) soul or life ;

2) *a-kokkiti-tu ajia-hu,* the lively oracles, *(a-)kokketo-* to quicken (J. V, 21, VI, 63) ;

c) R. *kalli,* cassava cake, *keheli,* expressed cassava juice, *kereli,* the chewed fresh cassava bread, *cashiri,* a beverage manufactured from cassava etc. (A. M. § 182, 120) ;

d) *a-koto,* to eat, also : feeding swine (L. V, 32) ; G. *a-koto-* is used when no fixed object is meant, for instance *da-kóto fa,* I go to dinner, *bu-koto|bi|da ?* hast thou already dined ? *da-kutá-ia-bi|da,* (yes), I have already dined.

§ 171. a) *eke, eki, ike, iki,* food, to eat ; G. *eke* is used when a fixed object is meant, for instance *d-iki fa,* I shall eat (answer to the question : shall you eat this ?), *kalī (hīme, kūta) d-iki fa,* I shall eat cassava (fish, meat), *d-ekee bi|da|n,* I have eaten it already ;

b) *eke, eki,* clothes, *na-wakaia eke,* a clothe for their sin, *plata eke,* a purse, *t-eke,* its vessel (for oil), the sheath (of a sword), *oniabu eki,* the waterpots, *t-eke-loko-tu-alaiti abu, alaiti-adaia abu,* with lanterns and torches, Sm. *aku-ke,* the eyelids, G. *ēkĭ,* bladder, *ékĕ,* amnion, *sá-hī,* uterus. *kúdibiyu sá-kĕ,* empty egg-shell, *kúši-ke,* spectacles ;

c) *c-ikihi,* its fat, *k-ikihi-tu baka sa,* the fatted calf.

§ 172. *Ako,* entering into (§ 128).

a) 1) I) *ako-si,* eye ; *(i)si,* seed (A. M. § 182, 15);

II) *yuho-li m-akosi-ci l-akosita ia n-adeki-n bia,* and unto many that were blind he gave sight ;

2) *abaren l-ako-loko warea t-itikida isogo-tu t-eda jiamutu* (S. *ikka -ké t-illipe ti dia t-a a-ttikida t-aku-lukku-waria),* and immediately there fell from his eyes as it had been scales, *kena n-akera l-ako-loko-ji,* and when they had blindfolded him ;

3) Sm. *aku-ke,* the eyelids ;

b) 1) *akonnaki,* a loud sound, *akonnakita,* to make noise, *akonnakita-hu,* uproar ;

2) *akonnabo- (bia-*form : *akonna-bia),* to hear.

§ 173. *Ade, adi,* strong, independent appearance (comp. § 88).

a) 1) R. *adibua-hu,* omen, token, auguries, Sm. *addibóa-hu,* ein Gespenst; *boa,* abnormal appearance, § 120 d) :

2) *adeki-, adiki-,* to see ;

b) B., G. *a-dimisi-,* Sm. *a-dimissi-,* to smell : *eme,* the smell, § 136 e) 3) II).

§ 174. a) *Adunku-, adunko-.* Sm. *adumki-, adunuki-* is a general A. M.

word (§ 182, 147) ; it may be in its origin an imitation of the sound of heavy breathing or snoring, but it may also be related to *a-odo-*, to die (§ 122 e) 1)) ;

ᵇ) *A-butado-(n-wa)*, to faint, to fall in a trance ; *bu* appearance, *t* flowing (?) ;

ᶜ) *Adaie-li angel ka-raia goba Joseph o-mun lo-tobonia*, the angel of the Lord appeareth to Joseph in a dream, *hui habe-ci o-toboni-wa fa*, your old men shall dream dreams, Sm. *wakáia dá-ttubü-n*, I dream (an evil dream), *óakai-u-ttubbü-*, to dream (A. M. § 182, 140) ; presumably : *tobo*, having the character of the fluent, the liquid *(a-toboti-*, Sm. *a-ttabatti-*, G. *a-thábati-*, to trickle, *a-tobodi-*, *a-tobadi-*, to cast, to dip, to step into a fluid, comp. also § 119 ᵇ)), *nia*, continuing in a free manner, or for some time. [In olden times the Arawaks believed that in sleep the soul left the body and experienced all sorts of things, and also received forecasts.]

§ 175. A great many object-words show one of the endings *-li*, *-ri*, *-ro* or *-ru*. Wherever it is possible to analyze such words, it is found that these endings indicate the general character of the thing denoted by the word.

Examples (for the meaning of the roots, see Alphabetical Index) :

ᵃ) *li*, freely streaming forth : *akorakali*, thunder, *koreli*, smoke, *auaduli*, wind, *oroli*, clay ;

ᵇ) *ri*, fixed, hooked : *kaiiri*, island, *hori*, snake, G. *wayuri*, a tick ;

ᶜ) *ro, ru*, stopping : *bilibiliro*, lightning, R. *kabadaro*, jaguar (with-claws), B. *adedisaro*, earthquakes ;

ᵈ) *bali* is the ending of several names of trees, for instance G. *dakama-bali*, Andira inermis, *ite-bali*, Vochysia tetraphylla, *širua-bali*, Nectandra ; according to Baptist, *širua-bali* means : a tree resembling the *širua*-tree, or belonging to the same family. *Bali* might depict trees standing in a row, comp. § 60 ᵃ) ;

ᵉ) *kili*, is used in the names of natural phenomena etc. (§ 130 ᵃ)) ; also : *tibo-kili*, a bush (A. M. § 182, 111), *amudi-kile-hi jiamutu*, a shore (Acts XXVII, 39), Sm. *amudü-kil*, the landing-place *(amodi-*, to go up), *su-muli-kile*, drunkenness, *ma-mulikile*, temperance ;

ᶠ) *koro*, in *ifiro-koro*, feast, R. *wiwa-k-ihi-koro*, (Halley's) comet.

It has not been found that the masculine or feminine gender is concomitant with these endings : *isa-be-tu* (f.) *akodoonali*, the fair havens, *kia akodoonali isa-tu* (f.) *koro*, the haven was not commodious, *auaduli a-fuda alon jiaro t-* (f.) *ansi-n*, the wind bloweth where it listeth, *adaili abato fa oriroko-n bia n* (f.), the sun shall be turned into darkness.

G. *hadáli futikidah-te-da ?* has the sun already risen ? answer : *ma-futikidi(n koa th-a-ya-te-da*, the sun has not yet risen. Baptist said that here the feminine prenominal prefix should be used, notwithstanding the sun is masculine according to the myth (§ 213).

§ 176. In other forms, however, these endings do indicate the gram-matical gender :

a) m. *-li*, f. *-ro* :

1) *adaie-li*, lord (*d-adaie-n*, my lord), *k-onyi-li*, the owner (of the ship), *isa-i-li* friend (Vocative), *d-onnaka-ro*, my burden, R. *ka-shikwa-lli* house-master ;

2) Proper names : R. *ka-iinasa-li* (boy), *ka-iinasa-ro* (girl). "big buttocks", *ka-bara-li* (boy), *ka-bara-ro* (girl), "plenty of hair", etc. ;

3) *abar-li, aba-ro*, § 152, *yuho-li, yuho-ro*, § 151 b) 4) ;

4) Superposition of the suffixes *-ci* and *-li* or *-ro* :

ifi-li-ci, great (a man), *ifi-ro-tu* (a woman, a non-rational being or a thing), *adaie-l-ci*, a nobleman, *k-abue-l-ci*, householder, citizen, Sm. *likia ándâ-l-te*, der da kommt oder gekommen ist (also *likia ándi-ti*, der da kommt, *kia andi-tu, kia andá-ru*, die da kommt) ; comp. § 95, *-l-te*.

In B.'s texts these endings rarely occur ; S. uses them frequently :

b) S. m. *-li*, f. *-ru*, plur. *-nu* ;

1) *a-hudá-li irei-tu*, his (the dead man's) wife, *a-uttika-ni|n a-hudá-ru*. and found her dead, *l-anniká-ru platta*, the price, *Petrus u-ma anda-nu*, they ... as came with Peter ;

2) *likidaha Jesus, hu-parrü-kubá-li*, (this) Jesus whom ye slew, *Gott ani-kubá-ru l-abbu*, [the signs] which God did by him, *l-a kuba-ru a-buleti-n Prophet David u-llukku-di*, Acts I, 20 (his-do past-*ru* writing prophet David in-place), *Jesus u-ma-tti-kubá-nu*, [they took knowledge] that they had been with Jesus, *Dai bu-ttinutti-kuba-nu U-mallita-koan-ti kéwai de*, I am the God of thy fathers ;

3) *andi-tti-pa-li*, him which should come, *b-aku-te tuhu dai da-waja da-dukuttu-pa-ru hurruru-muniru*, come into the land which I shall shew thee ;

4) *abba Gott u-mün a-kujaboa-koana-ttu añika-hü-ssia bia-ru bahü-kan*, the tabernacle of witness, lit. one God to worship-instrument taken-thing to-be-*ru* house-small ;

5) *w-addiki-ssiá-ru*, things which we have seen (B. *w-adeki-sia*) ;

6) *tu-maqua n-adia-ssia-bi-ru da-ijalugku*, the things whereof they now accuse me, *hamatalli h-adia-bi-ru*, these things which ye have spoken ;

c) S. m. *-ki-ll(i)*. f. *-ku-rru*, plur. *-ku-nnu* :

1) *Simon na-ssa-killi Zelotes*, Simon (they-call-*killi*) Zelotes, *bu-lesida-bu-kurru*, what thou readest ;

2) *Jesus ... Gott u-ria andi-tti-kill*. Jesus ... a man approved of God. *k-aima-tti-kill l-ibiamate-tti u-mün*. he that did his neighbour wrong, *Jehovah a-raijattoá-li ibitu-ttu-kurru kuñuku-mün*, the angel (Jehovah) which appeared to him in the (burning) bush. *adinamu-tti kunnu*. them that stood. *ihittira-tti-kunnu lü-jalugku*. his accusers. *ka-pparka-tti*. a murderer, *bibiti tausend ka-pparka-tti-kunnu*. four thousand men that were murderers ;

3) *Jerusalem-mün-li-kunnu Apostel-nu*. the apostles which were at Jerusalem, *miaka h-issika-buna-nu-kunnu Siba u-llukkumün*. the men whom (yesterday) ye put in prison.

§ 177. The pronouns are symbols for the different "persons". Their proper meanings are :

Pronominal prefixes :

I   *d(a)-*, firmly established ; will-power ; "I"-feeling (§ 184) ;

II   *b(u)-*, the quiet, expectant one ; or : deictic gesture (§ 184) ;

III m   *l(o)-*, *l(u)-*, *l* masculine, *o* not moving, potential ;

III f.   *t(o)-*, *t(u)-*, *t* feminine, *o* „   „   „   ;

I pl.   *w(a)-*, vast ;

II pl.   *h(u)-*, *h* deictic (comp. §§ 44 b), 45 b)), *u* vast ; or : deictic gesture, of a broader, a more solemn, character than *bu* ;

III pl.   *n(a)-*, continuity, or person (§ 187).

End-point pronouns

I   *di*, the same as the pr. pr., but as a principle *(i)* only ;

II   *bu*, „   „   „   „   „   „ ;

III m.   *i*, masculine ;

III f.   *n*, end-point ;

I pl.   *u*, the same as the pr. pr.;

II pl.   *hu*. ..   „   „   „   „   „ ;

III pl.   *ie*, perhaps originally *ne*, continuity, or person (§ 187).

§ 178. Class (gender and number) is expressed only in object-words and pronouns.

singular, human, male	—, *l(o)-*, *l-i-hi*, *i* , *-ci*, *-di*, *-li*
„ „ female	} —, *t(o)-*, *t-o-ho*, *n* , *-tu*, *-du*, *-ro*
non-human	
plural human	*-no*, *n(a)-*, *na-ha*, *ie*, *-ci-no* or *-no-ci*, etc., *-di-no*.

Consequently :

i	*l*	*u, o*	*t*	*r*
free, lively	loose	at rest	limited motion	impeded motion
(active)	—	(passive)	—	—
human	human	nature	nature	nature
man	man	woman	woman	woman

Certainly, those authors which considered the gender distinction in Arawak and in related languages as evidence of the low mental and social condition of these nations, were on the wrong track. See further § 188.

In B.'s translation of the bible, God (*Wacinaci*, lit. our-father) and angel *(angel)* are put in the human (rational) class : devil (*yauhahu*, nature-spirits) is put in the nature (non-rational) class.

For The Word *(Ajia-hu)* the m. pronoun *lihi* has been used (Jl. 3) in accordance with the English text. Otherwise *ajia-hu*, the speaking, and other words denoting "abstraction" are put in the class of non-rational beings and things. J. XVI, 13, in accordance with the English text, *lihi kidua-hu Ialoko*, he, the Spirit of truth. Elsewhere *Sa-tu Ialoko*, the Holy Ghost, the Spirit (Acts II, 4).

The sex of animals is distinguished as follows : Gen. VII, 2, 3 the male and his (the) female : *wadili hiaro mu-tu*. lit. man wife with-*tu* (non-rational).

§ 179. ‚Expressions used only by men (m.) or only by women (f.) :

a⁾ greeting "bist du da ?" : m. Sm. addressed to a man, *büi-l-uai*, to a woman, *büi-ru*, to several people, *hü-n-uai ;* answer "ich bin da", m. Sm. *da-ú-li, da-ü-li-si, da-ili-sé,* f. Sm. *da-ú-ru-ra, dâ-ü-ru-ra ;*

b⁾ I ! m. Sm. *dái,* f. Sm. *dai-ra ;*

c⁾ surely, certainly : m. R. to a man, *ta-de,* to a woman *ta-shi,* Sm. *ta-sè. ta-êssè,* v. C. *ehé* (= yes), *ta-si,* f. R. to a man *ta-shi,* to a woman *ta-ra ;* Sm. *ta-ra,* v. C. *ta-ré ;*

d⁾ o yes, so you say ; m. R. to a man, *d-a-i-do,* to a woman *d-a-dai,* f. R. to a woman *b-a-bui ;*

e⁾ "vielleicht, ich glaube" : m. Sm. *bahâ-sse,* v. C. *baha-ssi-da.* f. Sm. *bahá-ra,* v. C. *bahá-ra,* B. *d-ibibidi faroka baha l-eke,* if I may but touch his garment (Mt. IX, 21) ;

f⁾ "freilich" : m. Sm. *dú-ke-si, dú-ke-ssè* (comp. § 61 d⁾), f. Sm. *dú-ka-ra ;* "allerdings" : m. Sm. *he|du-ke-ssi* (also used for "ja, freilich"), f. Sm. *he|ki-ssá-i-ra, ki-sse-i-ra ;* "ja, allerdings" : f. Sm. *he|du-ka-ra, hé ki-ssé-i-ra ;* Pen. *wa-the-fa-do dokara,* we will go drink as usual, *wa-the-fa-do dokase,* do. (probably the first sung by women, the second by men) ; "gethan" (fertig) : m. Sm. *hébbi-ssè,* f. Sm. *hébbi-ra.*

a—f⁾ Many of these short words contain emphasizing particles which we have already met with. It seems that the sharp *si, se* (§ 116 d⁾ ¹⁰⁾) is used especially by men, the perhaps somewhat softer *ra* (§ 104), especially by women. See further § 191 a⁾.

g⁾ Sm. *akkubani-hü* or *ukubanni-hü,* a garden (§ 128 ⁵⁾) ; with pronominal prefixes : I *da-kkuban,* I pl. *wa-,* III pl. *na-.* When addressing men, one says : II *ba-,* III m. *la-,* III f. *ta-,* II pl. *ha.* when addressing women : *bu-, lu-, tu-, hu-.* Baptist considers this difference is owing to the fact that women articulate better than men.

CHAPTER XIX

FOREIGN WORDS. ARAWAK AND ARAWAK-MAIPURE

§ 180. The Arawak language has appropriated several foreign words. The Spanish words may be regarded as such, and also the creole-Dutch words which occur in Brett's texts, and partly those in Schultz' texts. Brett uses a great many English words (as: *hell, paradise, prophet, temple, angel, incense, praise, apostle*, etc. etc.), and Schultz several German words (see list of these words at the end of the Alphabetical Index), but these may not be regarded as having been assimilated.

All these words are — see Alphabetical Index — expressions for post-Columbian ideas. Penard (17c) is of opinion "that there is a tendency, though not a strong one, to replace foreign words by others of Arawak origin. Taken all in all, the Arawak language of Surinam does not appear to have been affected so much, as close contact with civilization might lead us to think".

The Arawak does not recognize foreign verbs as such; he makes an action-word from them, by means of the usual affixes:

From creole-Dutch words: B. *a-dankido-(n-wa)*, to thank, S. *a-lesedi-*, to read;

From English words: B. *a-baptizedi-*, to baptize (*baptism*, baptism), *a-circumcisedo-(n-wa)*, to be circumcised, *a-praisedi-*, to praise, *a-prophesido-(n-wa)*, to prophesy, *a-sacrificedo(-n-wa)*, to do sacrifice, *a-sweardoa*, to swear, *a-ridi-*, to read.

There is no direct proof that Arawak has appropriated words from other Indian languages. However, in Guiana and adjacent territories one often finds that a certain word for a pre-Columbian domestic article, a plant, an animal, or even a supernatural being, is used by tribes belonging to different families of languages. Such regional words also occur in Arawak (see §§ 197—200, where they have been marked [r]), and it may be that some of these are not of Arawak origin.

Next come those words, that only occur in Arawak, but the etymology of which could not be traced (see §§ 195—200, where they have been marked [u]). We are met here by the difficulty that we mostly do not know which peculiarity is described by a word. For instance, a land-boa is called "the slow one", *ma-hŏle-ru* or *mawleru* (§§ 112 [d], 175 [c]), but we should perhaps never have found this out, if the word had not been explained to us by an Arawak. [This snake is also called Sm. *kule-kunna-ru*, weak-walker.]

Finally comes the great majority of words (among them nearly all particles, pronouns, quality-words and action-words), which are constructed in the manner as shown in our examples in § 20. Although a slight doubt may be entertained here and there, as to whether our interpretation is the correct one, yet on the whole, the evidence that these words are really sound-pictures, complexes of sound-symbols, seems overwhelming.

§ 181. The Arawak words found in the oldest writings (ll. 9, 14) do not differ in any perceptible degree from the words as they are used to-day. The differences between the translations of Brett and those of Schultz, are to be attributed to the different views of the translators, and perhaps to a difference in the dialects, in regard to which Schumann says: "Man findet darin verschiedene Dialekte", and Brett : "There is at present some variety existing, principally in the pronunciation of words by people of different districts. But there is no difficulty in the way of their understanding each other, and in all material points there is little difference". This latter is also the author's experience.

We may, however, still find out something about the early history of Arawak from a comparison with the other languages of the Arawak-Maipure group.

As a result of a superficial examination of these languages, we venture to make the following remarks :

All the A. M. languages use pronominal prefixes and pronouns consisting of an emphasizing particle with a pronominal prefix : in some of them end-point pronouns, differing but little from the pronominal prefixes, have been met with.

Several A. M. languages apply a pronominal prefix, even when the person is already indicated by an object-word :

Palikur : *ri-wasiri Palikurene*. Land der Palikur, *Toussaint ri-pina*, Toussaint's Haus ;

Goajiro : *jamúsa nu nöike Maréigua nu mui Adam ?* (*su mui Eva, su mui úri, nu mui yaröjá*), I qué habló Dios a Adan ? (a Eva, a la culebra, al diablo), lit. what he said God him at Adam (her at Eva, it at snake, him at devil), *nu-doctrina-ka Jesucristo*, la doctrina de Jesucristo, *su-rauráka körésia*, el Jefe de la Iglesia ;

Kampa : *naçhi no-tomi*, hijo mio, *i-umbari Juan*, el amigo de Juan, *i-bango Juan*, la case de Juan, *i-gina*, su mujer, *o-gime*, su marido, *i-cachita-te pi-gimme ?* esta enfermo tu marido ? *o-cachita-te pi-ginna ?* esta enfermo ta mujer ?

Baure : *r-orani ehiro*, or *ehiro-coremo*, el vestido de varon, *r-orani eteno*, or *eteno-coremo*, el vestido de mujer, *re-puyi iscini*, or *iscini-puyi*, el pie del tigre ;

Moxo : *ma-muiria ehoiro*, el vestido del varon, *su-muiria esseno*, el vestido de la muger, *ta-ibopé ichini*, el pie del tigre, *ta-ha-ce to-bea ma-cpiya-co Maimona eto ?* paraque crio Dios essas cosas ? lit. what it-for he-creates God that ?

The pronominal prefixes are :

I sing. generally *n(u)-*, with the exception of : Arawak *d(a)-*, Goajiro *t(a)-*, Paraujano *t(a)-* (it is doubtful whether Baure *di*, which has only been found in d'Orbigny's vocabulary, is of the same origin) ;

II sing. generally *p(i)-*, *b(i)-*, Arawak *b(u)-* :

I plur. *ua-*, *oe-*, *u-*, *v-*, *ab(i)-*, *a* :

II plur : some languages use the same pronominal prefix as in II sing., others use *yi-*, *ye-*, *i-*, *e-*, Arawak *hu-* ;

III : A difference is made, more or less distinctly, between one man, one woman, more than one person, and one or more non-rational beings or things ;

III sing. Palikur m. *ri-*, f. *ru-*, Wapisiana m. *i*, f. *u*, Goajiro m. *n(u)-*, f. *s(u)-*, Achagua m. *ri-*, f. *ru-*, Maipure m. *i-*, f. *ju-*, Kampa m. *i-*, f. *o-*, Baure m. *r(e)-*, f. *r(i)-*, Moxo m. *ma-*, f. *su-*, a woman speaking of a man *ñi-*, non-rational beings and things *ta-* or *to-* ;

III plur. mostly *n* (with different vowels).

Plural suffixes are applied to all object-words; however, in the grammars of Baure and Moxo, it is stated that they are but little used, when referring to non-rational beings or things.

Other indications of gender are found in the names of family-relations and such like, and in :

Goajiro : *kasáichir ni-chinka parajá-chi-ka jashia* ? como se llama el primer hombre ? *kasáichir ni-chinka parajá-te-ka jiér* ? como se llama la primera mujer ?

Moxo : *mo-chijcha-re*, (man) sin hijos, *mo-chijcha-ru* (woman) sin hijos.

In Wapisiana, in Maipure, in Ipurina, in Kampa and in Moxo inter-jections are used which differ according to the sex of the speaker and of the hearer.

In Arawak *i* has, amongst others, the meaning of "small", *u* or *o* the meaning of "great". In Moxo we find *achipi*, small, *achope*, great.

In Maipure the ending *-au* is used in order to indicate "for, or of, itself" ; in Baure *-bo* or *-bobo* is used for the same purpose, and in Moxo *-bo*. It seems quite probable that these forms are of the same origin as Arawak *-oa*.

Moxo has numerous words in which the prefix *v-* means "great", for instance *v-a*, guevo largo, *v-i*, fruta larga, *v-pai*, campo, tierra larga, *ti-ve-quiené*, hay mucha distancia de aqui allà. Probably this is of the same origin as Arawak *wa-*. Comp. also : Arawak *wa-i-kille*, Kušitineri *wa-s(y)ö-ra*, Piro *hua-še-ra*, Moxo *ebo-i-re*, far.

Almost all A. M. languages use the prefixes *k(a)-* and *m(a)-* to indicate "being present" and "not being present".

Goajiro uses *-uma*, to indicate "with" (Arawak *o-ma*), and *mui*, in order to indicate "at" (Arawak *mun*). Ipurina uses *-muni* to indicate "at", "to" and "from", in the same manner as Arawak uses *o-mun(i)*. Piro uses *ima* to indicate "with".

Otherwise the suffixes indicating mood, tense and case are rather different in the several A. M. languages, but it appears not at all improbable, that they may have been built up originally from primary elements which have a similar meaning to that which still prevails in Arawak.

§ 182. Several works dealing with a language of the A. M. group, contain a comparative vocabulary. We here give a summary of corresponding words, in order to illustrate the position of Arawak.

Words that are only found in languages belonging to the same sub-group, have been left out. Moreover not all the various transcriptions for a given word have been copied, and complicated phonetic spelling has been simplified. Students who desire to go deeper into the matter, are recommended to consult the original sources.

For the sake of clearness, the languages have been classified into four geographical groups (which do not correspond with the linguistic sub-groups of the A. M. family), viz.

I. NORTHERN GROUP
(ANTILLES, GUIANA, MARACAIBO)

Abbreviation		List of literature
A	Arawak	different sources (phonetic spelling)
—	Arua	49
At	Atorai	15, 21a, 41
G	Goajiro	33A, 33, 40a, 44, 51a, b
IK	Island Karib	
IKf	do., women's language	31, 55
Map	Mapidian, Mawakwa	15, 41
P	Palikur	15, 49, 53
Par	Parauhano	44, 51b
—	Taino	6, 15, 42, 50
W	Wapisiana	15, 36, 41, 45e

II. NORTHWESTERN GROUP
(ORINOCO, RIO NEGRO, YAPURA, IÇA)

Ach	Achagua	40b, 42
Ad	Adzaneni, Izaneni	45c, 60
Am	Amarizama	40b
Av	Avane	42
Ban	Baniwa	15, 30, 32A, 34, 38, 45a, 60
—	Bare	15, 34, 38, 45a, 60
Ca	Caouiri	38
Car	Cariay	15
Cau	Cauixana	15
—	Cavere	42
Gu	Guinau	15, 21a, 45c
—	Guipunave	42
Ip	Ipeka	45a

Ja	Jabaana	15 (Part D)
Ju	Jumana	15
Kar	Karutana	45a
Kat	Katapolitani	45a
Kau	Kauyari	45a
Maip	Maipure	29, 42
—	Manao	15, 32b
Mand	Mandauaca	45c, 60
Mar	Mariate	15
—	Pareni	30A
Pa	Passe	15
Pia	Piapoco	34, 38, 45c, 64
Si	Siusi	45a
Tar	Tariana	15, 36, 45a, 60
Uai	Uainuma	15
Uar	Uareca, Uarekena	45a, 60
Yav	Yavitero	15, 38, 40c, 45a, 60
Yuk	Yukuna	15, 45a

III. SOUTHWESTERN GROUP
(BETWEEN THE AMAZONS AND THE RIO MADEIRA)

Ar	Araicu	15
In	Inapari	54
Ipu	Ipurina	35A, 45b, 52
—	Kampa	28c
Kan	Kanamare	15
Kun	Kuniba	54
Kus	Kušiti-neri	54
Man	Maneteri	35A
M	Marauha	15
Pau	Paumari	35A, 39, 52
—	Piro	54
Yam	Yamamadi	39

IV. SOUTHEASTERN GROUP

B	Baure	28a, b
—	Chané	50a
Gua	Guana	15, 56a
Ku	Kustenau	59
Me	Mehinaku	59
—	Moxo	28a, 29, 42, 46
—	Mucoxeone	(37)
Pai	Paiconeka	32a
—	Paunaka	(37)
Pare	Paressi	59
Sar	Saraveka	37
—	Waura	59
Yaul	Yaulapiti	59

COMPARATIVE VOCABULARY OF ARAWAK-MAIPURE LANGUAGES

THE BODY

1. Blood, § 191.

I. A *ite* (*itena* as a part of the human body), IK f *ita*, G *isha*, P *mera*. W *reine karu, irei ;*

II. Ju *itta*, Pa *yta*, Cau *isa*, Car *zanhy*, Bare *aya, iya*, Gu *ea*, Yav *miyari*, Kar, Tar *irai*, Uai *ira, irahi*, Mar *yray*, Manao *yraty*, Kat, Si *irana*, Yuk *ra*, Uar *ila*, Ad *ira. irena*, Pia *irai, irana*, Mand *-rami ;*

III. Ar *ithon, isa*, Kan *ürra*, Kampa *iraja*, Piro *xcrari*, Ipu *eerenga*, Kus *slali :*

IV. B *iti* (*n-itina*, mia sangre), Moxo *iti* (*n-ijtine*, mi sangre), Gua *iti, iddina*, Pare *itimarane.*

2. Juice, §§ 125, 107.

I. A *ura, era*, (*urali*, curare, arrow-poison), IK *ira ;* acou-*ira.* a tear, G *sira*, broth, P *nra ;*

III. Piro *ihixa, ixa*, broth, Kus *tra, tla ;*

IV. B *ore*, Moxo *oro.*

3. To drink, § 91.

I. A *a-ti-*, I K f *ata*, G *asi. aza*, P *hirap*, W *tir*, Arua *cta-lc ;*

II. Bare *dia*, Yav *ziya*, Uar *ila*, Ad, Kar, Kat, Pia, Si, Tar, Uai, Yuk *ira*, Mand *jira-ni. -ra*, Manao *tüira*, Ju *ita.* Gu *ucta ;*

III. Kampa *irhe, iri*, Piro *rani, reuači*, Kan *rcoatschy.* Kun *runc.* Ipu *ŋati*, Ar *iratschy, p-ito*, Kus *ratkarii ;*

IV. B, Moxo *cro.*

4. a) Flesh, b) Heart, c) Male genital, d) Female genital, c) Worm, grub, §§ 115, 116.

  I. a) A *isi-roko*, G *shi-ruku ;*
     b) A *oassini-hü*, W *ishene.* lunge ;
     c) A *issin*, W *tiye ;*
     e) A *isehü*, I K *l-iche ;*

  II. a) Pia *inazi*, Mand *ijeshi.* Ban, Yav *mitsi ;*
     b) Maip *nichini*, Pa *saua*, Uar *(n)aseni*, Gu *inišini ;*
     c) Kat *iži*, Ip, Uar *ihi*, Kar *ichiti*, Pa *tschyu-any*, Si *iši*, Uai *chy*, Yuk *hi.* Gu *senizi*, testicle ;
     d) Uai *ynaro-sache*, Pia *aitzci ;*
     e) Bare *enisi ;*

  III. a) Ipu *ishini, isene*, Kampa *aicha ;*
     b) Kan *natoxy*, Kun *wayi*, Piro *huaxi ;*
     c) Ar *chy*, Kan *same*, Marauha *isy*, Piro *simeči*, Yam *dzoui ;*
     d) Ipu *otseniki ;*
     e) Pau *sumi*, Yam *soomi*, Kampa *chitzane ;*

  IV. a) B *enascie*, Moxa *eeche*, Pare *inete ;*
     b) Sar *i-vihine ;*
     c) Pare *sc ;*
     d) Gua *oze ;*
     e) Moxo *ichepi.*

5. Bone (presumably : figure, stature, § 60 ff.).

I. A *abona*, I K f *abo*, G *jimpu*, P *api-ti*, W *une-wiire* ;

II. Ban *piuna, api*, Bare *abi*, Cau *bimi*, Ju *pina*, Uai *pihra*, Ad, Pia, Tar *api*, Gu *abe*, Mand *yahiži* ;

III. Kun *hapö*, Piro *xapui* ;

IV. B *inepe*, Gua *api, hopeeti*, Ku *anapi*, Me, Waura *inapü*, Moxo *eope, ope*, Pare *nahe*, Sar *nahaxe*, Yaul *napi*.

6. Skin (*ma, soft, nos. 12, 17, *eda, bark, no. 7 ?).

I. W *mada, mad*, P *mali*, G *imata*, lip ;

II. Ban *mada*, Yuk *(u)ma*, Pia *imasi, imami*, Jum *matsche*, Uai *mami* ;

III. Piro *mita*, Kun *muta*, Kus *šima* ;

IV. B *chomo*, Moxo *umomo, mo*, Pare *meli*, Me, Ku, Waura *mai*.

7. Skin, bark, § 89.

I. A *eda*, I K f *t-ora*, G *suta, pata* ;

II. Bare *ida*, Gu *eda, ita* ; canoe : Pia, Uir, Kar *ida*, Ad, Kat, Tar, Si, Uar, Mand *ita*, Yuk *hita*, Bare *isa* ;

III. Ip *itanta, utanta*.

8. Hair on the skin.

I. I K *iou* ;

III. Kampa *ibiti*, Kun *(yewe-)ti*, Pia *waziwi* (on the pubes) ;

IV. Gua *etšeo*, Moxo *hiyoo*, Sar *(i-)tihi*.

9. Feather.

I. P *sipri*, W *id*, G *sumure-ra* ;

II. Ban *uidoho*, Kar *(l-)idžu*, Kat, Si *(l-)idzu*, Gu *elidzu*, Ip *l-iyu*, Uar *(n-)idu*, Mand *idoshi*, Yav *junetzi*, Gu *hipiaži* ;

III. Ip *ipiti*, Kampa *ibiti* ;

IV. Gua *etšeo(-šoopeno* = bird), Moxo *pobo*.

10. Hair of the head : (head-)hair, §§ 100, 107.

I. (A *iyehe-riti-*, to shear), A *ba-ra*, W *(ruei-)re* ;

II. Manao *(küüna-)itschy*, Mand *(uati-)quishi, (a-)tiki*, Pa *(ole-)sa*, Uai *itzihi*, Uar *(iue-)si*, Gu *itši*, Ad *tsikule* ;

III. M *hoty*, Kampa *eçhi, içhi*, Kan *pity*, Kus *(šiwe-)sa*, Piro *(iwe-)tsa, (xihue-)sa* ;

IV. B *chohihi, ichi-jiji*, Moxo *chuti-si*, Yaul *(putaku-)yati*.

11. Eyelash : (eye-)hair, § 90 f).

I. A *(iki-)ti*, I K *(acou-)iou*, W *depian* ;

II. Bare *(biuiti-)bite*, Ip *(ti-)piyu*, Kar, Kat, Si *(ti-)pitsi*, Manao *(konika-)itschy*, Mand *(disi-)uishi*, Pa *(tschila-)ntschoy*, Pia *(tui-)zimi*, Uar *(bo-)siuiole* ;

III. Ip *(ke-)meipi-piti*, Kampa *tosio-ki*, Kan *pity*, Kun *pity* ;

IV. Pare *(dose-)nivari*, Yaul *(yeoka-)?ti*.

12. Moustache : hair(-mouth), § 90 f).

I. A *iti(-ma)*, I K *iti(-ouma)*, At *hin*, G *li(-ma)*, Par *(m-)i-(a)*, P *siu*, Map *(tci-)namu*, hair, W *de(-no), te(-nu)* ;

II. Ban *sa(-noma)*, Bare *si(-noma)*, Kar, Mand, Si, Tar *tsi(-numa)*, Uar *si(-numa)*, Yav *za(-numa)*, Ad *chi(-numa)*, Gu *tsa(-numa)*, Pia *ussi(-nume)* ;

III. Ipu *šamputa-piti* (Kampa *açhpatuna*, Kun, Kus *šaptu*, Piro *sapto)* ;

IV. B *ich-(aona)?*, Gua *etsa (-kiri* = nose), Ku *(kira-)pi*, Me *(kiržaa-)pienu*, Moxo *hiyo(-sumu)*, Waura *ma-pi*.

13. Excrements. § 90 A ; comp. also nos. 23, 149 A.

I. A *itika*, I K f *itica*, G *chaa*, P *isiki*, W *dikie* ;

II. Bare *isike, sikahei*, Kar *iziate*, Ip *itsuka*, Kat *ža*, Si *iša*, Manao *tya*, Mar *ytschuka*. Tar *ihe, tsukude*, Yuk *hie*, Gu *tšikahi*, Pia *itsoka* ;

III. Ar *yakye*, Ipu, Kan *itika*, Kampa *itiga*, Piro *yǒki* ;

IV. Gua *ciquee*, Moxo *ichiqui*.

14. Head, § 116 b): comp. nos. 119, 118.

I. A *ɩ̆ši*, I K *ichi-c*, P *tɕu-ti*, At, W *ruair*, Map *rɕku*, Par *ki* ;

II. Bare *dosie*, Yav *si-hu*, Uar *i-ua*, Kar *i-ta*, *gibi-da*, Kat, Ip *ui-da*, Si *ui-ta*, Tar *ahui-da*, Yuk *ui-le*, Maip *chibucu*, Ad *ui-da*, Pia *ivi-ta*, Mand *iua-shi*, *ui-da*, Manao *kü-una*, Car *küuy-sata*, Gu *in-tšɕuɕ* ;

III. Piro *xi-hue*, Kan *c-hüy*, Kun *yi-hwö*, Ipu *iki-wi si-uy*, Ar *g-hy*, Kus *ši-wɕ*, *ši-wö*

IV. Moxo *chuti*, Sar *hɕvɕ*, Me *tɕu*, Ku *tɕui*, Waura *tɕur-zata*, Yaul *kurɨu*. Pare *sɕviri*, Gua *tutiie*, *dooti*.

15. Eye, §§ 116 b), 172.

I. A *ako(-ši)*, I K f *acou* ;

II. Bare *aci-ti*, Gu *aui-ši*, Manao *kurika*, Uir *acu-que*, Gu *aui-ži* ;

III. Ar *oky*, Ipu *uky*, Kampa *oqui*, *oque*, Kan *chii*, *ako-sy*, Pau *kui* ;

IV. B *qui-se*, Moxo *uqui*, Pai *ihuikis*.

16. Nose, § 116 b).

I. A *iširi*, I K *ichiri*, G *ichi*, Par *yi*, P *ikirti*, W *iribe* ;

II. Maip *chirri*, Yav *siui*, Car *küty*, Manao *kiria*, Uir *que* ;

III. Ar *chit*, Kan *chiry*, Kus *širi*, *siry*, Piro *siri*, Ipu. *kirita*, Kampa *quiri*, Pau *iridi*, Yam *uidi* ;

IV. B, Moxo *siri*, Gua *girii-ti*, Ku, Me, Pare *kiri*, Waura *kidzi*.

17. Mouth, § 83 a) (see also n⁰. 12, moustache and n⁰. 20, neck).

I. (A *ema*, *uima*, the mouth of a river), I K *iouma*, G *anöka*, Map *unau*, *numiya* P *numa* ;

II. Ach, Ad, Am, Bare, Car, Gu, Ip, Ju, Kar, Kat, Manao, Mand, Pia, Si, Uai, Uar, Yuk *numa*, Ban, Yav, Tar *anuma*, Kau *nomo*, Maip *numacu*, Mar *nuna*, Uir *luma* ;

III. Ipu, Kus, Piro, *nama*, Kan *nahma*, *comako*.

18. Tongue, §§ 83 a), 184.

I. A *ye*, I K *inigne*, G *ye*, *shie*, Par *benye*, P *nɕnc*, W *nuba* ;

II. Bare, Car, Cau, Ja, Mand, Pa, Pia, Uar, Uir *nene*, Gu *neni*, Ju *nena*, Ip, Kat, Si *enene*, Kar *inene*, Mar, Uai *nenepe*, Kau *nanipa*, Yuk *lena*, Manao *ncta*, Maip *are*, Ad *nene*, *niñe* ;

III. Ar *elon*, Ipu *nene*, Kampa *anene*, *nene*, Kan *nuny*, Kun, Kus, Piro *ne*, *iaya* ;

IV. B *epenene*, Gua *nene-ti*, Ku, Me, Waura *nei*, Moxo *nene*, Pare *nini-se*, Sar *niñe*, Yaul *nya-ti*.

19. Tooth, § 100.

I. A *a(i)ri*, I K f *ari*, G *ari*, *(a)i*, P *aibu-ti*, Par *(a)i* ;

II. Ad *etsa*, *yeihei*, Am *e*, Ban *aši*, Bare *ahai*, Car *aü*, Cau *e*, Ja *aida*, Ju *ihi*, *iy*, Kar *yai*, Kat *etsa*, Kau *a*, Maip *ati*, Manao *ay*, Mand *e*, *ieshi*, Mar *ai*, Pa *see*, Pia *uayex*, *yai*, Tar *ye*, Uai *ahai*, *aei*, Uar *ye*, Uir *adi*, Yav *azi*, Yuk *i*, Gu *ahe* ;

III. Ar *itschy*, Ipu *serin*, Kampa *agi*, Kan *aü*, Kun *hi*, Kus *ihe*, M *atu*, Piro *ii*, *se*, *ixi* ;

IV. B *isero*, *isera*, Gua *oe-ti*, Ku *tevoe*, Me *teve*, Moxo *oe*, Waura *itseve*, Yau *tsoa*.

20. Neck, § 79 a) 3).

I. A *ono-ro*, G *nu-lo*, W *k-una*, At *k-anei* ;

II. Cau *noza*, *naza*, Kar *nu-ro*, Kat, Si, Tar *nu-ru*, Mand *nu-li*, Maip *inu*, Manao *noby*, Mar *nunape*, Pa *noto*, Yuk *nurupi*, Bare *nu* ;

III. Ar *no*, Kan *nopy*, Kun *nuye*, Piro *nuxi* ;

IV. Gua *anu*, Pare *hino*, Sar *xiiñu*, Yaul *rhinyu-ti*.

21. Heron, etc., § 79 a) 3).

I. A *honoli*, Tigrisoma, *anula*, Ardea *cocoi*, W *arunau*, Tigrisoma, I K *omanomali* ;

II. Kat, Si *unuli*, Ardea brasiliensis, Tar *unoli*, A. b. ;

IV. B *tinore*, Platalea.

22. Navel, § 128 h).

I. A *kuyu* ;

II. Cau *pahare*, Ip, Si *epure*, Pa *sipohry*, Tar *puleka*, Gu *žipulu* ;

III. Ipu *šoronke*, Kan *puluchy*, Piro *puro*, Yam *dzubori*;

IV. B *poyi*, Moxo *tuyu*, Waura *peze*.

Liver, see n⁰. 113.

23. Bowels.

  I. A *ite*;

 II. Kau *tre*, Car *itschaba*, Pia *te*;

III. Kun *satö*, Kus *sate*, Piro *sati*, Yam *turu*;

IV. B *etise*, Ku *tšitšu*, Me *tšikiu*, Yaul *tsityu*.

24. Male genital (*p* = striving, aspiring ?).

 II. Manao *puia*, Mar *pijhi*, Ad *piži*;

III. Ipu *pitsi*, *pichinchi*, Kampa *chibichi*;

IV. Me, Ku *pei*, Yaul *puhi*, Gua *keo*, B *pepe*, Sar *i-tihiyu*.

25. Arm, lower part of the arm, § 86 *g*).

  I. *a*) A *adina* I K *areunna*, G *töna*, Par *dene*, *adne*, W *anub*, At *anubai*, P *wani*;

 II. *a*) Ach *natuer*, Ban *nano*, Bare *dana*, Car *tanu*, Gu *dana*, Ja *tana*, Kat, Ip, Si *napa*, Kau *unapi*, Maip *ana*, Manao *tana*, Mand, Pia *ana*, Uar *nana*, Uir *tanaabe*, Yuk *napita*;

      b) Yav *kanu*, *cano*, Ja *canu*;

III. *a*) Pau *dabunui*, Yam *yedabu*;

      b) Piro *kano*, Kun *kana*, Kan *ghano*, Kus *kanu*, Ipu *canuke*;

IV. *a*) Pare *ötane*, wing;

      b) Pare *kano*, Sar *kahano*, Ku, Me, Yaul *kanu-tapa*.

26. Branch, § 86 *g*).

  I. *a*) A *adina-bo*, G *sutuna*, P *tauni*;

 II. *a*) Si *haiku-itena*;

      b) Cau *ghoe-kona*, Manao *ata-akura*, Mar *yru-kary*, Uai *apana-ghae*, Bare *ada-uako*, Tar *heiku-kena*, Mand *iuaco*, Gu *damun-uaku*;

III. *b*) Ar *aky*;

IV. *a*) Moxo *to-tabo yucuqui*.

27. Hand, § 134 *e*).

  I. *a*) A *akabo*, G *hap*, *japo*, I K *cabo*, Map *kuba*, Par *(a)p*, W *kabu-rei*, palm or back of the hand;

      b) P *waku*, At *kuei*, W *kake*;

 II. *a*) Ach *caje*, Am *cagi*, Bare, Gu *kabi*, Car *ghai*, Cau, Ju *gabi*, *kapy*, Ja *khapi*, Kar *kapü*, Ip, Kat, Kau, Si, Tar, Uar *kapi*, Ad, Maip, Pia, *capi*, Manao *kaita*, Mar *ghapy*, Pa *ghapohli*, Uir *caue*, Yav *kahahi*, Uai *gaapi*, *ghaby*, Pareni *cavi*, Mand *kahi*;

III. *a*) Ar *kabu*, *kabesuy*, Pau *kabo-tini*, palm of the hand;

      b) Ipu *wacu*, Kampa *aco*;

IV. *a*) Me *kapu*, Pare *kahe*, Waura *kapi*, *kabü*;

      b) B *baqui*, *boqui*;

Nail, see n⁰. 114.

28. Foot, § 129 *b*).

  I. A *kuti*, I K f *goutti*, P *kurku*, At *kheti*, W *kudi-be*;

 II. Maip *chii*, Manao *kiy*, Uir *cauque*, Pareni *cizi*, Gu *žipc*;

III. Ar *ghutschy*, Ipu *kiti*, Kampa *guiti*, *kiiti*, Kus *šiti*.

29. Tail, § 112.

  I. A *ihi*, I K *ili*, P *ribu*;

 II. Ban *biši*, *piši*, Bare *ihibi*, Ip, Kat *itsipi*, Kar, Si *itipi*, Tar *isipi*, Uar *sipi*, Gu *ibi*;

III. Ipu *ishipi*, Kus *nsii*;

IV. Me *inepiu*, Moxo *hiqui*, Pare *enihu*, Yaul *ikipina*.

MAN, FAMILY, RELIGION.

30. Man (h, homo, v, vir), § 166 c).

I. (A wadili, § 164 e)), I K f eyeri, v, P awaili, hinyeiri, v also "clan", Par eitsch. eiy(e), v ;

II. Bare heinari, h, v, Ban, Yav enami, h, v, Cau zinanni, h, Gu k-enaue, h, hanale, v, Manao herenary, yrinaly, h, Kar atsinari, h, v, Kat atsinali, h, v, Uar asinali, asinari, h, Uir atinare, v, Uai achijari, v, Si, Tar atsiali, h, Yuk asie, h, Pia naiyei, h, aziali, asieri, v, ouenaica, h, Ca ouenaouica, h, Pa schimana, h, Ad naiki, atchinali, h, tsiali, v, Mand aˇinahe, v ;

III. Piro ineri, h, Kampa cherari, chirampari, v, Ar etyalo, h, Kus yehyi, seˇsi ;

IV. B ehiro, v, Moxo ehiro, v, achane, h, Me erinau, v, Ku erina, eniza, v, Waura enyau, v, Yaul örinau, erina, v, Sar eˇceena v.

31. Husband (lord ?).

I. I K f amachi, chief ;

II. Bare mi, Ban meuale, Gu yeme, Ja imigi, imiri, Pia, Mand niri, Ad iniri, Manao imiry, Maip (nu-)mina(-ri), (my) lord, Bare maba-mina-ri, bee, Yav cuadiguao-mina-ri, jaguar ;

III. Kampa o-gime, o-chuema, Piro aneri, Ipu umane, chief ;

IV. Moxo ima, Gua uma, Moxo Maymonâ, God.

32. Woman, wife, § 166 c).

I. A hiaro, woman, ireyu, to be wife § 164 f), G hierhe, Par h'niere, P eru, tino. I K inno, ani, At beanaro ;

II. Kar, Kat Si, Uar inu, wife, inaru, woman, Tar, Uai inaru, Yuk inanaru, Pia inanai, woman, inu, wife, Mand inalutˇza, woman, yu, wife, Mar ynana, Uir inau, Manao ero, wife, ytunalo, woman, Car henitaky, netschu, Yav sariinaifemi, woman, Ad inaru, woman, inu, wife, Gu henau, woman, naune, wife ;

III. Marauha runo, Piro, Kun anendu, wife, Kus hanando, wife ;

IV. B eteno, Moxo esseno, woman, yeno, wife, Gua tseeno, Me, Waura teneru, Ku tineru, Yaul tinau.

33. Mother, § 124 b), 163 a), 166 c).

I. A yu, yo, G eyu ;

II. Maip ina, Pa ainyu, Manao ena-kony, Pia atoua, otue, Ad ndoa ;

III. Kampa ina, inero, iniro, Kan atu, Kus nato, Piro ndo ;

IV. B eno, Gua, Moxo eeno.

34. Child (male), § 164 b).

I. A korilia-ˇci, At curaitze ;

III. Kar koliliapu, Pia kirazei, Mand kirahere.

35. Son, § 163 a).

I. A ai-ˇci, I K f iraheu itaga, Par tschon, G chon, P haisu, W bitci ;

II. Ban tani, Manao tany, Maip ani, Cau oay, Ad, Pia iri ;

III. M tisy, Kampa tomi, Piro teri, Kun, Kus tori, Kan türy ;

IV. Moxo chicha, B scera.

36. Daughter, § 163 a).

I. A o-tu I K f iraheu, P serhu, W udanrin ;

II. Ad, Kar, Kat, Pia, Si, Tar itu, Yuk utu, Uar itu(x)ni, Mar, Uai ito, Manao tairu, Maip ani, Gu itxu ;

III. Mar tay, Kus mtero, Kun setiu, Piro ˇcicu ;

IV. Moxo chicha ;

37. Father-in-law, § 163 e).

I. A madukure, W imidukur, P mökerhu ;

II. Si kuiru, Kar, Tar kiri, Kat keri, Gu ku, Ad nxaueri, Pia yeru ;

III. Kus hemaˇciri(ö), Piro ximatieri ;

IV. Gua imetˇsako.

38. Mother-in-law, § 163 e).

    I. A *akiru, akürü.* I K f *couchourou,* P *maturu-hu,* W *imirdukur ;*

    II. Si, Tar *kuiru,* Yuk *yaxneru,* Kat *r(u)ixneru,* Kar *xneru,* Uar *xiyelu,* Gu *axku,* Ad *nxeru,* Pia *yeru,* Mand *koro ;*

    III. Kun *yiru,* Piro *ximaxiru,* Kus *hemaširo.*

38 A.   Stranger, white man (n⁰. 70 **parana,* sea).

    I. I K *balanaglc,* Christians, P *parahana,* Brasilian, W *parinakari,* G *parainsishi ;*

    II. Bare *yaranave,* Ban, Kar *yaranaui,* Mand, Yav, Uar, Kat, Si *yalanaui,* Ad *yalanai,* Tar *hearana,* Maip *jaranavi,* Portuguese, Gu *yalanaui,* Venezolan, *palanaxkele,* Englishman etc. ;

    III. Ipu *imbaraniri ;*

Karib languages in Guyana **paranakiri.*

39. Slave, § 164 h).

    I. A *(h)aiero,* I K f *hai,* female slave ;

    IV. Moxo *ahire.*

39A.   a) the soul, b) the late, the former ;

    I. a) W *durima ;*

          b) A *-mi ;*

    II. a) Maip *amita-mine* (Ban *amita,* to fly), Ban *no-minana-te :* remembrance, *ma-minana-rro :* without reason, Si *auakata mina-li :* bush-spirit ;

          b) Maip *-mine,* Bare *duh-amini :* a corpse, *kihi-amini :* the waning moon, Kar *ker-ami :* the w.m., Si *ker-amina-ku,* the settling moon ;

    III. a) Ipu *c-amyry,* Kun *usa-mene,* Piro *uza-mena ;*

    IV. b) B, Moxo *-ini.*

40. God, demigod, § 166 e) 2).

    I. A *kururuman, kulimina,* W *tuminkar ;*

    II. Maip *purrunaminari,* Tar *pirikuli,* Tar, Si *yaperikuli.*

41. Snake, § 108 A.

    I. A *hori, wuri,* I K *hehue,* G *uri, willi, guiri ;*

    II. Cau *höuwari,* Bare *huyaue,* Boa Cenchria, Tar *yolema,* B. C., Gu *udži ;*

    III. Kampa *oragon ;*

    IV. Me, Yaul, Waura *ui,* Pare *ui, uini,* Moxo *churu,* big snake, Sar *uhuvi,* boa.

42. Snake (comp. nos 41, 43).

    I. A *mawleru* (§ 180), Boa Cenchria ;

    II. Ban *mauaya,* Boa scytale, Si *umauali,* B. s., Ad *umauali,* Boa murina, Uar *auadamali,* B. s., Yav *zorema,* B. s.

    III. Kampa *marangua,* Pau *mabüdiri,* B. c.

Karib languages : Oyana *ulamali,* Trio *alamali,* Kaliña *arimouori,* Makusi *palaraima.*

43. Snake ; animal which casts its skin, "renovation" §§ 74 f), 168.

    I. A *emena-hu,* worm, *imina-ri,* scorpion ;

    II. Ban, Yav *omeni,* Maip *umeni ;*

    III. Ipu *imini, imina,* Kun *himuna,* Kus *imöna,* Piro *amuini, himane.*

Karib languages **munate,* scorpion.

44. Water-boa, Eunectes murinus (comp. nos. 42, 43).

    I. A *kamudu ;*

    II. Bare, Kar, Kat *hamu,* Mand *amu,* Pia *manu ;*

    III. Ipu *keanti ;*

    IV. B *comiti.*

45. Nature-spirit, demon, § 166 b) (comp. n⁰. 41).

    I. A *oriyu,* water-spirit, goddess, G *yaröja.* Par *dyörgua,* W *urupiru,* mythical great serpent ;

    IV. B *yuvire,* Moxo *ereo-no,* evil spirits.

Karib languages **yoroku,* etc., Tupi *yurupari ;* I K *ioulouca,* God.

46. Nature-spirit, demon, 166 j) (comp. n⁰. 42).

I. A *mahui*, I K *mapoya* (I K f *opoyem*, good spirits), P *maipoko*, *yumauali*, W *maatiahi*, (Nourague, Acoqua *maire*, god) ;

II. Ban *mauari*, Car *maihinauy*, Manao *gamainha*, Pia *oumaouari*, Uir *mapa*, Car, Manao *mauary*, god ;

III. Ipu *camyry*, Kampa *camagari, camaari, tzamari*, Kan *ghamatschy*.

Karib languages : Makusi *emmawari, emiwary*, Akawai *imawari*, Paravilhana *maualü*. Taulipang *mauari* ; Kaliña *alamali*, serpent-grandfather ; god : Mapoyo *maiuca*, Paravilhana *mauarouba*, Tamanaco *amalivaca*.

47. Etherical, § 169.

I. A principle of life, shadow : *üya*, I K shadow : *(t-)iaoua*, G *juya*, Taino spirit of the living : *goeiz* ;

II. spectre, demon : Yuk *hiya*, Bare *iyehe*, Tar *iyei*, Si *ieyeimi*, Kat *iyemi*, Mand *inaui-inaui* ; nature-spirits : Kat *piori*, Si *biuli* ;

IV. god : Moxo *biiya*.

48. Rainbow (comp. nos. 45—47 ; in South-America the rainbow is often considered as a manifestation of nature-spirits).

I. A *yawali*, § 166 i) 2), I K f *chegue-ti*, G *ka-sipo-rin*, W *kiweir* ;

II. Ban *biuali*, Bare *miali seuebini*, Manao *ghenaiy*, Pa *gheseu*, Tar *iyenunite mauali*, Uai *hechpy*, Uar *iuili*, Gu *yihabutanaua*, Ad *heuiya* ;

III. Ipu *kiesi, inkisi*, Kampa *uye*, Kun *kše*, Kus *kšö*, Piro *kči* ;

IV. Me *iyepe*, Waura *iyäpe*, Moxo *oe*.

Karib languages : Kaliña *palamu*, I K *alamoulou*.

49. Medicine-man, § 74 d) 8) *mali, mari*, knowledge ?

I. W *marinau*, P *yihamuli* ; *yihamulu*, medicine-woman ;

II. Kar, Mand, Tar *malili, mariri*, Ad, Kat, Si *maliri*, Maip *marirri*, Pia *kamalikeri* ;

III. Piro *mueraya*, divine, witchcraft ;

IV. Pare *otahariti, tihanale*.

THE HOUSEHOLD

House, see nos. 116, 117.

49 A. Plantation, field (§ 168 f); W *pineari*, newly made).

II. Maip *meni-ti*, Bare *miyu-re*, Ban *miu-li*, Yuk *mena*, Gu *menahi*,

III. Yam *kamini*, to plant.

Hammock, see nᵒ. 148.

50. Cassava grater, § 116 c) 2).

I. A *samali*, I K *chimali*, P *timali*, W *tcimari* ;

II. Bare *dayama* ;

IV. Pare *timare*, Me *imia*, Waura *imya*, Yaul *inya*.

Karib languages : Oyana, Trio *simali*, Makusi *chimiari*.

50 A. Cassava-baking pan, § 67 c).

I. A *budali*, I K *boutalli*, I K f *bourrêlet* ;

II. Bare *bodari*, Ad, Kat, Si, Tar *poali*, Gu *betali*, Mand *hali*.

50 B. Mortar, § 128 aA).

I. A *hako*, W *aku* ;

III. Kun *hiha*, Piro *igxa*, Yam *huo*.

51. Rafter, § 104 g).

I. A *yurada*, I K *ioulla* ;

II. Si *yura, yurama* ; a long bench, Gu *kalata* ;

IV. Me *yulakakati*, Waura *yulakakate*, Yaul. *yula, yola*.

52. Boat, § 76 b).

I. A *mihu*, ship, I K *meoulou*, pumice-stone, P *omuhu*, boat ;

III. Kampa *aho*, ship.

53. Paddle (comp. nos. 25, 26).

    I.   A *nalihe,* Par *ane-ti,* I K *(ne-)nene,* Taino *nae ;*

    II. Ban *neyupa,* Bare *neheu,* Cau *denare,* Maip *nau,* Mand, Uai *dena,* Pia *tena,* Yav *nehu,* Gu *meha ;* to paddle : Pia *tena,* Ad *dena-ka,* Mand *dena ;*

    III. to paddle : Piro *aniexare,* Kus *nikate ;*

    IV. Moxo *naurope ; nu-nau-co,* I paddle.

54. Bow, §§ 116 c), 76 d), 109.

    I.   A *simar-abo,* I K f *chimala,* W *sumara-u, sumara ;*

    II. Gu *tshimari,* Pia *lema-po, dema-pu.*

Club, see n⁰. 141.

55. Axe (comp. n⁰. 134 B).

    I.   A, W *baru,* G *pore ;*

    II. Yuk *peru,* Pia *tžipali ;*

    III. Yam *bari, pari.*

56. Fish-hook, § 67 a).

    I.   A *bodi,* I K f *boute,* Arua *pučare,* P *ipunti ;*

    II. Ban *bodesi, putersi,* Pia *puivi,* Yav *kotezi,* Maip *icuria,* Gu *mbuti.*

57. Hat, § 120 e) 5).

    I.   A *kwa(w)ma,* G *huomo,* W *kwomai, couame ;*

    II. Gu *koamihi,* Mand *kauarihire.*

58. Comb, § 175 d).

    I.   A *ballida,* I K f *boulera ;*

    II. Bare, Kar, Kat *mauida,* Si *mauide,* Gu *maueda,* Mand *mauirita ;*

    III. Yam *masera,* Kun *mösiri,* Piro *mčiri,* Kus *möširi ;*

    IV. Ku, Me, Waura, Yaul *palata,* Pare *halata.*

59. Panpipe.

    I.   A *λeru,* P *elelu,* I K *touromba,* trõpe de bouche, W (Roth) *tilele ;*

    II. Kat *peruma,* Si *peluma,* Mand *abedaru ;*

    IV. Pare *dero.*

NATURE

60. Heaven, high §§ 166 c), 83 a), 71 b) 6).

    I.   A *aiomun,* I K *inou,* P *ena ;*

    II. Ban, Bare, Kar, Maip *eno,* Ad, Kat, Mand, Si, Uar, Yav *enu,* Gu *uenu,* Cau *yunuhary,* Tar *enukoa ;*

    III. Kau, Kus, Piro *tenu,* Pak *tenuᶜa,* Ipu *itanotìsi, itanushiti,* Kampa *geno,* Pau *nama;*

    IV. B *ani,* Gua *vanoke,* Ku *enutaku,* Moxo *anumo,* Pare *enukua,* Waura *enunako,* Yaul *onyunako.*

60 A. Day.

    I.   I K *oubecou,* sky, heaven [also Kaliña (Pelleprat) les nuees, *bécou*] ;

    II. Maip *pecumi,* Ad, Kar, Kat, Si *hekoapi,* Tar *koapi.*

61. Sun, § 134 f).

    I.   (A *kalime,* light, glory, to be bright, to shine), At, P *kamoi,* Map *kamu,* W *gamu;*

    II. Ban *amoši,* Bare *gamu, gamoho,* Car *ghamuy.* Gu *ɣamuhu,* Ad, Kar, Gat, Manao, Pia, Mar, Si *gamui,* Mand, Uar *kamoi,* Uai *gamuhi,* Uir *camoe,* Yav *kamozi,* Yuk *kamu.* Maip *camo-ti,* Year ;

    III. Ar *ghuma,* M *kumctu,* Yam *mahi ;*

    IV. Ku *kami,* Me, Waura *kamc,* Pare *kamai,* Sar *kahame.*

62. a) Moon, b) Sun, § 134 f).

    I.   a) A *kači,* I K f *cati,* At *kaishe,* G *kashi,* Par *keitschare,* Map *kirsu,* P *kairi,* W *gaere, kaere ;*

         b) I K f *cachi,* G *kai,* Par *kei-kei ;*

II.   a) Car *ghaizy*, Cau *ghezy*, Maip *chejapi*, Pa *ghischy*, Am *kede*, Bare *ki*, *Manao ghairy*, Mar *gheery*, Ad, Pia, Tar, Si, Uar, Yav, Yuk, Kar, Kat, Kau, Mand *keri*, Uai *gähri*, Uar *querli*, Ad, Yav *queri*, Pareni *keri*, Gu *keuali ;*

    b) Tar *keri*, Pia, Kau *eri*, Maip *chie*, Am *keybin ;*

III.   *a*) Ipu *kasiri*, Piro *kačiri*, *kus*, *kserö*, Kampa *caçhiri*, Ar *kairy*, In *kaire*, Kun *ksörö;*

    b) In *tukuati*, Pak *xukati*, Piro *kaši*, Kan *ghasiry*, Kus *tökači*, Kampa *quienti ;*

IV.   *a*) Gua *koɣeee*, Moxo *cohe*, Pare *kayö*, Sar *kače*, Ku, Waura *keri*, Meh *kerzi*, Pai *kejere ;*

    b) Gua *kaɪše*.

63.   *a*) Star, *b*) Pleiades, § 125 *d*).

I.   *a*) A *wiwa*, (Sm.) *wijua*, Map *wishi*, W *wir ;*

    b) A (Sm.) *wijua*, W *wiñau*, G *igua ;*

II.   *a*) Am *wine*, Ban *hiwiri uiminali*, Bare *uinati*, Ad, Kar *hiwiri*, Kat, Si *hiuisi*, Gu *yuwinti*, Mand *euine*, Tar *uisune*, Uar *iuiri*, Yav *uine*, Yuk *hiuiri*, Mar *ipitze*, Cau *pirita*, Uai *ibihitschi*, Si *upitsi* (part of Orion) ;

    b) Car *eounaua*, Manao *ynau*, Uar *iuine*, Uai *hypitsche*, Gu *yewente ;*

III.   *a*) Pau *buiri*, Piro *piri ;*

    b) Ipu *uminaua*, Kan *putachy ;*

IV.   *a*) Yau *uitsitsi ;*

    b) Gua *ovä*.

64.   *a*) Star, *b*) Pleiades.

I.   *a*) G *siliguala*, *siruara*, *shuru*, At *watsieirhe*, W *aikaer ;*

    b) P *kusupui ;*

II.   *a*) Maip *urrupu*, Kau *uiruyo*, Pia *duruputa*, *nuluputa ;*

    b) Kar *oariperi*, Kat *oaliperu*, Si *oaliperi*, Tar *oalipeda*, Pa *pulay ;*

III.   *a*) Ar *ymiru*, Ipu *yuyryky*, Kampa *impuquiro*, Kan *tschy*, Piro *siri ;*

    b) Kan *nuchiry*, *sele ;*

IV.   *a*) Gua *šipere*, Moxo *hara-iriqui ;*

    b) Moxo *chuzi*.

64 A.   Venus, morning-star, evening-star (*oa-ri* = great, § 121 ?).

I.   A (Pen.) *iarowia*, I K *ouainamala ;*

II.   Kar *oariua*, Si *oaliua*, Tar *halianita*, Ad *ualiua*. star.

65.   Fire, § 112 *c*).

I.   A *ikihi*, At *tegherre*, G *sigui*, Map *tshikasi hikesia*, P *tiketi*, Par *guiei*, W *ikeire ;*

II.   Cau *ickiö*, Gu *tšeke*, Ip *tiye*, Ja *ikaɣi*, Kar, Kat, Si *tidze*, Maip *catti*, Pareni *kasi*, Mar *ytschepa*, Pa *heghüe*, Pia *kidzei*, Tar *tšiaua*, Uar *ixside*, Uai *itschipa*, Uir *jixe*, Yuk *tsia*, Ad *tidge*, *dzidze*, Mand *izide ;*

III.   Ar *yghe*, Piro, Man *čiči*, In, Kun, Kus *titi*, Kampa *chichi*, *yrisy ;*

IV.   B *yaki*, Gua *iuku*, Chane, Moxo *yucu*, Sar *tikiahi*, Pai *chaki*.

66 A.   Ash, § 116 *b*) 1).

I.   A *balisi*, I K *ballichi*, G *pari*, W *parite ;*

II.   Ban *palitzi*, Bare *baritzi*, Gu *balidi*, Kar *pali*, Kat, Pia *bali*, Kau *pari*, Mand *hali*, Si *paliate*, Tar *paliaua*, Gu *mbalidi ;*

III.   Piro *čici-paxi* (= fire-dust).

67.   Wind, § 121 *c*) 5).

I.   A *auaduli*, At *awarre*, G *suguaru*, W *auale ;*

II.   Ad *kaualere*, Pia *kauli*, Uir *maua*, Gu *hauidzi*, Bare *hauisi ;* storm : Kat *kaualere*, Si *kaualeri*, Tar *kaleru*, Yuk *karena ;*

III.   Ipu *ketaoliri*, *cataware*, Kus *hanate*, *kanipöari ;*

IV.   Gua *onauoti*, Pare *kahula*, Sar *kavihiena*, Mucoxeone *kavirian*, Pai *ovira*.

Rain, see n⁰. 151.

Rainbow, see n⁰. 48.

68.   Water, § 125 *a*).

I.   A *oini*, *wuin*, At *win*, *wuan*, G *güin*, Map *win*, *wune*, P *une*, *uni*, W *uene*, *wuane;*

II. Ban, Maip, Yav *ueni*, Bare, Gu, Kar, Mand, Uar *oni*, Ad, Ip, Ja, Ca, Kat, Kau, Pia, Si,Tar, Yuk *uni*, Manao *unüa*, Ju *uhü*, *uy*, Pa *oy*, Cau *auuwi*, *ouy*, Uir *uune*, Uai *auny*, *oohni ;*

III. Ar, In *uni*, Kan *weny*, Kampa *niya*, Ipu *wyny* (river), Marauha *uny*, Kun, Kus, Piro *une*, Man *huni*, Pau *waini* (river) :

IV. B *ine*, Gua, Ku, Me, Pare *one*, Chane, Moxo, Sar, Waura *une*, Pai *ina*, Yaul *u*.

69. Lake, lagoon, § 107 *b*) 3).

I. A *kiraha ; kulisa ;* pool, W *kerice ;*

II. Bare *kariahabuku*, Ban *cauiya*, Car *ghabitscha*, Ju *carica*, Kat *galidza*, Maip *cavia*, Manao *ghaliau*, Mand *kalisa*, Pia *caritsa*, Pa *ghaiya*, Ad *kalita*, Si *galita*, Tar *kalitsanei*, Uar *cauiya*, Yav *cabiya*, Yuk *karisa*, Gu *kaliha ;*

III. Kampa *ingasane ;*

IV. B *chaki*, Moxo *caquiure*.

70. Sea, § 107 *b*) 6).

I. A *bara*, G, Par *para*, P *palawa*, W *paranabauk*, I K *balanna*, Taino *bagua ;*

II. Maip *parana ; parrava*, Orinoco, Pia *barawa*, Orinoco.

71. Island, § 100.

I. A *kairi*, I K f *acaera*, Pal *kaiwuripra ;*

II. Kat, Tar, Kar *keueri*, Si *keueresi ;*

IV. Pare *kahihuruhe*.

72. *a*) Haven, § 128 *c*), *b*) Island.

I. *a*) A *akodona-li ;*

II. *b*) Ban, Mand *kadonori*, Ad *kadonuli*, Bare *kadonoli*, Uar *katonoli*, Yav *catonori*.

73. Earth (comp. n⁰. 75).

II. Cau *oipo*, Maip *peni*, Mar *ypai*, Uai *ypay*, Ad *hipey ;*

III. Ipu *kybachi*, Kus *kašpa ;*

IV. B *pay*, Moxo *payre*.

74. Mountain (comp. n⁰. 75).

I. G *urapa ;*

II. Ban *yapa*, Bare *siaba*, Kar *hidżapa*, Ad, Kat, Si *hidzapa*, Mand *idaha*, Pia *iba*, Maip *japa*, Tar *ixiapa*, Yav *auabo*, Guipunave *dapa*, Cavere *sciapa*, Gu *tsapa*.

75. Rock, stone, § 116 *a*) 3).

I. A *siba*, G *ipa*, P *tipa*, W *keba*, *kuib*, Taino *ziba ;*

II. Ban, Kar, Yuk *hipa*, *ipa*, Bare *diba*, *tiba*, Car *ghüpai*, Gu *żiba*, Cau *pahla*, Ad *hipada*, Kat *hipade*, Ja *iba*, Ju *zepa*, Maip *chipa*, Manao *ghüa*, Pia *hiba*, Mand *siba*, Si, Tar *hipata*, Uar *ipa*, Uir *cuiba*, Yav *siba*, Mand *iha ;*

III. Ipu *kai*, M *ghoeba ;*

IV. Gua *marihipa*, Me Waura *tepa*, Yaul *teba*, (Moxo *mari*), Sar *ehexa*.

76. Forest, § 127 *e*).

I. A *kunnuku*, W *kanoku ;*

II. Pa *uakaluga ;*

IV. Pare *koluhu*.

76 A. Road, (comp. n⁰. 5).

I. A *abonaha*, P *aheni*, W *dinap* [A *inabo* (to follow) behind] :

II. Bare *dinabu*, Ban *tanepo*, Yav *daneho*, Uar *anipu*, Kar *enipu*, Kat, Si, Tar *inipu*, Yuk *hiiepu*, Mand *enuhu*, Maip *anepu*, Ad *anipo*, Gu *tenabo*, Pia *ayapu ;*

III. Kun *hatönö ;*

IV. Moxo *achene*.

ANIMALS

76 B. Animal, § 129 *b*) 2).

I. A *kuta ;*

II. Maip *queti*.

77. Howling monkey, § 124 b).
   I. A *ittuli;*
   II. Gu *dʾæleue;*
   III. M *ytury;*
   IV. B *iyore,* Gua *toʒoro,* Ku, Me Waura, Yaul *kapulu,* Moxo *iyo,* mono pardo.
78. Monkey (one or more species).
   I. A 1⁰. *fudi,* 2⁰. *kaboaši,* Arua *puat;*
   II. Ban *poatsi,* Cau *pauay,* Ad, Kar, Si, Tar *pue,* Kat *bue,* Mar *puːero,* Pa *poehe,* Pia *pouoi,* Uar *poe,* Yav *juatzi, püache;*
   III. M *poete,* Kus *pöseri.*
79. Bat.
   I. A *buhiri,* I K *bouliri,* G *posichi;*
   II. Ad, Kar, Si *pitiri,* Kat *pitseri,* Tar, Uar *pitsiri,* Mand *hiːiri,* Yuk *pisiri,* Gu *mbesaue;*
   III. Kampa *pigiri,* Ip *šiepiri, šiu;*
   IV. B *huitere,* Gua *viteete,* Moxo *bite.*
Karib languages **rere.*
80. Jaguar, § 183.
   I. A *kabadaro,* G *kanapur;*
   II. Kat *kadanane,* Uar *kabanaro.*
81. Dog, savanah-dog, fox.
   I. A *ualiro,* I K *anli,* G *er, guariː,* Par *ieri.* At *din,* Taino *aon,* At *walir,* W *anir.*
   II. Ach, Maip *auri,* Kau *šani,* Mar *ynary,* Pia *aouri.* Ban, Bare, Si, Tar *tšino.* Kar *džino,* Ad, Kat *tsinu,* Mand *tžinu,* Uar *tšinu,* Gu *yunali,* Ach *isarito;*
   III. M *nira.*
82. Otter (= water-fruit ? nos. 68, 118).
   II. Ban, Bare *inevi,* Uar, Yav *neiui,* Kat, Si, Tar *hieui,* Yuk *hi(n)ycui,* Maip *nevɪ* Mand *neibi, ineui,* Pia *yewi;*
   III. Ipu *ene;*
   IV. Me *uveːe,* Pare *inaue,* Gua *everetše.*
83. Rat, mouse, § 129 c) 3).
   I. A *kuli,* I K *couli,* W *kori, kari;*
   II. Gu *kusitiu;*
   III. Piro *kuči;*
   IV. B *cajachi.* mouse, Chane *covo,* Moxo *coːa,* Mucoxeone *kosio,* Pai *kusa,* Paunaka *koso.*
84. Agouti, Dasyprocta, § 129 c) 3).
   I. A *pukuleru,* I K *picouli,* Map *tukula,* P *bukutru;*
   II. Ban *uayuru, picouroua,* Bare *guayuru* Cau *giahoui,* Pia *piːi,* Ad *pidːi,* Mand *hiːi,* Ju *puütschi,* Pa *poütːy,* Uai *pihtːi,* Jav *guaioto,* Gu *uayulumidː*
   III. Kun *pehiyöri,* Kus *peʾširi,* Piro *pehiri, pexiri;*
   IV. Me *pekirːi, peköʾːo,* Waura *peköorːi,* Yaul *pikiri,* B *pirɪ.*
Karib languages **akuri.*
Tupi languages **akuti.*
85. Paca, Coelogenis Paca. § 69 b).
   I. A *laba,* G *paüia,* Map *caba;*
   II. Ban *liapa,* Bare *yaba,* Ad, Kar, Pia *dapa,* Kat, Si, Tar *(n)dapa,* Uar *bapa* Uai *tahpa,* Pa *lapa,* Yav *iafa,* Mand *daha.*
Tupi languages **paka.*
86. Capybara, Hydrochoerus capybara.
   I. A *kibiolc, kibiwaːa,* G *shikuire;*
   II. Bare *kxihuiri, siwiri,* Pia *dːiwiri,* Cau *geha,* Ju *gäho,* Ad, Kar *ketu,* Kat *ketsu* Mand, Uar *kesu,* Yuk *k(i)esu,* Manao *kiu,* Uai *gesso,* Gu *keyu;*
   III. Piro *ipeti,* Kan *hypetu,* Kampa *ibeto;*

IV. Gua *evakat̆su*, Me, Waura *ipiehü*, Moxo *uchu*, Pare *oli*, Sar *huhuri*, Yaul *iruti*. Tupi languages **kapiwara*.

87. Armadillo.

I. A *yesi*, Arua *yudu ;*

II. Ach *che*, Ban *uetsi*, Ju *yetu*, Kar *(t)se*, Maip *see*, Mar *tschee*, Pa *yetu*, Pia *tse*, Tar *iye*, Yav *tzeh*, *sece*, Yuk *yee ;*

III. M *yeschy*, Ipu *iśiuati*, Kun, Kus *kŭiwana*.
Karib languages **kapaśi*.

88. Tapir, § 134 *f*) 3).

I. A *kama*, G, Par *ama*, horse ;

II. Ach *emayenesi*, Ban, Kau, Mand, Pia, Uar, *ema*, Ad, Kar, Kat, Si, Tar, Yuk *hema*, Bare *tema*, Ju, Gu, Mar *zema*, Pa *sehma*, Uai *aehma*, Uir *cama*, Yav *kema ;*

III. In *xama*, Ipu *kiama*, Kampa *quimalo*, Kun *hyema*, Kus *hyema*, *śema*, Man *čema*, M *gama*, Pak *sama*, Pau *dama*, Piro *xiema*, *siema ;*

IV. Gua *mayane-kamo*, Ku, Me, Waura *täme*, Yaul *tsâma*.
Karib languages **maśipuri*.
Tapir, see N⁰. 142.

89. Bush hog, peccary, Taitetu, Dicotyles torquatus.

I. A *matula*, Arua *urumaru ;*

II. Ach *chamu*, Ban *tsoara*, *soara*, Bare Mand, *arua*, Gu *inarra* (D. lab.), Ca *samouri* (D. lab.), Kar *samoliti*, *soara*, Ad *dzamulitu*, Kat *tsamulitu*, Pia *dzamu*, Tar *yamulitu*, Si *samoliti ;*

III. In, Piro *merič̆i*, Ipu, Kus *meriti*, Kan *merity*, Kun *möriti*, M *arua* (D. lap.), Pau *myṙycy ;*

IV. Moxo *simoru*, Sar *imiaxare*, B *simori*.

90. Bush hog, taiasu, Dicotyles labiatus, § 65 *b*).

I. A *abüya ;*

II. Bare, Uar *abida*, Maip, Tar *apia*, Kar *apit̆sa*, Cau *putzya*, Ju *apuya*, Mar *apytza* (Dic. torq.), Pa *abaeghua*, Ad, Mand *apija*, *ahida*, Uai *hapychtsche*, Uir *abiaxe*, Ad, Pia *apidza*, Si *apitsa*, Yav *ahiya ;*

III. Marauha *abia* (D. torq.), In *irari*, Kun *iyarö*, Piro *xihari*, *ilavi*, Kus *ialö*, Ipu *irari*.
Karib languages **puinike*.

91. Bird, § 129 *a*) 2).

I. A *kodibiyu*, I K f *oulibignon*, *oulibignum*, G *uchi*, P *kuhipra ;*

II. Ban *udsipie*, Pia *madzibe*, *couipira*, Ad *tepira*, *kepiren*, Yav *kotsiheasi*, Cau *uipiza-hinabe*, feather (bird-arm), Gu *kuripiu ;*

III. Marauha *ghimpu*, Piro *kuš̆ič̆i*, *kusič̆i*, Kus *kuš̆ič̆i*, *kuśiti*, little birds :

IV. Gua *śoopeno*, *dyaopeno*.
Karib languages **tukuž̆i*, humming-bird, colibri.
Bird's nest, see n⁰. 111c.

92. Humming-bird, colibri, § 58 *d*) 2).

I. A *bimiti*, G *chumuchau*, W *pimud ;*

II. Ad, Kat, Si, Tar *pimi*, Gu *humidi*, Mand *bumidi*, Pia *zipi*.

93. Pigeon, § 125 *e*).

I. A *wiru*, P *wirusi ;*

III. Kampa *çhiro ;*

IV. Moxo *siriu*.

94. Powis, curassow bird, Crax *a*) not specified, *b*) C. globulosa, *c*) C. tuberosa, *d*) C. Urumutum.

I. *a*) A *hič̆i*, G *ishu ;*

II. *a*) Kar *koitsi*, Kat *kuit(s)i*, Manao *uiu*, Pia *kuiz̆i*, Ad *kuidz̆i*, Mand *kuiz̆i*, Si, Tar *kuitsi*, Uar *kuisi*, Uir *itite*, Yuk *kusi*, Yav *zoita*, *itiri ;*

b) Cau *ghozy*, Ju *koezy*, Mar *ghuitze*, Pa *ghotsue*, Uai *ghuikzy ;*

c) Cau *pinozy*, Ju *poyory*, Mar *pytyaka*, Pa *püyury*, Uai *pytschaga ;*

    d) Cau *nazyry*, Kat *itseri*, Mar *auziry*, Pa *agho*, Si *itsiri*, Tar *yatsiri*, Uai *uzyry ;*

III.   *a)* M *piury*, Pan *piyung*, Piro *kiuli*, *kiunti ;*

    c) Kan *piury*, Ipu *payuri*, Kus *kiurö ;*

IV.   *a)* Sar *uruxu.*

Karib languages *a)* **pahuići.*

95.   Duck, § 69*b*).

  I.   A *ipa*, *ifa*, W *bai ;*

  III.   In *xupai*, Ipu *opai*, Kun *upsi*, Piro *upći*, Kus *opsi ;*

  IV.   B *ipahi*, Gua *pazi*, *pohahi*, Moxo *upohi*, Yaul *upuelyu*, Waura *upi*, Sar *oxaću*

Karib languages **rapono.*

96.   Tortoise (one or more species), § 129 *c*) 2)

  I.   A *hikuli ;*

  II.   Ju *yko*, Kat, Pia, Si, Tar *ikuli*, Kar *icurli*, Maip *curita*, Uar *exkuli*, Uir *ocolle.*

Yav *curia*, Gu *kulimalu*, Mand *kulimaru ;*

  III.   M *ykury*, Piro *krüa ;*

  IV.   Pare *ikore*, Sar *kore-zahuaku*, Gua *yukeelu.*

Karib languages **kuriźa.*

97.   Tortoise (one or more species).

  II.   Ban *puri*, Bare *tibuli*, Yav *sifori ;*

  III.   Ipu *sempiri*, In *piri*, Piro *sipree*, Kus *sepörö ;*

  IV.   Me, Waura *ipiu*, Gua *ovoe.*

98.   Alligator, § 134 *h*).

  I.   A *kaikući*, G *kaiushi*, Par *keibih*, Taino *caiman ;*

  II.   Kat *gatsiri*, Mar *ghatschury*, Pia *katsuiri*, Ad, Si *katsiri*, Mand *kadiri*, Tar *katsiri*,

Uai *gatschaery*, Uar *katuili*, Yav *katsohiti*, Gu *kaimana ;*

  III.   Ipu, *cayukyry*, Kan, Kun *siusery*, Pau *kasei*, Piro *coyuseri*, *cioxe*, Kus *k* *iuyörö ;*

  IV.   B *cahire*, Moxo *cahiure*, Ku, Me, Waura, Yaul *yaka*, Pare *iuwakare.*

Tupi languages **jakare.*

Karib languages **aribe.*

99.   Lizard (one or more species).

  I.   A *lobu ;*

  II.   Kar *dopu*, Kat *(n)do(u)pu*, Mand *doojo*, Tar *(n)dupu*, Uar *bopo*, Yuk *lupu*,

Ad *doku ;*

  IV.   Pare *dohi*, *zohi*, Sar *zooxo.*

100.   Toad (sound-imitation ?).

  I.   A *siberu*, P *tipuru*, G *iperüre ;*

  II.   Bare *tibau*, Kar, Si, Tar *hiparu*, Pia *baruta*, Gu *zibau ;*

  IV.   B *sipori*, Moxo *peru.*

101.   Toad (sound-imitation).

  II.   Ban, Uar, Yav *tororo*, Mand *tora*, Gu *tukuro :* frog ;

  III.   Kun, Kus *turuyöri*, Piro *toloxiri ;*

  IV.   Sar *katorore*, Gua *turumo.*

Karib languages **poreru.*

Tupi languages **kururu.*

102.   Fish, § 76 *b*).

  I.   A *himi*, *hime*, G *jime*, *jima*, P *ima ;*

  II.   Ban *simche*, Maip *timachi*, Yav *simasi*, *jimaa ;*

  III.   Kampa *çhima*, *gima*, Kan *schima*, M *eme*, Piro *cima*, Ipu *shimaki*, Kus *śima ;*

  IV.   B, Moxo *himo.*

103.   Fish, § 69 *b*).

  I.   W *kopai ;*

  II.   Bare *kobati*, Kar, Uar *gope*, Kat *gupe*, Pa *kouhoby*, Pia *kubai*, Si *kupe*, Tar *kope*,

Gu *kadźepe ;*

  IV.   Me *kupa*, Pare *kohasa*, Sar *koxahe*, Yaul *kubati.*

104. Perai, piranha, Serrasalmo (comp. n⁰. 102).

I. A *(h)uma*, P *umayane* ;

II. Ban *paruma*, Bare *baumehe*, Cau *pohma*, Jum *oma*, Kar *omai*, Ad, Kat, Mand,
Pia, Si *umai*, Mar *ypuma*, Pa *auma*, Tar *ume*, Uai *ygpuma*, Uar *ome*, Yuk *mai*, Gu *umahe;*

III. Kan *humah*, Kun *uma*, *huma*, M *sebieama*, Kus, Yam *uma*.

Karib languages *poune.

105. Honey, § 134 d) 2).

I. A *maba*, I K *mamba*, G *mapa*, W *mala*, bee ;

II. Ach, Ban, Bare, Gu, Kar, *maba*, Ad, Kat, Maip, Si, Tar *mapa*, Uar *maba*, bee,
Yuk *mapa*, bee, Mand, Yav *maha* ;

III. Ipu *mapa*, bee ;

IV. Gua, Yaul *mapa*, bee, Moxo *mopo*, bee, Para *maha*, Sar *maxa-hine*.

106. Big ant, Cryptocerus atratus.

I. A *muniru* ;

II. Kat, Si, Tar, Uar, Yuk *mane* ;

III. Kun, Kus *manahi*, Piro *manaxi*, Yam *yumu*, Pau *manei*.

107. Umbrella ant, Atta cephalotes (perhaps also other species).

I. A *kasisi*, *kuse*, P *kasisi*, W *kacur* ;

II. Ban *catsitsi*, Bare *kasisi*, Uar *kazizi*, Gu *kuse*, Maip *cuchi*, Mand *cajita-carero*,
Pia *kue*, Yav *cauijitzo* ;

III. Ipu *katsepokere*, Kun *katiti*, Piro *isiki*, Kampa *catitori*, Kus *kačiči* ;

IV. Moxo *cahisi*, Sar *arihiš*.

107 A. Wasp, § 124 b).

I. (A *hanuba*, a small fly that stings, *hayu*, ant that bites painfully) ;

II. Bare *hani*, Ban, Uar *ani*, Kar, Kat, Si, Tar *aini*, Yuk *hai*, Pia *aini* ;

III. Ipu *sane*, Kampa *sani* ;

IV. Moxo *hane*, Pare *ani*, Sar *anina*, B *ane*, Mucoxeone *dane*.

Karib languages honey, bee *huane.

107 B. Gnat, mosquito (one or more species), § 124 b).

I. A *haniju*, I K *aetera*, G *mein*, P *aniyu*, W *demese*, *mistu* ;

II. Cau *nhitscho*, Ban *aneio*, Pia *anatsa*, *anoteho*, Maip, Yuk *aniu*, Mand, Uar *anidu*,
Ad *ainidzu*, Kar, Si *ainitsu*, Uai *hanitschu*, Jum *ayu*, Pa *alikyu*, Kat *siniru*, Tar *ainiu*,
Mand *annido*, Yav *aniio*, Gu *haniyu* ;

III. M, Ipu *aniu*, Piro *axiu*, Kun *ahiu*, Kus *aiu*, Pau *pythaη* :

IV. Moxo *aniu*, Gua *niu*, Pare *aniotö*, Me, Waura *eyu*, Sar *ahazu*, Mucoxeone *anihure*,
B *ini*, *huajai*.

108. White ant, termite, § 129 f).

I. A *kumučiri* ; white ant-hill, I K *commotiri* (A *maba o-komodi*, honeycomb ; in
some Karib languages in Guyana *okomo, wasp) ;

II. Ban *amara*, Gu *kamada*, Kar *gamare*, Kat, Si *gamara*, Ad, Pia, Tar *kamara*
Uar *camara*, Yav *camata*, Yuk *kamarala*, Mand *kana*, Si *gamamota*. white ant-hill :

III. Ipu *kamara*, Pau *dyumah*, Piro *kamala* ;

IV. Pare *munuli*.

Worm, grub, see n⁰. 4.

PLANTS

109. Tree, § 89.

I. A *(h)ada*, P *aha*, W *ataman*, wood ;

II. Ban *atabi*, Bare, Mand, Uir *ada*, Car *atamina*, Gu *damuna*, Manao, Yav *ata*.
Maip *aa*, Mand *innana*, Kau *aha*, Uai *abana*, Ju *auana* ;

III. Ar *a-ata*, *aara*, Pau *aua*, Piro *axamuena*, Kun *amuena*, Kus *aömöna* ;

IV. Ku, Me, Pare, Sar, Waura, Yaul *ata*, B *ala-se*, fruit.

110. Tree.

I. W *luakare*, firewood, (A *egura*, root, §§ 124 a) 3), 107 b) 5)):

II. Ad, Kar, Kat, Si, Tar *haiku*, Mand *ahico*, Pia *ahicu*, Cau *aghozo*, *gazo*, Pia *ahicu*.

III. (Ipu *ecu*, *akotsa*, root, *icaty*, branch, Piro *itski*, root), Kampa *inchato*, *enchoto*, M *uguaschukuna* ;

IV. Moxo *yucuqui*, Gua *tikoti*, B *yokise* firewood.

110 A. Root, § 89.

I. A *duli*, W *ulud*, I K *f role* ;

II. Bare *iduli*, Manao *ataüety*, Ad *eliri* ;

III. Ar *azaly*.

111. a) Branch, b) Bush, c) Bird's nest, § 90 f) 4) (comp. nos. 11. 12).

I. b) A *tibo-kili* (I K *itibou ouattou*, fire-brand, *itibouri*, hair) ;

   c) A *itiboko*, I K *itibouca* ;

II. a) Tar *tapu*, riverbranch ;

   b) Ban *tauape* Uar *auakapi* Kar *tsakape* ;

   c) Si *lie(f)-erupuku* ;

III. a) M *batiberu* ;

   b) Ipu *itopa* ;

IV. a) Moxo *tabo*, branch (of a tree, a river, a path).

Branch, see n⁰. 26.

Bark, see n⁰. 7.

112. Leaf, (tree-)leaf, § 64 a) 4).

I. A *banna*, I K *(arou-banna*, G *pana*, P *(ru-)pana* ;

II. Cau *(a-)banna*, Kat, Si, Tar *panape*, Manao *(ata-)ana*, Mand *(a-)nape*, *(aha-)nahe*, Mar *(aa-)pana*, Pa *(a-)panama*, Pia *(a-)bana*, Uai *(apana-)pahna*, Ad, Uar *(a-)panape*, Yuk *(hauana-)pana*, Gu *(da-)bana* ;

III. Ar *(atu-)puena*, Kampa *(chi-)pana*, Kan *(sa-)pahna*, Pau *(aua-)φani*, Yam *(a-)φani* ;

IV. B *epone*, Ku, Me, Waura, Yaul *pana*, Sar *(ata-)xana*.

113. Liver, § 64 a) 4).

I. A, I K *bana*, G *pana*, W *k-uba* ;

II. Ban *pane*, Bare *kabale*, Kat *zupana*, Tar *inape*, Uar *toapaini*, Gu *yewana* ;

III. Kun *upana*, Piro *xupuna* ;

IV. B *perana*, *eperrena*, Gua *apakana*, Moxo *(ta)upono*.

114. Nail, § 64 a) 4).

I. A *bada*, I K *bara*, At *pari*, G *patau*, W *bare*, P *kinwirara*, *kipurara* ;

II. Bare *eba*, *apa*, Uir *bi-bata*, Car *pata*, Ju *pa*, Yuk *fino*, Pa *sopah*, Cau *paha*, Gu *abauidya*, Pia *ba*, Mand *ha* ;

III. M *para*, Ar *(ni-)kpia*, Kan *seoata*, Piro *sabata*, *seuata*, Ip *çawata*, Kus *sewata* ;

IV. Moxo *hipoño*, Ku *patata*, Me *hupatata*, Waura *huparata*, Yaul *barata*, Gua *dšibo* Sar *xauti*, B *tipo*.

115. Hair, § 64 a) 4).

I. A *bara*, I K *f iti-bouri*, head-hair, G, Par *walla* ;

II. Ban *dzi-banna*, head-hair, Ip *(niu-)detsi-pa*, do., Kar *(no-)sito-pe*, do.

116. House, § 130 e) (comp. n⁰. 112).

I. A *bawhu*, G *pia*, Taino *bohio*, *boi*, *boa* ;

II. Ju *bahü* ;

III. Yam *yobä* ; *baiä*, village ;

IV. Me, Ku, Pare *pai*, Sar *ahi*, Paunaka *ovia*.

117. House (comp. n⁰. 112).

I. I K *banna*, *bonoco*, G *pinche*, P *pinhu*, *pina* ;

II. Ban *paniši*, Bare *pani*, Cau *bagnö*, *painyoe*, Gu *bani*, Ju, Uai *pana*, Kau *paneti*, Ad, Kar, Kat, Si *panti*, Maip *paniti*, Mar *panizy*, Pa *pahna*, Tar *panisi*, Uar *panizi*, Yav *hanizi*, Mand *haniži*, Yuk *pasi* :

III.   Kampa *pango-chi, bango,* Kan *panitschy,* Kun, Kus *panti,* Piro *panči ;*
IV.   Gua *peti,* Moxo *peti, peno,* Waura *pune.*
118.   a) Flower ; b) Fruit, (tree-) fruit, § 125 c) 1).
   I.   b) A *iwi,* I K *(huehue)im,* P *(ra-)riwi ;*
   II.   a) Kar, Kat, Mand, Tar, Yuk *iui,* Maip *ivi,* Si *iui, yivi,* Manao *iby,* Bare *hiwi,*
Gu *hibiukuži,* Pia *iwina,* Ad *eliui ;*
   III.   a) Kus *iawö,* Piro *ka-xuere,* Kun *ka-huwiri ;*
         b) Piro *exi-n-exi,* Kus *čowayi.*
119.   Seed, § 116 b) 1).
   I.   A *isi,* G *sö ;*
   II.   Kar, Si *iši ;*
   III.   maize : In *is,* Kan *schi-schy,* Kun *čihi,* Piro *šixi ;*
   IV.   B *se, ese-ki,* Sar *ehe,* Pare *esö.*
Juice, see n⁰. 2.
119 A.   Bignonia chica, red paint, § 135 d) 1) VII).
   I.   A *karraüru ;*
   II.   Bare *kiaui,* Kat *karauitu,* Tar *keraweyu,* Uar *kilauiru,* Maip *chirraviri,* Gu *kayali.*
120.   Cassava (§ 170 c)).
   I.   A *kalli ; kanneki-ddi,* Cassabistöcke, § 83 a), I K f *canhim,* Map *kase,* P *kineri.*
W *kanir, kanen,* Arua *kait,* G *aik, aii ;*
   II.   Ach *quenirro,* sweet cassava, Ban *ašihi,* Bare *kaniti,* Gu *kani,* Ju *ghey,* Ad, Kar,
Kat, Si, Tar *kaini,* Kau *kanyi.* sweet cassava, Maip *cattichi,* Mand *cajinaji, chachi,*
Manao *ghanury,* Pa *ghanya,* Pia *kaini, caina,* Uai *ghany,* Uar *ka(x)ni,* Uir *calli,* Yav
cafesi, Yuk *gahiru ;*
   III.   Ipu *komiri, kumürü,* Kampa *caniri, cañari,* Kan *ghanury, ghunury,* Piro *ximeka,*
In *kemeka,* Kun *kande.* Kus *kandö, komiri ;*
   IV.   B *cajapa,* Me, Waura *mukura,* Pare *ketoso,* Sar *ketehe.*
Karib languages **kišere.*
121.   Cotton, § 121 c) 10).
   I.   A *yahu ;*
   II.   Ban *ahuali,* Bare *huakaoari,* Ca *saouari,* Kar *kauarie,* Ad, Kat *tauali,* Mand
cauarli, Pia *fawali, saouari,* Tar *tsauali,* Gu *kanaližži ;*
   III.   Kun *wapöhö,* Pak *apau,* Piro *goxapuxe,* Kus *wopö, wapeh ;*
   IV.   B *cajahuare, cohobore,* Moxo *cohore,* Pare, Sar *konohe,* Ku, Me, Waura *ayupe,*
Yaul *aliupö, ayupö.*
Karib languages **atakuare.*
Tupi languages **amandyu-b.*
121 A.   Genipa americana, black paint.
   I.   A *lana,* I K f *chaoua ;*
   II.   Si *tana ;*
   III.   Yam *ora,* Kampa *ana ;*
   IV.   Pare *dana.*
122.   Maize, § 116 b) 1).
   I.   A *mariši,* I K f *marichi,* G, Map *mariki,* P *mahiki,* Par *mai.* W *marique,* Taino
mahiz, maysi ;
   II.   Bare *mai, makanasi,* Ban *makanatsi,* Mand *makanaži,* Kar *makanadži,* Uar
makanasi, Maip *jomuchi,* Ad, Tar, Ach, Yav *kana,* Yuk *kane,* Kat *gama,* Si *kama,*
Pia *kanai ;*
   III.   Ipu *kiema, kimy,* Yam *kemi ;*
   IV.   Ku, Me, Waura, Yaul *maiki.*
Karib languages **ašinaᶜi.*
Tupi languages **abati.*
123.   Ite (muriti) palm, Mauritia flexuosa (comp. § 90 f)).
   I.   A *itte,* P *isawi,* W *duer, yure ;*

II. Ban *teui*, Bare *izehui*, Kar *iteuina*, Kat, Pia *ideui*, Ad, Mand, Si, Uar *iteui*. Tar *teuira*, *teuida*, Yav *tehui*, *tegui*, Yuk *hiteui* ;

III. Kun *yende*, Kus *hyinde* ;

IV. Pare *isoe*.

Tupi *miriti*.

124. Manicole (assai) palm, Euterpe oleracea, § 74 *e*) 2).

I. A *manaka* ;

II. Ban *manaha*, Bare, Gu, Kar, Mand, Tar, Uar *manaka*, Ad, Kat, Si *manake*, Pia *manakei*, Yuk *manakala* ;

III. Kus *yusiköl(r)ö*.

124 A. Papaya, Carica Papaya, § 69 *b*).

I. A *papaya*, I K *ababai*, G *papaya*, P *papayu*, W *mapaye* ;

II. Gu, Mand, Maip, Pia *mapaya*, Ad *mabaya* ;

III. Kun *kapayu*, Piro *kapayo* ;

IV. Gua *tsapaiu*, Moxo *opopohi*.

125. Paxiuba palm, Iriartea exorrhiza.

I. A *buba* ;

II. Tar *pupa*, Ad, Pia *puba*, Mand *koha*.

Tupi *paxiuba*.

126. Cayenne pepper, Capsicum (comp. to sneeze : Arawak *a-tte-di-*, Kechua *achhi*).

I. A *haci*, I K f *ati*, Arua *at*, G *jashi*, P *atiti*. Taino *axi* ;

II. Ban *tsitsi*, Bare *hadi*. Mand *hati*, Ad, Kar, Si *ati*. Kat *at(s)i*, Maip *ai*, Pia *aasi*, Tar *atsi*, Uar *asi*, Yav *atsitsi*, Yuk *haasi*, Gu *adzi* Pia *azi* ;

III. Pau *kasi*, Piro *tasso* ;

IV. B *iyeti*, Gua *tati*, Ku, Me, Waura, Yaul *ai*. Moxo *acheti*. Sar *otzotzo*.

Kechua *uchu*, *achi*.

127. Reed, § 112 *a*).

I. A *hihi*, I K *hipe*, arrow, A *hiwa*, bamboo ;

II. Bare *ixi*, *ihi*, Tar *iua*, bamboo ;

IV. Pare *tiua*. B *evise*, bamboo.

128. Sweet potatoe, Ipomoea Batatas, § 126 *a*).

I. A *halitsi*, G *jaishi*, Map *kasai 'i*, P *kairi*, W *kari*, Taino *hage* ;

II. Bare *gahau*, Gu *kauo*. Mand *kahau*, Kar, Uar *kariri*, Kat *galiri*, Ad *kaliri*, Maip *chei*, Pia *kalidi*, *carirri*, Tar *kalidie*, Yav *kaliti*. Yuk *koayu* ;

III. Ipu *kepare*. Kun *yipari*, Kampa *catzari*, *curiti*, Piro *xipali*, Kus *hipale*, *sipale* ;

IV. Gua *koe*, Moxo *coerepa*, *coere*. Pare *kaye*, Sar *kace*.

129. Tobacco, § 124 *a*).

I. A *yuli*, I K f *iouli*, G *yülli*, *yüri*, P *airi* ;

II. Ban *eli*, Bare *ali*, Gu *ili* ;

III. Ipu *awiri*, In *airipi*. Kampa *tzeri*. Kun *hiri*, Pau *hädyiri*, Piro *iri* ;

IV. Gua *tchahi*, Moxo *sabara*, Pare *azieho*, Sar *ace*, Yaul *airi*.

130. Tobacco.

I. At *schuma*, W *suma* ;

II. Ban *djeema*. Ca *sema*. Kar *ndzema*, Ad, Kat *dzema*. Maip *jema*, Mand *dzema*, Pia *tsema*. Si *(n)dzema*, Tar, Avane *yema*, Uar *dema*, Yav *shema*, *dyema*, Guipunave *dema*, Cavere *scema*, Gu *nyama* ; cigar.

Karib languages *tamu*.

Tupi languages *pety-m-a*.

NUMERALS, INTERJECTIONS, WORDS DENOTING PLACE, ETC.

131. One, § 152.

I. A *aba*. I K *aban*, Map *apaura*, W *baulau*. another :

II. Ach *abai*, Ad *apekutza*. Ban *peyaro*. Ju *aphülla*, Kar *aapetsa*, Kat *apadatsa*,

Manao *ababy*, another, Pia *aberi*, Pa *apeala*, Si *apaita*, Tar *paita*, Uar *apabasa*, Gu *abaamedža* ;

   III. Kampa *aparo* ;

   IV. Ku, Waura, Yaul *paua*, Me *pauitza*, Moxo *opo*, another.

   132. *a*) Two, *b*) Half, § 153.

     I. *a*) A, I K *biama*, G *biama, piama*, P *pitana*, Par *piam* ;

        b) I K *tibiri* ;

    II. *a*) Ju *biagma*, Yuk *hiama*, Gu *abiamaka*, Tar *hiamepa*, Si *dzamapa*, Ad *dzamana*, Kat *(n)dzamata*, Kar *ndza(x)me*, Pia *putsaipa* ;

        b) Bare *ihia*, Kat *bamutsoa*, Tar *pamuyoa*, Yuk *peyo* ;

   III. *a*) Ar *puyabana*, Ipu *ipi*, Kampa *apite*, Kus *hepi* ;

   IV. *a*) Ku, Me, Waura *mepiaua*, Moxo *api*, Pare *hinama*.

   132 A. Yes, § 109.

     I. A *ahe, ehe*, I K *hanhan*, G *aa*, P *ye, ihe*, W *uh, euheu, anhan* ;

    II. Pia *ahae, haa*, Bare, Ban *ehe, hehe*, Kar *ehe*, Ad *ohu*, Kat *uhu*, Si *oho*, Yuk *he*, Tar *haha-ye*, Mand, Yav *eje*, Ju *aeae*, Gu *hai* ;

   III. Ip *ei*, Kampa (women) *he* ;

   IV. Moxo *eè*, Gua *e, êê*.

   132 B. *a*) Verb or interjection expressing pain or sorrow, *b*) Pain, §§ 136 *e*) 5), 134 *a*).

     I. *a*) A *aka*, I K *cayeu* ;

        b) A *kari*, I K f *cari*, G *ais*, W *kario, kalini* ;

    II. *a*) Kar *caica*, Maip *cavi* ;

        b) Uar *keui*, Yav *cauiji*, Ban *cauina*, Mand *cauiri*, Uar *ueuiqueui*, Pia *caoure*, sick ;

   III. *a*) Kampa *accaia* ;

        b) Piro *kačindi*, Ipu *catçui*, Kampa *cariba*, a cudgel ;

   IV. *a*) B *acai*, Moxo *aco* ;

        b) Moxo *cati*, Gua *karinai-ti*, sick.

   132 C. Here, § 45 *b*).

     I. A *yaha*, G *yaya* ;

    II. Si *ayaha*, Ad, Kat *aya*, Tar *ahe*, Gu *auhu*, Pia *tsahei* ;

   III. Ipu *wai*, Kus *ewi*.

   132 D. Yonder, § 45 *b*).

     I. A *taha* : far, G *sasa* ;

    II. Ban *uitaha*, Ad *ayata*, Kat, Si *ataha*, Mand *eteha*, Uar *akada, atida*, Yav *te ie* : far, Gu *džuahe* ;

   III. Piro *tekka*, Kus *töka*.

COLOURS

   132 E. *a*) White, § 126 *a*), *b*) Light, day, § 161 *a*).

     I. *a*) A *(h)alira*, I K f *alou-ti*, G *kasutai*, P *seine* ;

        b) A *alaiti*, a light, *aranaha-i, harunaha*, the dayspring ;

    II. *a*) A *haledali*, Bare *balini*, Ban *aliri*, Kat *haalide*, Si *halaite*, Tar *ahalite*, Uai *ariri*, Uar *aleli*, Yav *ga-halimi*, Yuk *hareni*. Manao *palyhaty*, Pa *sareu*, Cau *jathiri*, Pia *kabaleri* ;

   III. *a*) Kus *kratarö*, Ar *ghalikate*, Kampa *quitamaro-ri* ;

        b) Marauha *ary* ;

   IV. *a*) Moxo *hapu* ;

        b) Moxo *hara*.

   133. Black, § 135 *b, c*).

     I. A *karime, uelihi*, I K *ouli-ti*, G *guitse*. blue, W *kuli*, blue ;

    II. Bare *kuli-ni*, blue, Ca *kouride*, Maip *curi-chini*, black, blue (*mari-chini*, white) Pia *curiri*, Yav *koyoni-mi*, blue ;

III.   Ar *ghuli, kuryhy.* Piro *saxiri,* Kus *ksayirö.*

134.   Yellow.

I.   A *hae-hae,* P *ayeweye,* I K *houhere-ti ;*

II.   Ban *t-cua-li,* Ad *euadali,* Kat *eua-de,* Maip *eva-chini,* Pia *everi,* Si *eua-da-li.* Tar *eua,* Yav *t-eua-mi,* Yuk *heua-ni,* Manao *t-aua-ty.*

III.   M *uauy,* white.

VERBS

134 A.   To be afflicted, § 29 e).

   I.   A *amunaiga,* I K f *imonheme ;*

  II.   Mand *uremi-cashi,* Yav *jata iomijina,* Kar *saum-queita ;*

 III.   Piro *amuneuata,* Ipu *amiyanata,* to be sick ;

 IV.   Moxo *miypone-re-reico,* to cause affliction.

134 B.   a) To beat, b) To kill, § 69 e).

   I.   a) A *a-boragi-,* I K f *apara,* W *bairi ;*

       b) A *a-forri-,* I K f *apara, aparo ;*

  II.   a) Pia *ibalaka ;*

 III.   a) Kampa *patza ;*

       b) Piro *haxali,* cudgel ;

 IV.   a) B *i-buicho,* Moxo *epucheico ;*

       b) B *iporocho,* Moxo *co-paraico,* Chane *parapiti,* the river of killing.

134 C.   To give birth to a child, § 124 b).

   I.   A *himeu,* I K f *emeigno ;*

  II.   Bare *meno ;*

 III.   Ipu *emeakore ;*

 IV.   Moxo *imino-co,* Sar *imiae-tsani,* male child.

135.   To bury, § 134 c).

   I.   A *akarata ;*

 III.   Ipu *nekatapiri ;*

 IV.   B, Moxo *ecoro.*

136.   To carry, § 79 c) 3).

   I.   A *aniki-,* I K *annegui ;*

  II.   Pia *enu-li,* Ad *anu-li,* Mand *anu-lu ;*

 III.   In, Piro *anika,* Ipu *anica,* Kampa *anaque, anaje.*

137.   a) To cure, b) Remedy, charm, § 58 d) 2) VI).

   I.   a) A *ibihidi- ;*

       b) A *bina ;*

  II.   a) Bare *binada ;*

       b) Ban *pinasi,* Bare *binihi, abinadani,* Kar *tape,* Kat *uetape,* Maip *epenati,* Si *dape,* Tar *l-itape,* Yav *epinatzi ;*

 IV.   a) Moxo *ca-ipu.*

138   To die, § 122 e) 1).

   I.   A *a-(h)o-do-,* I K *ahouce,* G *a-utu-,* Par *a-otida,* to slay ;

  II.   Yav *uauioa, uiyua,* Bare *adauikana,* Ban *uyoamiha.*

139.   To do, to put, § 78 e) 3).

   I.   A *ani,* I K *ani-ra,* G *ainy,* to make ;

  II.   Pia *anu,* to give, Uar *aini,* do., Kat *ani,* do., Maip *nua.*

To drink, see n⁰. 3.

140.   Dream, § 174 c).

   I.   A *toboni,* I K f *toboüi,* G *rapo ;*

  II.   Ban *tabonihi,* Bare *sabonini,* Kar *tapuinke,* Kat *taponika,* Si *hitapune,* Tar *tapuli ;*

 III.   Ipu *pi-tapunawa-tapinawa,* you dreamt ;

 IV.   Moxo *echopu.*

140 A. To eat, § 171 a).

  I. A *eke*, I K *aica*, G *eka*, Par *aghi*, W *nik* ;
  II. Bare *nika*, Pia *yaca* ;
  III. Ipu *nica*, Kun *nekane*, Piro *nike* ;
  IV. B, Moxo *nico*, Sar *inihǐca*, Mucoxeone *nika*. Gua *niige*.

140 B. To be halt, lame, § 129 c) 1).

  I. A *ikori*, I K *icou*, W *tukurai* ;
  II. Bare *aculrunani* ;
  III. Piro *hečuri* ;
  IV. Moxo *capuri*.

141. To be heavy, § 129 e).

  I. A *kudi, kudu*, I K *keurre* ;
  II. Uar *tokoli*, Bare *dokuni*.

142. Tapir (comp. n⁰. 141).

  I. Map, W *kudui* :
  IV. Pare *kote, koite*, Sar *kuti*.

143. Club (comp. n⁰. 141).

  I. W *couidarou* ;
  II. Ad *kudaru*, Mand *kuidaru*, Yuk *kutiua* ;
  III. Piro *kakonda*.

143 A. To know, § 133 a).

  I. A *aici-, aditti-*, G *atöj*, W *aitapan* ;
  II. Ban *(no-)tze*, Pia *ieouari*, Maip *via* ;
  III. Kampa *iute, iu* ;
  IV. Moxo *itu*, B *ite-ri*.

144. To leave, § 58 c) 2).

  I. A *a-iibi-* ;
  IV. B *ibio*, Moxo *beo*.

144 A. To make, to create, § 74 d) 5).

  I. A *a-maliti-* ;
  II. Maip *uma*, Uar *(b-)uma-ni*, Bare *(bi-)modasa*, Pia *mani* (?) ;
  III. Ipu *cama*, Piro *kamerete*, Kun *kamha*.

145. To plant, § 91.

  I. A *abone-*, I K *abona*, G *apunaja*, to sow, W *pauna* ;
  IV. B *ipono*, Moxo *bo-co*, to sow.

146. a) To be sharp (a knife), b) To sharpen, § 74 e).

  I. a) A *ka-mana*, W *dimin* (blunt *mameu*) ;
      b) A *a-manti-* ;
  II. b) Ban *n-amenota*, Kat *ke-mina-kane*, Uar *pi-meleta-ni*, Si *ke-manati*, Tar *pi-maneta*, Bare *ki-manada*, Maip *manu-ri*, a *knife* ;
  III. a) Ipu *ca-nwana* ;
      b) Piro *pu-xe-nana-teri*.

147. To sleep, § 174 a).

  I. A *adunku-, adunuki-*, I K *aronca*, Arua *domakalc*, G *a-tunku*, P *himaka, himeka*, W *dau* ;
  II. Am *nu-imaca*, Ban *tsima*, Bare *domakari*, Cau *w-emakya*, Gu *demakaini*, Ju *uymaka*, Kar Pia, Si *imaka*, Kat *imakaua*, Mar *magha*. Manao *uatümaka*, Pa *n-imata*, Si *imaka*, Tar *iemaka*, Uar *imama*, Yav *ua-tsima uera*, Yuk *pi-kiemato*, Ad *manimaka*, Mand *imake* ;
  III. Ar *timka*, Ipu *imaca*, Kan *macho-atschy*, Kampa *amajc. magaye*, Kus *re-möka*, M *temeka*, Piro *mka*, Yam *amo-nini* ;
  IV. B, Moxo *imo-co*, Gua *hime-ka*, Sar *i-tiemeka*.

148. Hammock. (comp. n⁰. 147).

  I. A *hamaka*, G *jamataure*, Par *hamach*, W *ramac*, Taino *amaca* ;

II. Kau *maka*, Maip *amaca*, Pia *hamaca, amaka.* Tar, Uai, Yuk *hamaka*, Mand *amakatža*, Uir *amma*, Yav *amaiha*;

IV. Ku, Me, Waura, Yaul *amaka*, Pare *maka.*

(It does not seem at all impossible, that the first European who saw an Indian hammock and asked the name for it, got the answer "to sleep", A. M. **imaka,* and that the word *hamaka,* which is met in a few vocabularies of A. M. languages, is really the creole word. The Arawaks, though they know the word *hamaka,* have also a word of their own for a hammock, § 129 *d*) 2).)

148 A. To be sound, good, § 114 *a*).

I. A *(i)sa*;

II. Maip *so-ni-rri* (*ma-isu-ini,* bad), Yav *yo-nihihi.*

149. (To steal). Thief, § 118 *a*) 1).

I. A *ka-čiki-be-či*;

III. Piro *ka-čunxe-ri.*

149 A. To stink, § 115.

I. A *(h)isi,* I K f *inchi,* G *ke-jushi,* W *depus*;

II. Maip *isi(-che)*;

III. Piro *puse,* Kampa *echte*;

IV. Moxo *heche.*

149 B. *a*) To be true, *b*) To be good, § 48 1).

I. *a*) A *kidua*;

II. *b*) Bare *doali,* Ban *anedoaha*;

149 C. To urinate.

I. A *a-dahaka,* I K f *arago,* W *tatakan*;

II. Ad *dakaka,* Gu *dzzakaini,* Pia *ataiteka,* Mand *adake*: penis;

III. Ipu *tcinaca*;

IV. B *itapa.*

150. To weep, § 91.

I. A *a-ii-, a-iya,* I K f *aya,* G *ayara, eira*;

II. Ban *yaya-ha,* Bare *ihiya-ni,* Ad *idza-ka.* Kar *itša-ka,* Pia *itse-ka,* Kat, Si *itsa-ka,* Tar *iiha-kanuka,* Mand *ida-ke,* Uar *ida-ka,* Yav *haya.* Yuk *iya,* Gu *aia*;

III. Kampa *irha, iraa,* Ipu *chiinta,* Yam *ahini,* wimmern, Kus *čiaata*;

IV. B *iya, iyo.* Moxo *iiyo,* Gua *jaho-ti.*

151. Rain (comp. nos 150, 2, 1).

I. I K f *oya*;

II. Bare, Gu *hiya,* Kar *itša,* Kat *ida,* Ad, Si *idza,* Tar *iya,* Uar *ida,* Yav *ziya.*

CHAPTER XX

ORIGINS OF THE ARAWAK LANGUAGE

§ 183. A few words which are in use in most A. M. languages, are not found in Arawak. These are : I, me, A. M. *n(u)-, Arawak d(a)- ; man, A. M. *e(š)ina-ri, A. loko (human), wadili (male) ; sun, A. M. *kamu, A. (h)adaili ; mountain, A. M. *yapa, earth, A. M. *ipai, A. (h)ororo ; mouth, A. M. *numa, A. areroko ; hair, A. M. *(b)itiu, A. o-barra.

The language of the Lesser Antilles, which was closely related to Arawak, and of which important remains have been preserved in Island-Karib, has not undergone these changes. Goajiro and Parauhano have the pronominal prefix t(a)- for the first person singular, which evidently is the same as Arawak d(a)-.

We surmise that Arawak, which is a very living language, has discarded the old words, because their inner meaning was no longer felt. The economical use of pronouns (§§ 16 c), 19) may also be an Arawak innovation.

In a few cases in which an Arawak word may be readily explained from the general principles of the language, the same explanation.is not applicable to the corresponding A. M. word. Most often, however, the explanation of the Arawak word also holds good for the A. M. word, and this, with what has been mentioned in § 181, makes it very probable, that in primitive Arawak-Maipure, the vowels and consonants were used with a similar meaning to that which they still have in Arawak.

In their vocabularies the A. M. languages show a wide difference, when compared with each other.

Now, an Arawak word is a description of a few salient features of the thing, and the same thing can also be described by mentioning other features belonging to it. And in this way synonymes may come into use, without there being any deviation from the principles of the language.

In other cases the feeling for the inner value of the parts of a word may have been weakened, and as a consequence decaying influences got a chance to creep in. This has perhaps taken place to a considerable extent in Goajiro and Parauhano, and in Wapisiana.

The language of the Lesser Antilles has assimilated great quantities of foreign (Kaliña, Karib) words, and it is possible that a few more originally A. M. languages have undergone a similar fate. However, the opinion of Max Schmidt (56b, 105) "Ebenso erklärt sich die Verschiedenheit der

Aruak-Dialekte aus einer Verbindung der Aruak-Sprache mit jeweilig verschiedenen anderen Sprachen", goes perhaps a little too far.

Many new words may have come into use, when existing words became tabooed. Concerning the Arawaks, R. (19a Sect. 194, 19b Sect. 881) mentions the following :

"in case of certain animals the Arawak use different names according as they speak of them by day or by night. Thus, during the working hours a jaguar is *aróa*, but when darkness sets in it is *kabadaro* (claws). Similarly, *kamudu*, a boa constrictor, becomes *akkara* (a coil) ; *yéshi*, an armadillo. is paraphrased into *andajika* (*anda*, close, *tejika*, ear, i.e., ears close together), and so on." And :

"The surest way of offending the Water Spirits, however, and thereby getting caught in a storm, and being capsized, wrecked or drowned by way of punishment, is to utter certain words strictly forbidden under the circumstances. Thus, among the Arawaks of the Pomeroon and Moruca Rivers, there are certain terms which must never be employed when on a boat : they have to be paraphrased. The majority of these tabooed words are evidently of foreign (mostly Spanish) origin : a few are certainly indigenous. Thus, the occupants of a corial will never be heard to use the term *arcabuza* (gun), but they will speak of a gun as *kataroro* (foot, referring to the stock) ; they talk of *kariro* (the one with the teeth) instead of *perro* (Span., dog) ; of *kanakara-shiro* (load on the head, the cock's comb) instead of *gai-ina* (Span., *gallina*, fowl) ; of *akwadoa-kotiro* (round foot) instead of *kawai-yo* (Span., *caballo*, horse) ; of *kakwaro* (horn) instead of *bakka* (Span., *vaca*, cow) ; of *tataro* (something hard) instead of *sereri* (grindstone, or saw, probably from Span. *sierra*) ; of *majeriki* (the untrimmed one, referring to the hair) instead of *hó-a* (monkey) ; of *ehedoa* (frothing, brimming over, in reference to its snarling or growling) instead of *aroa* (tiger) ; of *katau-chi* (the one with wisdom) instead of *semi-chichi* (medicine-man) etc.".

Pen. (17a, I, 45) mentions crab, tortoise, bird, arrow, as forbidden words when one is at sea.

G. An Arawak who is on the tracks of a tapir, calls this animal *kulihi* = rat or mouse ; he is convinced that, if he were to pronounce the real name of the tapir, it would then run away.

§ 184. Numerous Arawak words are comparisons and descriptions, several of which may have come into use as paraphrases (§ 183) or nicknames. Examples : G. *šilótoo wayurĭ*, a padlock, lit. lock (creole word) [resembling a] tick, R. *baiyari-shiri*, a certain fan-design, lit. sawfish-snout. G. *unábuse*, a certain blindworm, lit. ground-worm. R. (§ 183) *k-ari-ro*. dog, lit. with-tooth-one, *ma-jeriki*, monkey, lit. un-trimmed.

All these expressions contain a root which is a word in itself.

(H)ala, an Indian seat or bench, also designates a characteristic quality of the thing, viz. "movable", but in order to express this quality the Arawak

resorts to making an imitative gesture with the organs of speech. The loose
or free movement of the tongue (the loose or free part of the organs of
speech) which causes the *l* sound to be produced, is consistently used to
indicate the principle : willing (and able) to move, loose.

In this case there is a direct correspondence between (1⁰. the thing),
2⁰. the mental (emotional) image, 3⁰. the "gesture" of the organs of speech,
(4⁰. the sound).

A still more intimate connection may perhaps be seen in the root *le*,
talking, occurring in the words Sm. *a-leledü-*, durch einander plaudern, G.
lŏlŏ-ka adia-hü, he contradicts, S. *a-llepeikattoa*, Sm. *a-lllepekattoa*,
angeben, verklagen, verklatschen, in gutem und bösem Sinne, es sei wahr
oder falsch, S. *ue-llerukku*, B. *areroko, ireroko*, mouth (*roko*, fixed place),
a rather new word, § 183 ! B. *lihi k-areroko-ci*, this babbler, G. *tata
lŏ-léroko*, he is impertinent.

In a similar way the act itself is imitated in the roots of the words G.
da-thúnda, I cough, *da-čida*, I sneeze *da-ěerådoa-ka*, I yawn, *da-raráida*, I
belch, *d-iwíwida-ka da-leroko abu*, I whistle (with my mouth), *a-thethédi-n*,
to whisper, to whisper in the ear *(a-tekeda*, to advise), *·hatáta-η*, to stammer
(comp. also § 109, *hata*, to stick fast), *hŏkŏküli-šia de*, I hiccup (*hadülikülí-
šia de̜*, I have an eructation), Sm. *a-hüküdü-n*, to clear one's throat.

Sometimes it seems as if the sound results from pointing out the
representative part of the organs of speech ; this may be the case in A. M.
*enene, tongue, and in *ana (-ka, -ku)*, the midst.

Further we have a strong suspicion, that the Arawak in saying *bu*, thou,
ebebe, older brother, etc. (Vocative), *aba*, other, one, a, etc., indicates the
person by sending a mild explosion in his direction. The *f* or *p* in S. *pahia*,
Sm. *poi*, interjection of astonishment, and in *sipe*, bitter (*seme*, sweet).
G. *fȳ(h*, a thing no longer fit for use, might be the blowing away of the
undesired thing. The *m* in Sm. *emè*, interjection of astonishment, and
generally the *m* indicating hesitancy, might be the act of secluding oneself
from the unknown or dangerous. The movement of the lips in producing the
oa sound, by which the principle "self" is expressed, reminds one of an
instinctive withdrawal ("in itself"), and bears a slight resemblance to an
animal showing its teeth.

In a similar way the *h* is used to indicate "breathing out" (*ahakobu*, to
breathe), and as a gentle affirmation (*ahe*, yes) or deictic movement
(*n-aha*, these, *hu*, ye), and sometimes these functions merge into each other
(*ahaka*, to tell, to command, *-hu* forms abstracts, etc., *a(h)a-li-kibi*, joy).
Often the *h* only serves to put a slight emphasis on an initial vowel, and is
written in one vocabulary and omitted in the other (examples in § 111).

The feeling "uneasy, unquiet" is expressed by *onno, hunna* (§ 127, comp.
also Island Karib : he murmurs, *hom hom tiem l-ariá-ngle*, lit. *hom hom*
it-does he-speaks). The feeling "inner peace" is expressed by *ansi* (§ 80 ᵇ)).
Light is expressed by *a-li*, dark is expressed by *o-ri* (§ 126). Though each

of the component parts of these roots may be accounted for, they are also as a whole rather suggestive.

The use of the *d* to express a shock, appears to be almost a direct imitation. Examples : G. *dŏ(idŏ(i ka i*, he is limping, *hóɣoɣo dŏrŏrŏsi-(η*. B. *adedisaro*, earthquake, B. *a-dehada*, to be leaping, *adaridi*, to run, Sm. *dúbuli*, sting-ray, *issimuddu*, electric eel, Wyatt *eduólah*, a knife (Dudley *yeddola*, Sm. *jadolle*, Sagot *iadoala*, G. *yadoala ; oala*, a shiver, § 120 ᶜ)).

Closely related to this is the use of *d* in words like G. *miyu ŏ-dĭli*, a ship's anchor, and furthermore the Arawak *d*, expressing : will-power manifesting itself by remaining firmly established, standing, stiff ; "I" ; emphasis.

In Arawak the *r* is used to express : motion being impeded. $R = l + d$. and on account of this relationship, we can understand that often Arawak *d* ⁓ Island Karib *r*.

§ 185. See now the following synopsis of Arawak sounds :

i expresses (§§ ·2, 190) 1⁰. high tension, time is contracted, 2⁰. the pointlike aspect or central point ; when pronouncing *i*, 1⁰. the muscles of the tongue are tightened, 2⁰. the resonance chamber imitates a point in the centre ;

o or *u* expresses 1⁰. low, or negative tension, time is expanded, 2⁰. the periphery-aspect ; when pronouncing *o* or *u*, 1⁰. the tongue withdraws to the lowest position, 2⁰. the resonance-chamber imitates a hollow sphere ;

a expresses 1⁰. the regular flow of time, 2⁰. the world in its common, everyday aspect ; when pronouncing *a*, 1⁰. the muscles of the tongue relax, 2⁰. the cavity of the mouth takes on its natural form ; according to Steiner (71 a, b, c) the *a* is the natural means for expressing astonishment, "Ver-wunderung an der Sache" ; the Arawak *a*, indicating "the world in its aspect of continual change" agrees very well with this ; comp. also § 13 and the interrogative words, *ama, alika, alo*, § 139.

The *e*, which indicates something like : sickly, delicate, tender, lingering, quality, may really be felt as an *a* lacking health, or an *i* lacking energy.

The following consonants illustrate by degrees the contrast which we found to exist between the *k* principle and the *b* principle, and which we expressed by way of comparison by saying : "the *k* reminds one of 'creation at work', 'the idea or principle that becomes phenomenon', the *b* of 'the manner in which that which has been created manifests itself', 'the appearance' ".

H, k, passionless force :

h, gentle affirmation or emphasis ;

k, a strong force, making its appearance in a positive manner.

N, l, r, personality begins to appear, with a mild, innocent character : metamorphosed vowel + -*n*, the vague, an ending ;

n-, the neutral, a beginning, a continuation :

l, willing (and able) to move, loose ;

r, willing, but not able, to move, motion being impeded.

D, t, s, the personal will-power which already interfered in the *r,* appears, acts, and is checked, cumulates :

d, firmly established, standing, stiff ; forms causatives ;

t, motion directed towards an object, limited motion(with a touch of force) ; forms causatives ;

s, form, surface, shale or cuticle.

M, b, f, gentle feelings : timorous — placid — aspiring :

m, not daring, hesitancy, new, mild ;

b, a separate appearance, quiet, passionless ;

f, striving, aspiring, airily, lightly.

Furthermore the character of "pointing out" may be seen in : *s,* the scale or surface formed by the teeth ; perhaps the *m* in Sm. *ué-imihi-ruku,* the corners of the mouth, and A. M. **numa,* mouth ; also in *b,* the outer surface.

The character of imitating may be seen in : *f* or *p,* the pointed form of the protruding lips ; *d,* the tongue imitates or produces the vertical, the standing ; *t,* the tongue imitates or produces the horizontal, the moving.

N, l, r and *h,* see § 184.

Concerning the place where the sounds are formed, and tension and relaxation of the muscles of the tongue, there is also a relationship between the *d, y-* and *i* and between the *b, w-* and *u,* having its parallel in relationship in meaning.

§ 186. Words like R. *baiyari-shiri,* a certain fan-design, G. *unábu-se,* blindworm (§ 184), are of course deliberately invented compounds. But it seems scarcely possible that *(h)ala,* Indian seat or bench, has been quite consciously constructed from *a,* time-reality and *l,* loose, movable. The selecting of the "gestures" of the organs of speech in order to express different feelings and wishes, and the compounding of them into words, must be an intuitional, instinctive action.

The resemblance between Arawak and primitive Arawak-Maipure tends to the conclusion that these instincts are very persistent, and must be inherent in the nature of the people. They might be related to the instinctive, automatic imitating, which may be observed with young children, with monkeys, and with natives of Java suffering from the neurosis called "lata". In a wider sense it might be connected with the imitative tendency which we see in nature.

Now it is interesting, that a sound-symbolism in which the sounds represent something very similar to their meaning in Arawak, seems to be present not only in the Karib languages, but also to a certain extent in Dutch, French, etc. [1] ; sometimes we even find the same sequence of

---

[1]   And in African languages, see D. Westermann, Laut, Ton und Sinn in West-afrikanischen Sudansprachen, E. M. v. Hornbostel, Laut und Sinn, both in Festschrift Meinhof. Hamburg, 1927. (Professor Uhlenbeck was kind enough to draw the author's attention to these articles.)

sounds as in the Arawak word. Also the value of Arawak sounds corresponds more or less with the value of sounds as exposed by R. Steiner (71a, b, c).

We now begin to see, that there might be some reason for the special importance which the Arawaks, and many other peoples, attach to names.

Be that as it may, the important fact remains, that i n A r a w a k w e h a v e a w e l l - d e v e l o p e d l a n g u a g e, i n w h i c h t h e r e i s a n i n n e r a n d e s s e n t i a l c o n n e x i o n b e t w e e n t h e i d e a a n d t h e w o r d ²).

— In our discussion of Arawak speech, we have paid but scant attention to the sounds which result from the "gestures" of the organs of speech. But of course the auditive faculty plays an important part in the learning of speech, in guiding pronunciation, and perhaps also as an inner function which has something to do with the preparation of the word before it is pronounced. In this connection we may mention the sound-imitative words, of which Arawak possesses several, for instance *wakokwa*, a pigeon, *yohau*. a gnat, Sm. *húnnu-húnnu-li*, a bumble-bee (comp. Karib *were-were*. a fly).

Some other words, which may express a sequence of elementary principles, are so very suggestive, that they constitute as it were a link between built-up words and direct imitations. Examples : Sm. *a-ssürdü-*. *a-ssurrisürridü-*, to spin, to whirl the spindle, B. *a-soroto-*, to suck. *akoraka-li*, thunder, *a-fudi-*, to blow, *bili-bili-ro*, the lightning (comp. Jespersen. 65a Chapter XX Sound symbolism, "No wonder, then, that the Germans feel their word for 'lightning', *blitz*, singularly appropriate to the effect of light and to the shortness of duration"). See further the duratives, formed by prolonging a sound (action-words, *a* group), and the reduplications (§ 93).

---

¹) In order that no misunderstanding may arise, the author wishes to state that he did not seek for such a connexion.

The formation of the Karib verbs, suggested the idea, that in Arawak the *a* might also be the verb, indicating "time" or "happenings". Then the thought occurred, that the *i* and the *o* must have a different meaning from the *a*, and so on. Gradually it became clear that in a great many forms, each vowel and each consonant represents a certain principle, which is, roughly speaking, always the same. — The writings of H. Beckh have been of some assistance in finding the value of Arawak *s* and *n*.

It was soon apparent, that affinity between sounds is accompanied by an affinity between the value of those sounds, but only after reading L. Bloomfield's "An introduction to the study of language" (New-York), did the author hit upon the idea, that the Arawak in speaking. reproduces the thing or the event, by making a series of imitating "gestures" with his organs of speech.

This book was already in the press. when the writer for the first time read R. Steiner's lecture held at Penmaenmawr, August 26th, 1923 (11.71*b*, p. 33 ff.). and the articles of D. Westermann and E. M. v. Hornbostel. mentioned in note ¹), p. 240. It says much for the fundamental soundness of the explanations, that several investigators. working on different lines, come to similar (though not identical) opinions.

Of course we must not expect that the Arawak system of sound-symbolism represents the very earliest form of speech : moreover the author's description needs to be perfected.

Also : *k-okkituka-tu*, a thistle, in contrast with *maba*, honey ; *tata*, hard, in contrast with *bele*, soft, jelly-like, lame.

§ 187. Concerning the scale of consonants, we still venture the following remarks, by way of hypothesis.

The Arawak calls the lung Sm. *tutulla* = the deep (§ 122 c)).

His gutturals *h*, *(g)*, *k* have the value of the impersonal, of the spiritual, of a creative force ; comp. *ahaka*, to tell, to command, *oini ... iki*, Moxo *tikui-bo*, to rain.

The consonants *n*, *l*, *r*, *d* and *t*, which are formed by an action of the tongue, are used to express will-power and related ideas :

n, end-point pronoun III f., "a thing", *n(a)-* pronominal prefix III pl., *ie* (from an ancient form **ine*), end-point pronoun III pl., *-no* plural suffix human class, A. M. **n(u)*, I, me ;

l(o)-, pronominal prefix III m., *loko*, man, *-li*, *-ru* form substantives ;

d(a)-, pronominal prefix I, *di*, end-point pronoun I, *adaia*, to be a ruler, *ajia*, S. *adia*, to speak (this might also point to the "gesture"-character of speech, comp. *adi*, an appearance, § 173 a), *jia*, S. *dia*, as, like, § 88 a)) ;

t(o)-, pronominal prefix III f., *-ci*, *-tu*, suffixes forming agent nouns, etc., *tata*, hard, *tata ... o kona*, strong, *(hi)ti*, to desire, etc..

The *s* expresses as it were the cumulation of the creative forces, or of the will-power ; comp. *-sia*, the result of an action, etc., *siba*, rock, *isiroko*, flesh, *isibo*, face, *isi*, seed, *(i)sa*, child, egg. The word *(i)sa* is also used in order to indicate "sound", "good", „beautiful". It seems that the Arawak considers creation as being good, or even holy (§ 114 a) 4)).

In the series *m*, *b*, *f* we may feel the new life of the created, gradually unfolding ; comp *amaro*, to be afraid, *aburi*, to be ashamed, *ibara*, to be left, *a-fitikidi-*, to go forth, *da fa*, I will.

§ 188. It appears that the Arawak language discriminates between facts which form part of the central government of the cosmos, and facts which show independence or free-will ; the latter are distinguished by the particle *oa* (*ua* or *wa*).

To this last category belong, amongst others : *atenwa*, the beginning, *onnawa*, to choose, *o-loa*, heart, mind, *kidua*, truth, Sm. *a-buledu-nn-ua*, a source, a well (*a-buledi-*, to throw away, to lose), and further the "middle voice" of the Arawak verb. [May not this be also the origin of the middle voice in other languages ?]

The Arawak expresses "evil" by *wakaia*, lit. *wa*, the separate, the free-will, *ka*, strongly acts, *ia*, flowing out into time-reality ; the word might then depict pride, non-cooperation with the central government of the cosmos.

§ 189. a) The use of the particle *oa*, shows that independence or free-will is to the Arawak something worthy of special mention ; comp. also *b-oa*, abnormal appearance (§ 120 d)).

Related to *oa*, the separate, is the word *aba*, which means : that which has the aspect of the created, of a separate thing. The Arawak uses this word (with suffixes) as the numeral 1. He gets at the conception of 2 by dividing the one, of 4 by repeating the same process (§§ 152—155) :

b) The Arawak says : "they killed him" (*na-forra goba i*, lit. they-kill past-occurred him), but "fear occurred them" (*amaro goba yuho-li loko-no o-bora ie*, lit. fear past-occurred many men future-event them), and "you-with me" (*ho-ma di*, lit. your-humble place me), corresponding to English "they killed him", "they feared [the multitude]", "I am with you".

Evidently, the Arawak is not so strongly possessed by egocentric feeling, as the European.

For the Arawak the "person" is very important : he mentions it in cases where the European would deem this to be superfluous (§§ 10, 16 b), 19), and he has several kinds of pronouns (§§ 7, 44). But his pronouns, and generally also the object-words, are not oa forms (however : *o-koborokwa*. consciousness, § 120 g) 7)). Moreover, he depicts even the person par excellence, the "I", by elementary principles *(d-a, d-i)*, which also occur with the same meaning in the names of all kinds of other objects, actions, etc. It seems as if the consciousness of his own personality, his "I" feeling. does not essentially differ from the feeling evoked by a sensual perception or a remembrance.

In addition to this, we found that there are no sharp lines of demarcation between object-words, quality-words and action-words, and it seems as if in Arawak even object-words express qualities or describe events ;

c) From a) and b) we might perhaps conclude that the Arawak feels the cosmos, himself included, more or less as a whole ;

d) One cannot imagine that words as, for instance *ala*, a bench, *ororo*, earth, *furi*. a blade of grass, are the result of logic reasoning. Evidently the Arawak felt the salient qualities of these objects, and when he wanted to name them, his instincts or intuitions prompted him to put his organs of speech into such successive positions as evoked similar feelings.

The old Arawaks — this has already been discussed in § 20 — probably lived far more in the sphere of feeling and will-power than we do. To the sensitive creature, the world is all life and activity, and this may account for the fact that those same Arawaks whose language is so very systematic, logical, sincere and philosophical, before they were christianized, described the world in terms of gods, spirits, souls and magic forces.

Similar beliefs are found all over the world. It may be that they will cease even to seem absurd, when we succeed in interpreting them in the way they were originally meant. Comp. also the following extract from de la Borde's description of the Island Karibs : "Ils s'offencent quand on les appelle Sauvages, & qu'on leur dit qu'ils n'ont point d'esprit, & qu'ils vivent en bestes : Ils répondent que nous le sommes encore plus à leur égard, parce que nous ne vivons pas à leur mode : qu'ils ont leur science, & nous la nostre, comme si il y avoit deux façons de sçavoir les choses dans la vérité."

§ 190. One of the most important elements of the Arawak language, the discrimination between the *i* and the *u* principle, expresses the cosmic fact, that energy (or whatever we should like to call it) manifests itself in two forms : *u* or *o*, expanded, great, slow, inactive — *i*, contracted, small, quick, energetic ; also : *u* or *o*, fertile matter, the spirit in an enchanted form — *i*, the free spirit.

This cosmic fact is described with great clearness in Chinese philosophy (perhaps also in the Indian and in other philosophies).

In Arawak, we find :

u	*i*
great, space, the permanent, motionless, not changing (*w* vast, far away)	tiny, quick, instantaneous, free, principle, idea, intensively, accentuated (*y*, here)

[comp. *(u)* the slow current in places where the bed of a river is broad and deep, *(i)* the rapids and falls in places where it is narrow and shallow, *(u, w)* a curve or curved surface, the periphery, *(i, y)* the focus, the centre]

o-ri, dark	*a-li*, light
nokonne, sad, merciful	*a(h)ali-kibi*, joy
mule, to be drunk, *muri, muli (-ka)*, to be false	*mali, mari (-ko-ta)*, to be able, to know
oie, lazy	*imi*, willing
roko, female genital	*isin*, male genital
o-iyu, mother	*ici*, father
o-tu, daughter	*aiici*, son
o, u, female class	*i*, male class
o, u, nature class	*i*, human class
o-iyu (u-i-u), mother	*iwi (i-w-i)*, fruit
iwi, fruit, *o-tokoro*, flower	*isi*, seed
yu (generally *u*), moisture	*ikihi*, fire
ororo, earth	*adaili*, sun.

Something of a similar nature as the Arawak contrast between the *i*, (the *a*,) and the *u* or *o*, might be presumed in that which Trombetti (72, § 281 ff.) has described in his chapter Il fenomeno della polarità[1]). Comp. also de Josselin de Jong (66, 213) : "In Indo-Germanic, the higher class is grammatically characterised as active-transitive, the lower, on the other hand, as passive-intransitive".

§ 191. The following coincidences may be quite accidental, but yet it seems worth while to mention them :

a) Anguish, astonishment, they express by saying *aboko-(n-wa)* ... *ia*,

---

[1]) And perhaps in the contrasts found by D. Westermann (op. cit. p. 328) in West-African Sudan languages.

the soul (or principle of life) boils (§ 169 a) 2)). The soul is here considered as having the nature of a fluid. (Comp. also § 80 b), vexation, trouble, haste, *yula* or *yura* ... *ansi*, presumably : the soul is stirred).

The word *hiaro*, woman, literally expresses : soul-female thing, or life-female thing, and again in our enumeration in § 190, the female, nature and moisture (fertility) appear in the same class.

T, which is used to indicate the female or nature-class, also describes "flowing" (*ite*, blood, *a-ti-*, to drink, etc.), and the suffix *-ra*, used by women (§ 179) also appears in connexion with fluids (§ 107), whereas *si*, *se*, the suffix used by men, appears in words denoting matter, flesh (§§ 116, 115) ;

b) The female *(u)* principle we find in *Oriyu*, the virgin-mother, *aiomun*, heaven, *o-yu*, the animal-mother-spirits, in the water-female of the Taruma legend (Farabee, 41, 143), who became the mother of the human race, in the clan-system in which descent is traced through the mother, in the woman who caused man to descend to the earth (§ 167 b)), and in the woman whose inadvertency caused the big flood, and who became an *oriyu*, a water-spirit (§ 216).

The male principle we find in *Harliwanli*, the saviour (sun-deity ?).

APPENDIX

Information collected in Surinam in 1907 and in 1928

I

§ 192. The author collected :

in 1907 vocabularies, communicated by an Arawak woman at Albina ;

in 1928 a few words and forms, communicated by an Arawak woman at Zandery I ;

in 1928 a great many words, sentences, tales etc., communicated by the Arawak Johannes Baptist, assisted by his cousin Alphons, both from Mata.

The phonetic spelling, mentioned on p. 14 has been used, with the exception of §§ 202, 204, 212, 216—222 and parts of §§ 203 and 214, which have been written down by Baptist in the Dutch spelling ; in these the author has inserted hyphens according to the system adopted in this work.

Short sentences from which nothing new can be learned, have not been included in this work, and as a rule the Appendix does not contain such words etc., as have already been mentioned elsewhere in this volume.

§ 193. A few words of Sm., S. or B. they did not understand, or called them antiquated ; a few of the words collected on this occasion, do not occur with the older writers. The pronunciation approaches very nearly that of Sm.'s vocabulary (in which not all Arawak sounds can tell to full advantage, because Sm. does not use any special phonetic signs ; also the Moravians persistently write *p*, where nearly all other authors recorded *f*).

The following deviations from the language of the bible-texts have been met with :

a) The words are often abbreviated, for instance *to* ∼ B. *toho*. The following is often heard :

-n ∼ B. *-mun, -nro* ∼ B. *-muniro, -ron* ∼ B. *-robuin ;*

-m-bia, -m-bena, -m-bo ∼ B. *-n-bia, -n-bena, -n-bo ;*

-sa ∼ B. *-sia ;*

-kona ∼ B. *-koana, -dona* ∼ B. *donwa ;*

-(n or *-(η* ((means : indistinctly articulated) ∼ B. *-n ;*

b) *ma-či, ma-tho* ∼ B. *mi-ci, mu-tu ;*

　mihira ∼ B. *mahera,* Sm. *meherên ;*

　ka-yara and *ka-raya* ∼ B. *ka-raia ;*

　kapása (sword) ∼ B. *kaspara ;*

c) In the stories *bia* (§ 39) and *fa* (§ 5) are often used where the English does not use the future ; *ya* ∼ B. *ia* is also very often used ;

d) Very often the suffix -da is used, probably for the sake of emphasis (comp. § 47A). Also *thada* is often met with ; perhaps this expresses : th, it, a, is, da, emphasis. The end-point pronoun, however, always comes at the end of the sentence :

e) The word *baikia* which is frequently used, possibly means "there happened", or "there was" ;

f) As an end-point pronoun III f. *no*, as well as *n* or *η* is used.

§ 194. As much as possible the accent has been marked and indicated by '. Let us, however, not lose sight of the fact that the words, sentences and texts have been pronounced under abnormal conditions, whereby the accentuation may have been influenced. Probably this is the cause that in words that have been separately given, the accent often falls on the first syllable, even if this is a pronominal prefix (the same is the case in Sm.'s vocabulary). Apparently the accent never falls on suffixes such as *-či, -tu-, -li* etc.

II. VOCABULARY, ETC.

In these lists of words, the following abbreviations and signs are used :
cr. creole (Surinam "taki-taki" or "negro-English") ;
Sp. Spanish ;
r) regional word ;
s) sound-imitative word ;
u) origin (etymology) uncertain.

§ 195. **The body**

blood (as a part of the body)	*ü-thena*
„ (outside the body)	*ü-the, úe-ti*
my heart beats	*da-lóa dŏda*
„ pulse „	*d-akubo-η dŏda*
vein	*ü-the boná* (blood-path)
nerve	*dá-üküra* (roots ?)
bone	*ú-bona, dá-buna*
marrow	*da-bona-loko-do*
joints	*d-ándaka*
skin	*da-da, bú-ęda*
nail (finger or toe)	*da-báda, dá-băda*
hair on the skin	*da-bára-kona*
hair of the head	*da-bára, da-bála*
crown of the hair	*da-bára si-kéru*
a man with curly hair	*kakáliči*
eyebrow	*da-kúsa bóna bara, u-kuši bála*
eyelash	*d-akíti, d-ikiti*
moustache	*da-tíma*

beard	*da-tála-tīma*
the hair under the armpit	*bára-daná-ǫoko*
the hair on the pubes	*da-yóǫo-roko*
flesh (of a man, an animal, a fish)	*široko*
fat	*d-ikíhi*
saliva (in the mouth)	*úraroni, dá-urarun*
spittle (outside the mouth)	*da-kúi*
to spit	*a-kŭĭdi-(n*
tear	*d-ikíra*
I perspire	*hadufuči ka de*
urine	*éhĕ*
I pass water	*da-daká ka, da-daháka* u), A. M. § 182, 149C)
I go to stool	*d-ikiá ka*
matter, puss	*t-ŏ́kŏ*
a wound that matters	*šúbuli*
head	*da-ši*
forehead	*da-šiba-roko*
brain	*da-ši-toko*
eye	*d-akuši*
eye-ball	*d-akúši káleme* (my-eye-shine)
ear (the lobe)	*d-ádikĕ, d-adíki*
earlap	*d-adikĭ yodo-n* (my-ear hanging)
ear (organ of hearing)	*da-kúyuko*
ear-hole	*da-kúyuko hólai*
nose	*da-širi*
nose-hole	*da-širi hoolai*
nose-interior	*da-širi-lóko*
cheek	*da-oála-ši*
upper lip	*da-léroko-ú-da*
lower ,,	*da-léroko-ú-da únabo-maria*
corners of the mouth	*d-imi-roko*
upper jaw	*ayumú maǫia tála*
lower ,,	*da-tálȧ-bona*
chin	*da-tála-bóloko*
opening of the mouth	*da-lé-roko*
tooth	*d-ári, b(ü-ári*
fronttooth	*d-ári-šibo*
backtooth	*d-ár-ina*
tongue	*da-yé*
uvula	*da-matabára* u)
larynx	*da-yúlĭ*
throat	*by-yurĭ-roko*

neck	*da-nólo*
breast	*dá-lua, da-ló-bana*
rib	*d-ádura*
pap (man or woman)	*dyó, dá-dyo*
belly	*d-adibéyu*
back	*d-ābo*
lower back	*dá-iri*
backbone	*d-ādo-būna*
collar-bone	*da-rẹ-sáλi*
hip	*da-tába*
buttock	*iná-sa*
anus	*d-éna-ko-léroko* (my-behind-mouth)
lunge	*da-thúla*
breath	*d-ākubo-η*
heart	*da-wášina*
stomac	*da-té-firo*
,,	*ü-tē-hŭ*
liver	*da-bána*
milt	*da-dabă(η*
bile	*da-kúlira*
bowel	*ü-te-íbera, da-té ibira*
kidneys	*da-búλiu* u)
bladder	*d-ēkĭ*
penis	*d-íwisi*
testicle	*b-íwisi loko-do*
sperm	*da-kχẹ*
pudenda	*dá-roko*
womb	*da-sá-kĭ*
embryo	*da-té-loko-koan-ši*
amniotic fluid	*le-ñále* u)
amnion	*l-éke*
placenta	*ló-ba* u)
navelstring, navel	*kóyo*
to cohabitate	*nánika* (they do ?)
she menstruates	*kači-nanika|n* 1)
,, ,,	*tō čikoá-ka to hiáro* (at the house is that woman)
he keeps the couvade 2)	*lo-mayaudo* (he keeps quiet)
shoulder	*d-adŏna-ina, d-aden-éna*
arm	*d-adŏna*
biceps	*da-kuliyĭ*

---

1) According to the ancient Arawak belief, the moon is cohabitating with the woman ; see also § 134 *f*) 1), and R. 19a, Sect. 198.

2) If a man did break the couvade, the child would be ill.

arm-pit	*d-adŏna-lóko*
elbow	*d-adŏna sále*
cavity under the elbow	*d-adŏna-kuyule-roko*
wrist, lower arm	*d-a χabo-kóto*
palm of the hand	*d-akhabo-róko*
I have a wound in the palm of my hand	*d-akháb-roko kakóloko-ka*
I make a hollow of my hand	*d-akhábo o-lokotoá*
the lines of the hand	*d-akhábo-roko th-üyada-η*
back of the hand	*d-aχabo-dyáko*
finger(s)	*d-akabo-ibíra*
I thumb	*da-kóna* (my instrument ?)
II index	*da-kŏlŏka-kóna, da-kiλika-koana* (my-stretch-forth-instrument)
III	*anakabó-koro d-akabo ibira* (middle my-finger)
IV	*da-khóle denăn-koro* (my little finger arm-thing)
V	*da-khóle, da-kúle* (my weak)
thigh	*da-bukŏ*
knee	*da-kóro*
hollow of the knee	*d-adana-kuyŏlé-roko*
lower leg with foot	*ú-turu*
lower leg	*d-adáne, d-adána*
shin-bone	*d-adán-siri*
calf of the leg	*d-ibíto-n-a* ᵘ)
ankle	*da-sále*
heel	*da-iána*
foot	*da-kuči*
sole of the foot	*da-kúti-roko*
upper part of the foot	*da-kúti-áboroko*
toe(s)	*da-kuti ibíra*
I—V	same names as the fingers
mouth of a horse-fly	*tu-lēroko*
a bird's bill	*kudibyi iširi*
fish-bone	*hīme búna*
skin of an insect	*th-éke*
horn	*ó-koa, to-koá*
comb of a cock	*kálina sepére* ᵘ)
crest on a bird's head	*tu-kúlise, kalina kuliši*
tail (of a monkey, a bird, a fish)	*íhi*
wings of a fly	*tú-dena*
legs ,, ,, ,,	*tu-kuti*
fin	*hime u-wádawáda*
pincer of a crab	*to-kóna, kua-kóna* (its-instrument ?)

egg of a butterfly	*kambána-uesa*
white ant-hill	*kumučiri*
the white ant-hill emits foam	*kumučiri kúta, ká-kuta-či-ma-ru árara*
cow-milk	*baka udyūre, baka udyo ura*
honey	*mába*
wax	*makório tika* (bee excrement). *fíntyika* (airily excrement), *mába fé* (honey rubbish)
bird's nest	*kudibiyu tíboko*
daylitter of a stag	*kuyála bitóla, ts-ibitúla* ᵘ)

§ 196. **Man**

Some names of Arawak families :

Uraši
Uraši yúbutá-na } (belong to a group of 7 families)

Káluafu
Kabubú-na } (belong to a group of 8 families)
Úralike-na

Sìwana-no
Atyukána-no } (form a group)

Arámuküito
Besoǎ (§ 224)
Hayáwafo
Máratákayu
Nikériyu
Kabolefu or *Kabólena*
Sábayu ; these people are said to be descendants of a group of Indians who are neither Arawaks nor Karibs, who in the disturbed times when these tribes were continually at war, have left their abode at Saba, and mixed with the Arawaks. Saba is said to be "an island in Central America" (the Dutch island Saba ?).

§ 197. **The household**

village	*ašikwá-hŏ*
(my) house	*da-šikwa*
house	*báhü(ŏ*
house of the medicine-man	*tokai* [Brett *bo-tokaini,* thy closet. *lo-tokaini,* the (his) secret chambers (Mt. VI. 6. XXIV. 26 ; ʳ)? Kaliña *tokai.* Tupi *tokaya,* a hiding-place where one lies in wait when shooting game. a poultry-house.]
„ „ „ „	*ká-takára t-a báhü* (§ 104 ᵉ)

temporary shelter	bána-bo
deserted village	bahŏ ŏdiki (house-trace)
thatch	th-ádà (§ 109 Sm. adu, parasol)
Indian bench	hála
(my) hammock	da-kūra, da-kúla
canoe (coorial)	kuliála
paddle	nálihe, nāle
steering-paddle	bokódo-kona
a ship's rudder	mīyo bokodo-kona
(my) pole	da-čirikídi-kuána
a ship's sail	miyu wéla-n, thŏ-wĭla
,, ,, anchor	miyu ŏ-dĭlĭ
bow	simárabo
arrow	simála
,, with bamboo or iron lanceolate head	siparáli
arrow with iron point	wayakáši (§ 117 b)?)
,, ,, three prongs	sárapa
,, ,, wooden barbs	širita
,, ,, loose iron point	hotómo u)
,, ,, blunt head	mároa
,, ,, ,, ,,	t-abolokó-do
the feathers of the arrow	šimal-o-koáma (arrow-hat?)
poisoned arrow	urali (§ 182, 2)
blowgun ; arrows for blowgun	súdi
club	múši
broad wooden sword	sapakána
European sword	kapása
cutlass	kasipáọa
old stone axe	ọóli u)
axe	báọo, bálu
knife	yadoála
gun	arakabúsa
gunpowder	kúlabáọa
cartridge	arakabúsa o-lokó-do
I will charge the gun	arakabúsa da-lokóto ɸa
scissors	ili-kóana
razor	dri-koána
nail	påtåtåli
needle	akósa
bell	kampána
watch	kasákabo č-ikisi [day-time (signal)]
telephone	ɸaleto üdya-kóna (stranger-speak-instrument)

telephone	*kalĕ́-loko (-koro?) th-üdyá-kona* (quick its speak-instr.)
bycicle	*fáleto to-koná-kona* (stranger its-go-instr.)
automobile	*kále-kóɡo faléto akoná-koná* (quick stranger go-instr.)
chain	*kaɡéna*
padlock	*silótoɡo wayurĭ* [lock (resembling a) tick]
lock, key	*silótoɡo* (cr., from Dutch slot, sleutel)
,,	*tẹ-tatade-kắno* (its-securing-instr.)
pair of pincers	*ardĭtĭkĭtĭ-kona* (bite-cause-instr.)
airplane	*aiumún-di koná-koro faléto kanan* (high go-thing stranger instr.?)
steamship	*ikī-bo koná-koro mīyu* (fire-with go-thing ship)
man-of-war	*kaimá-ɡin mīu* (wrath-stop ship?)
telescope	*adŏkŏ̆-kona* (see-instrument)
fish-trap	*tambo* (bowed, § 73 b) 9)?)
bait for a fish-hook	*búde ména*
field	*kabúya*
my field	*da-kubaη*
cassava-bread	*káli*
European bread	*brĕde* (cr.)
,, ,,	*fáleto kháli* (stranger cassava)
farina	*kuák* r)
starch	*háɡu*
tapana, fermented drink	*kašíri*
strong paiwaru	*kari-tu ü-ta-hü* (painful beverage)
,, ,,	*tata-tú* ,, (strong ,,
rum	*sópi* (cr.)
strong rum	*kari-kóro sópi* (painful rum)
kassiripo, pepperpot	*kēri*
salt	*pámu* r)
barbecue, rafter	*yúɡada*
fan	*wáliwáli*
earthen pot	*duádo*
big earthen pot	*kána* (cr.)
earthen dish	*kárubu*
spatula, stirrer	*hálalu*
cassava grater	*samaλi*
,, squeezer	*yóro*
,, sieve	*mánali*
mortar	*háko*

pestle	háko-ére-či (mortar-husband)
knapsack	wăyali
basket, trinket-box	bórodi, bólodi
cotton	yáho, yahu
cotton-spindle	kírōdoli
silk-grass	ŏkŏli, ŏŏkili
a ball of cotton thread	kunulíma ʳ)
tobacco	yūli
a cigar that is ready for use	yūli síribidá-sa
covering of a cigar, made from the leaf of the manicole palm	wūina
cigar used by the medicine-man	sīribi
European cigar	yūλi a-maǫitá-sa
comb	bálida, balĭda
mirror	dikī-kuana, adekŏ-kona (see-instrument)
crab-oil	kalába-kihi (crab-tree fat)
painting of the face	úmbali ᵘ)
down for adorning the hair	mólise ʳ)
feather headdress	kárusa
hat	kuáma, kwa(uma
nose-feather	na-širi-loko-do
garter of the Kaliñas	to-kolo-loko-do
woman's apron	kiwéyu
clothing	bokóloko (cr. or Dutch "broek", trousers?)
shoe	sapátu
bamboo flute	béyuka ᵘ)
,, ,,	baladakor ᵘ)
,, ,, (small)	tílili ˢ)?
,, ,, , a kind of sliding-trumpet	sĕnde ᵘ)
panpipe	λēru ˢ)?
tortoise-shell, musical instrument	héruhéru ˢ)?
rattle of the medicine-man	maráka
church-organ	ʄaléto béyuka (stranger flute)
,, ,,	,, aikitá-kona (str. music-make-instrument)
map of a country	hólolo ǚiya (earth-picture)

§ 198. Nature

sky, heaven	hayúmu
cloud	uraro, ulálå
haze	ulálo-tikidi-η (cloud falling)
fog	uraro-u-kili (§ 130 ᵃ))

rainbow	*yauále, yáwali*
,,	*oni simalábo* (rainbow)
rain	*ūni*
it rains hard	*uni kyá masoŋ*
drizzle	*uni uribita* (rain dirt ?)
thunder	*kúlakani* [s])?
lightning	*bélebelíru*
sun	*hadáli, hádali*
eclipse of the sun	*hádali ōdo-n* (sun dies [1]))
the sunlight	*hadáli kŏndŏ̆-n*
,, ,,	*hadáli kumolokoto-n*
the sun shines	*te-kŏnda-tĭ hādaλi*
the sun shines in the house	*hádali kuindá-te bahü o-loko-nro*
moon	*káči*
eclipse of the moon	*kači ōdo-n* (moon dies [1]))
full moon	*kači kóroboda*
waning moon, dark moon	*kači ulikada-ká* (moon darks)
new moon	*kači ka-iára* (moon appears)
star	*wīua*
Milky Way	*wåya-naka-či bonaha, waya-nake-či bona.* (clay-carriers path) [2])
Pleiades	*wīwa yó-koro* (star many-thing ?)
Hyades	*kama-tále* (tapir-jaw)
Orion	*ma-buhkú-λi* (without-thigh-person)
belt of Orion	*katálu-kuya* (tortoise star-spirit)
Scorpion(?), lower part	*warubuši* [u])
,, upper ,,	*kasóroa-kuya* (fish Anableps st.-sp.)
Southern Cross	*hitsi-kuya* (currassow st.-sp.)
Great Bear	*ánula-kuya* (heron st.-sp.)
morning-star, evening-star, Venus or (and) Jupiter	*wálukuma* [r])
Halley's comet, 1910	*wīwa k-ī-koro*
one month	*ába kači*
,, week	*aba Sondaka* (one Sunday. cr.)
,, day	*ába kasákabo*
dry season	*makarellike* [u])
long dry season	*hádali-ka* (sun-when)
short rainy season	*šo-koro uni-ka* (small-thing rain-when)
,, dry ,,	*awora-dá-li-te* (§ 161 ; *awora,* a certain palm)
long rainy ,,	*firo-koro unébera* (great-thing swamp)
,, ,, ,,	*firo-koro ūni* (,, ,, river)
morning	*mauča*

[1]) An eclipse arises from a conflict between sun and moon ; see also R. 19a. Sect. 195-202.
[2]) The way spirits went ; R. 19a, Sect. 205 ; B. 5d, 107 : D. S, 343 : Pen. 17a, I. 105.

noon	wá-n-dali, wa-n-dáli (wa-mun hadalı, § 161 d))
afternoon	bakĭlama
evening	kasákoda
midnight	kasákod-anáka
fire	ikíhi
spark	ikíhi tháro u)
smoke	kuλéli
charcoal	budálilisi
ash	bálisi
fire-wood	ikíhi o-kódo
„ ; my f.w.	imehe ; da-íme kódo
the air around us	må-u-kili (§ 130 a))
wind	awadúli
water	oni-abo
river	ƒiro-to úni
a small river, a creek	oni-khaη
tributaries of a small river	th-údaku u)
a source	hóǫoǫo koboǫokwá-ǫi to oni-ábo u- bunáha (earth among-thing the water's path)
high water (in the river)	wuini-ábu hēda-ka (water very when)
the water of the river flows to .the sea)	to oni-abu oni loko-área mála bára-nro
current of a river	wuini-abo maladi-n
strong current	malali
rapid	wuini-ábu sórokodo-n (water spouting)
high waterfall	ƒiro-to wuni-ábu sórokodo-n
„ „	málali-dókoto (fall-grandfather)
whirlpool	tę-káikai
the small waves caused by a waterfall or by a moderate wind	sibá-ṣibá-ru
the bend of a river	thę-debó-loko (its-waterside-inside)
water-side	un-élebo, th-élebo
landing-stage	amudü-kĭle
mouth of the Surinam river	Sulináma iima-loko
upper „ „	„ ši-roko
swamp	un-ebera
swamp or pool	kiraha
pool or puddle	kulisa r)?
sea	báǫa
sea-shore	balá-lebo
the sea has waves	bára oǫomurida-(n

the sea is rough	*bára k-áima-n*
,, ,, roars (surf?)	*bára kaľŏkakŏdo(n, kalŏkalŏdoa(ŋ* (sea curling, § 134 cᴬ)?)
spring tide	*t-iſhírota-n* (*iſiro*, great)
neap ,,	*t-ušukuta-n* (*isogo*, small)
incoming tide	*bára kodó-no* (sea entering)
outgoing ,,	,, *kuyo-na* (sea returning)
island	*kairi*
the ground	*unabo*
mountain	*hololo*
mountain-top	*holólo ši-n*
rock, stone	*šība*
sand	*motóko*
clay	*wáya, uáya*
quartz	*halira-to šiba* (white stone)
a crystal of quartz	*sibŏ kalĭmĭ* (stone shine)
forest	*konóko*
savanah	*kaláo*
a bridge	*abonáta* (bone, or path become ?)
a ditch	*háčia* (B. aciga)

§ 199. Animals

animal (four-footed)	*kuta, kutá-hŏ*
howling-monkey	*ituli*
couata-monkey, Ateles	*hádafe, ádafĭ* (tree-decay ?)
monkey, Cebus	*ſudi* (§ 182, 78, quick-one ?)
,, , Chrysothrix	*kaboaši* (§ 182, 78, with-abnormal-head?)
,, , Pithecia leucocephala	*húa* ᵘ)
,, , ,, chiropotes	*bísa* ᵘ)
,, wanaku, Pithecia sp.?	*hóloe* ᵘ)
,, Nyctipithecus	*wísęwísę* or *wi-wála* ˢ)
sackewinki monkey, Hapale	*siǫíǫe* ʳ) or *ŏsúĭtŏ* (French ouistiti)
bat	*bŭiri, búhüri* (§ 182, 79)
,, ,big species	*waǫu-maká(nre* ᵘ)
jaguar	*aróa ; kabadáǫo* (with nails); *mabúledan šibo-ro* (un-pointed face)
puma 1.	*kuyáǫa u-ǫuá-te* (deer tiger)
2.	*kaboánama u-ǫoá-te* (monkey Crysothrix t.)
tiger-cat 1.	*kulí-ǫua-te* (rat t.)
2.	*laba-roá-te* (paca t.)
3.	*abúya-roá-te* (bush hog t.)
4.	*dódole aǫoá-te* (bush hog t.)
5.	*ſirobéru aǫoá-te* (tapir t.)

6.	*háka-ǫoa* (aira-t.)
7. (hunting in herds)	*warakabe aǫoa-te* (trumpet-bird t.)
dog	*péro* (Sp.)
savanah-dog, Ictyon	*ualíro* (§ 182, 81)
aira, Galictes barbara	*háka* ᵘ⁾
otter	*asíro* ʳ⁾
1., big species	*aširu firobéro*
2., small ,,	*saǫóǫa* ᵘ⁾
Procyon cancrivorus	*krabu-dágo* (cr. crab-dog), *koa-péro(η* (crab-dog)
coati, Nasua socialis	*kíbihi* ʳ⁾
squirrel	*kálio, káǫiu* ᵘ⁾
rat, mouse	*kúli, kulihí*
porcupine	*aǫóǫo*
acuchi	*hadúǫi* ʳ⁾
aguti	*fukuléru*
paca	*lába*
capybara	*kibiwáǫa, kibiola, kibiole* ʳ⁾ (§ 182, 86)
sloth	*uthábo* ᵘ⁾
,, 1. Bradypus tridactylus	*háu*
,, 2. Choloepus didactylus	*walimédu* ᵘ⁾
armadillo, 1. giant do.	*baǫakatá-yu* (small a.-mother) or *waǫoǫóima* ʳ⁾
2.	*yese-érï*
3.	*yési* (§ 182, 87)
4.	*báǫakata* ᵘ⁾
5.	*kayudúkuli* ᵘ⁾
ant-eater, 1. big species	*tamanoa* ʳ⁾
2.	*walíti* ʳ⁾
3. Cycloturus didactylus	*wáliti maka(ηro*
opossum	*yawáǫe* ʳ⁾
horse	*ási* (cr.)
deer, 1. Cariacus rufus	*kuyáǫa*
2. ,, savannorum	*béyu* ᵘ⁾
3. ,, simplicicornis	*wiribisíri* ᵘ⁾ (the word implies "small", "quick")
goat	*krabíta* (cr., Sp.)
sheep	*skápu* (cr.)
cow	*báka* (Sp.); *kakoáro* (with-horns); *kayulēru* (with-larynx or throat)
tapir	*kama* : *firubéru, fürẹbéru, pirubéru* (big belly ?); *katóroro* (with-feet); *kainako* (with-rump), *kúlihi* (rat, § 183)
tame pig	*porku* (Sp.)

bush hog, peccary, taitetu	abuya or matúla (§ 182, 89)
,, ,, , taiasu	kēerun (stinking, or navel-thing ?) or dódole (stampeding, § 184 ?)
manati	koyumóǫo
dolphin	kásekuya
bird	kudibiyu
parakeet, 1.	širiširi ᵘ) ¹)
2.	šikišiki ᵘ)
3.	kirekíre ʳ)
small parrot, 1.	solisóli ᵘ)
2.	kúǫiakúǫia ʳ)
3.	yaleyaléro ᵘ)
4.	kayakáya ᵘ)
5.	bálǐsi ᵘ)
green parrot, Amazone, 1.	kulewáke ʳ)
2.	saláma ʳ)
ara, 1. red	káro ʳ)
,, 2. blue and yellow	káλaλa ʳ)
3.	kúyali ʳ)
,, 4.	aléru ᵘ)
,, 5.	wáyęwáyę ᵘ)
toucan, 1.	buǫádi (bill-strong ?)
2.	šíro ᵘ)
3.	yánakáli ʳ)
Coccyzus, 1.	hikaǫuána ᵘ) ²)
2.	hikanúǫi ᵘ)
Crotophaga major	húye ᵘ)
kingfisher, 1.	sakasákali ʳ)
2.	kalasúli ᵘ)
3.	unitíbiǫi ᵘ)
goatsucker, 1.	wåkoláyu ʳ)
2.	kokobéru ᵘ)
3.	sipío ᵘ)
4.	kakuádabayo ᵘ)
humming-bird	bímiti ; (furthermore each sort has its particular name)
woodpecker	hodódi (hanging, § 122 ᵉ⁾ ²⁾, or ˢ⁾ ?); there are six sorts, each of which has its particular name.
eagle	hau baǫíǫi(a (hau. sloth)
caracara, Ibycter aquilinus	búlitata (§ 166 ᶠ⁾)

---

¹) Probably many names of parrots are sound-imitations : the reduplication either imitates the repeated screams, or it describes a pair, or a flock of these birds.

²) This bird produces two different sounds, and so presages good or evil.

condor	*anuanŏ̆ áɾoko(η* ᵘ)
vulture, Cathartes	*anoāne, anoána*
owl	*moɾokódi* ʳ)
„ , 1. big species	*áɾŏ̆* ᵘ)
2.	*kaiháiɾo* ᵘ)
3.	*maláro* ᵘ)
(there are several other species)	
rice-bird	*tiɾiɾiáne* ˢ)?
kiskedee, Tyrannus	*itiki* ˢ)
mocking bird, Icterus, 1.	*búiña* ᵘ)
2.	*bokoɾoli* ᵘ)
3.	*asáwako* ʳ)
4.	*iábani* ᵘ)
swallow, 1.	*solóya* ʳ)
2.	*samália* ᵘ)
bemtevi, Lathria cinerea	*ʃayeʃáye* ʳ)
Cotinga sp. (?)	*ŏ̆ɾikako* ᵘ)
pigeon	*wakukuá* ʳ)
1., big species	*yabúλe* ᵘ)
2.	*wakúkua* ʳ)
3.	*wiɾu*
4.	*adíri* ᵘ)
5.	*mália* ᵘ)
partridge, Odontophorus guianensis	*dolokwálu* ʳ)
fowl	*kalina, karina* (Sp.)
curassow	*hǐči* (§ 182, 94)
marudi, Salpiza	*marúdi* ʳ)
„ , 1. big species	*marúdi ʃirę́béru*
2.	*kolók* ᵘ)
Ortalis motmot	*káloba* ʳ)
Penelope pipile	*koló* ʳ)
maam, Tinamus	*mámu* ʳ), or *kasáleru* (with-elbow, because in a sitting posture they, as it were seem to rest on the elbow)
frigate pelican (?)	*wárakána* ᵘ)
flamingo (or red Ibis?)	*kórokóro* ʳ)
Ibis infuscata, 1.	*koɾokóɾobudyiro* ᵘ)
2.	*kaléo, kaléu* ᵘ)
Mycteria americana	*jáuru* ʳ)
heron, 1.	*anula*
2.	*sáumaru* ᵘ)
3.	*wakála* ʳ)
4., bittern, Tygrisoma	*hónoli*
5., bittern	*tókoli* ᵘ)

trumpet-bird	*waǫakába* ᵘ)
sun-bird	*wáyakoya* (clay-shy animal; it makes a nest of clay)
water-hen, Aramides cayanea	*kótaka* ʳ)
duck	*ifa*
tortoise, 1. sea do.	*katálu* ʳ)
2.	*hikúli*
3. small bush do.	*alásu* (stool-form ?)
caiman,1. big species (not found in Surinam)	*arára* ʳ)
2.	*kaīkúči*
lizard, 1. Thecadactylus rapicaudus	*sóko-sóko aǫakwaíru* [cut off the root of its tail (which is supposed to be venomous)]
2. Polychrus marmoratus	*yēmoǫo* ᵘ)
3. Tupinambis nigropunctatus	*marǎ(nro* ᵘ)
4. iguana	*iuwana* ʳ)
5.	*sararę* ᵘ)
6.	*lobo* (§ 182, 99)
blindworm, 1., living in ant-hills	*kúseúyu* (*kuse*-ant mother)
2., living under the ground	*unábuse* (ground-worm)
snake	*ūri, wūri*
venomous snake	*ka-kári-to ōri*
land-boa	*mahǒléru* (not-rapid), or *khólekonáru* (weak walker)
water-boa	*kamódo, kamudu*
Coluber corais	*fukuléǫu úǫia, fukuléǫuǫia* (aguti-snaʀe, because its tail is yellowish, like an aguti's)
Oxybelis acuminatus	*yawokayorǐ* (? -snake)
Elaps	*makúǫakúǫa* ᵘ)
rattlesnake	*kasikì(nro, kasakéru* (with-egg-shell-snake ?)
bushmaster, Lachesis	*wadibéru* (big-belly, or long snake ?), or *konokosǐ* (bush-worm)
labaria, Bothrops atrox	*laba-uria* (paca-snake)
parrot-snake, Bothrops bilineatus	*kuliakáǫia* (parrot-snake)
toad	*šibéǫo* (§ 182, 100)
(there are many sorts, each of which has its particular name)	
big toad, Pipa americana	*arabáyu* ᵘ)

trog, 1.	*walekĭ* [u])
2.	*ádaba* [u])
(there are many other species)	
fish	*hīme*
Acanthicus	*wátawáta* [r])
eel	*ihíri*
electric eel	*šimodo, simadå*
Erythrinus Erythrinus	*waꝗápa* [u])
,, Unitaeniatus	*yaꝗáu* [u])
Macrodon Aimara	*ayumúꝗa* [r])
Mugil brasiliensis	*kweriman* [u])
perai, Pygocentrus, 1.	*úma* (§ 182, 104)
2. small do.	*kaliáši* [u])
Rhamdia sebae	*káši* [u])
Sciaena amazonica	*bášia* [u])
shark, 1.	*morokáimö* [u])
2.	*maruári* [u])
Silurus callichthys	*kaꝗiwàꝗu* [u])
,, Parkerii	*wiꝗokotóꝗi* [u])
sting-ray	*dúbuꝗi*
Torpon allanticus	*kumúꝗeda* (bright skin ?)
iridescent beetle, Euchroma gigantea	*kamayoli* (bright, § 129 [f]) ?)
sawyer beetle, Macrodontia cervicornis	*adūĭrŏ̃* (strong ?)
fire-fly; also: Fulgora lanternia	*yuλíwi* [tobacco (burning cigar) luminous point]
wasp, bee	*makóꝗio* [u])
1. umbrella-wasp	*budaléhe* (its nest has the form of a cassava-baking pan)
2.	*búꝗišiꝗi* [u])
3.	*buraburádo* [s])
4., bumble-bee	*ånằnåli* [s])
queen of bees	*kåyå* [u])
ant	*háyo*
1. Ponera clavata	*muniꝗi* (§ 182, 106)
2. hunter-ant	*háuꝗére* [u])
3. sauba-ant	*kóse* (§ 182, 107)
4. ,, ,, , other sort	*hárakúli* [u])
5. the ant which is used for the ant-test, § 210	*yóko* (strike, § 123 [c] [1])?)
6. ant living in the Cecropia	*fukę* [u])
7. ant, the nest of which is used for tinder	*foŋko-óyo* (tinder-mother)
8.	*walumúli* [u])

9. small black sugar-ant	*kásisi* (§ 182. 107)
10.	*kúlebéli* ᵘ)
11.	*mautĭ* ᵘ)
butterfly	*kambána* ʳ)?
caterpillar	*kumakáti* ᵘ)
pupa	*titíbadona* (§ 90 ᶠ))
gnat, 1.	*yuwáw* ˢ)
2., Anopheles	*kašiǫiǫo* (with snout that stings)
3. grey do.	*kathúliǫo* (with-dust)
mapire, Simulium	*maǫiu* ᵘ)
horse-fly, Tabanus	*alimúlimu* ᵘ)
fly, 1.	*mabúǫi* ᵘ)
2.	*mapáǫawa, máparoá* ᵘ)
3. (this sort stings)	*hánuba* (§ 124 ᵇ))
4.	*kabáuru*
jigger	*míbiki* (§ 58)
dragon-fly	*bibīri*
white ant, termit, 1. (which makes a sort of hollow passages)	*aǫáǫá* ᵘ)
2. (lives in decaying wood)	*haǫáǫa* ᵘ)
queen of the *aǫaǫa*	*tĭseŋ* ᵘ)
cockroach	*hokóko* ᵘ)
locust	*kuǫatáka* ᵘ)
grasshopper, 1.	*sikisiki* ˢ)?
2.	*fúti* (quick ?)
cicada	*líalia* ˢ)
louse	*uyĭhĭ*
centiped	*báyabo*
scorpion	*ananáka* ᵘ)
,, . 1. big species	*emenáli*
2.	*muláto* ᵘ)
spider	*aráia, aiára* [appears (suddenly) ?]
bird-spider, Mygale	*koáta* ᵘ)
tick	*wáyurĭ*
ticks, just hatched from the egg, in a heap	*maibúli* ᵘ)
bete rouge	*kuléme*
lobster, 1.	*isåǫo*
2.	*sále*
crab, 1.	*koá* ʳ)
2.	*saǫáǫá*
any worm	*üséhĭ*
periwinkle	*kuluboále*

§ 200. Plants

the stem of a tree ; tree ; wood	*ada*
the core of a tree	*thó-koba*
the wood between the core and the bark	*tho-má-koba*
bark	*úda*
root	*thŏ̆-kŏ̆ra*
,, of cane	*tíriti-duli*
buttress	*ada událĭ*
sprout	*t-iširi-loko móϱomóϱo* (§135 d) 2))
thorn	*yuϱua*
straight thorn	*tŏ̆-kŏ̆tŏ̆ka*
branch	*ada dínabå*
leaf	*to-bána*
flower	*tó-tokoro, to-thokólo*
fruit	*č-íwi*
seed	*t-iši*
a grain of maize	*mariš u-kuši* (maize-eye)
,, ,, ,, ,,	*mariši ari* (maize-tooth)
resin	*th-ŏ̆kŏ̆*
sap of a tree	*th-éloko*
a plant, a shrub	*abuĭnękará*
a maize-plant	*mariši daya*
a tobacco-plant	*yūli dáya*
liana, bush-rope	*míbi* (§ 58)
ananas	*nána* r)
annatto, Bixa orellana	*šírabuli* (flesh-paint ?)
avocado	*avokáti* (cr.)
bamboo, 1.	*hīwa* (§ 182, 127)
2.	*kamoáti* u)
banana	*manikina, mánikini* u)
Bauhinia	*hikúli múdi-kona* (tortoise-mount-in-strument)
bean	*kumáta* r)
breadfruit tree	*bredeboη* (cr.)
bullet tree, Mimusops balata	*búlue* (coloured ?)
cactus, Melocactus	*ka-kŏ̆tŏ̆ká-tu* (with thorns)
calabash-tree	*iwida-bali* (fruit-skin-*bali*)
cashew	*merei* r)
bitter cassava	*kali*
sweet ,,	*bosali* u)
red cedar, Cedrela odorata	*akúyali* (resembling a deer ?)
Clusia	*kof̣á* (§ 215, 17)
cocoa	*kakao* (cr. or r))

copaiva	*kopáiwa*
cotton	*yáhu*
silk- cotton tree, Ceyba pent-andra	*kúmaka* [r])
crabwood, Carapa guyanensis	*kálaba*
Bignonia Chica	*kalawíru, koláiro*
fishpoison, 1. Clibadium surinamense	*kunalí* (instrument, § 120 [a]) [?])?)
2. Euphorbia cotinoides	*kunapálu*
3. Longocarpus (liana)	*hayáli*
4. Tephrosia toxicaria	*yóro-kona-ŋ* (employed for a fish called *yoro* or *yarrau*, R. 19*b*, Sect. 212)
grass	*kaǫáu*
sharp grass	*yiroka* (shave ?)
greenheart	*wasiba* (very stone ?)
guava	*máliaba* [u])
hyawa, incense-tree	*hayáwa*
lana, Genipa americana	*lána* (§ 182, 121A)
leaf of life, Bryophyllum	*kála-bana* (scar-leaf)
letterwood	*buǫĭ kóǫo* (speckled ?)
lime	*lémone* (Sp.)
Long-John, Triplaris surinamensis	*yekuna* [u])
a sort of love-vine (Quamoclit pinnata?)	*kalubákulĕ* (coiler, § 108A)
Macrolobium acaciaefolium	*manáli-báli* (sieve-*bali*)
maize	*mariši*
Mammea americana	*mámi* [r])?
mango	*mā̃ña*
masusa, Renealmia exaltata	*masusa* [u])
Montrichardia arborescens	*yulika*
mushroom, agaric	*kamalasána* [u])
okra	*okru* (cr.)
orange	*arānsu* (Sp.)
paddlewood	*ayálolo* [spatula or stirrer (-wood)?]
palms: 1. Astrocaryum segregatum	*awara* [r])
2. Euterpe oleracea	*manaka*
3. Geonoma	*dáli* [u])
4. Ireartea exhorrhiza	*buba* (§ 182, 125)
5. Mauritia flexuosa	*ité, ītĭ* (§ 182, 123)
6. Maximiliana Maripa	*kokoliti* [u])

papaya	*papáya*
Para-nut, Bertholletia excelsa	*tútuka* [r])
pea-nut	*pīnda* (cr.)
Cayenne pepper	*háči*
plantain	*puǫatana* (Sp.)
wild plantain, Heliconia	*háliči-bana* [u])
sweet potatoe	*halitsi*
purpleheart	*kóǫobcǫéli* (red colour ?)
arrow-reed	*ihi*
basket-reed, 1.	*itíriti* (§ 90 [f])
2.	*mokóǫo* [u])
rice	*alési, rési* (cr.)
,,	*káǫau-wi* (grass-fruit)
ricinus	*melona* [u])
sapodilla	*sapatiya* (cr.)
silk grass, Bromelia	*uhikili, ŏkili*
Spondias dulcis	*pom siteri* (cr. or French pommier de cythère)
,, lutea, hogplum	*hobu* [u])
sugar cane	*sikalu* (cr. or Sp.)
taro	*taya* (cr.)
tobacco	*yuli*
tonka, Dipteryx odorata	*kumaru*
trumpet-wood, Cecropia	*uanasoro* [u])
vanilla	*kamaye*
wallaba	*wálaba*
yam (cr. "napi") Dioscorea trifida	*himikona*
,, (cr. "jam") Dioscorea cayennensis	*dolokwaru*

§ 201. Old forms, genteel forms, salutation

come here ! (old)	*b-akó-the yáha*
(modern)	*mira-ba-te,* or *mihíra-ba-te yáha*
(very polite)	*mihíra-ba-te yá-mara*
(when addressing a child of five years)	*kó-the,* or *kó-the yáha*
wives (genteel)	*iréi-no-či*
(ordinary)	*iréi-to-be*
give us this ! (old)	*bu-báto wa-ne*
(modern)	*b-ŏkŏlŏka-te wá-di,* or *b-okói-ba-te wá-di*
fetch that thing ! bring it here (old)	*ba-thé|no*
(modern)	*bú-kŏlŏka-te|no,* or *bú-ʃika-the|no*

come, and welcome them ! (old)	b-ákobā-the ye
(modern)	b-o(hodidá-té ye (from cr. odi, good-day)
greeting on arrival	mayáukwa b-á bo ? or mayáukua b-a bú ?, pl. mayaukua h-a bú ?
answer :	mayáukwa d-á bo !
greeting when meeting	sa-u-ka-kwa-bó (§ 130 a))
greeting on arrival	d-andá-bí-the, or d-andá-ya-bí-te
answer :	b-anda-ra-bí-te-khán ?
greeting when meeting early in the morning	himili-wábu súwe (very cold, friend)

(when addressing a person older than yourself, da-lŏkŏnči is used instead of suwe ; when the person is younger, sá-či is used)

| the younger one answers the older one : | hadiá-ke|t-a himili-wabu dúku-či (indeed, cold very, grandfather) |

§ 202. Sentences
(Dutch spelling)

good-day !	sa-wo-ka-kowa-bo-teh !
how are you ?	halika-dja-khan-koba ?
good evening !	sa-wo-ka kowa-bo bakkelaman !
where are you going to-day ?	halonro b-ose fa tanoho ?
I 'm going nowhere to-day	halonro khoro da-osa-ja-fa tanoho|da
I should like to visit you	hadjake da tiena to osa-tie-n b-iebitjiro
where have you been to-day, I have not seen you the whole day	haloron b-osa-bi tanoho, toh kasakabo m-addekhi-n da|ja d-a|bo
you are a virtuous man, that is why I like you so much	bji toda sa-tjina wadili da, kijadoma hadjake|d-a k-ansie-n bo
will you come with me a moment to the waterside ?	h-osa-the da-ma sjo-khanie onie rlebonro?
where have you been so long, I have been waiting for you a long time	halonro b-a|khana kebenan|da, d-aobada-ja mebenan khoro bo-bora
listen I have something to tell you	b-akanaba-teh amathali d-a ti-ka bo-moen
I like you so much	hadjake|da k-ansie-n bo
I have not seen you for a long time	wakharo khoro m-addekh-n da|ja d-a|bo
I have been hunting, but I have seen nothing to shoot	da-osa jokha-nro barlie-n, to-mora amah-khoro d-adekha da-jokho-n bija daba

I am so hungry	*hadja kha-ke|da-hammesja-n*
I want to drink	*da-tha-ti-ka*
I want to eat	*da-khota-ti-ka*
I am going to play	*da-bira-ʃa*
I shall go with you	*da-osa-ʃa ho-ma|kowa-n*
you are a deceiver	*bji ammrlida arlien* (§ 141)
you are also a liar	*bji mrlieka-tsi kie daba*
I cannot understand foreign languages	*ʃarletho dja-he khoro da-kanaba-ma*
I am so poor	*dai hadjake-ma kammenika*
men and animals are not alike	*khotah ma-thji kakhitsji khoro herreke-ka* (§ 104 b) 2))
what nice shoes you have	*wakhathora toh b-sapato-n daba*
the tide has come in	*barla kodowa-ja|da*
how wicked you are	*halimoro b-a wakhaja-n*
the sun is so hot to-day	*tanoho hadjake|tha hadalie there-n*
what bad weather this morning	*hadja|thaja abo-w-ka toh mawtsja*
men and women	*wadili-no ma-thsi hijaro-no*
the dog barks	*pero simaka*
the children cry	*na-simama-ka iebilie*
what do you talk the whole day	*hamaha-ron b-dja ka toh kasakabo*
I bore you	*hadja d-a-ja|da miteh tien b-iekiradie*
I have been ill	*kari-tsia koba da de*
what is your name ?	*hama b-ierie ?*
my name is difficult for you to pronounce	*mienka-kho ʃarletoh d-ierie hessa-n-bija no*
I am going for a walk	*da-jadowa-ʃa*
my foot hurts me	*da-kotti kari-ka*
the plant grows quickly	*tho abennekaraha borlo-ka* (§ 69 d) ?) *wabbedien*
I was out hunting and saw a big tiger advancing on me	*jokha-nro aba-ka* (one time ?) *da-ose-n kenda ʃiero-tho arlowa osa-teh d-iebitsji*
where is your gun ?	*halon-ka khana b-arrakabosa-n da ?*
have you also brought arrows with you ?	*b-siemarla abo ma-n-tsji kiekhana da bji ?*
we have caught much fish	*wa-othsjika-ja joho-ro hieme*
why do you want to stay here ?	*hama bija khana jaha ti-ka|da bo ?*
where is your right hand ?	*halomarija khana b-sa-marija b-khabo ?*
we shall see how it happened	*wa-dekha-ja ʃa-khana aba halika|th-a-n-ʃa balie-n*
he is still living	*kaki-kwa l-a-ja*
no, he is already dead	*manien l-oda-ja hibie-n*
I'm sorry	*kari-ja th-ańdi-n da-khonan*

walk a little quicker	*bo-kona kale sabo khanien*
the water flows	*oni abo mala*
the water is sweet (fresh)	*oni abo seme-ja*
I pass	*da-bali-ka-teh*
I go away	*da-osa-teh*
the birds fly in the air	*torah kodibijo-be moroda-ka ajomon-die*
I have no clothing	*ma-bokorlo ba da de*
have you already dined ?	*bo-khotho bie da ?*
I am going to town	*th-ojo-sikowa-nro da-osa-bo*
the trees bear fruit	*toh ada-be k-iwi-ja*
the fishes swim in the water	*toh hime-be tiema oni rakho-die*
do people act like fishes ?	*naha kakhitsji hime dja-ma|ma kikhana daba ?*
I am going fishing	*da-bokoto fa hieme-be*
are you not afraid ?	*m-amaro-n-ka khanada bo ?*
I am afraid of nobody	*hama koro boro hamaro-ka de*
I go hunting	*jokha-nro da-osa-bo*
where are you ?	*halonro ba bie da ?*
I have been nowhere	*halon-khoro da-ose bie*
come and see me	*bu-ddikhe ba-teh de*
I have heard of you	*dai kanaba-ja bu-khonan*
he lied when he said he would go	*ousoro l-a-ja da-ose-fa ma-n|da*
oh, what a liar he is	*ma. hadia l-a-ja merlieka-n|da*
we shall go thither	*wai ose-ja-fa jonro*
who goes with us ?	*halikan ose-fa wa-o-ma ?*
we have seen him there	*wa-dikkha ja jon|da ie*
a snake has bitten him	*orie otoka ie*
what is the matter ?	*hamah ron khan tora ?*
you deceive everybody	*bu-mmerli da|ja*
it is not true, what you say	*kidia tahja khoro, hamah bu-ddia-sa*
I have been so glad that day	*dai kiaja kasakabo hadiake ma-koba halikhebe-n|da*
I shall come back again	*da-anda-bo-teh kida ba*
I like my parents	*da-a-marlita-kona-tsi da-ansi-ka*
can you tell me anything ?	*b-akka koma amathali da de ?*
I have seen two men there	*da-uddikkha-ja bijanma-no wadidie jomon*
what has that woman in her hand ?	*hamaron tho-khabo-roko tho hijaro ?*
she has a knife in her hand	*jodowala tho-khabo-roko ka*
I have had a dream	*ka-tobon ka|de koba*
I am going to dance with you	*da-bieni-fa bo-ma*
he has died	*l-oda-ja da*
no, he is not dead	*manien. l-oda-ja-khoro da*
I squeeze a lemon	*lemona da-samooodá* [u])

§ 203. Proverbs and mottos
(1 a), 1 b), 2, 3 a), 4 Dutch spelling.)

1 a) *Jarah-ki wiribisiri adeda-fa*
there deer spring-shall

1 b). *Jarah-diki tho wiribisiri akona-fa da*
there the deer walk-shall

2. *Hebe-tho arowa tho-mora th-berleda khoro tho b rle-wa*
old tiger but it-lose not its colour-own

3 a). *Ad-o-ba a-tikida oni-rakon, toh-mora to-khona-khwa khoro*
tree-leaf fall water-in but sink yet not

kholo-ka|n
soaked it

3 b). *Ká-tho adá-bona abárakoná úni-rakó(ŋro abāre thákoro akónom*
when tree-leaf throw(?) water-in at once is-not go(?)

4. *Awadoli a-foda ade-be-ro-toh ada, toh-mora ada ina khoro*
wind blow high trees but tree stump not

toh-roko-sa.
it-shakes

5. *Kχ há-to awadúli fúdi(ŋ to hāū koná-ka.*
when wind blows the sloth walks

---

1. There the kariaku-deer (Cervus simplicicornis) will spring (is said, if anyone has done evil, and Nemesis is awaiting him).

2. A jaguar may be old, but it does not lose its colours (the fox may lose its hair, but never its tricks).

3. When tree-leaves fall into the water, they do not sink at once (an evil deed is not soon forgotten ; punishment may still follow).

4. The wind blows against big trees, but tree-stumps it does not shake.

5. When the wind blows sloth walks (people are going to exert themselves only when they are obliged to ; R. 19a).

§ 204. Letter, dated Mata, March 20th, 1928
(Dutch spelling.)

1. *Mynheer, Jaha da-sikita fiero-tho akoba-he b-iebithi-ro.* 2. *Toho*
sir here I-give-cause great greeting thou-to this

b-oso-n-koba Paramaribo o-khonaria hadiake d-a nekamon bo-nani,
thou-go-past P. from very I-am sad thou-with (?)

da-koborokowa towa-ka bo-kani.
I remember continually (?)

---

1. Dear Sir, I send you kind greetings. 2. When you departed from Paramaribo, I was very sad [because you have treated us kindly], I have continually thought of you.

3. *M-aneki-n b-a   kaima bia'no kidian|toh mani d-a-n   joho-ro*
not-take   thou-do wrath   it   true   that not   my-doing   much

a-berleti-n   b-iebitsiro.   4. Da-anika   abakhan   amathalie   b-iebitsi
writing   thou-to   I-bring   one-small   thing   thou-to

a-mikodo-n da.
sending

5. *Jaha b-onaba   toho, da mon-tsi a-sikiti-sa akohba-he b-iebitsiro da.*
here thou-answer this   me-with-person send-thing greeting   thou-to

6. *Dai a-thikita|bo, kia, kha-toh da-sikitie-n b-iebitsiro aba   mathalie*
I   advise   thou that when   I-give-cause thou-to   other   thing

a-berleta-djaro, n-ani.   koma kha aba-no kaketsi manthan addikhe-tsi
write   they-do   may   some   man   all (?)   see-person

mekhebo o-khona   da-berleti-n da ?   7. Kidia da a-koborokwatowa-ni,
work   concerning   my-writing   such   I-remember

matie   da|badia mani.
not-willing   also   not

8. *Bo-berleta-lie da-mon kwan ama-ha b-ansi-sa   da-ani-bia bo-mn.*
thou-write!   me-to   yet   what   thou-like-thing I-do-to be   thou-for

halikhebe lokho-di da-ani-ti-ka bo-mn   mathalie.
joy   in   I-do-wish   thou-for   thing

9. *Aba khan-o-ma   k-emekhebe thia khan d-a ba,   da-sikitie-n bia*
one   small-with   work   small I-do   again   I-give-cause to-be

joho-ro   b-iebitsiro.
much   thou-to

---

3. I beg your pardon that I have not written much to you.   4. I have, however, done my best to send you something [1]).

5. Receive also greetings from my family [specially from Alphons, who accompanied me].

6. I tell you, that if ever I should again send anything, it would be better if some other person, or rather an overseer, were to control my writing. 7. Because it does not turn out as I desired it.

8. Write to me whatever you still wish that I should do for you ; I will gladly do whatever you desire of me.

9. At present I am doing some small work ; therefore I have not the time to send you much.

---

[1]) The stories given in §§ 212 and 222, and a few sentences (§ 202), accompanied this letter.

III. MYSTICISM, ETC.

§ 205. In former times — perhaps even yet in a few places — there were real, able medicine-men *(semeči)* ; Baptist has known one in his youth. The Kaliñas have not exactly the same medicine-knowledge as the Arawaks, and that which they practice (— see the detailed description by Pen., 69f —) is said to have been partly of Arawak origin.

A course in medicine-knowledge is as a rule attended by several persons. First they construct a small house for their study (*na-oroá-kona* ; I am studying for medicine-man, *da-orowá-ka*). Each pupil digs a hole in the ground, and is obliged to keep this hole moist for forty days [1]) by continual vomitting. During this time his whole food and drink consists of tobacco-balls and tobacco-water.

Then a pot is placed outside the hut, filled with the juice of the takini-bark, and the pupil inhales the fumes arising from it (see for tobacco and takini, §§ 167 [a) 4)], 169 [c) 2)], and D. 8, 285). Now visions appear to the pupil, and the medicine-man explains their signification.

Afterwards the novice is allowed to shoot humming-birds with a blunt-headed arrow ; he may only eat the heart and the head of these birds, one bird per day, divided over three meals. After this, he may eat Trogon viridis. And then crabs, and so on.

§ 206. When anyone is seriously ill, and the aid of the *semeči* is called in, the *semeči* examines him in the evening, and concentrates his thoughts on him. After that the *semeči* goes to sleep, and in a dream the sort of the disease is revealed to him [2]). On the second evening the *semeči* blows tobacco-smoke over the patient, etc. (presumably he now enters into communication with the rattle-stones-spirit, the water-spirit, bush-spirit, etc.).

Singing by which a spirit is called up :

bo-kóna-thǐ da-múni yúλi-no, come to me, tobacco-spirit (vocative),
adóŋko-ro|dá-ʃa-do bu-burá-di, thou shalt find me sleeping,
ánda-thu|bá-te-kána, I request thee earnestly to come,
dá-muŋ yúλi-nu d-adiá-ka bú-konaŋ, I request thee earnestly to come to me.

The *semeči* now sends a good spirit *(lǐ-sémehe)* to find out what evil spirit, or what human spirit, has caused the illness. If he finds it, he brings it to the *semeči*, who asks it, why it has done that, and moreover he asks the good spirit to punish the evil one.

§ 207. A child receives its name eight days after birth. The parents or the family consult the *semeči*. The latter examines the child, and in a dream the sign of the child's future appears to him. According to this sign the name is given (*li-sémiči a-ribirita-ya da|i*, or *lŏ simiči a-šiká-ya l-irí-wa*, the medicine-man has given him a name). If the child received a wrong name, it would be ailing all its life.

---

[1]) "Forty days", comp. R. 19a, Sect. 276, quoting Gumilla.
[2]) Dream : see also §§ 174 c), 207. 211. 220.

A few names :

clan	Arawak name	baptismal name
Káluafu (his mother was a Kaluafu, his father a Šiwena)	Sásanáli (sa, good)	Johannes Baptist
Úraši	Sibanáli (siba, stone, possibly the pebbles in the rattle)	Alphons
—	1⁰ (seldom used) Máǫakeli	
	2⁰ Tokódi or Tokódo (the lovely one; flower?)	Evelina Josephina

§ 208. In former times, when a chief had to come to town in order to visit the Governor, he first rubbed himself with the bulb of the peace-plant (sáika-bina, §§ 29 e), 58 d) 2)). Whoever must appear before the judge, does it also (kirtyádu-bína, white-people-charm, § 164 j) 2)). For similar purposes a Kaliña will rub his body with red paint (from Bixa Orellana), in which the charm is mixed. Presumably the old Arawaks did this too, see Q. 18, 239 and R. 19a, Sect. 240A).

§ 209. A swollen place (ahé-kuna ; my hand is swollen, da-kabo ákoa), is treated with the plant "touch-me-not" (ayákü(h), in powder form. As the leaves of this plant can shrink, its properties must cause a swelling to shrink or decrease.

§ 210. A girl having her first menstruation, is isolated by the parents for three weeks in a hut. All this time there is feasting. Then a piece of matting is prepared, in the mashes of which ants of the species yóko are caught. An old man or an old woman applies this mat (ná-rabáioda-n, § 104 c)) to the skin of the girl. By this means the girl will become quick and industrious like the ants. After this, she is adorned (comp. R. 19a, Sect. 269).

In the same manner they also have children bitten by ants : "this is good for them".

§ 211. An Arawak chieftain went to town and there received presents from the Government. Some Kaliñas asked his wife to give them some of the presents, but the woman refused, whereupon the Kaliñas by magic power sent an evil spirit to that chieftain. He became ill, and died on the way to his village.

The people of his village became suspicious of the brother-in-law of the chieftain, a medicine-man living in an adjacent village. That man had requested to accompany the chieftain to town, and when his body was brought home, he had said : "look here, brother-in-law, before you went to town, you were not ill ; how is it, that you have come back as a corpse (a-udó-či abúdia-či)?"

They prepared a beverage, and invited the inhabitants of other villages to a feast : two youths were appointed as executioners.

The spirit of that medicine-man had told him everything (lę-séme|tha *haká-ka|da|i)*. The messenger said that no evil would befall him. That night the spirit appeared to him in a dream (*lę-seme|tha a-yárato-sa-yamun|da|i,* or *l-ętębuŋ lokoá|tha le-séme a-káya|de),* and said to him : go, but some evil will befall you. Thereupon he went with the messenger.

He was kindly received, but when he drank his third gourd [1]), one of the executioners stabbed him with a sword (which had been presented by the Government to the chieftain) in the abdomen, and after that the other beheaded him. The blood bespattered everything, also the vessel containing the beverage.

The feast was stopped, and the beverage poured out. The two executioners immediately began a tobacco-fasting-cure for him, *(na-uroá-fa|tha lę-diki)* in the same way as the medicine-pupils do (§ 205). Afterwards they buried him.

But the man knew the Arawak medicine-knowledge, and also the medicine-knowledge of other tribes, which he had learned on the Orinoco ; if he wished, he might transform himself into a tiger. His inspiring spirit had left him ; had that not been the case, he could not have been killed. After his death, the spirit returned *(lo-ódo-n-bena|thá lę-séme ánda).* And then the man caused the death of one of his executioners as soon as the new moon appeared ; and he caused the death of the other a month later. The population were visited by sickness ; the remainder was scattered ; the place was forsaken. Baptist himself has seen the vestiges of that village.

"This is a true story, which happened when my (Baptist's) grandfather was young (14 or 15 years)".*("t(k?)idyán-tho a-báli-ŋ-koba, de-kuthú|da bikidólia-th-a-ŋ-ka").*

---

[1])   "Three times" ; also in §§ 212, 213, 219 and in many other Indian tales.

IV. MYTHS, ETC.

§ 212. The story of the founder of the medicine-art.
Dutch spelling.

(§ 166 ᵈ, ᶠ), and comp. v. C., Ant III, 485, R. 19a, Sect. 3—8, B. 5e, 18, 5d, 401.)

1. *Aba ukkha koba toh m-aithie-n kowa m-a-n-kha semetsie khonan ;*
one time was not-know yet being med.-man concerning

jon koba aba wadilie tah, a-sikithi ƒa djan-tsi, atenowa bia kidia
there was a man give-cause like first to-be thus

th-a-n ƒa|da. 2. *L-ieri tah lie aurokot-arlien lu-ssakhotah*
shall his-name he med.-art-learn-cause-artisan he-call-cause

Harliwanlie. 3. *Harliwanlie tah ussa kaki-n lo-jono o-ma: ukkha tah*
H. H. good live his-family with time

n-aka-n lokho-die, jawahe koba tah ka-here-ka koma kakhitsie o-ma da ;
they-say in devil was friendly may man with

4 *kidia tah wadia djaro aba hereke jawahe sa-be aba amathalie*
thus by and by about one company devil children a thing

wakha-tho th-anika naha kakhitsie da, 5. *th-ani-ka tah hadian-tho*
bad they-put those men they-put such

ballihie-n amathalie keben-toh ietika wabo thu-rlanta n-abojo-n-a
certainly thing very excrement exceeding they-mix their-food

o-ma nah kakhitsie da. 6. *Kiadoma kida, nah kakhitsie mienkhoro*
with those men therefore those men very

aimato-n-a kidian-tho o-balie-n o-khonan, toho th-ani-sa na-ma da :
angry suchlike pass concerning that its-doings they-with

7. *ken khoro nah kakitsie adia-ƒa n-abokwawa da, hali th-a-n-ƒa o-balie-n*
then those men speak among each other how shall pass

---

1. There was a time when the art of the medicine-man was not yet known; there was a man who as the founder, did it for the first time. 2. The name of that founder was Harliwanli. 3. H. lived in peace with his family; at that time — so people say — the devil was on friendly terms with man ; 4. later, some children of the devil played a dirty trick upon mankind, 5. they behaved very badly, and even mixed excrement with the food of man. 6. Therefore the men were very angry on account of the things they had done to them 7. and the men considered what was the

kidian-tho.   8. Ken   toho   iebiro-be   wakhaja-be-ro   ma-iebowa-tie-n
suchlike   then   those   little ones   wicked ones   not-cease-wish

tho-malokonia da,   naha kakhietsie a-bokoto-n bia|tah be|da|no, nah-fari-
its-with-in-continual   those   man   catch   it they-kill

n-bia be da|n,   9. kiadoma   tho-marli t-akona|tho be toho wakhaja-be-tho
it   therefore its-parent it-walk   those wicked-ones

iebi-ro-be mienkhoro aimatowa-sabo-ren baikia naha   kakhitsie o-khonan.
little-ones   very   angry-very-being   those   man   concerning

10. *Ken tah tho jawahe adia-n bia fa o-balie-tho-fa   amathalie khonan|da.*
      then   that devil speak   occurrence-future thing   concerning

11. *tho-makwa amathalie hikorlie-hie bia-wo,   kari-hie khonan, ma-tho*
      all   thing   lameness   to-be we (?) sickness like   with

amathalie sabo ande-tho fa   kakhitsie diako-n,   12. toho jawahe adia-n
thing   more come-thing future man   upon-at   that devil speak

bena da kidien tho|ma-jarado-n-a-bia|tah abakharen tho-makwa|da, nah
after da   thus   it dis-appear   suddenly   all   the

kakhitsie m-adikkhi-n sabon bia tho jawahe da. 13. Ken baikia jawahe da,
man   not-see   more   the devil   then   devil

a-jorlathi-n bia nah kakhitsie ansi|da,   14. kia doma khoro lie
disturb   those man   peace   therefore   that

wadilie, da-ussa-bo-kilie, adia-fa lo-ma-n-tsie kakhitsie o-ma, halika
man   I-named-person   speak   he-with-persons man   with   how

n-a-n-fa toho jawahe o-ma da. 15. Ken khoro liehie Harliwanlie na lie
they-do-shall that devil with   then   that H.   they he

mn adia-ka|tah da, 16. jawahe-be o-ma wa-fara-li, hadia wa farokha
at say   devils   with   we-war   thus   we-do if

a-ibie-n toho amathalie harlaja-fa   wa-ma-sido-n-a ahdon. 17. Ken
leave   that thing   appear-shall (?) we-beheaded (??)   then

lu-ddia kika da ba bija-nieno l-okiejotsie o-ma, aba tokai   wa-marlita-
he-says again   two   his-brothers with   a   medicine-house we-make

---

best thing to do. 8. As these children did not leave off playing their dirty tricks, the men caught them, and killed them ; 9. therefore the parents of those wicked children became so very angry with men. 10. Then the devil prophesied : 11. all accidents, diseases etc. will come upon mankind ; 12. after the devil had spoken thus, they all disappeared, men have seen them no more. 13. Then the devils began to vex men : 14. therefore the man I have just mentioned, told the people what they should do with the devils.

15. H., as he is called, said : 16. let us make war on the devils, for if we tolerate this, we all shall perish.

17. He said to his two (younger) brothers, let us make a medicine-house,

teh   18. *lo-koborokwatowa-n lokho-die da, kia tah na owrowa-n bia,*
       he-planning   in   that   they medicine-art-learn

halika n-a-n ʃa   a-ʃeliedo-n-a toh amathalie o-loko-waria ande-tho
how   they-doing-shall loose   that thing   in-from   come-thing

ʃa-the na-diako-n, tho-jomede-sa-koba toho jawahe tho-bora-di-wa.
will   they-upon   it-prophecy   that devil   it-before

   18A. *Kiadiki   jorlie-sie   l-unneka, lo-bona tah|no. wa | tha-khoro*
         thereafter tobacco-seed he-take   he-plant   it   long was-not

borlondan ;   atenowa-tho tah tho-bana tho jorlie   l-unneka, woinatah
(*furi,* sprout?) first   its-leaf   that tobacco he-take   (beginning.

olo   lu-ssiribidie-n bia tah da no.
sprout ?)   he-roll up   it.

   19. *Ken baikia iewida   n-aneki-n bia kibona   ourowa-kona bia,*
        then   calabash they-take   that-past medicine-art-instrument to-be

jo-waria tah aba-lokho-die-kho mathalie kidaba. toho m-aithie-n
there-from   different   thing   again   that not-knowing

d-̣a-sa   ussa-n aka bia kida.   20. Kidiatah koba a-inato-n-a, halika
my-do-result well speak again   thus   was beginning   how

n-a-n-koba nah   loko-no seme-tsie   aitie-ni.
they did   those men   medicine-man knowing

   21. *Lihie, na-sa-kili   Harliwanlie tah, a-inati-n-ʃa|tah osa-ren*
        he   they-name-person H.   begin   go-stop

l-ani-ti-sa-ʃa da ;   22. l-onnaki-n bia tah naha bija-nino l-okiejotsie
his-do-wish-result-future   he-take   those two   his-brother

lo-ma-wa,   kia lo-ma   nah-ouwrowa-n-bia.
he-with-own that he-with they-medicine-learn

   23. *Aba kha koba kakke ka tah toh hiaro be o-ma da ie ussa-n; 24. Toh*
        a   time was live   that women with he well   that

---

18. his purpose being that men should learn (be initiated) how to be delivered from the things that were going to happen to them, as the devil had prophesied.

18A. After that he took tobacco-seeds and sowed them, and they grew quickly ; first he took the leaf of the tobacco and enveloped it with a leaf of the manicole-palm [thus it was formed like a cigar].

19. Then he took also a calabash to serve as an instrument to work with, and other things which I am not able to repeat.   20. Thus was the beginning of men (Arawaks) knowing the medicine-art.

21. He, the so-called H. began to attain his purpose ;   22. he took his two brothers also to study the medicine-art with him. [After having put everything in order, he took two women as his wives].

23. Some time he lived in peace with his two wives.   24. But the fire

hiaro be|da a-inata-fa iekihie a-kojakoto-n 25. *wakhaja kakke-he abo,*
women begin-shall fire collecting evil life with

wadia kida toh   bijan-be hiaro da a-inata-n wakhaja-tho o-loko-n na-ma
soon those two woman begin wicked-thing in-at they-with

nah   bija-nino lihie wadilie okijotsie.
those two that man brother

26. *Toho wakhaja da, nah ani-sa, kebena sabo   jamada   khoro*
that wickedness their doings short time very (maya, public?) not

aitha-n-bia da|no. 27. *Okojoko loko-n th-itikidie-n bia tah, kiadoma tah*
know it ear in-at it-whisper therefore

l-iematowa-koba mienkhoro lihie wadilie, l-iematowa-sabo ka tah masowan
he-angry-was very that man he-angry-more very

l-okijo-no o-khona-n. 28. *L-ieri tah lihi Harliwanlie abalie l-okitsie :*
his-brothers against his-name that H. one his-brother

Orlowama, l-ierabo   l-okitsie   ieri kho   da-aitha ; 29 *kabi-nino*
O. his-second (§ 104c)) his-brother name not (?) I-know three

Harliwanlie erejonotsi n-aito   balien, bijan-be wa|tah toh l-erejonotsie
H. wives they-heed indeed two own that his-wives

koba. 30. *N-ieri-be tah nah   bija-nino hiaro-be|da. Orliro. Sibarlojen.*
were their-names those two women O. S.

31. *Harliwanlie tah aithsie fa|da|no halika n-a-n   wakhaja-n l-erejonotsi,*
H. know it how they-were wicked his-wives

kiadoma   kidia l-a-koba lo-monowa a-koborokwatowa-n, halika l-a-n-fa
therefore thus he-did him-for-self planning how he-do-will

na-ma o-balie-n fa|da. 32. *The ibokota-n bia tah da l-ajarlodokoto-n bia fa*
them-with pass shall ? punish he-enslave-cause

---

of discontent began among those women ;   25. they began to lead a bad
life with the two brothers of that man.

26. The wrong they had committed, could not remain hidden. 27. It
reached the ear [of H.], and therefore that man was very angry [with his
wives] and he was more angry with his brothers. 28. The name of H. 's
first younger brother was Orlowama, the name of his second younger
brother I don't know, 29. it is said also that H. had three wives, because
he had two wives for himself only [1]). 30. The names of those two women
were Orliro and Sibarlojen.

31. H. noticed how wicked his wives were : therefore he made up his
mind, what should happen to them. 32. In order to punish his brothers,
he exercised his medicine-art at night.

---

[1]) The meaning of this may be, that a man is not fully the master over his first wife,
because she is protected by her clan.

l-okijotsi, orli-ka|tah lo-marlakada-n-bia,   33. atenowa-lie l-okitsi|tah aba
his-brother   night   he-rattles   first-one   his-brother   one

ka   m-awso-ni aba-nro. ken khoro baikia koba bahi-n l-a-n-kha|da,
time   not-going   one-at   then   house-at   he-was-when

aba   sjoko-tho kodibijo   khan   andi-n-bia|tah   l-iesikowa   kiradi tahda,
a   little   bird   come   his-house   round-about

th-omoromorodi-n bia ʃa tah, jaha-n, taha-bo-n man ansentowa-n|da.   34.
it-fly-fly-ing   here-at   there-at   all   warbling

Ken kia kodibijo-khan ajento-n-owa-bia|tah. akanabi-n-bia th-ejento-n-a
and   that   bird-small   singing   hear   it-singing

kidaba k-akaneki-n lihi Orlowama ieri a-sa-ʃarokha dia-tsie-n   35. hama !
again   loudly   this O.   name call-if   like   what

l-a|tha liehi wadilie, bjie sjoko-tho kodibijo. bjie tatarleko da|dien teh
he-do   that   man   thou little   bird   thou strong   thus

da-ieri loko ussa-n|de.   36. Kharoho|da l-a|tha da-unneka-ʃa da-simarla-wa
my-name in   call   me   now   he-do   I-take-will   my-arrow-own

da-ʃare-n-bia a-jokho-n bia|bo ;   37. tho-morodo-n-bia a-siʃodabo-ren.
I-kill   hunt   thou   it-fly   turn about

38. ken l-unneki-n-bia tah l-iesimarla-wa   39. lu-bbenati-n-bia atenowa
then he-take   his-arrow-own   he-be after (?)   first

tah lo-koboda|tha da|no l-iebijantehdo-n-a lo-koboda kika da ba|n. kabinnie
he-miss   it   his-second   he-miss   again   it   third

lo-bonate-n | kida, l-unneke ka ʃa lu-ssima, lu-ssiʃeda-n-bia lu-jabomaria.
he-be-after (?) again he-take will   his-arrow   he-turn about   his-back-side

lu-ddeki-n-bia|tah ʃiro-tho onie ebera barlaa da kidian-tho amathalie
he-see   great   swamp sea   thus-thing   something

a-bali-tho lo-ma, aboka-n bia l-uja.   40. Ken da lu-ddekhe ʃa tha
happening he-with boiling   his-life-spirit   then   he-see

ʃiro-tho oniabo akhausa-tho da ie, lo-bokona-n bia tah mienkhoro|da,
great   water   surround-thing him he-boil   very

---

33. His first brother once not having gone out to any other place, and
being at home, a little bird came near his house and began to warble.   34.
When that little bird began to sing, it was as if the sound of his song called
the name of O.   35. What ! said that man, you little bird, are you so
insolent as to call my name.   36. Now, he said, I will take my arrow to
kill you ;   37. then it flew to and fro ;   38. then he took his arrow;   39. after
that the first time he missed, the second time he missed again, the third time
he shot, and as he intended to pick up his arrow, he turned round and saw
a big lake, and was amazed at the things that happened to him.   40. When
he saw that big water which was round about him, he became greatly

m-aithie-n   l-a-n-bia|tah   halika   l-a-n-ſa   da.   41.   Jomon,   jon-tho
not-know   he-doing-to-be   what   he-do-shall   there   the place

lu-ddinamo-n, sikowah koba|tah, atako-tho   abalokho-die tah kho tiebokili
he-stand   house   past   covered-thing different   shrubbery

abo da kia horloro.   42.   Kia hororo koba tah, halon toh kobibijo sjoko-tho
with   that country   that country   where that bird   little

o-kojaha kakki-n :   43.   kia|tah sjoko-tho kodibijo toh lu-ddekha-ro da,
spirit-place (§ 167)   that   little   bird   that he-see

kia tah khoro kodibijo ja|da|no, ujja-he ron tah.   44.   Kia adiba-thie-n-
that was not bird   it   spirit only   that apparition-per-

tho   kodibijo ussa kidian-tho lo-ma   amathalie iebira-ka, kiadoma,
son-being-thing bird   go   thus   he·with thing mock   therefore

lihi thojokilie   nah-bokintsi   a-jorlateke-ti-n mienkhoro
that (family-chief, § 164 k) 3) ?) their-older brother stir-cause-wish very

l-ansi.   45.   Kidien|tah, jomon koba hajarlo-tsie dien iebara-ni.
his-peace thus   there past slave   like remain

    46.   L-iebijanteh l-okitsi   kitah da Harliwanlie mansowa k-aima-loko
           his-second   his-brother also   H.   very   wrath-in

a-jarlodokota,   47.   kenkhoro l-ossokota koba jowaria   a-majaradi-n
enslave-cause   then   he-go-cause past there-from disappearing

aba wakhaja-tho sikowa-nro da ie,   jon-tho haliman-tho ukkha hadien
a   evil   place-at   him there how-long   time thus

mansowan k-amenika-ni,   48.   ken khoro baikia toh sikwa-he jawahe-be
very   suffering   then   that place   devils

ron m-abena-be-tho da, kakhitsi dian-tho tah.   49.   Ken da jon   atenowa
only without-bone-things man   like   then   there first

l-andi-n bo, jon-khondo-be tah, a-bokoto-n bia da ie,   tho-roboti-n-bia
he-come   there-persons   catch   him   it-extract

lo-bona l-iesiroko koboroko-waria lo-kona-sabo ka khoro wadilien
his-bone his-flesh among-from   he-walk-more was not (mamarin, not at all)

---

alarmed and did not know what to do.   41. At the place where he was
standing, there was a waste, covered with all kinds of wild shrubs.   42.
That was the country where the spirit of that little bird dwelt ;   43. so that
little bird which he had seen, was not a bird, but a spirit.   44. That
wonderful bird had played with him, because his older brother had wished
to trouble him.   45. So he remained there in exile.

    46. H. also severely punished his second brother ;   47. he caused him
to disappear to a desolate country, where he had to suffer heavily for some
time ;   48. it was a country of spirits which had no bones ; they were
like men.   49. When he came there at first, the inhabitants extracted all
the bones from his body ; he could not walk any more, because he had

m-abena-ja   ie sabo khana da.   50. Ken baikia naha ka-hoketsi kakke
without-bone-being he more   and   those brethren   live

kowa-ma-ja hajarlo loko da.
still-may   slave   in

51. Naha biaja-nino hijaro authika|tah n-ajarlodo-n-a bia kida ba.
those two   woman find   they-enslaved   to-be also

52. Aba-kka tah lie-dia-n Harliwanlie l-erejonotsi bija-nino o-mon. 53.
one-time   he-say H.   his-wives   two   to

wa-ossa-lie kieraha-nro, da-dikkha koba hime mienkhoro jo-ni, 54. kidia
we-go   lake-to   I-see   past fish very   much   so

n-ah koba auso-n jo-nro, ken hime sabo-ren mienkakhoro n-ahothikie-n da.
they-did go   thither and fish very   very   they-find

55. ken khoro iekihi firo-tho na-marliti-fa, kidia tah adia-he. kidia tah
then   fire great they-make   thus   word thus

a-marlito-n-a|n. 56. Nah ienate-fa toh a-jabodi-n. 57. aba|tah toh
done   it   they begin that broil   one   that

hijaro da Sibarlojen tho ieri kia tah hadofethi-ka   toho iekihi a-theretie-n
woman S.   her name   oppressed (§ 109) that fire heat-cause

da ; 58. Kidia|tah fa adia-n th-ieretsi   mon, da-ukka-fa banja : 59.
thus   speak her-husband to I-bath-will first

kenkhoro th-oso-n oni rako-n thu-ttimatimada-bo. 60. Jowaria l-osa|ba
then   she-go water in-at she-swim-swim   thence he-go again

adikkhi-n lie Harliwanlie th-iebitsiro, lu-ddia-n bia tah tho-mon, tora
see   this H.   she-at   he-speak   she-at that

hadja-ro b-a-lie l-a-n-bia tahda, 61. kha-ki|tah abakharen toho lie-dia-n
so   thou-be he-do   time-this! suddenly that he-say

o-ma ki,   hime bia th-ebesowa da toho hijaro Kasekojah bia,
with this! fish to-be she-change that woman porpoise to-be

62. toh-rabo hijaro addikkhe kidian-tho a-balie-n toh-bokowa uja,
the-other woman see   thus   pass   she-boil   life-spirit

---

no bones. 50. So both brethren lived in bondage.

51. The two women also got their punishment. 52. One day H. said
to his two wives, 53. let us go to a pond, I have recently seen a lot
of fishes there ; 54. so they went thither and caught many fishes.
55. and he said : make a big fire ; no sooner said than done. 56. They
begin to broil those fishes. 57. One of those women, S. was her name.
became oppressed by the heat of the fire ; 58. Thus she said to her
husband, I will take a bath ; 59. when she went into the water, she began
to swim. 60. After that H. came to look at her and spoke to her : thus
you will be transformed. 61. At the same moment he spoke, the woman
was changed into a porpoise.

62. When the other woman saw this, she was seized with fear. 63. she

63. *tho-khojabi-n bia tha lihi th-ieretsi-wa tata-n,   amaha th-ani-sa-koba*
    she-beg   that her-husband strongly what her-doing-past

amathali wakhai-tho, lu-ssikie-n-bia ussa-loko|no.   64. Ken baikia sa-thie
thing   evil   he-give   good-in it   then   good

l-a-ſa adia-n tho-ma da   65. d-ani-ſa khoro wakhaja-tho amathali
he-do   speak   she-with   I-do-will not   evil   thing

bo-ma   l-a|tah, 66. kia diki da, a-bira-tsi l-a-n-bia tah tho-khona,
thou-with he-said   that after   mock   he-do   she-at

th-imithamithada k-akkaneki-n. 67. Ken khoro toh hijaro da akhojaba-
she-laugh-laugh   loudly   then   that woman   beg-again

re-ma barlie-n da ie, l-ienati-n bia tah abalokho dien khoro toh-mon da, kia
    indeed   him he-begin   different like thing her-to   that

tah a-mithadakotho-n bia da|no tatta-sabo-n, aikasia-thi thana th-ieſiro-wa
    laugh-cause   her hard-more forget   her-body-own

ma-ibo-tie tah a-mithada-n da. 68. Halika mo-tho adi-he-ron|tah lie-dia-sa
not-cease   laugh   whatever   word-only   his-saying

tho-mon th-iebowa-ti-ka-khoro a-mithada-n ;   69. kenkhoro baikia l ſa
she-to she-cease-wish-not   laugh   then   he will

adia-n : mitha|da b-ansi-a hadien, haliman|bo-ſa a-mithada-n bu-kkakke
speak   laugh   thy-wish so   how   thou-shalt laugh thy-life

man. 70. Kia diki lie-dia-n bena kidien, th-ebeso-n-a-n-bia kodibijo
whole   that after he-speak after thus   she-change   bird

dien. 71. Ken kia kwan kodibijo kharo-ren-man bia n-aithie-n da. 72.
like   and that   bird   now   they-know

T-ah koba toho l-iereitho iebijanteh Harliwanlie|da kodibijo-bia a-beso-n-a
it-was this his-wife second   H.   bird   changed

koba. 73. Th-ieri tho l-iereitho|da th-sa-kho : Orliro, ken toho kodibijo
            her-name that his-wife   it-call   O.   and that bird

th-ebeso-sa   koba loko-n th-ieri|da : Beletatta.   74. Kidia l-a koba
she-change-result past in-at its-name   lame-strength (?) so   he-did

---

begged her husband to pardon her the sin she had committed. 64. Thus
he spoke with kind words to her, saying 65. I shall not hurt you.
66. But after that he begins to tell her all sorts of jokes, and then she
laughed loudly. 67. When the woman begged him again, he began to
say many talks, so that the woman forgot herself and started laughing
again, and could not cease laughing. 68. At every word he said to her,
she laughed incessantly ; 69. then he spoke thus : you like laughing and
so you shall laugh your whole life long. 70. After he had said that, she
changed into the shape of a bird. 71. And to this day that bird is well-
known. 72. Thus H.'s second wife was transformed into a bird. 73.
The name of that wife was Orliro, and the bird whose shape she took is

Harliwanlie   l-erejonotsi   bija-nino   a-jarlodokoto-n,   na-wakhaja
H.   his-wives   two   enslave-cause   their-wickedness

khonaria   n-anie-sa-koba.
for the sake of their-doings-past

75. *D-aakah ki-fa Harliwanlie khona kowan.*
    I-tell   further H.   concerning yet

76. *Toho   tah   da,   naha   bijanino   l-iereitho-be   l-ebesokoto-sa-koba.*
    thòse   two   his-wives   he-change-caused

atenowa-ro tah kasekoja bia-koba da, th-ibijanthe tah l-ireitho da, beletata
the first   porpoise became   the-second   his-wife   caracara

bia koba kharo-ren da.
become   now

77. *Naha tah bijanino l-okijotsie l-ajarlodokota-koba no,   lo-joo tah da,*
    those   two   his-brother he-enslave-caused   plur.? his-mother

a-khojab-n bia tah da ie, lo-robeti-n bia jowaria,   jon-tho koba
beg   him he-extract   from thence   place

l-iemikodokoto-n da je. 78. tatta-n doma tah lo-joo   a-khojab-n da ie.
he-send-cause   them   strongly because his-mother beg   him

l-onaka koba kidaba je. 79. Naha tah   bijanino l-okijotsie ieri|da :
he-took   again   them   those   two   his-brother name

Orlowama ma-thi Hiwanaka.
O.   and   H.

80. *Hiwanaka tah da ma-bena-li-jo   mamn-thsi koba, mawadilija*
    H.   without-bone-spirit there-person   *mamari*, impossible

aba-nro   l-oso-n tho-rija-be|da, belle l-a-nnada ma-bena-n   doma da ie.
other place-at he-go they-from lame he-was   without-bone because he

81. *Lo-wa   wabo|tah, l-onake-fa l-okitsie-wa. 82. Kenkhoro   baikia*
    he-self very (?)   he-take   his-brother-own   then

---

called Beletatta (caracara-falcon).   74. In this way H. punished both his wives for the sin they had committed.

75. I shall now continue the story of H.

76. Well then, he had metamorphosed his two wives, the first into a porpoise, the second into a caracara-falcon.

77. His two brothers, whom he had banished, had sighed in exile for a long time already, when on a certain day his mother came to him, and begged that they might be released from their place of exile : 78. because she entreated him so strongly, he made up his mind to release them. 79. The names of the two brothers were Orlowa and Hiwanaka.

80. Hiwanaka was exiled into a country of boneless people (spirits ?) ; he could not walk any more, because he had no bones in his flesh. 81. He went there himself, in order to deliver his brother. 82. Before he

lo-maraka da ʃa ʾlie dikowa|tah l-oso-n-bora jomnro da.   83. Waboroko
he-rattle   he after   he-go-before   there   path

lokko   tah   l-otsikie-n-bia   ma-benalijo-be   da,   a-jokhatho-bo   ʃirobero
in   he-find   boneless people   hunting   tapir

kanbanna-ron tah, th-iʃirobero-n doma tah no,   84. lo-jjoko-n-bia|tah,
butterfly-only   tapir   because (?) it   he-hit

tho-bora be da|no ; kia doma toho kanbana   ʃirobero kharo-ren th-a-n-bia
it-before   it   therefore that butterfly   tapir   now   it-being

ballalla   thsi-dien   kerouwakowan   anekebo   da.   85. Lo-bali-ka|tha
round   as   § 108 A   midst   he-pass

th-iesikowa-nro da, lu-ddikkhe-bia tah, l-okitsie wa, kawa-u-ka tha jomn da,
the-house-at   he-see   his-brother own absent-were (?) there

kia doma tah, lu-dkhi-n jon-tho da ie,   lo-bena tah leta leta ba-n tho bahe
therefore   he-see   there   him his-bones   put-put   the house

khona|da.   86. l-unneki-n-bia tah da|no,   lu-lletadi-n-bia   lo-mn kida
at (?)   he-take   them (Sm. a-ltadü-, to put on) he-at again

toho lo-bena,   abaren tah tattabedi-n bia da ie.   87. L-onaki-n bia tah da
that his bones   forthwith   make stiff   him   he-take'

ie,   th-ujjaʃidi be toho mabenalijo da.   88. Ken khoro baikia, l-osso-ʃa
him they-were out (? § 69) the b. p.   then   he-go

l-okitsi   abo|da a-tede-ni, wa|tha khoro-tha-i th-a-n l-a-wa|da, kiadoma
his-brother with   flee   long is not   being   himself (?) therefore

tho-kojo-wa bahe-nro, addikhe-ren kawa wa   kolan.
they-return   house-to   after (?)   each other (?) swift (?)

89. *Ken na-wso-n bena da, toho mabenalijo-be, awso ʃa na-ienabo.*
          and   they-go   after   those b. p.   go   they-after

Th-osa|tah abenan da je,   kija doma tah, nah-osabo-ka.   90. Toho
they-go   moment (?)   them therefore   they go-very (?)   those

---

went, he practised his medicine-art.   83. On the way he met the boneless
people, who were on the hunt ; a butterfly as big as a tapir went before
them [they were hunting for a butterfly ?]   84. He shot it with an arrow,
and the place where he shot it may be seen to this day : a circular spot
[on a rock, or in the wood ?]   85. He passed by and came to the place
where his brother was. He saw his brother, having no bones at all ; other
people he did not see ; his bones had been extracted from his body by the
inhabitants ;   86. he took the bones and put them again in his brother's
body.   87. Then he took him along with him, whilst the inhabitants were
still from home.   88. After that he fled with his brother ; when the
inhabitants came home, they perceived it.

89. The boneless people pursued them, therefore they ran swiftly.   90.

mabenalijo-be	*osabo-ka*	*tah*	*na-ienabo,*	*t(?)-ohtsika*	*tah*	*nah*	*khona,*	*aba*
b. p.	go-very (?)		they-after	they-find			they concerning	an

jesi sikowa	*loko-nro*	*nah-kodon-a-n bia tah da.* 91.	*Ken khoro baikia,*
armadillo hole	in-at	they-enter	then

th-a-n|da	*be*	*jomn*	*kia*	*jesi sikowa*	*lokowaria tah,*	*l-dena-wa,*	*lo-fetikitie-n*
being		there	that	armadillo hole	in-from	his-arm	he-put forth

bia teh	*lu-kkabo-wa|da,*	*orie*	*dien tah*	*th-iebitsiro.*
his-hand		snake	as	they-to

92.	*Kenda*	*Harliwanlie*	*l-okitsi*	*o-ma*	*toho*	*jesi sikowa*	*loko*	*l-a-*
then	H.	his-brother	with	that	armadillo hole	in	he-

n-kha,	*jon-kowa*	*tahtha*	*kia*	*mabenalijo-be*	*da,*	*abaren*	*tah*	*korlijaka*	*bia*
being	there-yet		b. p.			suddenly		parrot	to be

l-ebbesokoto-n	*lo-ma wa*	*l-okitsi da.*	93.	*Kia diki da,*	*nah-moroda*	*koba*
he-change-cause	he-with own	his-brother		that after	they-flew	

korlijaka-dien tho-rija-be.	94.	*Harliwanlie*	*awonaka*	*koba*	*l-okitsi tah*	*toh*
parrot-as	they-from		H.	took		his-brother	those

mabenalijo-be	*oria.*	95.	*Nah-jonatho*	*tah*	*abarlitaja*	*da|je*	*mienkhoro,*
b. p.	from		their-mother		wait (?)|	them	very

m-aithie-n	*th-a-n*	*doma*	*amaha*	*balie-n*	*nah-ma.*	96.	*Nah-morodo-n*
not-knowing	she-do	because	what	pass	they-with		they-flew

koba	*toh*	*jesi sikowa*	*lokowaria,*	*nah-osa-koba*	*nah-sikowa-ron,*
	that	armadillo hole	in-from	they-went	their-house

bahjorl-adiako	*tah*	*nah*	*teni-n-bia da.*
house-tiebeam-upon		they	tread (?)

97. | *Kia diki kida. Harliwanlie* | *adia-ka* | *lo-jo* | *ma-tsi lo-jo-no o-mn da,* |
|---|---|---|---|
| thereafter | H. | say | his-mother and | his-family to |

n-iesado-n-a bia tah.	98.	*Aban diaro tah,*	*korlija-be*	*a-moroda-fa*	*nah*
they-prepare		one time		parrots	fly	their

The boneless people hotly pursued them, and they found an armadillo-hole and entered it. 91. When they were in the armadillo-hole, he put forth his arm and his hand was changed into a snake. 92. When H. with his brother were still in that hole, and the boneless people were waiting for them, he suddenly metamorphosed himself and his brother into parrots. 93. Thereafter they flew away from them, as parrots. 94. H. had brought back his brother, and delivered him out of the hands of the boneless people. 95. Their mother had been anxiously awaiting them, because she did not know what would happen to them. 96. When they had flown out of the armadillo-hole, they went back to their house.

97. After that, H. said to his mother and to his family, that they should prepare themselves. 98. One time parrots flew past their house: they

sikowa adi-ren, hijarlie tah iewi abo bierakhatowa-loko toh. 99. *Ken*
house   upon   takini-tree   fruit   with   play-in   and

bierakhatowa th-a-n-kha th-abo da th-etikidie-n bia thoria liehi
play   being   it-with   it-fall   that-from   he

Harliwanlie ren sikowa sibo, abaren tah lu-kkarati-n bia lo-koti abo da|n.
H.   house   before   suddenly   he-bury   his-foot   with   it

100. *Hadia th-a-n a-tikidie-n o-ma kida tho thokho bia aba korlijaka da,*
thus   being   fall   with   it   descend   one parrot

th-dia-n bia tah lo-ma a-khojabi-n tah da ie. 101. *Tho-kojaba tah da*
it-speak   he-with   begging   him   it-beg

ie tatta-n bo-ssika-li da-bierakha da-mn kidaba tha tah lo-mn, lo-kona
him strongly thou-give!   my-play   I-to   again   he-to   his-thumb

abo tah lu-kkarete-sa-ja da n. Barlien baikia tho-khojabi-n da ie th-osa
with   he-bury   it   really   it-beg   him   it-go

lo-rija da. 102. *Wa-tha-koro borlo-n toh hijarlie da fata katsie dikhidi-ron*
he-from   long is not   sprout(?) that takini-tree   moon   after-only

baikia firo-ja|da|n, k-adenabo ka|tah da|n. 103. *Ken wai lu-ddia-fa*
great   it   with-branch is   it   then   he-speak

nah mn da wa-ossa-li jahari toho horloro bana ria wa-robeto-n-a-n
they-to   we-go!   here   this   earth   surface from we-extract-ourselves

ajomn ron wa-oso-n-tsi. 104. *Jowaria kida nah ossa-koba a-medi-n toh*
heaven   we-go-person   therefrom   they went   climb   that

hijarlie iesie-nro nah-makowa-ren koba, kidia nah koba ajomn ro. 105.
takini-tree   top-at   they-all   thus   they did   heaven-to

Toho Hijarlie a-doladowa-koba nah abo da. 106. *Kidia l-a-koba*
that takini-tree   uproot (take root?)   they with   thus   he-did

Harliwanlie ajomonro lo-jo-no abo awso-n.
H.   heaven-to   his-family with   go

---

flew to and fro and played with a takini-fruit (§§ 167a) 4), 205). 99.
Whilst playing, the fruit fell on the ground, just before the house of H.,
who at once put his foot upon it and buried it in the soil. 100. Directly
the fruit had fallen, one of the parrots flew down, and spoke to him and
besought him. 101. It begged him that he should give it back its toy, but
he pressed it with his thumb deeper and deeper into the soil. Its begging
was of no avail, and so it left him. 102. The takini-fruit grew quickly;
after a few months it had become a big tree with many branches. 103.
Then H. said to his family: "let us go away, in order that we may be
delivered from this world." 104. Thereupon they all climbed up that
tree; they all went up. 105. The takini-tree had uprooted itself from
the earth. 106. So H. with his whole family went heavenward.

107. *Kia doma wakili be-koba toh hijarli da, mienkakho nah-kisida-n*
     therefore   formerly   the takini-tree   very   they-esteem

da|no.
   it

---

107. For this reason all true Indians in ancient times have always considered the takini-tree as being holy.

§ 213. The children of the sun; one of them becomes Orion

(§ 166 ᶜ· ᵍ), and comp. v. C. 7e Ant II, 682, Pen. 69e, R. 19a, Sect. 29ff, 142, 303, D. 8, 259, 339, B. 5e, 29, Koch-Grünberg 45d, nᵒˢ 35, 38, 64, 79, 80, 102, 106.

The sun was a man, who, every dry season, went to a creek where fish was plentiful. At that place there lived a man who had a beautiful daughter and the sun fell in love with that daughter and took her to wife.

The woman became pregnant with twins. She went to seek for her husband, but she lost her way. She came to a spot where there were many flowers, and the children in her womb said to her: "Mother, gather those flowers for us, the best of them". The mother carried many flowers with her in her hands. Then they came to a big bees nest, and the bees stung her. And the mother became very angry with her children, and scolded them, and the children grew angry also.

There were two ways; the woman chose the wrong way [1]; the children, who knew the right way, would not say anything to her. So the mother came into a desolate country, inhabited by cannibals. These put her into a cage, and there she gave birth to two boys.

These cannibals were vulture-spirits, for the vultures (carrion-crows) are (creole: *opete*,) eaters. The common vultures now said: if it is possible, we shall help you, for these people are bad; if they kill you, they will not give us anything of your flesh.

Then, on a certain day, the mother was killed and eaten. But the children were with an old woman in a hidden place. Then the other vultures said: "what is this we hear? is it the child of that woman?" But the old woman answered: "it is only a piece of intestine that I am cleaning, and this is what you hear as the sound of a child".

The old woman brought up the children, and these cared well for her. But when they were grown-up, they would not stay any longer with the old woman. For they said: these are no real people, but eaters; and they resolved to kill the old woman. They said that they had seen fruits in the wood, and that the old woman should go into the wood to gather those fruits. And there they have murdered her.

---

[1] In a Kalina version: the path of the moon.

Then they walked for many months in the wood, and they came to a place where people had lived ; but the people themselves they didn't see. Then they wanted to see what sort of people lived there, and they climbed up a high tree, and remained there. They saw how an old woman (*Taukelélelio*, the *anuanå-yo* or *anåno-yo*) came to fish with a big sieve. The woman saw the image of the boys in the water, and thought that they were men in the deep, and she tried to ladle them out with the sieve, but she did not catch anything. The boys reveled in this ; one of them laughed, and the old woman perceived that they were sitting in the branches of the tree. That woman could not climb up the tree ; she was not a real human being, but a devil. Therefore she went to her village to fetch something wherewith she could catch the boys, but she found nothing. Then she went back to the wood and fetched a great many pingo-ants. These climbed up the tree, and bit the boys, and when they could not stand it any longer, they fell to the ground. The woman immediately killed one, and ate him, and took the other in a cage with her.

That woman had a beautiful daughter, who always stayed at home, whilst the woman went out to look for food. The next day, when the woman had gone out, the girl went to the boy and began to talk with him. The boy promised the girl, that he would take care of her mother and her, if she would ask her mother permission to marry him. And so it happened.

But then the boy said : "what will happen, when your mother comes home and brings nothing? then she will eat me. Have you no place to hide me in ?" Then the young woman answered : "I have no hiding-place, but when my mother comes, I will put you on my body, under my *kiwéyu* (apron)".

The mother returned with an empty bag, and was hungry. Then she said to her daughter : "where is that boy ? you have allowed him to escape !" But the daughter said : "it is not a bad boy, he is good to us ; I love him ; he will take care of us ; don 't kill him, for I have known him as my husband". Then the mother gave her consent. And every day the boy went to the sea to catch something.

One day the mother followed the boy, in order to see what he would catch. He caught many fishes, but the mother ate everything and brought nothing to her daughter, and said : he has brought nothing. And this happened many times. And then the boy became angry, and one time he said to his wife : "spin much cotton for me ; I want it for some purpose". But he did not say for which purpose he wanted it.

He came to the sea-coast, and caught many birds, and with their feathers he made something like a wing.

After the mother had eaten everything up the third time more, the man came home, and said : "your mother must come to-morrow to the sea-shore, for I shall catch much, and she should help me to carry it".

He did not catch anything, but he brought the coorial (canoe) in the midst of the water, and told a shark to catch and eat the mother, when she waded through the water to the coorial. And so it happened. Her milt [1]) floated on the surface of the water, and began to cry. The daughter in the house heard this, and became afraid, and came running along. But the man tied the wing to his back, so that he would be able to escape, if necessary. When the daughter arrived, the milt spoke again, saying : "your husband has murdered me".

The daughter took some object with which to slay the man, but he began to fly. She could only get hold of his leg. And the man with one leg, flew upwards, and became the constellation of Orion.

§ 214. **The man who roasted his wife**
1. and 2. Dutch spelling

(comp. Pen. 17a, II, 39, 60 (with a noteworthy explanation), R. 19a, Sect. 131A, 207, Nimuendaju 49, 90.)

1. *Wakíli koba,   abá|tha wadili l-irethó-wa   lo-fára kóba kenda*
   long ago   one   man   his-wife-own   he-killed   and

l-iedibaléda da|no ; th-ekéreketi-n khonaria óni   kólo,   l-eimáto-n-a
he-roast   her   she-bind-cause   for   rain soaked (?) he-angry

doma   ki-dia l-a koba.
because   thus   he did

2. *Abá-ka|tha oni-sábo-ren a-khie-n, seme ke da fa do adónko-ni*
   one time   rain-very   (raining)   sweet   I will   sleep

l-a-bo|tha adija-n. 3. Ḳen thada t-ečilikiánoči-wá|da th-ónaḳe-fá-de
he-said   speaking   then   her-brothers-own   she-take

n-akŏrŏŋ-bia-te fá|da|i. 4. N-akörátá|da|i   khidoá-ni to óni ka-
they-bind   him   They-bind   him   verily   the   rain in

lokó|da|i   áradi-(n úri-ka. 5. Kien waitháda mauči-dia-ró|da na-dókoda-
him entire   night   then § 121 ᵉ)   morning   they-loose

ki kádoba|i.
again him

---

1. Long ago, there was a man who killed his wife, and roasted her, because he was angry that she had had him tied up in the rain.

2. Once, when it was raining heavily, he said : I will sleep sweetly. 3. Then she called her brothers to bind him. 4. They bound him really, and during the whole night he stayed in the rain. 5. Only in the morning did they untie him.

---

[1]) "Milt", as well as "liver" in § 214, probably has a symbolic meaning.

6. *Toho* *amátaľ* *a-bále-to* *lo-má|da* *sẹku-diáro* *l-a|tó|koro|da*
this thing pass he-with § 116 d)? § 140 c) he-do that not (?)

l-iimato-n-a *a-dokotú-n|da ;* *kiadomá|da* *l-iretú-dyaro* *ú-maŋ|kóro|da* *lu-*
he-angry show therefore his-wife § 140 c) to not (?) he-

masémedoána|koró|da. 7. *Kiadóma-kóro|da* *l-iiretó|da* *l-iimato-n-a*
not-sweet-be not therefore-not his-wife he-angry

aithána|da.
know

8. *Ki-adiki|tháda* *kasákabo* *balī-m-bena* *kǐ(η* *bena* *w-adóηka-bá-te*
that-after day pass-after then let us sleep

l-a-bo|tha *to* *l-iréito* *mún|da.* 9. *Kiadóma* *tháda* *th-osá-kuba* *lo-má|da*
he-say this his-wife to therefore she-went he-with

konoko-nró|da *adóηka-ηro.*
forest-at sleep

10. *Kidiančina* *baikiada|i* *a-yukháyukádi-(n.* 11. *Lo-yokhá-ka* *tháda*
custom, § 88 c) he hunt-hunt he-hunt

kuthá|tada *abálokodikó* *lo-fará|da.* 12. *Sa-m-bená|dẹ* *ka-dibáli-(η* *bena|*
animal all-kinds-of he-kill good-after with-roast-after

da|i, *kienbáikiáda* *aba(η-fá|da* *itíriti|tha* *l-ŏrŏká|da.* 13. *L-ilẹsá-ka|thada|(η*
he then other basket-reed he-gather he-split it

kéke-bia *lo-dorá|da.* 14. *Má-ibi-kwa|ta|(n* *kha|táda* *b-ikisitóa-*
basket-become, § 171 he-plait not-ready-yet it when thou-try

te *a-bira-lokó-či|di(n* *thu-múĭn|da.* 15. *Kienbáikiáda* *lo-balẹtŏkŏta* *kiawai*
joke-in-person as she-to then he-sit-cause § 48

lo-doro-sá-bo *ó-loko|dá|no.* 16. *Kidia* *l-a-n-béna* *tháda|no* *t-ohsa|kīka*
his-plaited-thing in her thus he-do-after her she-go(again)

thó-lokoária *dába.* 17. *M-ībi* *koa* *l-a-sána|da(n* *á-doro(n-bó|da|(n*
it-in-from again not-ready yet his-work (§ 30) plait it

---

6. He did not show for a moment that he was angry on account of what had happened to him ; therefore he did not show a wry face to his wife. 7. So his wife did not know that he was angry.

8. Some days later he said to his wife : let us go and sleep in the forest. 9. Therefore she went with him to the forest and slept.

10. As his custom was, he went hunting. 11. He hunted and killed many animals and other things. 12. After he had sufficient, and had smoke-dried it, he gathered basket-reed (Ichnosyphon gracile). 13. He split it and plaited a basket of it. 14. When the basket was not yet ready, he said as if in jest to her : try. 15. And he made her sit in the thing he had plaited. 16. After that she went out again. 17. He had not yet finished his work, when he called her again. 18. She went again into

yu-wária|ki|tháda(n̄ l-išimaka kikada ba(ŋ　l-ibiči-wa.　18.　*T-oso(ŋ-bia|*
there-from　　　　he-call　again　her　he-to-own　　she go

kidaba to ó|da lo-dóro-sá-bo　kiwéke o-loko-nre kidaba.　19.　*Th-aitána-*
again　that　his-plaited-thing　basket　into　again　　she-know-not

kóro amaha balli-n-fá-n da|no.
what　pass-shall　her

20.　*To-osoŋ|ki|táda tó-loko-nro|da m-aithó-n-a|t-a-ŋ|ka l-osa|mokodó-n-*
she-go　　　　it-into　　　not-knowing　　he-go swallow (?)

bia toho kĭkĭ|da m-ībi-koan-tó|da　abakári(n, l-ękŏrŏ-m-bia thada
that　basket　not-ready-yet-thing　suddenly　he-bind

t-ęšibo|da kiá|da kéke-lokó|da.　21.　*Tano|d-áučiká|da|bo　l-a-m-bia thá*
its-face　that　basket-in　　　now I-get　　thee　he-says

to-muĭn|da k-aimá-loko-di|da.　22.　*L-ŏkŏrŏ-n-doma t-išibó|da hálika|t-a-sa-*
she-to　　wrath-in　　　　　he-bind-because　its-face　how　(§ 30)

bó-ya ma koró|da a-bóratu-n-á|da.　23.　*Bąǫi-ya baikadę thu-kúyabuĭ(n*
can　not　deliver　　　really　　she-beseech

da|i　a-yę̄-n|tha lo-muĭ(n balīn, lę-kŏna-sa-bó-ya kóro thę-kuyabuĭ(n
him　weep　he-to　indeed　he hear-result　not　she-beseech

koná-n|da.
at

24.　*Kienbáikiáda kakŏ̆-iya lę-dibaledá-ya-fa|da(n　yom-báikiada.*　25.
then　　　living　he-roast　　　　　her　there

Yóǫada-bána th-á-n-ka|da kákŏ̆-kwa t-a-ŋ-ka|da adakwathá-ya kóyabŏ̆-in
barbecue-on　she-being　live-yet　she-being　ask　　　beseech

balī-n|da|i.　26.　*Lo-khóto-m-bia|ta ikihi th-a-bó|da.*　27.　*Kientháda*
indeed　him　　he-collect　fire　she-with　　　　then

th-ōdo-m-biá|da.　28.　*Th-odó-n-bena tháda lo-dókoda kiénbiadaba to*
she-die　　　　she-die-after　　she-die　he-loose　　　that

keké|daba tháwa.　29.　*Kiŋ kóba kiáda lo-kholobetá-da|ŋ　kutá-di(n.*　30.
basket　§ 120 ǫ) 3)　then　　　　he-cut up　　her　animal-like

---

the basket, which he had made.　19.　She knew not what was going to
happen to her.

20.　When she had entered into it, without her knowing it, he suddenly
closed up the unfinished basket, and tied her inside.　21.　Now I have got
you, said he to her in wrath.　22.　Because he had tied her, she could not
free herself.　23.　She besought him weeping, but he gave no heed to
her prayers.

24.　Then he roasted her alive.　25.　When she was on the rafter, and
still living, she was asking and beseeching.　26.　He collected firewood.
27.　Then she died.　28.　After she had died, he untied the basket.　29.
He cut her up like an animal.　30.　After he had cut her up, he roasted

Lo-kólebeti-m-bená|da|no   l-edibalede-fa|da|(n.   31. Sá-wabo   l-edíbale
he-cut up -after   her   he-roast   her   good-very   he-roast-

di-n-bená|da|no   lo-lokhóto   fa   wáyali   lokó|da|no   abā-bĭ   l-edibalĭ
after   her   he-put-in   knapsack in   her   others   his-roasted

kothá-(siroko ó-ma   a-her̥ek̥edr̥e (n.   32. Kie(nwáida   le̥-koyo-fá|da   yuwária-to
animal-flesh   with   gather   it   then   he-return   from-thence

thé|da|i   l-ĭ(sikwaǎ (nro.
flee   he (?) his-village-at

33. *L-ande-fa|tháda   bahǒü|n|da,   l-iréitu   o-yóno   ámuŋ.*   34. *Na-malitha|ta*
he-come   house-at   his-wife   family   at   they-make

a-tá-hǒü   lo-borā-n da.   35. *L-andā|tha   nā-mun|da.*   36. *L-andi-n-kona|*
beverage   he-for   he-come   they-at   He-come-when

tháda   ná-(sika   náha   bahü-n-či   le̥-táña   wa|da.   37. *Le-thá|ta|no*
they-give   these   house-at-person   his-drink   he-drink

méra-loko-či-di(n.   38. *Le̥-ti-m-bena|thá|no   yuo̥a-či   l-a   kikataba*
haste-in-person-as   he-drink-after   it   disturb   he-do   again

an(sí|da|ba.   39. *D-aúsa   kika   thédaba   l-a-m-biá|ta   na-múĭn|da.*   40.
peace   I-go   back-again   he-say   they-to

Da-onaká-fa   tūraha   ú-ma   l-a-m-bia|tá   na-múĭn-da.   41. *Hadiaki|tháati*
I-take-will   her   with   he-say   they-to   So

kúdu-ni   l-a-m-bia|tá   a-moλidá-n|da|ye.   42. *Kiantháda lu-kúyua kikádaba.*
heavy   he-say   deceiving   [them   then   he-returns again

43. *L-idiki-(nrĕn|tháda   na-kóloo̥oso-(η   bia   lo-woyáli-á|da.*   44. *Lo-*
he-after   they-shake out   his-knapsack   his-

woyáli-a   ú-(sibo|baikiáda   l-i(siká-ya   too|da   l-iréitu   o-banā|da.   45. *Funá(sa-*
knapsack face   he-put   this   his-wife   liver   Hungry-

(n-doma   tháda|yĭ   aredábo|kená|da   kutá-bana-bia   n-ikisi-ká|da|nǎ
because   they   bite   then   animal-liver   they-think   it

---

(smoke-dried) her.   31. After he had roasted her thoroughly, he put her into a knapsack with the other dried meat, and tied it together.   32. Then he returned from thence to his village.

33. He comes to the house, to his wife's family.   34. They make tapana for him.   35. He came to them.   36. As he came, the inhabitants of the house gave him to drink.   37. He drank hastily.   38. After he had drunk, he made haste again.   39. I go back again, said he to them.   40. I shall fetch her, said he to them.   41. She has a heavy load, he said, deceiving them.   42. Then he returned.

43. After he had gone, they emptied his knapsack.   44. Uppermost in his knapsack he had put his wife's liver.   45. Because they were hungry,

to-bánná|da. 46. *Kienbaikiáda n-ekei-ya to   to-baná|da.* 47. *N-iki-m-*
that liver   then   they-eat   that her-liver   they-eat-

bena(η sá-wabo   to kakŏ̆-tó o-bána, na-kóloọosó-m-bia to wáyali-loko-
after   good-very that human liver   they-shake out   that knapsack-in-

ária|da. 48. *Adẹχkẹ́-re|n-a-m-bia|tádẹ   to   kakhŏ̆-to|da   to-mákwa*
from   see   they do   that   human being   all

th-ánikō|da   to-kóti-dibaledá-sa má-tho the-kábo|de hara(n t-üši
her-things, § 78 ᵉ) ²) her-foot-roasted-thing with her-hand   complete her-

kowái   l-ẹdebalidi-sa to-mákwa th-üyédi.   49. *Kiatá n-adẹkẹ́(n*
head § 48 ᵇ) roasted-thing it-all   her-necklace, § 112 ᵉ)   they-see

domá|da n-ewedá-ti-ka-tǐ tatá-loko to   na-mŏkŏ̆dŏ̆-sá-wa balí-n. 50.
because   they-vomit-wish   strong-in that they-swallow, thing-own indeed

A-thŏ̆|ibaikia   na-thá-ya   bálí-n   n-ewedī-m-bia|thá|no. 51. *Kiaki|tháda*
beverage   they-drink indeed they-vomit-tobe   it   then

to   amáhtali bali-tó|da aimata(n bia na-kobóroko n-ausó-m-bia báikia
these things   reality(?) angry   they-among   they-go

wádi(n l-ibiči da.
seek   he-for

    52. *N-áucika-sá-bo-ya|kóro|da|i ;   firó-to|tha adé-be-ra-tú-ši áda*
         they-find-result   not him   great   high   top tree

lu-mudá-ya a-yakatú-n-a bali-m|báikia. 53. *Audá-bia diá|na a-wádi-(n*
he-mount   hiding   indeed   mad   thus   seek

l-ibiči. 54. *N-aučiká-ya kóro|de.* 55. *To-moróa thada ada ši-waria*
he-for   they-find   not   but   tree top-from

yóη-koro lü-yakatú|n-a, yuwária tháda l-ẹdẹkẹ-ša-kathǐda|ye. 56. *Balí-n|ta*
place   he-hide   from thence his-see-result-hide them   indeed

n-awádi-n l-ibiči-ro|da, ná-iboa lo-konáriaa|da. 57. *L-aiči-(n ná-ibo-n-oa*
they-seek he-for   they-cease he-for   he-know they-cease

---

they bit the supposed animal-liver. 46. Then they ate that liver [the
mother of the family ate first from the liver]. 47. After they had eaten
well that human liver, they shook out the remaining contents of the knapsack. 48. They saw all the things of that female : her dried feet with
her hands complete. her head which he had dried, all her necklaces. 49.
As they saw that, they strongly wished to vomit out that which they had
swallowed. 50. Tapana they drunk in order to vomit it out. 51. Then
they were very angry and went to search for him.

52. They could not find him at all ; he had mounted upon a high tree
and was well-hidden. 53. Frantically they sought for him. 54. They
found nothing. 55. But from his hiding-place on the top of the tree, he
spied all. 56. Really they sought for him. they stopped. 57. When he

lo-konária lo-thókodá-koba únabo-(ŋró|da yuware|ki|da(n lŏ-tŏ(üdá-koba
he-for　　　　he-descended　　　ground-to　　　from thence　　　he-fled

ába šikoá-(nro.
other village-to

---

knew that they had stopped searching for him, he descended, and fled to another place.

§ 215. **The man who killed the bush-spirits**

[In the corresponding Warau tale, recorded by R., 19a, Sect. 19ff.; the hero is called *Kororomanna* (this volume, § 166 e) 2)]; comp. also D. 8, 188.

1. *Abá|t-a   lokó|da.*   2. *Kónoko-n tháda ilasá-či-bu|da|líra l-ityirityá-*
one it-is　　man　　　　　　　forest-at　　　splitting　　he　his-cane-

wa, áda tháda ƒiró-tho diáko balákoa l-a-bó|da.   3. *A-hílasá-m-bo, kǐ(n-*
own tree　　　great　　upon sitting he-did　　　　splitting　　　then

kita lę-kánaba   lílěsa-ŋ   dǐ(n čikíšikíšidi-(n-bo|da.   4. *Kiadóma tháda*
he-heard　splitting　　　as　　(split-cane-sound)　　　　　therefore

l-ędęká-bó da : hamá-ro(n ikísida(n|da|i.   5. *Biámbǐ wa|tháda ibiro-bé|da*
he-look　　　　what　　imitate (?)　　him　　　a couple　　　little ones

kiá áda ká-loko-tu o-lokó-ya-bó|da.   6. *Konóko-kúya   üsa-be-wá-ya*
that tree hollow　　in-being　　　　　　bush-spirit　　children-own

tháda|no.   7. *Kiadóma   tháda   ló-dobada-thé|da   to   ibiro-bé-da*
they 1)　　　　therefore　　　　he-pull out　　　those　little ones

thó-lokaaria to ƒiró-to áda lo-ƒáro-m-bia|thá to   ibiro-bǐ|dę kónoko-kúya
it in-from　　that big　tree he-kill　　　those little ones　bush-spirit

üsa-bé dę.   8. *Uráli th-a-bó|da lu-čáda-ka tu-báda-lóko-di-a th-ódo-m-biá*
children　　　　curare it-was　　he-prick　　their-nail-in　　they-die

da.   9. *Kié(nbená lo-ƒára-be(n-domá|da|(ŋ ló-modę-(n bia tháda*
thereafter　　he-kill-just now-because　　them　　he-mount

aiómu(n ada-ši-nró|da th-idíki|da.
high　　tree-top-at　　it-after

---

1. There was a man.   2. In the forest he was splitting basket-reed, seated upon a big tree.   3. As he was splitting, he heard as it were the sound of splitting made with the mouth.   4. Therefore he looked to see what could be imitating him.   5. Two small children were in the hollow of that tree.   6. They were children of a bush-spirit.   7. Therefore he pulled them out of that tree to kill them.   8. Poisoned (curare-) arrow-points he pricked under their nails to make them die.   9. Then, because he had killed them, he afterwards climbed a high tree.

---

1) § 178, nature-spirits are regarded as belonging to the class of non-rational beings (nature).

10. *Ki(n kúbaikiáda k-ireákata   th-ánde-n|tu   kónoko-kuyahá|da.*
    then   married-couple they-come   those bush-spirits

11. *Th-ẹdẹke-m-bia|da t-üsa-be   á-udo-n da.*   12. *Kiádoma baikiáda*
    they-see   their-children dead   therefore

to-boná-ka|da|i.   13. *Lo-üya|tháda th-ẹ́dẹkẹ̀-m-biá|da   kulisá-črakó|da.*
they-follow (§ 64) him   his-image   they-see   pool-in

14. *Aiomó-ro ta-ko|dẹkẹ-thó-na-ma dá|no má(nsoa(n dóma|thada k-akúsa-*
    high-at   not   see-can   it   very   because   with-eye-

boná-n|da.   15. *T-ẹdẹkẹ-n-doma|tháde úni-rakó l-oyá|da   th-aithá|da|i*
surface   they-see-because   water-in his-image they-know him

áiomu(n ada-ši-n|da|i.   16. *Kiadóma tháda thu-múdẹ-fa tho   wadili-*
high   tree-top-at him   therefore   it-mount   that male

koró|da th-áboloka-nro thó-mode-fá|de l-ibitsi-ro|da to   áda khón-di|da.
§ 176 c) 2) the-top-at   it-mount   he-to   that tree-on-person

17. *Ká-šitódai-tō|tha thú-mudi-(n-bó|da ; či-tora-(nró da th-inaloko|tháda*
    upside-down   it mounting   head-foot-at   its-hind parts

kufá-iwi-abó|da lo-yoko-ŋ-biá|da č-iwiši dyako-ri(ŋ th-ódo-m-bia|dẹ.
kufa-fruit-with   he-strike   its-testicle upon   it-die

18. *Mǎ-mudi-(n koa|t-á-ŋ-ka   tohó|da kónoko-kuyá|da l-ibitsi-ro aiomó-*
    not-mount-yet it-do-when   that   bush-spirit   he-at   high-at

ro, kia-bóra-kwá-n|da to-soká-ti-ka|tá to áda   l-a-bó da.   19. *To-sokó-m-*
that-before-yet   it-cut-wish   that tree he-was   it-cutting

---

10. Then came the couple [man and wife] of bush-spirits.
11. They saw their children dead.   12. Therefore they followed him.
13. They saw his image in a pool of water.   14. They could not see
upwards, because their forehead protrudes over their eyes (do. R. 19a,
Sect. 23, 99).   15. Because they saw his image in the water, they knew
him to be upon the high tree.   16. Therefore the male bush-spirit began
climbing to the top, to get at the person that was on the tree.   17. Upside-
down it was climbing ; when he was upside-down, the man hit his testicle
(see R. 19a, Sect. 99) with a *kufa*-fruit (creole *abrasa*, Clusia sp. [1])), and
he died. (N°s 18—27 form part of the history which the narrator had
omitted).

18. Before the bush-spirit climbed towards him, he wished to cut down
that tree on which he was.   19. When cutting, the axe got loose from the

---

[1]) D. 8, 267 ["The nest of the humming-bird is a marvel of strength, lightness,
and beauty. It is skilfully plastered throughout with the clammy part of] the *cuffa* or
wild onion, the seeds of which resemble canary seeds, and afford food to some birds.
An Indian will avoid treading on an unripe fruit of the cuffa, dreading from its
acridity a sore called "stone bruise". At the risk of the stone bruise, the toes rubbed
with the cuffa are said to be safe from bat bites." See also R. 19a, Sect. 168.

bo ki l-a-bó|da   tho-baró-n|da   a-fúlido-n-á-bia   tho-daya-konária   kin|to-
  he-was (?)   its-axe   loose   its-handle-from   then it-

tóbadoa   to-baǫó|da   úni-rakó-(n.   20.   Kǐŋ   kúbakiáda   wadi-thó|da
 falls   its-axe   water-in   then   long

bokhóroná|da   t-ęthękękę-fa   th-ęnęka-ki-m-bia|to   tho-baró-ña wá|dę.   21.
 creeper   it-pulls   it-take-again   that its-axe-own

Bári-ka tháda abároko bokhórona(n t-ęthékędę-n|da.   22.   To ibi-n-doma
 though   several   creeper   it-pulls   it thin-because

to-bokórona|da   iera|tháda   uni-rakó|da   ka-úǫudárathá-ya-bo
the-creeper   there, § 45 ᶜ)   water-in   coming in a heap together, §§ 122 ᵈ) ²), 108 A

k-alebétu-n-a   uni-rako   toh bokóroná|da.   23.   Kiadomá|da mintóko tulá-ŋ
coiled   water-in   that creeper   therefore   very   deep

to   oniábo   morothá-ga.   24.   Kialokó|da   ibóro|th-a(n-bia   to-báro-n-
that   water   think   that-in   remain   its-axe-con-

kona|diá|da.   25.   Tóho   yawo-báro(ŋ   na-ǫomi(ŋ   álaso; to|
cerning   thus   This   devil-axe   they-call (§ 139 ᵇ· ᶜ) ?)   tortoise it

tháda   konok-uyá-kuba   o-báro-(n   thóra   thó-tobádi(n   koba|tháda|no
was   bush-spirit-former   axe   that   it-lett fall   long-ago   it

thu-baǫo-ña   kulisá-rako-(ŋro   kia|tháda   to   aláso   bia-kobá|da.   26.
its-axe-own   pool-in   that was   the   tortoise   to-be-past

Khaǫó-bia|da iawohŏ̌ baró-(ŋ n-á(m-bia to-múǐn|da.
now   devil   axe   they-say   it-at

   27.   *Tó(a   áiomu(ŋ   kasáko   o-loa-bána   uyáro-n-wa   th-ędękhá-na|da*
        the   high   heaven   heart-surface   reflecting   it-saw

mintoko tholá-n|toho t-a-m-biá|da a-ibī-n|da|no.
very   deep   it-did-to be   leave   it

---

handle, and fell into the water. 20. Then he tore off a long creeper (*bokhorona*, Arum sp. ?[1])) for measuring the depth of the water. 21. He tore off a great quantity of that creeper. 22. Because that creeper was very thin, in the water it came together in a heap in coils. 23. [He did not perceive that, and.] Therefore he thought the water was very deep. 24. He let his axe lie in it. 25. "Devil's axe" they call the (a certain species of) tortoise; it was the bush-spirit's axe which he let fall into the pool which became in ancient times the tortoise. 26. To this very day they call it "devil's axe". 27. He saw the blue sky reflected, and fancied that the water was very deep, and left the axe.

---

[1]) D. *bucuruma*, sarsaparilla; a similar name in Sm. *bukkurúmana hatti*, a species of very thick and long Cayenne pepper; comp. with this D. 8, 184, R. 19a, Sect. 103, the bush-spirit having peppers on its head, and Koch-Grünberg 45c, II, p. 148: the pepper plant on the head of Piaima.

28. *Th-ódo-m-bená|da   č-iriči|da,   č-ireitó|da   wade-fá|da   ibihi|da*
　　　 it-die-after 　　　　 the-husband 　　　 the-wife 　　　 seek-will 　　　 charm

č-ibidi-(n bia   líhida lokó|da úidiki. 　　29. *Atönoa|tháda m-ausó-ŋ-kwa*
she-practices magic 　　 that 　　 man 　　 footstep 　　　 first 　　　 not-go-yet

t-á-ŋ-ka   ibī-bia   wadá-(nro lü-díkita   th-ánaká|de t-edikíti-ŋ bia
she-was-when 　 charm-to be seek-at 　　 his-footprint 　　 she-take 　　 she-envelop

tháda ade-bóna lokó|da|(ŋ. 　 30. *Kie(n th-óso-n|da uwáda-ro ibi   ibitsí-*
　 tree-leaf 　 in 　　 it 　　 then 　 she-go 　　 search 　 charm for

ro|da   th-aikašía-ŋ-bia   thá-to   t-idikíti-wa. 　 31. *Th-óso-m-bena|tháda*
　 she-forget 　　　 that 　 her-package 　　　 she-go-after

liída lóko kilí|da a-tokodó-m-bia onabó(nró|da lo-dokodó-m-bia|tha tó(ho
that 　 man § 176 c) 2) .'escend 　　 ground-at 　　 he-loose 　　　　 this

dikitá-sa|da. 　 32. *Lü-díki-wa :   th-önakö̆-sa   ká-lokothó-n-á   da*
package 　　　 his-footprint-own 　　 its-take-result 　 within-put

kiadoma|tháda   l-ialókota   l-idíki-wá|da   th-oáya|tha   to   kónoko-kúya
therefore 　　　 he-changes 　 his-footprint-own 　 its-own 　　 that 　 bush-spirit

idiki|da l-eneke-(m-bia l-ediki   üyalokodówa.
footprint he-take 　　　 his-footprint 　 instead

33. *Thu-makwá-ro-m|báikia   ad-ubóna   ty-ikídi|tho   yúliwihi.* 　34.
　　 all 　　　　　　　 tree-leaves 　　 she-envelop this 　 fire-fly

Tho-máliti-sá-na to ts-ibiwá|da. 　 35. *To   th-ánde-n|da li(hi bá(ha 　 lóko*
she-make-result 　 this her-charm-own 　　 this 　 she-come 　　 this 　 perhaps man

idiki-koán-to mórothá-fa|ba th-oáya kwa(ŋ a-bído-n-á da. 　36. *Kĩŋkóbaikiáda*
footprint 　 think 　　　 herself 　 yet 　　 practice magic 　 then

líhi lokó|da lo-modá ki kádaba aiomó-ro ada-šī-nro. 　 37. *Yu(ŋ ada-si(ŋ*
this man 　 he-mounts 　 again 　 high 　 tree-top-at 　　　 there 　 tree-top

koa|l-á-ŋ-ka|tháda   th-ánde-m-biá|da. 　 38. *To-khóta|ta ikíhi|da firō-tho*
yet 　 he-is-when 　　　 she-come 　　　　 she-collects 　 fire 　 great

---

28. After the husband had died, the wife sought for a charm in order
to practice magic with the man's foot-prints. 29. Before she went to seek
a charm, she took his foot-prints and wrapped them in the leaf of a tree.
30. Then she went to look for a charm, and forgot the packet. 31. After
she was gone, that man came down and opened the packet. 32. He took
his own foot-prints and put the bush-spirit's foot-prints in their stead.

33. All [the magic things she used] were tree-leaves and wrapped in
them a fire-fly [which has the habit, if there is a fire, of flying into it].
34. From these the charm was made. 35. She thought that it were the
foot-prints of the man, but on herself she practiced magic. 36. Then the
man climbed again up the high tree. 37. He was still up that tree, when
she came. 38. She collected fire-wood and made a big fire. 39. If I

ikihi máliti(n. 39. D-ibídi-faroká|i l-etikidi-fa-té áiomu(nária toho
fire   make   I-practice magic-if him he-fall-shall   high-from   this

iki(hikolóko-(nro moro|tábа|da ; d-ibída | i muõthána|da. 40. Th-oǎya-
fire-in   think   I-enchant him she has said (§ 35)   she-self-

šia-ro|th-a-nbia|thada iki(hi kolokó-nro adalidí(n|da a-bitú-n-a. 41. Kiyatá-
result it-do   fire in   run   burn   this

koba-thára to konóko-kuya eréito ōdo-n-koba.
was   that bush-spirit   wife   died

---

practice magic on him, he will fall down into the fire, she thought ; I practice
magic on him, said she. 40. It was herself that ran into the fire and
burned. 41. So the bush-spirit's wife died.

§ 216. **The tortoise, the thrush and their mother-in-law;**
the great flood

Dutch spelling

(comp. R. 19a, Sect. 162C ; B. 5e, 10, Koch-Grünberg 45d nos 41, 49, 107)

1. *Lokoh   khona th-a-n-ka|tha hikorli ma-tho korlasiri, kaboja tha*
   man   like   being   tortoise and   thrush   field they-

tho-soko-fa th-mikketehnatho o-bora. 2. Kasakabo-noma|tha a-mekhebo-n
cut-will   their-mother-in-law for   day-all   work

ro ose-fa-be-n ; 3. Kenda th-mikkethnatho, bahe-n ka|tha obada-n
go   and   their-m.i.l.   house-at when   wait

tho-bora-n-be ; korlasiri tha mehra   andi-n, hikorli tha ajowa-
them-for   thrush   quick (§ 104 b) 1) II)) come tortoise   late-only

ron anda bah-m, kijadoma tho-mikketeh k-ansi ka tho hikorli, mika-kho,
come house-at therefore its-m.i.l.   loves   that tortoise hard

l-mekhebo-n mn thana.
his-work 1)   at

4. *Aba ka|tah korlasiri koro|kahlin bahe-n   andi-n, ken baikija ka-tha-n*
   other time   thrush   not   quick house-at come   then   with-drink

---

1. When the tortoise and the thrush were still men, they prepared a
field (plantation) for their mother-in-law. 2. Every day they went to
work. 3. Their m.i.l. waited for them at the house ; the thrush returned
early, the tortoise returned late, therefore the m.i.l. loved the tortoise,
because it worked so well. 4. Another time, the thrush did not return so
early ; the m.i.l. had tapana for herself, and she gave diluted tapana to

---

1) The pronominal prefix of the male class has to be used here, because the
mother-in-law speaks of her son-in-law.

th-oja th-mikkethenatoh, th-fa-te-sa   rontah th-asiekie-n-bija korlasiri
herself their-m.i.l.   her-do-future-result mixed she-give   thrush

mn. 5. *Hamakhoro l-mekhebo-ka mn thana korlasiri amon;* 6. *Hikorli*
to.   nothing   he-work   at   thrush   to.   tortoise

koro rontah th-keleke ti-n-bija th-imikketeh usa-tho th-era-wabo   ataha
not mixed she-reach-cause [1]) its-m.i.l.   good   its-juice-genuine drink

da. 7. *Kija tha-khoro a-mekheboto-hja toho hikorli, awsoron-tho baikija*
       that it was not   working   the tortoise   idle

sabasabadi-n jaraha-di ma-mekhebo tha-ja. 8. *Aba-li tha ka-sa-tho kija*
trampling   yonder   not-work   not-work   one   having-child that

korlasiri da, th-usa baikija aka-n-bija th-ietsi wa   amaha th-ikketeh
thrush   its-child   tell   its-father what its-grandmother

adija-n a-mirita-djaron th-ietsi jaloko. 9. *Kijadoma|tha th-imawtowa koba*
say   reviling § 140 c) its-father against   therefore   it-became angry

korlasiri th-mikketeh amoni. 10. *Korlasiri tha, a-hibida-tho kaboja a-soko-n.*
thrush   its-m.i.l. at   thrush   finished   field cutting

11. *Th-ibita tah tho kaboja hibien kiba.* 12. *Th-mikketeh a-kasirida*
    it-burn   that field already also   its-m.i.l.   prepare kasiri

kikaba, kija emelija-tho kaboja bana, 13. *firo-tho tha samako o-loko*
again   new   new   field on   great   pot   in

th-siki fa|da|no, tho-sonko-n-owa-bija. 14. *kija-tho tho-sonko-n-owa*
she-put it it-pour   that this   her-pouring

koba|tha tho barla bija da. 15. *Amaha a-tendo-tho-koba, kija|tha|to*
past   the sea   become   what sunken   was   that   the

orijo bija koba.
water-spirit became

---

the thrush. 5. "He has done no work, the thrush". 6. To the tortoise the m.i.l. did not give diluted tapana, but good pure tapana. 7. The tortoise, however, had not been working, but had idled, trampling on the grass. 8. The thrush had a child, and the child told its father how its grandmother was reviling him. 9. Therefore the thrush became angry with its m.i.l. 10. The thrush finished cutting the field. 11. It had already burned it too. 12. Its m.i.l. had again prepared kasiri on that new field. 13. in a big jar she put it. [She came to look at the field and collided with a big tree, which had not yet been cleared away; the vessel containing kasiri touched that tree, and the kasiri] ran out. 14. that spilled kasiri became a big lake. 15. The m.i.l. sunk and became a water-spirit.

[At that same moment a koata (Ateles) was planting a bixa-fruit (Bixa

---

1) The mother-in-law has the tapana given to the tortoise by a child: she may not do so herself, see § 165.

Orellana, red paint) ; when the great flood came, the koata not knowing what to do, rubbed the bixa-fruit on its forehead, after which it fled to the forest ; ever since that time, the koata has a red spot on its forehead. The m.i.l. had many things with her, among others a cassava-squeezer and grated cassava ; a cylinder of grated cassava which came out of the squeezer, then became the fish *kwériman* (Mugil Brasiliensis)].

§ 217.   The vain trogon and the industrious colibri
Dutch spelling

1. *Wakili-be-koba* (or *wakili-koba*), *loko   khona   th-a-n-kha,   tho-*
long ago   man   like   being   all

makowa-ron   khotah   ma-tho   kodibijo,   bokolawro   ma-tho   bimiti   kha-koba.
animal   and   bird   trogon   and   colibri were

2. *Da-marliti-ba|do   d-a|la-nnijawa   firo   ba   da-jakhoro,   a-baleta-ti-rro*
I make, § 60 b)   my-bench-own   great also my-soul (?)   sit-wish-only

da-ja-fa|do,   n-ahla-n   o-lokko, tah tha bokolawro adija-n, akanabokota-n
my-soul (?)-will their-bench in   said trogon   speaking hear-causing

tha   bimiti   da.   3.   Kasakabo-man   tha,   bokolawro   da,   amarli-amarlida-ka
colibri   day-whole   trogon   make-make

th-la-nnijawa.
its-bench-own

4. *Kidija   th-a-n   doma   bokolawro   adija-n|da,   bimiti   da,   arleke-fa   adija-*
thus   because trogon   speak   colibri   move(stir) word

he bokolawro adi|da.   5.   Bimiti baikija da akobantowa-ron mana, kija thada,
trogon   upon   colibri   field-make only   being

---

1. Very long ago, when all animals and birds were like men, there were a trogon [1]) and a colibri.   2. I will make a bench [2]) for myself ; not only am I great, but I will also sit on a bench, on the people's benches, said the trogon, so that the colibri heard it.   3. The whole day the trogon was occupied in making its bench.   4. Because the trogon spoke so, the colibri spoke in proverbs (a side-hit) to ("upon") the trogon.   5. The colibri

---

[1]) The trogon (Trogon viridis) is a sacred bird, a medicine-bird. The trogons sit with their backs to each other, when eating, and after that example the Indians formerly also sat with their backs to each other when eating ; they might not look at each other (comp. R. 19a, Sect. 223).

[2]) In several tales and customs an Indian bench appears as a sign of distinction. D. 8, 264 "The *hahlah* was the divining stool used by Piai priest-doctors during their incantantions, ornamented with fanciful designs of animals, chiefly the tortoise and the alligator. It is now one of the few ordinary articles of furniture in every Indian household."

6. *da-soko-ba do da-koba-nijawa si   th-a-n bija to   bimiti adija-kien daba;*
   I-cut, 60 b)?   my-field-own   § 179 become   the colibri said again

7. *amaha dokho da-sa-be   eke-ja-fa da-moni, awosoro da-be-ja   ka-sa-*
   what   ?   my-children eat-shall I-by   idle   I-am (§ 59 ª) ³)) having

nie,   mawadilija   d-a-dekhi-n nah khona.
children mamari, not at all I-look   they-for

---

was preparing a field, and said   6. I cut my field,   7. nothing shall my
children get to eat from me, [if] I cannot look after them.

§ 218. **The tortoise and the opossum**
Dutch spelling
(comp. R. 19a, Sect. 159).

1. *Hikorli ma-tho jawarle tha, a-kisidowa koba halika-n djaro tata-sabon-*
   tortoise ¦and   opossum   tried   which ever   ¦strongest

fa hammusia mn ;   2. *kijadoma tha hikorli, jawarle tha a-kkere-fa|da|n*
hunger   at   therefore   tortoise opossum tie   it

hobo abon|da|no. 3. *Ts-ikien   ka-tokorlo-n   bo-ren   baikija   tho   hobo*
plum   under   it   moment   blooming (just begin)   this   plum

t-ekkera|no jawarle tho hikorli da ; haliman|thatha tho hikorli k-ebena-n
it-tied   it opossum the tortoise   so   the tortoise long time

jomn hobo abon ma-khoto-nia, kijaron kakke kowa|th-a-n tha.   4. *Tho*
there plum under without-eating   live   yet   being   that

hobo da, ka-tokorlo-ja hibien, k-iwi-ka badijan, kijadoma thokololon
plum   blooming   already set-fruit   also   therefore   fallen unripe fruit

abo tha tho-bojowa-ja. 5. *Wadja wai tha|da th-dekhi-n-bija the tho*
with   it-feeds-self   afterwards very   it-look   the

jawarle da|nno. 6. *Awothiki-ren baikija|da|no tho hikorli kakke ren-tho|da.*
opossum   it   find   it the tortoise live   still

7. *Kijaloko   hebe-tho hobo iewi   th-mn, tho th-ikie-n bija th-tata ansi-*
   next-time (?)   ripe   plum fruit   it-at   it-eat   it-strengthen-self

wa|da, ma-odo-n th-a-n-bija.
not-die   it-to be

---

1. The tortoise and the opossum once tried which of them could best
stand hunger.   2. To this purpose, the opossum tied the tortoise under a
plum-tree (Spondeas lutea). 3. At the time the tortoise was tied up by the
opossum, the plum-tree was only just coming in bloom ; so the tortoise had
to stay a long time under the plum-tree without food, yet it remained alive.
   4. So the plum-tree bloomed and bore fruit, and then the tortoise fed
upon the unripe fruit which had fallen off. 5. A long time afterwards,
the opossum came to look at the tortoise. 6. It found the tortoise still
alive. 7. Next time, the plum-tree had ripe plums, and through eating
them, the tortoise had regained its strength.

8. *Ken   baikija   th-odokodo-n   bija   tho   jawarle   tho   hikorli   da ;*
then   it-loose   that   opossum   that   tortoise

th-jalokhota-n   bija   baikija   be,   hikorli   tha   a-kkere   bija   jawarle   ḳidaba
they-change   tortoise   tie   opossum   again

th-jalokhodo-wa   karowa|da   o-toro.   9. *Th-ikhien   ka-tokorlo-n   ren   bo|da|*
its-stead   agava   foot   moment   blooming (just begin)

no,   tho   jawarle   a-kkera-ka   jaraha   iebara-n.   10. *Ken   bena|da,   joho-ro*
it   the   opossum   tie   there   remain   thereafter   many

kasakabo   idiki|da,   hikorli   adekke-ḟa-teh   tho   jawarle|da.   11. *Athenowa|tah*
day   after   tortoise   see   the   opossum   first

awnobo-wa   khan   kowa   thatah   tata-noma   kha-toh   tho   hikorli   a-sa-
answer   being   yet   strong-with (?)   when   the   tortoise   call

nnoma|da|n.   12. *Kijaloko   ki|tha   kholen-bija   th-dja-n   khon|da.*   13. *Aba-*
it   next time   weak   it-speak   other

ka|tha   tho   hikorli   adekhi-n   kithe-sa|ba   no,   th-sa-ka   th-erie   tho   hikorli   da
time   the   tortoise   see   again   it   it-calls   its-name   the   tortoise

mawadili   sabo-ka|tha   th-onabo-n-a   tata-sabo|n.   14. *Jowarija   ki|tha*
mamari,   impossible   more   it-answer   hard-more   it   from thence

kasakabo-be   balie-n   bena,   th-anda   kikatha   tho   hikorli   tho   jawarle   amn   da,
days   really   after   it-came   again   the   tortoise   the   opossum   to

tho-oda-ja   koba   hibien ;   mabberie   ron   tah   awnaba-n-bija.   15. *Kijadoma*
it-died   already   flies   only   answer   therefore

tho   hikorli   mienthokho   tata   ansi   ḟenasia   mn   tora.
the   tortoise   very   hard   living-force   hunger   at   that

---

8. Then the opossum untied the tortoise, and they changed places, and
the tortoise tied the opossum to the foot of an agave. 9. At the time
when it was just coming in bloom, the opossum was tied up to remain there.
10. Many days afterwards, the tortoise went to look at the opossum. 11.
In the beginning, when the tortoise called it, it answered with a strong
voice. 12. Next time, its voice was weak. 13. Another time when the
tortoise went to see it, and called its name, it could no longer answer loudly.
14. Many days later, the tortoise came again to the opossum, it was
already dead ; the carrion-flies only answered. 15. And that is why the
tortoise can stand hunger so well. [It may do three months without food].

§ 219. The girl and the goatsucker (whip-poor-will)

Dutch spelling

(comp. Koch-Grünberg 45d, n⁰. 67).

1. *Wakilie koba|tha, abah-ka aba bikidolija-tho hijaro, bakkelama khan*
   long ago   one time   a   girl   female evening

ansa-n-bo.   2. *Kenkhoro baikija, wakorlajo a-moromoroda-bo waboroko*
grating   then   goatsucker fly-flying   path

siri warija.   3. *A-joroda th-a-n-kha baikija, waboroko-sirie-n|da kakkih*
begin from   squeeze she-being   path-begin-at   making

rethajabo wakorlajo.   4. *Kijadoma|tha iekihie josie tho hijaro|da*
noise   goatsucker   therefore   half-burned firewood the   female

a-bborle-borleda-bo th-ibitsi to wakorlajo;   5. *bijama-ka|tha tho-borledie-n*
throw-throwing   it-at   the goatsucker   second time   she-throw

to hijaro th-iebietsi|to hijaro.   6. *Ken baikija th-kabinteh okhoni da*
the female   it-at   the female   then   third   time

th-oso-n-bija|to hijaro waboroko-sierie-nro th-ienabo to wakorlajo,   7.
she-go   the female path-head-at   it-after   that goatsucker

abakharen|tha to wakorlajo a-beso-n-owa bija aba loko wadilie dien|da.
suddenly   that goatsucker   transforming   a   man male   as

8. *Kijadoma|tha to wakorlajo da adija-n-bija to hijaro o-ma ;*   9.
therefore   that goatsucker   speak   that female   with

kakkehitsi bija a-beso|tah|na.   10. *Dai ronnija|da hijaro ussa.*   11. *Da-sie-*
living man become transformed it   I   only   woman good   I-love-

n-doma|bo hadijaken da-jarratowa-bo b-mon.   12. *Khiddowahni bija*
because thee   with desire   I-appear   thee-to   verily

baikija bikidoliatsi loko wadilie dija th-a-n a-beso-n-a|n.   13. *Tho-ma to*
youth   man male   as   being transform it   it-with   the

---

1. One evening, long ago, a girl was grating cassava. 2. Then came a goatsucker and flew round and round the place where the road from the village begins. 3. As she was squeezing the cassava, the goatsucker made a great noise at the beginning of the path. 4. Therefore the girl threw pieces of half-burned fire-wood at the goatsucker. 5. She threw a second time. 6. The third time she went to the beginning of the path after the goatsucker. 7. Suddenly the goatsucker was metamorphosed into a man. 8. And the goatsucker spoke with the girl; 9. it had become a living man. 10. It is only I, good woman. 11. Because I love you, I appear thus before you. 12. Really he had become a young man. 13. The

wakorlajo da kijawai hijaro.   14. *Th-eben loko wadilie dija|thana baikija*
goatsucker   that   woman   its-full   man   male   as

ussa-n dikkih-ni th-iereitoh khona.
good   looking   its-wife   like

    15. *Wahdijarontha kebenan disijan | to hijaro tho-ma;*   16. *Tete-*
      afterwards   long time accustomed the woman it-with   mother-

khanni d-adikkeh ʃa banja, b-ossa-li da-ma th-a-n-bija koba|tha to
small   I-see   for a time thou-go   I-with   said   the

wakorlajo anmrlidie-n to hijaro tho-ma-wa.   17. *Kenkhro baikija|to*
goatsucker   deceiving   the woman it-with-own   then   the

hijaro osa-koba tho-ma tho-jo mamonro adikkhe-ren baikija to tho-jo da.
woman went   it-with   its-mother to   see   that its-mother

18. *Kija tha th-kerre   adijakema k-ansie-n da no, abalokhodie thako,*
     that   her-mother-in-law thus-very love   her   all kinds of things

aklekatsidija, th-tiejo   o-mon.
reach   her-daughter-in-law   to

    19. *Aba-ka tha aba dnaroko rethan th-ietyo mn iekihi-khodo a-sikie-n,*
      one time   a   armfull   her-d.i.l. at   fire-wood   give

kija|tha khoro iekihi-khoda wabo-jada|n, odo (owdo-tsi)-bona ron wa|tha.
that was not   fire-wood   genuine   it dead   bones only

20. *Aba-kka|tha ata-he (kasiri) th-iesikie-n th-ietjo mn kiba, owdo-tsi*
    one time   drink (kasiri)   she-give   her-d.i.l. to again   dead

urraro-n ki|tha|da|ba,   21. *ma-thi-n thatha|da|no, mienka khoro da-te-loko*
liquid again   not-drink said   she very   my-bowels

karie-ni kijadoma da-tha makhoro t-ah da,   22. *th-ieretsi wa|tha*
aching   therefore   I-drink   nothing   she-said   her-husband-own

a-ttekeda-ja da|no.   23. *Akkaratana-le ron nija baikija jomn da,*   24.
advise   her   burying   only   place

---

goatsucker took the girl to be his wife.   14. He was like a real man, **and**
took good care of his wife.

    15. A long time afterwards, when the woman had got accustomed to
him,   16. He said: I will visit my little mother, go with me; so the
goatsucker enticed the woman to accompany him.   17. So the woman
went with him to his mother, and saw his mother.   18. Her mother-in-law
loved her very much, and gave many things to her daughter-in-law.   19.
Once she gave her d.i.l. an armfull of firewood, but it was not real firewood,
they were bones of dead men.   20. Once she gave her d.i.l. kasiri, but it
was the fluid from dead bodies.   21. She did not drink; "I have colic,
therefore I cannot drink", said she.   22. Her husband had advised her to
act in this manner.   23. [At the place where they were, there were no

kijadoma|tha|to loko-hijaro, th-ieretsie da a-sikaa koba toho hijaro-kon
therefore   that man-female   her-husband   gave   that   woman-small

o-jo amonro|da.   25. Kidija|tha koba|to loko hijaro tho-jo amn   anda
mother to   so   that man-female her-mother to came

kiendaba.   26. Kija doma loko-no odo-tsi jalokko moro m-a-ssa , to
again   therefore men   dead   spirit   think possibly (§ 30) the

wakorlajo mn.
goatsucker at

---

real men, but] it was a burial-place.   24. Therefore the husband of that human female gave that little woman back to her mother.   25. So that human female came back again to her mother.   26. And that is why the Indians call the goatsucker "dead man's spirit". [The narrator added : "superstitious people fear these birds".] [1])

§ 220. The man and the goatsuckers

In 1910 I was working in the balata-trade at the Wayombo, and slept in an Indian village. About half past nine, when everybody was asleep, I heard a goatsucker, and when he came near, I heard two. When they were very close, they shook my hammock as if a man was doing it. I felt as though I had been struck by an electric current ; for a quarter of an hour I did not know whether I was alive or not. — I lighted a lamp, and asked the birds whether they were living men or spirits. Then I dreamt that they were two men. — The day after, I told this to the inhabitants, and then someone said : two persons, a man and his wife, have been buried here, at the place where you have slept.

§ 221. The dead woman who became a deer
Dutch spelling

1. *Wakilie koba, aba|tha loko wadilie, l-iereitho owda|tha, lu-karata|tha*
   long ago   a   man male   his-wife died   he-buried

da|no ; Na-wah kowan-tsi tah daba nara   2. lu-kkarati-n bena|to lo-
her   they-alone (§ 120 a) [3), a) 2])   he-bury   after that

bodija-wa|da l-ose-fa aba-nro|da th-idiki.   3. Atenowa|tha l-osa konoko-nro.
his-corpse he-go-will other-at it-after first   he-go forest-at

---

1. Long ago, there was a man whose wife died : [when] he buried her, they (he and his dead wife) were alone.   2. After he had buried her, he went to another place.   3. First he went to the forest.   4. When evening

---

[1])   Comp. also R. 19a. Sect. 103 : a bush-spirit's brains were scattered, and from each piece there grew a *wokorai-yu. Yu* = spirit ? § 167 d).

4. *ken kho baikijada, bakkelama khan jokha-waria l-anda ki-ſa l-sikowa-n,*
   then   evening   hunt-from   he-come   his-house-at

jon-tho bie wabbeka l-iereitho-wa lu-kkarati-n ; 5. *bakkelama wabo-*
where just now now   his-wife   he-bury   evening   very-

ron|tha konoko-sie-n-bo hadali da, lo-balie ſa aba-nro da.
only   forest-begin   sun   he-pass will other-to

    6. *Ken khoro baikija, sjokhan l-a-n-bena oso-n|ki|tha ma-tato-n-a kowa*
       then   somewhat he-be-after go   not-far-being   yet

l-a-n-kha, lu-kkanabi-n bija|tha a-siemaka-he l-ienabo-wa|da.
he-be-when he-hear   cry   he-after

    7. *Lu-kkanabana baikija, l-iereitho be-koba o-jorleroko dija-tsi|th-a-n*
       he-hear   his-wife past   throat-in   like

barlie-n. 8. *Amaha-ron b-ieba | de !! tah tha kakonon ben a-simaka-n*
indeed   what   thou-leave me said   loudly   calling

l-ienabo. 9. *Toho|tha lu-kkanabi-n doma tata-n th-isimaka-n kakhitsi*
he-behind   this   he-hear   because hard she-calling   living man

dien|da lu-ddarliedie-n bija tha da.
as   he-run

    10. *Wa-tha-khoro l-ienabo th-oso-n, lu-darlida|tha tata-n ken barlie-n.*
      long-is-not   he-behind she-go   he-run   hard   very indeed

waa-ja-khoro baikja, th-ose-n l-ienabo. 11. *Homoni doma thee no, lo-*
long-not   she-go he-behind   near because   she he-

borleda-ka|tha tho-bora-die, addekhe-ren baikija|no, hodo-hodo khoren ;
throw-away   she-before   see-distinctly   her bowed   very

12. *lo-joko-n bija baikija siemara abo|da|n, th-owda|kika th-a-sa-ba.*
he-strike   arrow with   her she-die   again § 30

13. *Kojərla dijatsie-n a-beso-n-a|tha,* 14. *kentha lu-darlidie-n-bija*
deer   as   she transformed   then   he-run

lo-jono-mamonro, l-akka-n-bija tho-khonan 15. *nah oso-n-bija*
his-family-to   he-tell   her-concerning   they go

---

came, he intended to return home, where a short time ago he had buried his wife. 5. It was late already ; when he came to the edge of the forest, the sun went down, and he passed on to another place.

6. When he had gone a short distance and was not yet far away, he heard a voice behind him. 7. He recognised the voice of his late wife. 8. "Why have you left me !" cried she loudly behind him. 9. When he heard her crying like a living being, he began to run.

10. She followed him very fast, and the more he ran, the faster she followed him. 11. When he was close by, he went to the wayside and saw distinctly that she was bent. 12. He hit her with an arrow, and she died. 13. She was metamorphosed into a deer (see § 167 a) 1) II)). 14. He ran to his family, and told what had happened. 15. They went

th-iebitsi-ro. 16. *Kijadoma khoro loko-no wabo ieki-sa'n-a'to kojarla,*
she-to therefore not men genuine eat they-do deer

owdo-tsi jaloko mora nah tho-mon.
dead-person spirit think they it-at

---

to her. 16. And that is why true Indians do not eat deer : they call it "dead man's spirit".

§ 222. The two bushmaster-snakes
Dutch spelling

1. *Aba-ka tah aba wadilie wakili koba a-jokha-ro ose-n.* 2. *ken baikia*
once was a man long ago hunt-at go then

orie o-toko fa|da ie, lo-kojowa tah bahhi-nro|da, wadili sabo-ka|tah
snake bite him he-return house-to mamari, impossible more

khoro|da ie, kari thana l-mn mienkhoro da no. 3. *Mawtsi djaro tah*
he pain he-at very it morning about

aba ose-fa jokha-nro kidaba, 4. *lu-ddikhi-n-bia tah bian-be kakkitsi*
other go hunt-at again he-see two men

djan-toh lu-rrabodikke-wa-teh. 5. *Ken khoro baikia ajakado-tsi th-a-n bia*
like he-encounter then hide

aba ada a-tikidi-toh koba waboroko-loko be ren-toh da ujjabo khona tah
a tree fallen path-in just now behind

tho-jakado-n-a bia be ; 6. *lu-ddikhi-n bia tah bianma firo-be-toh orie|da,*
it-hide he-see two big snakes

konoko-se-be|tah. 7. *Kia boro|tah kakkitsi dja|th-a-n lu-ddikkhi-n lu-*
bush-worms that before living man as being he-see he-

rrabodikke-wa be da|no. l-kanabi-n bia tah th-dia-diadi-n th-one-kwa be;
encounter just now them he-hear they-talk-talking among each other

awsa-n|da se th-abo adiadiadi-n tah th-onekwa-be. 8. *mijaka-bena*
going § 116 d) 10) them-with talk-talking among each other yesterday-after

a-tokota-ro d-a-ja|no, korlihi arlien-ron abo da-jokho-sa-ja da|no th-abo
bite-cause I-do it rat artisan-only with my-hunt-result it it-with

---

1. Once upon a time, a long while ago, a man had gone out hunting. 2. He was bitten by a snake, and returned home because he could no longer stand the pain the bite caused him. 3. Towards morning, another man again went out hunting. 4. he saw what he took to be male persons coming to meet him. 5. When he saw them coming, he hid behind a big tree which had just fallen in the middle of the path. 6. He saw two big snakes, so-called bushworms (Lachesis rhombeata). 7. Before he had seen them coming to meet him as if they were living men, he had heard them talking. 8. Yesterday I missed him, because I shot at him only with

tah aka-akadi-n th-iebia teh-wa|da.   9. *Lieh baikia miaka bna th-arrede*
    tell-telling   he   yesterday past they bite

bena lie akah tho-jabo khonan|da.   10. *Lu-dikkhi-n doma tah tho orie-be*
after   he   tell   it-behind   he-see   because   those snakes

da lo-fari-n bia tah tho   orie-be.
  he-kill   those   snakes

---

an arrow which is used for shooting rats.   9. They talked about the man,
who they had bitten yesterday [for the snakes had assumed bodies or
shapes of men].   10. Because he really saw the snakes, he has killed
them both.

§ 223. The man and the savanah-dog

There was a man ; his name was Long John. One day, when he returned
from a *kaširi*-feast, about 3 or 4 o'clock in the morning, he heard cries as
if coming from savanah-dogs *(oaliru)*. First one, then a second. The man
was somewhat drunk, and when still another cried, he reviled against them.

A moment later he saw a man coming to meet him, who said : "what did
you say just now, don 't you know who I am ?" The man was not
frightened, because he was drunk, and answered : "I did not speak to you,
I only scolded the savanah-dogs. But where do you come from ?" The
other said : "I have come, because you have deeply offended me".
Thereupon they wrestled. When both were exhausted, the man who had
come to meet him, said : "I am stronger than you are ; I go away now,
but you must not abuse me any more".

The man did not know whether it was a man, or only had the shape of
a man. But it was a spirit *(üyáhŏ-wa|tháyada|n); [na-yáloko-wa|yatháda*
would mean : that was the spirit of a human being].

§ 224. The origin of the Besoa-family

(comp. B5e, 176, v. C. 7e Ant III, 484.)
There was once a man who lived quite alone ; he had no wife, but only
a small delicate dog that remained at home the whole day. Every day the
man went hunting, and when he came home, he saw the dog lying there.

It is a custom with the Indians, that when the husband comes home, his
wife has prepared a beverage for him. Now, one day, the man came home,
and saw a vessel with a beverage. He did not know who had prepared that,
for only the dog was there.

He made up his mind to watch who had done that for him. He said to the dog : "I am going away for two days". But he came home earlier. and then he saw a woman baking cassava in order to make a beverage from it. He said : "what woman is that ? I should like to know where she comes from". He walked softly behind the woman, and there he saw hanging over a beam, the skin of his dog. He took the skin secretly, and threw it into the fire. Thereupon he said to the woman : "you belong to me. and you will remain here".

The woman began to cry and said "why have you done that ? give me my skin back". The man said : "I have burned it ; if you want to be a human being, you should live like one." And so he lived with her ever afterwards, and she became the mother of the *Besoa-na*.

CPSIA information can be obtained at www.ICGtesting.com
Printed in the USA
BVOW081915081011

273125BV00002B/5/P